From Clee to Eternity

M. A. Jenkins

Pubished in 2014

© 2014, A.E. Jenkins

ISBN: 978-0950-9274-7-3

Printed in England by Orphans Press Ltd., Hereford Road, Leominster, Herefordshire

This sceptered isle,

This earth of majesty

This seat of Mars,

This other Eden, demi-paradise,

This fortress built by Nature for herself

Against infection and the hand of war,

This happy breed of men, this little world.

Shakespeare

Foreword

Alf Jenkins has the rare ability to educate, inform and entertain through his writings based on the life and industry of the Shropshire Clee Hills. However, "From Clee to Eternity" he elevates this genre into an important social historical record of life along the Welsh borders in the twentieth century. Through Alf's own personal life experience and recollections the reader is taken on a journey from a simple but rich rural upbringing to that of an influential ambassador for the heritage and values of his Shropshire landscape.

Alf's keen observational skills of both people and crafts enriches the work in a manner that becomes invaluable as a reference document for readers wishing to fully understand the skills and processes which made up village industries now long abandoned. Through this book many such activities can be unearthed through the comprehensive array of period photographs and illustrations often cross referenced to surviving archaeology today.

Whilst such information is a peerless addition to local records its true value is gained through the enrichment of the documentary by Alf's personal life story and the characters he has come into contact with on 'the hill' and beyond. Alf's great love and respect for his father, his national service, his working life and his love for his own family leap from the pages and become so tangible to the reader. It is a life passage familiar to many families in the Marches area but rarely told with such passion, enthusiasm and graphic detail which allows the reader to be engaged with Alf in the many experiences he describes. He genuinely uses words to paint pictures and evoke the atmosphere of a time when people had a closer association with the landscape and community of which they were part.

From Clee to Eternity is a story which in part can be transposed to any part of Britain in the twentieth century. However what makes it special is that it is rooted in the Shropshire Hills and in particular Alf's cherished Clee Hill. It is reputed that man first trod in these hills some 5000 years ago, few will have left such a valuable legacy as Alf Jenkins-a real Shropshire lad.

Colin Richards MBE September 2014

Acknowledgements

David Postle – Kidderminster Railway Museum.

Keith Beddoes – Photographer.

Mrs Marina Clent, MBE. - Photographs.

Mr John Clent – Indentifying individuals.

Mr Alan Johnson – Articles.

Major Adrian Coles, TD. MBE – Parish Council minutes.

The Sutton Family – Oreton Brick Kiln, and much more.

Mrs Daisy Passman – Cleeton St Mary School.

Miss Freda Pugh – Photographs of Cleeton School.

Mr and Mrs Mick Oliver – Information and photographs of Leintwardine Endowed School.

Mrs Aileen Jordan – Photographs of Tenbury Primary School.

Mrs Marion Bassett – Photographs of Tenbury Primary School.

Mrs Pat Edworthy – Photographs of Canon Pyon School.

Mrs Mary Hall – Photograph of Canon Pyon School.

Mr Alan Brisbourne – Researcher (Newspaper snippets).

Dr David Higgins. Honorary Research Fellow, University of Liverpool.
   (Field Archaeologist; Chairman of the Soc. For Clay Pipe Research).

Harold Parker – Clay Pipes.

Marjorie Hammond – Ex Head Teacher of Clee Hill Primary School. An enabler.

Mr Ted Blackwell – Woolhope article.

Edwina Guest – Clee Hill Boy's Cricket Tournament.

Sally Yapp – Computer work and much more.

Colin Richards – Fount of information.

Ann and Brian Harris - Proof readers.

Derek Crowther - Information and photographs.

Tom Massey – Hydro Scheme.

Liz Howard – photo of Authors on cover.

Clifford Pearce

Desmond Key – Lorries.

The Sloan family – Excavating Coal.

Contents

Introduction

"Grandad, I can see the whole universe from here."

I can't tell you how thrilled I was to hear grandson Sam say that at the age of five when we took him for his first outing to the highest point of Titterstone Clees.

His reaction took me back to the time when I was a small boy, running across that fantastic promontory, accompanied by my faithful sheep dog and experiencing that phenomenal vista. I wouldn't have used Sam's words because my vocabulary wasn't that extensive but his reaction summed up my sentiments; and looking from there now is just as special and awe inspiring to me.

How lucky I was to have been born in such an unsophisticated age, to experience tremendous freedom without fear, to be able to wander for hours without my parents having to be concerned and to have that amazing view – one of the best in the world and a hive of industry smothering the area too.

I would scan from Clent to the Cotswolds, to Malvern and the Abberley Hills with their majestic tower in the middle. On to the Skerrid and Abergavenny's Sugar Loaf, the Black Mountains, Brecon Beacons and 'Radnor Tump'; the Strettons, Wrekin and on the western, Welsh horizon Plynlimmon where the rivers Wye and Severn begin.

Nestled one thousand feet below was Ludlow, clustered around prominent St. Laurence's Church and mighty castle with the mini St. Pauls, St Peter's Roman Catholic Church to the right at East Hamlet.

I was a pupil at Ludlow Grammar School with the worries and apprehensions of a country lad but whenever I looked from that lofty summit my problems paled into insignificance.

But! I am racing ahead. What of the present. In spite of having Autumn tints I continue to look forward to so much I wish to do, remain optimistic and welcome new challenges. Those near and dear to me wonder why I seemingly never stop working, writing, continuing craft work, saying I should relax and slow down.

Life is finite and my hope is that zest will not entirely forsake me; but; I do reflect more on my patchwork of experiences. Those episodes of luck, good folk who have helped me along the way, opportunities, amazing co-incidences and most importantly being blessed with a wonderful wife, a real friend and encourager, plus our children and grandchildren – so precious.

My home area means more to me than ever and since publishing Titterstone Clees in 1983 changes have continued. I have more I wish to record and photographs in my collection to share.

From Clee to Eternity is an autobiography supplemented with events and people my wife Ann and I have met during our lives and careers, plus further interesting aspects of my beloved Titterstone Clee Hills, its industrial and social past.

Childhood

My childhood days were spent at the Dhu Stone Inn about 1300 feet above sea level in south Shropshire's Clee Hills. It was a small, country public house near the stone quarries in Dhu Stone hamlet, built for quarry men and miners of the Titterstone Clee Hill area.

The pub was, like most of those in rural areas a cider and beer house with basic amenities, scrubbed topped tables and spittoons under the seats. Of course it was devoid of electricity and mains water – quite a problem for public premises.

Sister Marina feeding the hens. Sitting on a Beer bottle crate:- These were utilised for many uses.

Life was extremely busy, my Mother seemingly running from morning till night. Her routine included organising the public house during the day time, cooking for the family on an oil stove, making scratchings and curing bacon when the annual pig was killed, making butter and in addition helping the community or giving to a hard pressed family by way of a jug of milk or a cake; and there were plenty of families who had virtually nothing.

She would commandeer my sister and I to carry water for drinking, washing floors, for the weekly family bath and clothes wash.

From an early age we were expected to keep a lone customer entertained in the bar with conversation or a game of darts until more people arrived. As a result we soon learnt to communicate and make small talk with anyone and everyone, a skill which has helped us both through life.

Dad ran our small holding which included cattle, sheep, pigs and poultry. In addition he worked long hours in his workshop. He was an excellent wheelwright, carpenter and local undertaker too. Sometimes he would rest his arm on the gate and take in that truly magnificent view to the far, distant hills of Wales and Herefordshire only to be jolted by Mum who assumed he was wasting time. But! that was not so. More often than not he would be working out the construction of his current project in his head before making it from beginning to end without even a sketch or drawing.

Both Marina my sister and I loved the animals especially feeding the calves with warm milk from a bucket. Dad taught us to put our fingers over the calf's nose and fold them into its mouth over its tongue. Then while the calf was busy sucking fingers lower its head into the bucket to drink. Occasionally the calf would jolt its head up, milk and froth slobbering from its mouth and its tail swinging rhythmically from side to side with contentment.

Marina playing in the poultry run

Marina with me in a doll's pram:- Behind is a gate going into one of our fields. Rear right our wash house where we had our weekly bath.

Feeding my pet Tiddling lamb, helped by Mum. I was broken hearted when Dad accidentally backed over the lamb with his car and killed him. Little did I realise sometime later that the lovely, fleecy mat by my bed had been the coat of my 'Lammy'.

(1938) My 'playpen'. A secure box where Mum would know I was safe while she got on with essential work.

Looks like wash day; (1937). Marina and Alf in our 'paddling pool' on the front lawn.

(1938) Alf and Marina:- Marina sitting in her doll's pram.

I had a little piglet which Dad encouraged me to feed from a bottle. I was very young at that time, not more than a toddler. We kept pet rabbits and guinea pigs. One of my rabbits died. I could not understand this was the end of its earthly life so naively placed him in a warm oven hoping he would revive.

We often had tiddling lambs which had to be bottle fed too and at the age of four one Shropshire lamb befriended me and followed me everywhere. I loved him and his strong, square back enabled me to ride him like a small pony. Dad was backing the car out of the garage one day, knocked my lamb flying and sadly it died soon afterwards. I was inconsolable and when a lovely, warm, woollen mat appeared by my bed, Mum did not tell me it was the cured skin and wool of my dear pet.

From a very young age I would wander into Dad's workshop where he encouraged me to recognise timbers by their smell, understand their grain structure and know their differing properties. Elm was for coffin boards and wyche elm for cart wheel hubs because of its wild grain that wouldn't split. I had my own tiny axe and tools.

One morning he told me Mum needed some morning wood and asked me to split a pile of short off cuts placed near his vice. I took each piece in turn and tried to split it, but, my axe barely penetrated the wood

Alf with Dad outside Dhu Stone Inn Workshop. Dad making a 5 barred gate and Alf making a cabinet for a sewing machine

more than half an inch. I looked up to see Dad's rye smile at my efforts and saying, "Now you know elm will not split easily. Here, try this instead."

Ash was pliant with an elasticity which made it suitable for his cart wheel felloes (the outside rim), axe and hammer shafts, also hay rakes, ladder rungs and sides too. He reminded me that when he was young he had worked at Malvern's Morgan Motor Works, where he had used ash for constructing the chassis of those wonderful cars. He said that the Morgans did not have a reverse gear in those early days. Ash was the only timber which could withstand road vibration without cracking and that was why it was being currently used for the body work of Morris 1000 Travellers.

Fine English oak he used for wagon wheel spokes, gates and other structures where strength was essential whilst its beauty and medullary rays when quartered (cut radially) were a joy to be seen in furniture and coffins.

Pine or deal as it is known in the trade was best and cheapest for windows, doors and painted items. It was easily planed and shaped and would last for a long time if properly protected with undercoat and top coat.

I loved going into that workshop, watching Dad's hands and learning to use the tools. But! he had few machines. Most things were cut out with rip and cross cut saws but from making farm wagons, wheels, wheelbarrows, hay rakes, gates, coffins and many other items with him I acquired an affinity with wood and hand skills I have used ever since (See Titterstone Clees). Whenever I am using a marking gauge or other hand tools I instinctively look at my thumbs. Immediately I reflect that they are just like my Dad's and I know that he is still helping me. By looking and running my finger along wood he taught me how to feel the wood fibres and plane "with the grain", essential to enable a smooth finish. Working against the grain tears layers from the timber destroying its appearance and leaving a rough finish useless for the cabinet maker. He would say, "It is impossible to obtain a smooth finish against the lie of the fibres."

He taught the correct proportions for strong joints and how to work out and cut all joints from halving, mortice and tenons and dovetails. I know of nothing more satisfying than to put a well sharpened plane along a piece of timber and produce a beautiful, tightly curled shaving. But! the secret is to have really sharp tools. This reduces necessary effort and makes the work look easy. I watched him scores of times put oil on a sharpening stone, hold the plane blade at an angle of thirty degrees, move it in a rhythmic figure of eight, reverse it to remove the burr, pick this out of the oil to avoid getting it embedded in the stone then say, "Now all I need to do is strop it." That meant stroking the blade back and forth over the palm of his hand to obtain a finely honed edge. It took me years to acquire this essential skill. The old saying that a poor workman always blames his tools is often heard but no craftsman can work effectively and with safety without learning to prepare his equipment to perfection.

There was always a list of workshop jobs waiting to be done for customers but these were often put on hold when a funeral arose or necessity called him to farms, shops or homes. Bitterley Court often had wagons which needed minor repairs on site. I loved to go with Dad during school holidays. Mum prepared a packed lunch for both of us and we would sit beneath a wagon in the shade eating our home grown beetroot and cheese sandwiches.

I learned a great deal sitting there listening to his countryside knowledge. He was always pointing out birds; wagtails, a nuthatch or wren. We enjoyed the brilliance of the occasional, majestic cock pheasant or a vixen slinking furtively along the hedge – sights not to be seen a few hundred feet higher at Dhu Stone. The lush trees of chestnuts and bannuts were not seen on higher ground either. I would forage for these beneath the trees in Autumn and my hands soon stained from peeling off their protective husk. Dad used his pen knife to insert into the end joint of the shell and with a quick twist revealed the juicy, milky, fresh kernel.

Shropshire Yeomanry:- Dad on Duty

Shropshire Yeomanry:- Sgt. Richard Jenkins.
So very young.

Bannuts are a small variety of a walnut. It was many years later that I saw my first large walnut. Only a little while ago a local, elderly Herefordshire lady said, "Alf I'm sure you can tell me the difference between a walnut and a bannut. A bannut is much smaller than a walnut isn't it?" I confirmed that this was so.

Dad helped me make a small pull along cart because he knew timber fellers were working in the 'Wallers'. They encouraged me to trundle it to collect wood chips which Mum found really good for kindling. Brother-in-law John Clent was well known for getting up to mischief when he was young and the timber fellers knew this. Pointing to the top of a tall larch one said, "Young John there's a drey up there but I think it is deserted." Of course John had to investigate. He climbed from branch to branch, eventually reached his quarry and put his hand inside. He gave a sudden yelp, quickly pulled his hand away to find a baby squirrel securely attached to his thumb – much to the hilarity of those looking on.

The Wallers (a local name for alders) was a large expanse of trees quite near my home with Dhu Stone Hamlet on the lower side of the lane which leads to Nine Springs Farm and Cottage. It was our favourite play area for fox and hounds and pirates. On the upper side of the track was an extensive wood which stretched past Nine Springs nearly to the foot of Titterstone. Years earlier it had been part of a considerable forest, essential for pit prop timber for the local coal industry, timber structures for brick making , stone quarrying and fuel for lime kilns too.

Sadly in 1942 the area was transformed. Forestry men and women appeared and spent many months felling with axes all the timber for the War effort. My Mother was persuaded to make sandwiches daily for this workforce and the lady foresters in particular appreciated her hospitality. By the end of the year our playground wood had disappeared, opening up the view from Dhustone to Bedlam Village and beyond to Ludlow and the hills of Wales.. All that remains is a small coppice by the side of Limers' Lane, the road which leads to the radar station on Titterstone's summit.

Shropshire Yeomanry:-Richard Jenkins (Dad) soon after joining up. My mother Marjorie Jenkins peeping through the curtain.

On windy days the air was filled with swirling, white dust belching from quarry stone crushers. The daily, detonated explosions necessary to produce enough stone to keep occupied the work force of many hundreds, sent shrapnel like fragments screaming through the air for a distance of half a mile. Fortunately everyone was warned to seek shelter by a bell being rung from a small concrete bunker above Dhu Stone's houses. Much damage was done to the cottage roofs but the repairs were a matter of course because most of them were quarry property.

Nearby tar macadam plants mixed crushed stone with bitumen to be transported down the Clee Bitterley incline railway for twelve to sixteen hours every week day to distant destinations for road surfacing.

It was thirsty work and my home was full to bursting with quarrymen each lunch time – consuming an average of eight to ten barrels of cider plus numerous casks of beer and porter every week.

The stories these sinewy quarrymen and miners recounted of bleeding hands from pushing wheelbarrows heavily loaded with stone when they began working in the quarries at the age of thirteen; and mining tunnels not more than two feet six inches high(80 centimetres) necessitating them crawling on hands and knees to and from the coal face, pulling 'carvs' on hands and knees in mud and water. Their resilience was extraordinary.

Illness brought extra hardship, forcing them "on the box" , having to manage on meagre handouts from workmates plus the almost impossible task of feeding a large family especially when the bacon pig had tragically died.

When a man was able to work he was requested to put whatever he could afford in a collection box. When ill he was permitted to ask for some sick pay – hence the expression, "he's on the box". I understood the bitterness which surfaced at the time of a General Election because it was felt that, "They dunnu do anything fer the likes of we." The very few pleasures these men gave themselves were cigarettes , a pint and chewing twist tobacco and without exception there was always a budget increase on these items. There was no escapism from the ceaseless round of work, living on the breadline with no foreseeable change. These childhood memories coloured my attitude and empathy with these ordinary, industrial people.

There was always a string of jobs waiting to be done during school holidays. My sister Marina and I never had time to suffer from the modern disease of boredom. Whatever our parents were occupied with we were encouraged and expected to join in with too so that play was work and work became our play.

It was second nature to help clean out the cattle; cut tightly compressed hay from the hay bay with Dad's sharp hay knife, fill bags to carry to the cattle and chop it up with a chaff cutter for the calves. The lethal blade of this machine could have easily cut off fingers but without the necessity of the protection of guards and 'health and safety' we learnt to be careful. Other seasonal jobs were hay making, butter making, carrying gallons of water down into the beer cellar and drawing it through the old lead beer pipes to make sure they were absolutely crystal, clean. The feeding of poultry, pigs and numerous other tasks filled each day. It always amused us to hear urban cousins ask, "What- ever do you do to pass the time in the country?"

Our seasonal jobs were hay making, muck spreading, hop and blackberry picking. Regular weekly routine included butter making. Each evening after milking, Mum took what she required for our daily use. The remainder was put into a separator. This had a large metal container on the top and lower down it was connected to two spouts. One emitted cream and the other skimmed milk hence the name separator. The cream was added to a container daily until Mum considered she had enough to make butter.

The cream was put into a churn and on Saturday it was our job to turn a handle to rotate the churn until butter was formed. Occasionally we pressed a valve to release air and longingly looked at a little inspection glass hoping to see bits of butter coagulating. I disliked the job because sometimes it seemed to take an eternity before I heard the welcome 'plop' of forming butter. I really enjoyed the next stage. Mum extracted the golden lump, beat it with butter patters, added salt, cut and formed the butter into one pound blocks finishing each lump with an artistic pattern along its top. There was nothing more mouth watering than that beautiful, smooth butter on warm toast. The churned 'butter'milk was put in the pig swill tub while the separator milk was used for cooking.

I referred in detail to the process of hay making in 'Titterstone Clees' and 'Jim's Journey'. The weather at harvest time being unpredictable always meant a race against time to cut, row, turn the grass with hand rakes, cock it up and carry it on poles to the barn for storage.

Hay making; Mum and me on the 'pig' trailer. Note the War time white band painted round Dad's Standard Nine to help the car to be seen at night time.

Neighbours helping to gather in the hay:- Having a well earned break. Note Railway Terrace in the background; the hay 'cocked' up ready for carrying on poles. Near neighbour Dick Beddoe on left, next to him in back Dad. Back row next to right Edwin (Skinnum) Lloyd. He lived in the squatter's cottage now a pile of stone at the top of Limer's Lane.

1939. We all gathered for hay making:- Betty Lloyd at the back. Left to right Marina, Derek Bytheway Alf and Bryan Bytheway (real neighbours and friends).

In the Hay field:- Friend Barbara Beddoe with her twin boys John and Alan. Mum back right. My sheep dog pal in the middle.

On reflection those old leys had never to my knowledge been ploughed. They were therefore special. As a child I would lie in the long hay grass with its diverse mixture of buttercups, vetches, clover, yellow rattle, knapweed, sorrel, thistle, docks, hill rushes and so much more. It all seemed to provide a mixture on which our shorthorn cattle thrived, gave good milk and suckled healthy calves.

School was about a mile away, quite a short distance to walk compared to our contemporaries from the hills. Many of them had to walk two or even three miles. We walked along the old quarry railway line, past the mammoth shed which housed the incline engine. This building was stabilised against gale force winds by large sleeper-like buttresses placed along each side.

A few yards further along a large metal sign read, "Trespassers will be fined 40 shillings." Why it remained there I don't know. It was the only route to school. Everyone had no option but to ignore it and cross the railway line.

Dhu Stone Lane 1940:- Mum with Marina and Alf. The snow having been cut through with shovels by quarrymen in order to get lorries to Dhu Stone Quarry.

1947 Snow:- The worst snow fall I remember in my life time. Me left, Dad middle and Marina on right. We are standing on the roof. See chimney background left. We used to start sledging from by the chimney and be stopped by a clothes line appearing just above the snow, two fields lower down Dhu Stone Lane.

Veering right on to cinder and scalping embankment we ran downhill, over two stiles and into The Pit Ground. This large field was pot-holed with many depressions two to three metres deep; the remains of coal bell pits. Over two thousand similar ones have been recorded in recent years forming a huge necklace around the Titterstone Clees. They had been part of a considerable industry which had existed since the Middle Ages and concluded in the 1920s. Local environmental and social history was not included in our school timetable so sadly we knew nothing about our local heritage and past industries.

When collecting frog's spawn from these depressions, sliding across their frozen ice in winter or hiding in them during a dry summer we had no idea that these pit shafts were just loosely filled with rubble which could and did collapse after extremes of weather. We did not realise either that the railway track we ran across every day had been developed in the 1860s to transport coal from the hill tops to Herefordshire, Worcestershire, Shropshire and beyond; before the huge local stone quarries opened and taken the 'coal' railway over. From where the Pit Ground joined the main road just a few hundred yards remained before reaching school. On the left we passed a lovely house of brick with an attractive garden and tennis court. This residence was the home of Mr Fred Edwards the manager of Clee Hill Rolling & Transport Company. It was indeed considered special, being very different from the multitude of squatter stone cottages which dotted the hillsides. During winter months we were clad like Eskimos to protect us against the elements, balaclavas,plus gloves and even old socks over our shoes and wellingtons to prevent us slipping on ice.

The school had two separate buildings. The first one a Methodist chapel was partitioned off to form the infants' classroom. Originally it had been a Methodist boarding school . The near by 'top' building was much larger and housed all the rest of the school up to the age of fourteen.

On arrival our wet clothes were spread to dry over a huge fender around open fires. At the end of the day I remember how difficult it was to force our fingers into dried gloves. Contrary to the general nostalgia of childhood, after enduring inclement storms and carrying every necessity including food and water, we really hated snow. But! in Spring and Summer days we dawdled home, stopping to collect frogs' spawn from those old pit shafts and peeing on the embers from the incline engine fire-box raked out by Mr George Price the driver. This created billows of obnoxious, yellow smoke which wafted towards other pupils following us home along the track. The following evening they would do their best to hurry to the engine shed first and make us cough and splutter by performing the same trick.

Memories of infant school are hazy but I do remember my first days sitting by an evacuee from Leeds by the name of John Turford. He had been sent for safety to live with an aunt. Wonderfully we met again in 2008. He was still six inches taller than me.

We became quite good friends in those early days because like virtually everyone else we had to have our tonsils out and for this operation we had to make the then enormous journey of thirty three miles to Shrewsbury ENT Hospital.

I was extremely apprehensive never having been in a hospital nor having travelled so far before. On being prepared for our operation we were walked down a corridor and put in separate small cubicles. I looked around thinking that some enormous machine would descend and somehow pluck out my tonsils. *Nothing* happened and when I arrived at the operating theatre the surgeon enquired, "Has this boy had his bowels moved?" It then dawned on me that I had been standing by a water toilet in that small cubicle; but I hadn't used it because I had never seen one before and did not know what it was. How life has changed!

My other clear memory at this stage is of Miss Selly the infants' teacher, the first adult outside my family unit to leave an impression on me. She was a kind, consistent, rotund lady who sang well, played the piano, taught us all to read and earned our respect. She re-enforced basic etiquette and discipline taught at home and my lasting humiliation was being mildly rebuked and corrected in Clee Hill village sweet shop. My response to the answer from Mr Tommy Davies the proprietor had been, "OK". I was jolted when Miss Selly's voice behind me remarked, "OK Alfred! Your reply should have been thank you very much Mr Davies." How our world has changed. I have tried very hard not to forget that early advice.

World War II Memories

Clee Hill School had to accommodate many evacuees and their teachers from Liverpool. Teaching areas were partitioned off in our existing classrooms making them cramped. Many of the city children did not readily settle to our rural environment. Their first questions were, "Where is the picture house and the chip shop?" They were more worldly wise and this led to fights and disharmony. But, many were happy and kindly received as was my friend in the Infants John Turford. During my junior school stage the Second World War ended and the evacuees disappeared from our midst with their teachers but many thoughts of that time are imprinted on my mind.

The War broke out when I was three years of age therefore it was war time for most of my childhood. There was much talk in the pub, daily about the progress or lack of it. Times were difficult but I knew of no other existence and the day to day worries fell on parents' shoulders.

Germany had a propagandist, Lord Haw Haw. He broadcast on our radio somehow, regularly, and frightened us beyond all sense and reason saying such things as, "Coventry will be bombed tonight and many people will be killed. You will soon be defeated." German intelligence was amazing and nine times out of ten raids did follow Haw Haw's predictions. It was uncanny. He really disturbed everyone. Thank God for Winston Churchill's strong defiance. Harry Downs a local came into our pub and said to my Dad, "Dick, what's a proper gander?" Everyone in the pub laughed because Harry thought it was some sort of farmyard creature.

Black out was a very important rule and we all knew of its importance. It was not too difficult to achieve in the countryside because we still had not got mains electricity. In fact it did not arrive on the Titterstone Clee Hills until the 1950s. It was quite natural for us to wander about at night in war time with only the help of the stars by which to find our way. Oil lamps in our homes were relatively easy to conceal. Every window in every home had to have a blackout and my Dad made a great number of framed fixings to attach to the inside of cottage windows. He was an ARP Warden (Air Raid Patrol). His duty was to patrol the neighbourhood and make sure no light was escaping which may attract the attention of enemy aircraft.

In school we had to have regular gas mask practices and many small children were really upset when a mask was fitted over their faces because breathing was restricted and difficult. Children panicked because they thought they were going to suffocate. Teachers had to have determination, patience and sensitivity

War Time Clee Hill and District ARP: Dad is in the back row next to the extreme Right. I do not think there is one person still alive pictured here. All were so much a part of my young life.

Back L to R:-George Morgan, Reg Martin, ...,. Sam Unit, Ern Bate, Cyril Clent, Charlie Davidson,Eli Brown, Jack Didlick Ben Wheel, Ern Bradley (Dad's friend and confidant), Mr Lloyd, Dick Jenkins, Bill Greenhouse. Middle Row:- Charlie Lucas,Sam Taylor, Billy Beeston, Joe Lewis, Jack Haynes., Arthur Wiltshire, Alf Butcher, Bill Hall, ...George Lloyd ,Bert Brown, Mr Crowther. Front Row:- Jack Baker, Mr Owen (Headmaster Clee Hill School).............., Walter Breeze, Bill Jordon, ..., Mr Lees (Court of Hill). Wilf Tommey (Village Baker) Lambert Matthews, Harley Everall, Walter Lloyd, ...

too. Our lounge was considered to be quite large being about sixteen feet by twelve and it was absolutely crammed with gas masks. It was part of Dad's remit to distribute them to homes. Some had Mickey Mouse faces others Donald Duck shapes. There were the ordinary shapes for adults and large incubators for small babies. They looked similar in shape to incubators that are seen in premature baby units today.

It was not permitted to carry a torch at night unless it had a hood to prevent its beam going skywards. Cars were not permitted to have head lights on. This led to many dicey situations. Every vehicle had to have a two inch wide, white line painted around the edge of mudguards, bumpers and along its running boards. Problems with traffic were minimised because there was very little petrol available. This greatly reduced traffic but the black market trade for petrol was rife. It was amazing where petrol turned up. My Dad was allowed an official allocation because being an undertaker was considered an essential service..

Food was scarce and rationing affected every family. Country folk being resilient helped themselves in every possible way. In their traditional manner they had to be even more self sufficient. There were no lawns to be seen. Even the vicar dug up his tennis court to be turned into a vegetable plot. Every crop that could be was preserved. The slogan issued by government was, "Dig for Victory". Even local common land was ploughed up and planted with potatoes.

There were no domestic refrigerators so runner beans were put in earthenware jars and salted; eggs were put in large containers with isinglass to preserve them; vegetables were clamped and every berry and fruit collected, put in kilner jars and also made into chutney and jams.

The bacon pig was gold and a very important part of our daily diet. Every scrap of left overs of food and peelings were put into the pig swill tub, ladled out and boiled for pig feed. We only had the luxury of fresh vegetables in season from our own plots. It is a peculiar thing that I still only enjoy produce that is produced at its natural time.

In 1940 there was a government department called the Ministry of Food. It laid down rules and regulations as to what could be allocated to every person. Everyone had a Ration Book, full of coupons and my goodness people guarded them like jewels. We had very little sugar and most people were slimmer in those days. Rationing went on for years and when the War finished in 1945 our ration allocation was still 4 ounces of bacon; 8 ounces of sugar; 2 ounces of tea; 2 ounces of cheese; 2 ounces of butter per week and the allocation of sweets for a month was 12 ounces.

However wartime measures which we accepted as the norm continued for some years. Only very small amounts of butter, cheese and other foods were permitted to be purchased weekly. Clothing coupons were extremely precious and my Mother saved them up to allow one substantial, special purchase annually.

Petrol was very scarce but people in business were allowed extra. The black market was rife and I soon cottoned to the fact that week-end customers came not only to get away from the cities and have a quiet country pub drink but to barter and obtain precious eggs and butter from locals.

Being a war time baby life had always been like this for me but the most treasured gifts were the ration book sweet coupons. These were really paper gold. I would take an eternity eyeing the various sweets available before making a choice and handing over a precious coupon to 'Tommy Toddles', Mr Davies at Clee Hill village sweet and paper shop. Incidentally he and his wife lived on Angel bank. Mrs Davies delivered daily papers, walking miles to do so. My vivid memory was her beautiful, white hair. It blended so well with the whiteness of newly fallen snow. Mr Davies was a well known Methodist preacher known by locals as 'Shouter Davis'. Local comedian Dennis Crowther amused me when he said, "E was a tod bellied mon (fat man) and e coudnu see over the front of Knowle Chapel pulpit."

He was however respected because he preached with sincerity and passion.

Many frugal families saved their coupons up for what was considered a special acquisition. Life at home was basic. There were no frills. My Mother, like most others in the area made any rugs and mats we had in our home. Her method was to cut up old clothes in to strips which were considered "past it". These materials were various colours. She would wash and iron a sack, pull short strips through a hole in the sack which she made with a bodger and gradually fill up the whole of the sack surface. All the strips were trimmed off to make them appear the same length. We all helped in the evenings to make these warm rugs.

If still in reasonable condition large trousers, jackets and overcoats were cut down to fit children. I do remember one being adapted to fit me. The material was extremely heavy and when I put it on I could hardly stand up.

Young children were encouraged to drink milk to help their bone structure and in school we had powdered milk. This was mixed with water but I never liked it because there was always an unpleasant taint left in the mugs because washing up facilities were very poor indeed. There were other War time items that were common such as dried egg powder and Woolton Pies. These were made from potatoes, cauliflower, turnips, swede, carrots, oats and spring onions all topped with potato pastry and grated cheese served with gravy. But! anything available was put into those pies.

In 1946 bread was rationed and in 1947 potatoes. Things did not ease for many years but in my opinion people in general were much fitter in those days. At home we were lucky because we had our own eggs, milk, butter and bacon. Occasionally there would be a prolapsed hen which Mum would soon feather and boil. As I have said the Dhu Stone Inn was quite a place for clandestine Black market transactions.

Many of our local families were very poor indeed. The Credit Crunch of 2009 onwards was nowhere near as desperate as those times. My Mum would often save a bottle of skimmed milk and give it to a local family and it was quite common to have a whist drive or dance to raise money for a family who had lost a pig or experienced a bereavement and had no funds for a burial.

Search lights criss-crossed the skies over the cities of Birmingham, Wolverhampton and Coventry and in the night sky we could clearly see them trying to track enemy aircraft and offer some protection from air raids. The rumble of bombers and enemy aircraft was common and the occasional explosion and vibration of the earth clearly heard. A number of German and Allied aircraft crashed into the quarry faces. I have seen wreckage scattered over huge areas on the tops of the hills. Quarrymen were often first on the scenes and were distressed to find dead crew members, some decapitated and others burnt to death with just their boots remaining.

German and Italian POWs working in the quarries made lovely brooches and model planes from perspex windows and scattered bits of metal. Quarry men used to generalise but they felt that the Germans were more content to work hard and soon gained the good will of locals. Some remained in the area and married. These prisoners were very relieved to be in Britain and often told us they thanked their lucky stars they hadn't been sent to other countries. The Italians were canny. The large pans for loading stone had two handles and one quarryman would lift a loaded pan into a truck. The Italians refused to do this and said that for two handles two men were required. Many of the prisoners were skilful and made lovely toys out of scraps of wood; jumping men and pecking hens etc. We thought these were marvellous because we really did not have commercial toys. My main toy was a metal hoop with a hook made by the quarry blacksmith. Most local boys had a similar one and we spent hours bowling them and having races. I also had a trolley which Dad had helped me to make using odd bits of wood and four small pram wheels.

Christmas time brought just one present usually wrapped in last year's Christmas paper which had been ironed then tied up with wool. This we were instructed to carefully untie so that the paper could be used again ; and a stocking received with perhaps a little chocolate, orange and an apple. Although it may seem very little by present day standards we really appreciated these gifts. I still try very hard to open my Christmas presents carefully whilst I see my grandchildren tearing the wrappers to pieces being surrounded by a pile of paper and their parents frantically trying to make a list of where each present came from.

Although away from city bombing all these things made us feel War was near. We were really saddened when news came that local lads had been killed. I remember the first young man for us to lose was Sidney Reynolds, a bright, good looking lad who had been in our midst just a few weeks previously.

Many quarrymen were called up or volunteered. As they said, "It was an opportunity for adventure and travel".   Locals had never experienced holidays. Fortunately most of those known to us returned safely some years later. Bill Jordan a quarry foreman was in the Worcesters and did service in Burma, Japan, Shikoka Island near Hiroshima and Malaya. Alec Evans was in the Royal Engineers and was a Desert Rat. As friend John Hughes and I discovered a number joined the Navy.   Was this I wonder because they had never visited the sea other than on the pub dart outing? Paddy Taylor was a fire fighter and stoker on the Davenport, a corvette escorting convoys from the Bay of Biscay to Scapa Flow. Bert Bounds from Knowbury was in the Italian and Greek campaigns, Singapore and Malaya as an Able seaman on a destroyer. Sam Lloyd who I only knew as a quiet, mild mannered lorry driver was drafted to a fishing trawler. He had been trained as a baker and was commandeered as a chef. He cooked for the crew of thirty eight. All fishing trawlers were fully armed and placed on the Northern Patrol for the Royal Navy. Sam spent much time near Iceland and he told John Hughes and me that although he had been regularly torpedoed and spent much time tracking submarines his most alarming experience had nothing to do with the enemy. He was off the coast of Iceland when his vessel ran into a force nine gale. It was driven by steam and the coal burner broke down. As a result they drifted for days, going round and round in large circles and doing everything but turn over. It was an incredibly frightening experience but at last the gale subsided and they drifted into 'Valyured' an Iceland port.

Older men and those not conscripted continued to produce as much stone as possible in the local quarries but their clothes were basic – corduroys, hob nailed boots and hands in a shocking calloused state. Suddenly there were many hundreds of white American soldiers deployed around the hills. At Dhu Stone they deployed near my home in a wooded area known as the "Wallers". They commandeered one quarry, brought their own mobile machinery and crushers and transported huge quantities of stone to construct their own run- ways and camps. Our quarrymen were extremely envious of the Yanks'superb winter clothing; fur lined boots, gauntlets and fur hats with ear flaps. They were very pleasant to Marina and me and would sit us on their knee and tell us stories about their children, home and life. We had a constant supply of chewing gum, a real treat for us, but they used to get fed up with people shouting at them while on the road. As a result they pinned large notices on their vehicles saying, "No gum chum." They brought huge containers of coffee into Dhu Stone Inn and filled the place every evening. I remember on one occasion a rabbit was run over and the troops brought it to Mum. She skinned it and made a typical English rabbit stew . They were thrilled and I remember them bringing their mess tins and shouting to their colleagues, "Come down here if you want to see something to make your mouth water." For appreciation of my parents' kindness we were all invited to their tented canteen and stores. Our eyes boggled when we saw stacks of tins of pineapple, peaches and other tinned commodities we had never seen.

Bruce Astbury who was about my age lived at another local public house near the top of Hopton Bank known as the Miners Arms. It became known as The Finger because Mrs Aimes who had lived there used to point her finger at anyone who misbehaved. Like me Bruce experienced tremendous freedom being able to run unrestricted for hours over common land. Again hundreds of White American soldiers were billeted on Catheron Common. They crammed into the Finger and the locals got so fed up that they asked the landlord to put a couple of barrels outside inthe yard so that they could have a drink in peace. Beer was seven and a half old pence a pint and cider four old pence. Bruce remembers they had a little dog which went missing. They need not have worried. The soldiers had taken a fancy to the animal and dressed him up in sergeant's uniform as a mascot before returning him to the pub.

When the white Americans left they were replaced by coloured American troops. As a small boy I remember hearing a knock at the back door of the pub and thinking it was a well known local person, opened it. I could see no one. Then suddenly I could discern four eyes moving in the dark. They belonged to two coloured troops. I ran to my Mum never having seen a coloured person in my life before. We were so saddened to learn years later that when they left the quarries they had all perished while crossing the English Channel.

Local business people certainly capitalised on this new found trade. One local baker made thousands of doughnuts and parked one of his vans outside the peripheral camp fence. He did a roaring trade every morning for weeks.

Scores of Italian and German prisoners of war were deployed on local farms. Initially all were transported from camps to the farms by lorry but as time went by certain prisoners were trusted and allowed to cycle to and from farms. Some even were allowed to live in and became almost like members of the family. Many were no more than eighteen or nineteen years of age. One local farmer's son had been conscripted and it was ironical that he had two young German prisoners sent to his farm. They knew nothing about country life or farm work and they had to be tought every basic job. He said to his wife on one occasion, "Look at these poor young lads. They are someone's sons just like our lad; are away from home in a strange place not of their own volition. " Local farmers did not bear these young prisoners any malice whatsoever.

School was punctuated with memories of Miss Fanny Manley, a severe, guant lady whose skill at teaching handwriting could not be questioned and which I now admire, but I found her hard manner frightening. When any pupil formed a letter incorrectly she would haul that child out, often by the ear; grab the wooden board rubber, hold the unfortunate child's arm under her armpit and proceed to rap knuckles as fast as a woodpecker could strike a tree.

Mr Owen the Headmaster was so different, hard but fair and compassionate. Anyone who stepped out of line would be caned but those who tried to conform and learn received encouragement and had nothing to fear. Mr Owen knew our parents well enough to encourage us to use appropriate adjectives when describing them and their occupations in our essays.

Of course classes were enormous with a wide age range but because of respectful obedience we learnt. Mr Owen loved the countryside and nature study. I remember his skill when encouraging us to be observant. As a result I thoroughly enjoyed nature study and art lessons. Each of us would have to pick a daffodil, leaf or 'sticky bud' in season but before he would allow us to draw it he would say, "Look at it, really look carefully at it. Look at the shape of the petals. Look at the curl of the leaves. What a wonderful creation! Only God can create such wonders. Now draw carefully all the detail you are able to see."

Because I enjoyed calligraphy and printing Mr Owen gave me a book of printing styles. Sixty five years on I still have it and frequently refer to it when sign writing.

When I was ten years old Mr Owen retired and a new Head fresh from the forces arrived. Mr Morris loved football, was a superb, tricky winger, played for Clee Hill United and took older lads who showed aptitude far and wide to improve their skills – quite unusual in those days. I liked him and he encouraged a number of us to sit the entrance examination to Ludlow Grammar School. This was a major step for us to be able to look beyond our familiar environment.

(1948) New Headmaster extreme right Mr Morris);- Clee Hill Senior School Football/Cricket Team. Mr Morris was very talented; excellent footballer who played for Clee Hill United. Back L to R Mr Ben Purslow, Leonard Butcher, Donald Davidson, Dennis Bowden. John Martin, John Thomas, Johnny Cleeton, Mr Badger (organiser) , Front Row L to R Roy (Commander) Brown, Nipper Brown, Stanley Martin, Alan Warrington, Bernard Key. Edwina Guest came up with this precious photograph. Mr Badger was responsible for organising a tournament for school boys in the Cleobury Mortimer area. Mr Morris coached the boys and took them far and wide to play. This was a wonderful novelty for Clee Hill youngsters.

A new Phase. The Grammar School

1947 was an atrocious winter. My Dad sold a cow in April and was really relieved because the very next day it began to snow and snow. Ultimately we could walk over hedges on hard packed snow and sledge from by the side of our wash house chimney where drifts were well over twenty feet deep. We had many weeks away from school. Everything was frozen up. Roads were blocked and telephone wires had collapsed from the sheer weight of frozen snow. I remember my father measuring some wires which were nine inches in diameter. It was the worst winter I remember in my life for snow.

The 11+ examination was postponed but eventually my school mate Gordon Breeze and I made the journey to Ludlow. We found ourselves sitting at old, mutilated desks in Ludlow Grammar School's ancient, beamed and panelled hall.

Some weeks later we were asked to return for an interview. It is an episode I vividly recall. Afterwards we caught the 192 Midland Red bus home from outside the Portcullis public house in Upper Galdeford, long time gone I am afraid. As we sat at the back of the bus we asked each other questions about our interview. I had been asked what reading material I had enjoyed. Although I did not understand the significance of 'material' I said that I read the Dandy and the Beano and recounted stories about Black Bob a Scottish,

Border Collie. This very limited choice must have sounded pathetic to my interviewers but it reflected our lack of resources and opportunities.

I asked Gordon about his questioning. He said he too had been asked about reading material but hadn't really understood what 'material' meant either.

He continued by saying that they had asked him an odd question which was, "Here lies the body of John Brown who was lost at sea and never found," and continued, "What do you find odd about that Gordon?" My friend said, "Well, e connu be lying ere if they annu found im."

Some weeks later our parents received a letter to say we had been accepted. The following September with much trepidation we cycled across the hillside, caught the bus to the 'city of Ludlow' to experience our first day of a new chapter, while many of our contemporaries transferred to Lacon Childe's School in Cleobury Mortimer.

For reticent, unworldly Clee Hill boys the impact of school in Ludlow was very significant. At the end of the first day my mum said, " Well, what was it like?" I told her that all the teachers wore gowns and that when you went to the toilet there was water running down the wall all the time and when you went to the lavatory the pans had water in them and you had to pull a chain to flush them. She said, "Everyone has one of those in town." I found this apparent waste of water difficult to accept because we had to carry every drop we required and never wasted any. I wonder on how many other children at the age of eleven water toilets made such an impact? I also said the school was enormous. In fact there were 212 boys.

I didn't relish the thought of my second day because it began to dawn on me that Ludlow Grammar School was where I was going to have to attend for the foreseeable future. I had been happy and felt secure in my local environment but boys were different in Ludlow. They dressed differently, spoke differently and appeared more confident, worldly wise and some even had pocket money to spend.

At lunch time we were instructed to wear our red and blue school caps at all times when walking to and from school. We were told to walk via Broad Street to the Angel Hotel which housed The British Restaurant. There after saying grace and collecting our lunch we sat and ate in absolute silence. Afterwards we walked through the streets back to our school in Mill Street.

As soon as I went through the gates two big lads grabbed me, forced my arms behind my back, threw my cap away and frog marched me across the playground to the toilet block where my head was forced into a toilet pan and the chain pulled. I came up spluttering, coughing, furious and breathless. In spite of my anger I could not retaliate but as a result of this initiation ceremony I was determined not to be defeated by bullies. As my Clee Hill friend John Hughes said, "We mountain goats are bent on survival."

The afternoon brought my first History lesson with local, eminent historian Fred Reeves, during which he asked me a question. He had a slight lump on his lip which made his speech somewhat indistinct but I answered as best I could.

My Clee Hill dialect, which was not really understood in Ludlow may have contributed to my seemingly, inarticulate reply but whatever the result Fred said, "Jenkins were you born in a cave?" This was a shock and further dented my already inadequate confidence. There was however a happy sequel to this incident and Fred became an inspiration and friend in later years.

Many teachers were fresh from war service and military experience, therefore some continued this flavour as part of their school discipline. One such person was a short, stocky Welshman A.J. David. When he shouted the whole place seemed to vibrate but generally I got along well with him and he was a consistent help to me.

He took us for PT (physical training) in some old cottages which had been converted into a gymnasium. It was well equipped and a real inspiration to watch AJD (The Beak) vault over apparatus with such ease and agility. We all did our best to emulate him. Swimming lessons were an ordeal. Previously I had only been in sea water up to my knees on the very occasional summer outing to Barry Island with our pub dart team, therefore I could not swim at all. During summer term when weather permitted we were marched to the bottom of Mill Street, through Harry Green's farmyard to a tin hut near the River Teme. Having put on our bathing trunks we struggled through mud holes which had been made by cattle on their way to and from the river while getting a drink. Here as a response to very direct Welsh accent demands we splashed about trying to do the breast stroke to no avail. Thank goodness after a brief period we were allowed out covered in goose pimples with mud half way up our legs. Needless to say I never learnt to swim a stroke. Of course we had to carry games and PT kit plus woodwork apron as well as all other necessities from home. In contrast to town lads we looked as though we were moving home each day. Each Wednesday was games day. After lunch we had to walk from Broad Street, round the castle, down Linney and across the fields to Burway carrying all our clobber, a distance of about a mile. The town boys had in the mean time been home to lunch and whizzed past us on their bicycles wearing pristine kit. By the time we arrived at the minute pavilion it had been commandeered. Not an inch of space remained. There was no alternative but to change under the nearest hedge and prepare for rugby. In spite of lack of practice and the accessibility the town boys and boarders had for extra tuition I enjoyed rugby with some minor success as a result of encouragement from The Beak. We were told that after games we could have a bath at Dinham Hall the home of boarders in town. Gordon and I being denied running water at home looked forward to this impending luxury. Often rain had fallen during rugby practice but we collected our damp clothes from under the hedge, dressed as quickly as possible and trudged all the way back up to Mill Street's Dinham Hall. Needless to

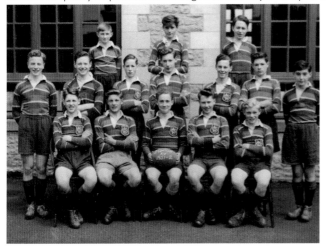

say the boarders and town boys with the aid of their bicycles got there first. By the time we arrived the warm, attractive bath looked more like a solution of sheep droppings and grass. For two or three weeks we immersed ourselves in this but from then on decided to go straight to the bus and have a sponge down at home. Beak was a superb rugby coach, gave us the opportunity to travel to watch internationals and made some tremendous players out of many who showed potential.

Under 15 Rugby Squad at Ludlow Grammar School(1951). Alf 2nd row; 3rd from Right. Some well known faces still around the area. Clee Hill mate Brian Bytheway 2nd from Left on Front Row.

I did ultimately become friendly with one or two town boys who were in my class one of whom was Clive Lewis. His mother ran a small, grocery shop at East hamlet and his father drove the railway engine on the Clee Hill railway near my home. Clive was an extremely good athlete, built for the job and well coordinated. His side step in rugby was outstanding and he was chosen to play for the Three Counties with other school chums. However he was also a good goal keeper and played for East Hamlet, a town football team. This resulted in a conflict. Clive was chosen for a school match which clashed with a football fixture. He mentioned this to Beak whose response was, "If you do not turn up for the school match I will never pick you again." This was a difficult dilemma for Clive but he did choose to play for school. As a result Beak really encouraged him and Clive went from strength to strength

Are you on this one? 1953/4:- Ludlow Grammar School Rugby squad: Alf Back Row on Left. Another Clee Hill lad and friend Back Row Right Clifford Prosser. Mike Wise middle Row Left. 4th along David (Razor) Dallow of Tenbury , Next friend Clive Lewis in England shirt. Bitterley friend -----Watkins. On far Right

Ludlow Grammar School Band 1951: Alf back row Left; next on right Clifford Prosser. Nine of the group were chosen for the National Youth Brass Band & to be conducted by Sir Harry Mortimer.

Grammar School Band 1953:- Alf back row third from Left. Some well known local faces here including Music Master centre front (Kewis) Mr Davis.

Grammar School Band:- Alf middle row third from Left. Youthful Gerald Acton extreme Left middle row.(1952/3).

culminating in playing for England schoolboys. It was something special for us all to go and watch him.

Our class was labelled 1B and after six months in the school we gathered that once every four years there was a double in take. I fell into that grouping and therefore was lucky to be there at all I suppose. My parents were surprised and disappointed to discover we had virtually no homework, no main sciences and only a smattering of French and that for only a period of two years. Our timetable had a preponderance of General Science, gardening and woodwork and this was the only subject I took throughout my time at Ludlow Grammar School. The corresponding A stream had a completely different timetable with trigonometry, languages including Latin and pure sciences.

After a year I was asked by Mr Davies the Latin master if I would like to join the band really because I enjoyed his 78s in our 'music appreciation lessons'. Here I found myself alongside A stream lads and to my surprise found that although they appeared more confident generally they were pretty well the same as me in many respects. Mr Davies encouraged us to progress, gave us the opportunity to join with the British Legion Band for evening practices by giving us tea at his house before making the journey home on the 9.30pm bus.

Arthur Powis the British Legion conductor was likeable, extremely enthusiastic and really keen to have a younger element in the band. I was learning the Eb Bass so I sat alongside Mr Lloyd who was the curator of Ludlow Castle. He never belittled my efforts and his kindly manner helped make sure I enjoyed the experience. I achieved some success and as a result was chosen with nine others to play in the National Youth Brass Band at Birmingham Town Hall under the baton of Sir Harry Mortimer. What a privilege! For one session we were joined by a contingent of blind musicians. I thought their ability without sight was remarkable. That experience is one I have never forgotten. "Kewis", Mr Davies was the first master at L.G.S. to give me a smattering of self belief.

The Beak, Mr David got to know through chatting in woodwork lessons that my Dad was an undertaker. Good timber at the end of the war was expensive and schools would only purchase little more than what pupils were prepared to pay for. I enjoyed my woodwork classes and although Beak was extremely hard and loud he encouraged me and I excelled in that department. The more he encouraged me the more Dad seemed to find a few oak coffin boards for the school's woodwork stock. This timetable pattern continued until I was fifteen when a buzz went round the classes that we were going to have a new Headmaster. We assembled as normal in serried ranks, youngest pupils at the front, oldest at the rear and gowned staff along the side of that ancient schoolroom. The new Headmaster, immaculately dressed, hair groomed and a real spring in his step descended a couple of steps of the staircase then stopped. He cast his eyes around the room. From that moment on we knew the discipline and ethos of the school was going to change. In fact everything changed.

Mr Sparshott our English teacher was a pleasant gentleman with a kindly manner; but the first thing I noticed about him was all that remained of his academic gown were the shoulders and a few straggly pieces hanging down his back with knots at the end. Apparently when a sixth former left school if he was on good terms with Squish, Mr Sparshott , he could request a piece of his gown. As a result all he wore was a tatty remnant. I am sure that like other staff Mr Sparshott must have been in the armed forces because his shoes were always beautifully polished. I was more interested in those shoes than the content of his lessons.

The following week after his arrival Mr Beeby came into our English lesson. We all stood up of course when he entered upon which he asked us to be seated.

Ludlow Grammar School visit to Chirk area 1953:- Mr Nixon (Second from the left) came to the school on secondment and was in the Art Department. He took me and others into Ludlow Town, unheard of; to look at the architecture of our wonderful castle, church, houses etc. We were encouraged to sketch and that knowledge which he passed on has been an inspiration to me ever since. I would love to tell him.Left to Right, Cleasby, Jones, Boulton, Miner, Davies, Jenkins, Dallow, Farrington, --------, Thomas, Wise, Morris.

He asked Squish permission to address us for a few minutes. I recall he began by saying, "You boys are all intelligent otherwise you wouldn't be in this school. Next year you will all be entered for an external examination at the same time as your A stream contemporaries. As from next week you will have a revamped timetable with regular homework. I expect you all to do very well." With that he left. We were all a little non-plussed or should I say shell shocked. That evening going home my companion Gordon said, "That's the first time at Ludlow Grammar School anyone has given me an indication I may have an atom of intelligence." When I arrived home I recounted the day's events to my parents. They were delighted we were going to have to work harder but I must say I was more than a little apprehensive.

DHUSTONE INN,
CLEE HILL,
LUDLOW.

DR. TO

A. R. D. JENKINS
CARPENTER & UNDERTAKER

M.r.s. *Lousia Charles*. 31-8-19.5-2
Caynham Rd Knowbury.

To making coffin with silver fittings, attending funeral, + conveying body of the late George Downton from East Hamlet Hospital to Knowbury Church 18.10.0
Burial Fees 2.0.0
Four bearers at 10/- each 2.0.0
 22.10.0

with thanks

A R D Jenkins

Alf on Left with life long friend John Hughes. John another Clee Hill lad from 'The Knowbury'. This photo was taken at a fete on the field of the Crown Inn Knowbury about 1952/3. John went to Ludlow Grammar School during Alf's time there and like true 'Mountain Goats' they have stuck together. Note the pens in the top pockets, part of the accepted uniform for teenagers in those days. Alf has obviously cycled to Knowbury.

Funeral Costs:- I mentioned that in the late 1930s Dad had charged £11.2.6d for a funeral. The bill above shows the details for a funeral he did in 1952. The whole affair cost £22.10.0. No wonder he wanted me to look at other possibilities for a career.

My Dad must have been thinking about my future possibilities because a week or so later he called me into his workshop and said, "Read this advert in the Ludlow Advertiser." It read that a schoolmaster was required at Ludlow School for the Art Department. Salary would be according to experience and could be £9 per week. Dad said, "Now that's what you should aim at. If you could earn that sort of money my boy you wouldn't want for anything for the rest of your life." Although I didn't use these words I replied that I couldn't possibly aspire to being a schoolmaster. It was such a revered position to us in those days and I did not exactly exude with confidence. Dad said my answer was rubbish and concluded, "My brother, your uncle Arthur is a schoolmaster. You could do the same I am sure, especially with the practical skills you have."

Dad had just finished making a large wagon wheel and had fitted strakes round the felloes. It had taken him the best part of a week of hard slog to do and I saw the bill to the farmer for £4.10 shillings which included materials. I knew therefore why he wished me to strive for other vocations. Recently I was shown an invoice for a funeral Dad had submitted for the father of Alice Jordan (nee Rubery) at about that time. The making, polishing and fittings for the coffin plus all other expenses amounted to £11.2.6d. My goodness in spite of inflation this seemed to me a very small amount. In 2012 it is expected to pay in the region

Dad ready to conduct a funeral: Outside home the Dhu Stone Inn with 1936 Austin 16.

of £2,000. No wonder his reasoning at that time to encourage me to use my craft experience and expertise seemed a possibility.

It was a rude awakening for our class and a great challenge to take an external examination in a year's time. Of course our A stream colleagues had been steadily preparing for four years. Some of us did surprisingly well and two years later I was able to apply for a teacher's training college place. Much to my parents' joy I was accepted at Worcester College of Education, now Worcester University to study Primary subject methods, Handicrafts and Geography at Secondary Level. Chance in life is fortuitous. Opportunities depend on good people. I have Mr Cecil Beeby to thank for opening up opportunities for me. He sincerely believed everyone should be encouraged and given a chance. His teaching philosophy became mine too. What a wonderful man! I owe him so much.

In 1953/54 many experienced quarry men were not optimistic about the future of the industry at this time. It had been decided to close Titterstone quarry and centralise all activities at the Granite and Dhu Stone. However considerable faulting was encountered and men were saying to me in the pub, "Three parts of what we are moving is clay, muck and not much good quality stone. The future doesn't look rosy." Production of road stone dropped dramatically, the Dhu Stone tarmacadam operation became redundant and only a few 'trips' were running daily down Mr Clark's railway incline to Bitterley. Many buildings including the Dhu Stone weighbridge were left to become obsolete. Suddenly Dhu Stone was quiet, dust free for the first time in my life; a ghost village. The pulse had been knocked out of my birth place.

I wondered what the situation would be when I was next able to return home. Little did I realise that nine years would pass before I had the opportunity to explore my beloved Clee Hill again.

National Service

The 1950s was a time when every fit young man was obligated to do two years National Service and a place at University would only be allocated on condition that an individual did forces service first.

With another Clee Hill lad Geoff Key I was called for a medical to Worcester. I filled in various forms concerning academic qualifications and which branch of the forces I wished to enter. I chose the Army Educational Corps. This was ignored because I was informed that a large number of graduates had already made the same request. Two medical discoveries noted were my slow pulse rate of 41 and flat feet. The former was considered an asset for endurance but the flat feet detrimental. Only the previous week I had heard that Colin Cowdrey failed his medical due to this problem and I half hoped for the same outcome.

However flat feet didn't prevent Colin from becoming a very successful batsman or prevent me from doing National Service.

Army papers arrived on the 2nd September 1954 just two weeks after my eighteenth birthday. With much trepidation I caught the train from Ludlow to Oswestry. From there I was transported by bus with many other apprehensive and unsure eighteen year olds to the Royal Artillery Camp at Park Hall. My first impression was of groups of denim clad soldiers marching hither and thither swinging their arms frantically; endless wooden huts all looking the same and very large tarmacadamed parade areas with huge 'guns' dotted here and there. This was going to be my home for the next ten weeks. I felt at rock bottom.

Following my settled life pattern on the top of Clee Hills the next few days were a confused, depressing upheaval.   I was continually rushed and cajoled from pillar to post; shouted at ; verbally abused, issued with ill fitting kit, thick woolly, itchy vests and pants which were hot and uncomfortable and heavily nailed boots with rough toecaps. The appearance of everyone was transformed by a bald off hair cut (short back and sides) and from that day on my spikey crew-cut never had a parting.

Our bedraggled group were, sort of marched to an office where we were issued with an individual army number, mine being 23065879. It seemed from then on every two minutes someone would shout, "What's your bloody last three Gunner ?" to which I had to respond, "879 sergeant; bombardier or sir." We were all so scared we would have saluted a tree or lamp post to avoid the possibility of being hauled before the powers that be and ridiculed yet more.

Every National Service man can no doubt re-call similar stories and experiences but it has to be remembered that everyone had to go unless registered as a conscientious objector. That two year 'stint' had an indelible impact; changed attitudes; broadened horizons and made everyone of us appreciate having had freedom of choice. Life was indeed hectic from each early morning until late evening, each day being punctuated with marching drill, arm's drill including the old .303 rifle, tests, lectures on a multitude of subjects including gonorrhoea, syphilis, French letters (condoms) all of which I had never heard of in the 1950s. This may seem difficult to believe in this 'enlightened' day and age. Other lectures on reasons for our short hair cuts to prevent the spread of lice, cleanliness to prevent scabies and how to have a proper wash. How humiliating to be instructed how to wash behind your ears, clean ones teeth thoroughly and shave properly. Being continually watched, cajoled and having someone bawling abuse about two inches from your face, insinuating you were the lowest form of life on earth was the norm. On reflection some of those basic ablutions and drills could be useful in modern parenthood and society where it is noted that so few consider any pride in their appearance.

There was so much futile information and worthless skills to assimilate including having to scrounge, cut and fix rectangular pieces of cardboard inside folded shirts and other clothes to 'square them all off' for inspections; how to collect grains of barrack room dust with an inadequate broom and another squaddy holding a piece of taut paper only to be insulted by the bark, "You shower; this bloody place is filthy. God knows what your pig sty homes look like."

After our first kit inspection we were given a demonstration on how to 'bull' (shine) boot toe caps. I was made to get down on my knees and look at Sgt Mc Caffrey's toe caps . He bawled, "Can you see your 'orrible mug Gunner? My nose was only a few inches away from his boots and yes I could see my reflection. Following this we were told, "Anyone whose toe caps aren't as good as these in one week's time will be put in the cooler (prison)."

Every evening of the next week , hours were spent with polish, spit and a blob of polish on a duster, moving it round and round in small circles working it into the leather, trying to build up a bull. Recruits who 'had got some in' that is, had been in the army a couple of weeks told us to use a warm iron to smooth out the toe cap bumps or use the back of a spoon.

Impromptu inspections at all hours of the day and night were regular. The door of the barrack room would burst open accompanied by the egoistic voice of an NCO (non commissioned officer) bawling, "Stand by your beds! Atten-----tion!" Half asleep and bedraggled, for the next half an hour all eighteen of us were subjected to a stream of personal abuse; our kit thrown all over the place; beds tipped over and being told, "You are the filthiest, untidiest bastards I have ever come across." We were all so tired, dejected and humiliated and it would take ages to collect and sort individual's belongings. But! camaraderie developed between us that was so united and strong we were determined not to break or be defeated. Some acquired skills of bulling, squaring off kit or obtaining perfect creases in trousers with a hot iron and brown paper quicker than others.   So articles were swopped around to 'specialists'. Pity was genuinely taken on less resilient buddies and help given with menial tasks they couldn't master. On reflection this was probably the aim of the army to make us a cohesive unit.

Sunday morning was the only time of respite and was quoted by one as being a moment of Heaven in Hell. I usually took the opportunity with one or two others to go to church because I knew my family would be doing the same. I felt I was able to share that time with them and it strengthened my faith. It was a place too where all ranks seemed to respect each other; every hat off and heads bowed – but not surprisingly I never saw any of our uncouth NCOs there.

On returning to the spider on one such Sunday mates were sitting on their beds blancoing belts and brassoing buttons while they listened to Jean Metcalfe and Cliff Michaelmore on Two Way Family Favourites. Suddenly Spud Murphy, a cockney boxer stood up, spun round and threw both his boots at the nearest radio speaker shouting, "Shut your f...in' rattle."

Absolute silence ensued. A buddy picked up Spud's bruised boots and placed them on the bed where he was sitting in tears. Other chaps collected numerous speaker fragments, intending to reassemble it. Alas it was beyond redemption. The incident led expectedly to an inquisition and reprimand but, no one would say who was responsible for the damage because we all could have reacted in the same way.   For the remainder of the day we were each given a metal egg cup, made to run buckets of water and fill two baths to their rim by dipping the egg cups into the buckets then tipping their contents into the baths.

We began to realise that an integral part of this training was to subject each individual to as much abuse, physical and mental endurance to test one to breaking point or provoke a reaction. This was to ensure that under pressure every recruit would automatically obey no matter how absurd the request; ultimately to achieve an unquestioning response necessary on active service.

Nowadays there would probably be numerous 'Deep Cut' enquiries, but we all assumed in our naivety that it was a system devised for the good of the army and country – not to be challenged.

After a few weeks we endeavoured to shut abuse from our natural emotions even when an NCO was hurling expletives, making derogatory remarks about one's parents and spraying your face with saliva from a distance of about two inches.

Those hulks of manhood, PT instructors, were the most feared. They oozed with muscles from every conceivable part of their body and put us through excruciating physical tests. Luckily as a country boy I carried no weight and was reasonably fit from having walked and run to school and naturally fulfilling many physical tasks at home. But! to watch a city lad or someone who had never lifted anything heavier than a pencil, collapse from the gymnasium wall bars into a heap on the floor was not a happy sight. Of course the more someone resembled a seven stone weakling the more the PT hulks played on his apparent limitations.

In a semi daze we endured circuit training, PT drill and full kit exercises with individuals constantly being picked on and blamed for the squad being given extra penalties and hardship. However I do recall our squad did not add to the 'culprit's' misery but in the main realised this regular discrimination was yet another tactic to break our spirit and develop camaraderie.

When acquired to perfection, drill and marching skills result in a considerable feeling of pride but the processes which National Service Recruits were subjected to were unbelievably arduous and humiliating. The continual bark from the sergeant or sergeant major to "Get fell in you miserable lot," and the "1,2,3, 1,2,3" which we all had to chant in time with our movements when learning basics were soon imprinted on our minds.

When starting to march the command "By the left qui....ck march" was given. Some poor chaps were so perplexed they would move left leg and left arm together. Try doing it. I found it physically impossible but it's amazing how confused one's movements and thoughts can become under pressure. The bawling abuse aimed to make us feel we were the "worst shower on God's earth" these tyrants had seen.

Each block of barrack rooms was known as a spider because from above, the long corridor had four squaddies' rooms on either side. In our spider we were indeed a mixed bunch both academically and physically. Giles Davidson was 6' 3", Barry Pagdin 5' 11" and me 5' 6". Some were articulate others unable to string a cohesive sentence together and even some Welsh lads to whom English was truly a foreign language.

In spite of these physical and academic variations I have to concede it was a logistic miracle that the army's methods moulded us within a week or two into a Battery able to march, wheel, dress to the right and left, slope arms, order arms, stand at ease, fall out, etc, etc and feel somewhat proud of our survival achievements.

The constant physical demands, being ordered from pillar to post; not having any freedom of choice or being able to make one's own decisions was a shock to the system. Our mutual thoughts were however that we were all in the same boat and thankfully our minds were becoming hardened and conditioned to absorb the insults. I have been asked by young people, "Why did you put up with such treatment? I wouldn't." What a foolish thing to say! We were forced to obey every command and absorb any abuse. To have reacted would have resulted in being put on a charge or confined to the "cooler".

Depression was experienced by some lads and virtually everyone had homesickness. As new recruits surplus boot laces, belts , ties and lanyards were taken from us to reduce the risk of attempted suicide.

Fatigues became a new experience. Army cooking was tolerable for me because thankfully I had been encouraged to eat anything and everything at home. I found the change easier to manage than many. Fatigues in khaki denims formed part of every day. Some occupations were stupid and pointless such as painting string or edging grass areas with the aid of scissors. Being on the end of a cookhouse dishwasher for eight to ten hours at a stretch was absolutely exhausting. Greasy, half clean, metal utensils were nauseating and after a few hours taking twelve inch dinner plates off a conveyor belt my arms ached like toothache and I longed for a rest. I was weighed again about this time and I had dropped from 8stone 10 lbs to 8 stone 6 lbs – not much more than skin and bone but fit.

As well as .303 rifle practice and the handling, firing and cleaning of other small arms we were introduced to 25 lb field guns. Now I realised why we were named the 17th Field Regiment Royal Artillery. Sergeant McCaffrey was our instructor and God. He explained the name of every part of these large weapons but like some others I couldn't take every detail in immediately. Eight men were assigned to each gun and each man had to have experience of the eight positions necessary to operate the 25 pounder. My first command was to set the correct elevation and obtain the correct firing setting for any given target. I just couldn't remember how to execute this, partly due to anxiety and fear created by Sergeant McCaffrey breathing down my neck. As usual we were all accused of being bloody useless and illegitimate, but the tirade culminated with us all being ordered to put a full pack on our back, hold a .303 above our head followed by the command, "You can see those elm trees at the far side of the barrack square. I want to see you all go across this square like a streak of duck sh.., rifles above your head and climb those trees. Those who are nearest the ground when I get to you will be put on a charge. Move!" I finished half way up a tree with my boots resting on another fellow's helmet. Exhausted but I was relieved I had avoided yet more trouble.

Sunday was next day and we were given an hour to sort out our kit and tidy up. Those who could, wrote letters home. I also helped some poor chaps who couldn't string a sentence together. Looking back I expect that was my first teaching experience. I told my Mum we were near Gobowen Orthopaedic Hospital and one lad had been permitted to visit a relative. He had been incredibly elated to experience an hour of freedom. I asked Mum if she knew of any relative or friend from home who was receiving treatment so that I could visit. Some days later I received a reply from both Mum and Dad accompanied by the name of a patient and a lovely home-made fruit cake. That was the best cake I had ever tasted and it was polished off by my newly found buddies in no time.

The Regimental Church was a peaceful sanctuary. I requested permission to go to services but before this was granted my records had to be checked to see that I had been a regular church attender. It was a strange experience. Rank did not matter. We were all saying the same prayers together. I felt very relaxed because I realised that my devout parents would be in church at home and for the first time in my life I really wanted to do the same as them and my faith became an important comfort to me.

We were back on the square next morning. More drill on the field guns and to the exasperation of Sergeant McCaffrey I could *not* remember the setting sequence. However he had his own effective method of making sure I did. He came up behind me grabbing my left ear with one hand and the right one with his other shouting, "You silly young b...... More degrees, less degrees," as he turned my left ear clockwise and my right ear anticlockwise. I *never* made the same mistake again; always recalling left ear clockwise, right ear anti-clockwise.

Within a week we were loading and unloading 25 lb shells. I was the number one on my gun giving instructions and we were off to Tonfanneau firing range for our first of many firing practices. Now we *had* to get everything right.

To set the gun on a target, load the shell, fire and see it explode very near its target nearly a mile away was exhilarating and the recoil of the gun tremendous.

Increased fitness gradually made demands easier to withstand and continual expletives and abuse had less impact. I began to enjoy rifle practice but the sight of scores of rabbits dying, dead and others with bulbous eyes from myxomatosis was distressing. We frequently put them out of their misery by hitting them on the head with a rifle butt. Millions of rabbits were wiped out in 1954/5 from that horrible disease.

Rabbits had been a staple part of our diet on Clee Hill all my young life but after this epidemic I never relished eating another.

I was unexpectedly called to the HQ office with the usual command, "123,123, Halt. What are your last three?   My answer of 879 was followed by, "Gunner Jenkins I see you play an Eb Bass. You will go to the Regimental band practice this evening." That was that. No polite invitation of course. So in addition to square bashing, field guns and fatigues I had some enjoyment playing with the 17th Field Regimental Band. I was fixed up with a gleaming instrument and had to learn for the first time to play while marching. This was fine apart from having my lips bruised when being jolted by potholes at our practice area.

Soon my eight weeks of basic training came to an end and we were allowed out of camp to visit Oswestry. We were like taut, wound up springs and I was the fittest I'd ever been in my life. The gates were opened and we ran, heavy boots and uniform all the way into town without needing to pause.

Woolwich

Our next move was to Woolwich, the Headquarters of the Royal Artillery. We were all re-assessed, asked where we wished to be posted and our attributes analysed. The world was a troubled place. Cyprus was in turmoil; the Korean War was in full swing and there was the Mau Mau unrest in Africa. I volunteered for the Far East thinking that I was unlikely to get to that part of the world as a civilian. We all had to wait and see if our choices had been granted.

Due to 'colour blindness' I failed the final tests for an officer's course. Again I was told there were no vacancies in the Educational Corps, that I was clerical material and instructed to take a six weeks clerical and typing course. Our Battery continued with square bashing and guard duty but we were allowed out of barracks to make use of Woolwich Public Baths.

This was much appreciated because Woolwich Barracks was a disgrace to the Royal Artillery; peeling plaster, dirty rooms, antiquated bunk beds and disgusting ablutions – such a contrast to pristine Park Hall. On reflection because Woolwich was mainly a transit camp the MOD were probably not prepared to keep the place in reasonable condition.

My visits to the bath house gave me first hand experience of London smog as well as a decent bath. Due to the extensive use of solid fuel in those days and low lying mist from the Thames the city was blanketed with thick, yellow fog. The pollution was appalling and public buildings completely blackened from soot.

The smog was as thick as pea soup. Most people walked around with handkerchiefs tied over their mouths and after breathing through these they became black in a few minutes. Chronic chest problems were

(Jan 1955) Having completed two months basic training at 17th Field Regiment Park Hall Oswestry; standing at ease ready to be inspected:- Alf second from Left in the front rank. Spud Murphy second rank on the right (the squaddy who threw his boot and smashed the radio speaker) and Trevor Nuttall back rank right. Both these chaps were in the same spider as me at Oswestry.

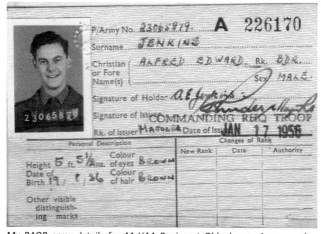

My BAOR army details for 44 HAA Regiment Oldenburg:- Army number 23065879 and rank at that time Bombardier.

common and everyone seemed to be incessantly coughing. Traffic continually came to a standstill. Only bus drivers, extremely familiar with their routes seemed able to cope. I remember talking to my brother-in-law John Clent some years later about the conditions and although he was a very experienced HGV driver the only way he could progress on occasions was to get out of his lorry, speak to a local bus driver and follow him. What a transformation has been made in our cities by banning solid fuel and cleaning wonderful architectural gems like St. Pauls and Westminster Abbey.

On application a six hour pass was available on a Saturday evening. Mum had told me that some of her friends, Davidsons, members of a Dhu Stone family, lived near Clapham Junction. London was the furthest I had ever travelled in my life and although I was becoming a little more confident the underground and London transport was still an enigma to me. However I took the plunge and travelled to Clapham to be very warmly received by Mrs Nancy Styles (nee Davidson), her daughter Norma and son Brian. It was truly special to enter their home and have tea in civilised surroundings and forget for a short while I was a National Service man. I was lucky enough to visit Nancy and her family a few times. They all loved Titterstone Clees so much so that one member of their family had his ashes scattered on the hills. The family visited Dhu Stone whenever they had the opportunity and we had lovely, nostalgic chats. On my last visit being very fatigued I dropped off to sleep on the train. I woke with a start to find myself sitting in an empty carriage in a siding. Everywhere was deserted. I looked at my watch. It was

23.40. Panic! I had to be in barracks by midnight. I ran up the stairs and hailed a taxi asking hurriedly how much it was to Woolwich Barracks. The taxi driver's reply was ten shillings and six pence. The sum total I had was ten shillings. The wonderful London cabbie took pity on a soldier in uniform and much to my relief delivered me to the barrack gates by 23.57 accepting my ten shillings as payment. That was the only time I was pleased to see Woolwich Barracks.

My clerical course was the least physically demanding period of my army experience. Instructors were human, knew their job and addressed us in a civil manner. With their encouragement most of us became competent typists, successfully took examinations, were designated B3 Clerks and assessed as suitable for future Regimental HQ administration.

A little later we received our postings. We were assigned to various parts of the Globe. My request for the Far East was ignored and my posting read, "23065879 Gnr Jenkins A – 44 HAA(Heavy Ack Ack) Regiment BAOR, Oldenburg." I collected my weekly pay the next day. The same procedure with an NCO bawling, "Gnr Jenkins; fo....ward; 123,123 halt. Salute the paymaster." This I did smartly shouting, "879 Gnr Jenkins , Sir." I received my 28 shillings , did a quick about turn and was ordered to collect a thirty six hour pass.

I was unbelievably excited at the prospect of seeing Mum, Dad and Marina. The journey however was tortuous and so time consuming, the route being via Birmingham, Shrewsbury and eventually Ludlow – leaving me just ten hours at home. What a joy it was to see my parents, my home, the Dhu Stone pub and the quarrymen but the first thing they said was, "When are you going back?"

Mum gave me a close inspection, said I was thin, asked where had all my curls gone and finished by saying, "My that's some hair cut."

I could not sit or relax because I had been continuously on the move and shouted at for three and a half months. Each time I 'perched' I really expected someone to bawl and have to jump to my feet.

Almost before I could collect my thoughts I was making my return journey to Woolwich Station realising that it would be at least six to nine months before I could be home again.

Germany

We were ordered to pack our kit bags ready to move out at 0600 hours the next morning; loaded into army lorries and transported to Harwich where we embarked carrying our kit onto a troop carrier. Thoughts of men leaving home during World War II came to mind. Their sadness of leaving wives and children and not knowing whether they would *ever* return helped me put my future into perspective.; but I can't say that it softened my blow much just at that moment.

None of us had ever been on a ship or out of the country before. I for one felt very apprehensive but surrounded by hundreds of like minded lads helped. The ship seemed huge and I marvelled how it could possibly float. Carrying our kit bags etc we descended flight after flight of stairs. Our studded boots made the steel treads above and below reverberate . It was hot and claustrophobic. Eventually we were shown into a dimly lit hull packed with row upon row of metal framed hammocks. Having been allocated one each we were ordered to grab our mess tins and line up for supper. It was stew, pleasantly hot, welcome and far better tasting than anything I had had while at Woolwich. Meal completed we were ordered back to our hammocks and told to lie down. There were a few uncomfortable thuds and bumps, the engines began to drone and we realised we were at sea. We were on our way to the Hook of Holland and the first of what was to be my eight crossings of the North Sea. The purring of the engines and the motion of the sea thankfully induced sleep.

Reveille sounded all too soon followed by ablutions, breakfast and the carrying our heavy loads up those stairs again for a roll call and inspection on deck. We disembarked, were herded onto a train and were soon off on our long journey to Oldenburg in West Germany.

I really enjoyed the first few hours travelling through Holland. The day was fine and to see vast, low lying areas which the Dutch had reclaimed from the sea made me recall my school geography lessons at Ludlow

Grammar School. This was an experience I never expected to have. The land was so flat, a real contrast to my home area and the Titterstone Clees. Dykes stretched for miles and huge herds of Friesian cattle filled the countryside. Everywhere looked so clean. Even the cowsheds had curtains at their windows and every inch of land was purposefully utilised. The ubiquitous windmills and hundreds of cyclists peddling furiously along billiard flat roads completed the scene. I could not believe that a country could be so flat. On reflection Holland was seething with windmills and obviously accepted as essential by the Dutch. No objection to them. Why not accept wind turbines in this country then to produce clean power?

Day wore on into night as we rattled and squeaked our journey into Germany in that antiquated, rusty train. Eventually we arrived at Oldenburg. As we assembled on the platform I saw huge, ancient engines soon to become a familiar sight. The last leg through the city by lorry took us to an imposing, high barracks which we were told had been previously occupied by German SS troops. This was to be our home.

By now we were really tired but had to carry our kit up seven flights of twelve steps to our allocated rooms. All I wanted was sleep.

!955 Oldenburg B.O.A.R:- Alf newly promoted as a B2 Clerk at Regimental Head quarters, 44 H.A.A.

The rooms were much smaller than Park Hall only accommodating eight people. But for those who have never experienced being in close proximity to others for long periods it is not easy. There has to be considerable tolerance especially when you do not have any control over who your companions are. I get along with most people but there are always one or two flies in the ointment. Fortunately I had Terry Joy next to me. He had worked at Cowley Oxford as a clerk. He was intelligent and good company but so depressed because he had just left his newly wedded wife. Terry and I became good friends. I had been very much a home bird and was still occasionally homesick. I did not however take kindly to Bombadier Hancock, a scouse Regular who seemed to resent all National Service personnel and who had been established in the corner of the room for a long time.

The purpose for us to be in the army was to be trained as soldiers and this continued. We still had parades and inspections but not so frequently and we had to learn to position huge HAA guns (Heavy ack,ack) into their firing position. This took all of nine minutes, no use whatsoever against modern aircraft. I marched along to the Regimental Headquarters Office where I was to be a

Christmas Time 1955 in the SS (Secret Service) Barracks, Oldenburg:- These barracks had formerly been used by the German SS. Alf on the Right with Friend Terry Joy from Oxford.

junior B3 clerk. I found that if I worked conscientiously and fulfilled my duties life was tolerable. Initially I used my typing skills to write letters for the Adjutant to approve and sign. Our old typewriters with their metal keys seem now to be so antiquated. I was always asked to produce three copies; one to post and two to file. Carbon paper of course was placed between each copy and all mistakes had to be erased on each copy with a very thin rubber. I soon acquired routine skills of the office including filing and preparing regimental and company conduct sheets. These were details of offences supposedly committed by soldiers which I had to prepare for forthcoming trials. It certainly was an eye opener for me being a comparatively naive country lad. Some incidents were hilarious and others extremely serious. Certain names occurred regularly and after each guilty offence a fourteen or twenty one day punishment was not uncommon. Some of those chaps must have served well beyond their stipulated two years because of their unfortunate company or stupidity.

After an established routine for a few weeks we were allowed a pass for a Saturday evening in pairs. Terry and I approached the guarded exit gate and were handed a packet each. Outside the gate I Investigated. I asked

Terry what these 'things' were. He laughed and explained that they were French Letters, contraceptives, to be used to prevent venereal disease and avoid a woman becoming pregnant. Being married Terry knew about these aids. I did not. How different our modern world is when even young school children are given instruction about contraceptives and to think I had never seen such a thing at the age of eighteen.

As we walked into town I was interested in the difference between architecture there and at home. Roofs were much steeper and there was not the range from medieval to present day design as experienced in our beautiful local towns of Ludlow and Leominster.

World War II bomb damage was still very evident and extensive but re-construction was really pushing ahead. Scaffolding was 'Heath Robinson' construction. Bits of timber of all sorts, lengths and thicknesses held together with nails and cord. It seemed so amateurish compared with home; but I realised that this defeated country hadn't got the resources they needed and had to make do. However we were truly amazed how destroyed shops quickly returned to business.

Provided we were in barracks and not on manoeuvres we were given some freedom at weekends to go into Oldenburg. Sadly young Germans our own age understandably resented us but I did eventually become friendly with a young civilian named Detre who came into our offices for various reasons. He invited me to his home. His parents were pleasant and polite and although his father had fought against the British he did not bear me any animosity. The invitation did allow me to see a domestic situation. The home was certainly not lavish but they introduced me to various varieties of sausage.

In general shop keepers and business folk were happy to see us and take our money especially when we made an effort to communicate in German. On the other hand I discovered to my surprise and detriment that frauen in particular did not queue at bus stops. It was a free for all when a bus arrived. Buxom women armed with umbrellas were really belligerent and just pushed us polite squaddies out of the way.

On our second visit to town we were in quite a group. It was at least three miles to the shops, pubs and restaurants and on arrival we needed to go to the toilet. Our phrase book enabled us to choose the appropriate door but we were taken aback because just inside the toilet entrance an elderly lady gave us three pieces of paper each. No wasting here I thought. Spud Murphy of Park Hall fame began to laugh and in his broad cockney accent said, "What's this for Mrs? One up, one down and one polish." We all appreciated the banter but the stern frau did not bat an eyelid.

During those visits two things made quite an impression. Firstly the cuckoo clock shops. I just loved to wander in and see the incredible variety and workmanship; some very expensive and elaborate and of course the ubiquitous cuckoos popping in and out everywhere. I made a vow to save up and take one home. This I did and fifty years on we still have it. The second lasting memory was the piano accordion. It was so common when walking back to barracks in the evening to hear the unmistakable sound of these instruments emanating from lighted homes. That made me think of home, the Dhu Stone Inn because as I had written in "Titterstone Clees" every Saturday at home was music night when every customer would sing, play an instrument, recite a favourite poem or perform a stunt. Flooding back would come the home scenes particularly of Christmas time. The singing in the pub was wonderful. Every man knew the words of all the well known carols. Would they nowadays I wonder? Mum would distribute trays of mince pies and the 'Minstrels' would arrive with Dick Beddoe playing tin whistles, Jack Williams the bone clappers, other instrumentalists and Dennis Crowther with piano accordion. The whole group had highly coloured clothes and faces completely blacked. Lovely thoughts! Will Cleeton was so good on the concertina and my old friend Dennis Crowther would bring tears to our eyes with his rendition of 'Little Johnny Brown.'

In our roll as HQ clerks we were inspected regularly; had to turn out smartly every day and be absolutely correct in our approach to our senior officers. However we never knew when Major Thomas, known to us as 'Black Tom' would be there to meet us on our arrival. He was cruel, had a condescending and curt manner, detested all National Service personnel and absolutely resented us being there. Everyone in HQ was extremely wary of Black Tom. We had no doubt that on active service, troops would have been tempted to shoot him. But! his attitude kept us on edge, made us determined to keep reasonable hours and drink very little. How our barrack room wished Bombardier Hancock was under his direct command. That despicable character was more often than not the worse for drink.

Remember our room was six storeys up. Hancock would open a window wide; stand up on the window sill and while hanging onto the central, stone mullion urinate on to people walking below. We were absolutely ashamed of him but could do nothing to affect that unpredictable bully's attitude.

One Saturday evening as usual he came in slamming doors, shouting abuse and waking us all up. We had had enough! He collapsed into bed fully clothed and was soon snoring. Terry, me and Trevor Nuttall got up quietly; lifted the front of his bed above our heads and dropped it. The cast iron frame smashed to pieces. We ran out of the room and locked ourselves in the nearest toilets before he came to. This tirade raged for some time before his inebriated state made him collapse on the floor. We crept back into bed, Hancock not realising what had happened. He was fined heavily for his broken bed and charged. Our room was relieved that he left us alone thereafter.

Hanover Military Hospital was where we were all sent for specific medical treatment. The increase of clerical work concentration brought some minor sight problems for me. I mentioned this to Sgt Williams my HQ office superior. He sent me to the MO (medical officer) who arranged for me to go by lorry to an eye specialist at Hanover. Since the age of seven I had worn reading and distance spectacles. I explained my occasional ' cloudiness' to the specialist and after various tests he asked, "Why do you use two pairs of spectacles?" I explained that one pair was used for close work and the other pair for rifle, HAA work and other distance requirements. He told me he could not understand why I had ever had two pairs because he was sure he could prescribe one pair of lenses I could use all the time. A week later I received my new spectacles; one pair perfect for all occasions. They were not bi-focal or vari- focal, just ordinary lenses. What a difference that discovery made to army life. How lucky I was to visit that military hospital and how grateful I have been to that optician.

I wrote home to tell my parents my good news. A week or two later Mum replied and suggested I should take advantage of such good treatment and get my teeth sorted out too. I duly applied for dental treatment and after being seen by the Regimental MO again I was dispatched to Hanover. I knew I needed a number of my lower teeth attended to. After inspection I was ordered to recline. Remember this was the early 1950s. An ether mask was put over my nose and mouth and I was soon in 'noddy' land. When I woke I was really uncomfortable and aghast to find I had just one molar and a few front teeth left on my lower jaw. From then on I was determined *not* to see the MO if at all possible.

Manoeuvres lasting fourteen days or more were a regular part of the Regiment's routine. Every vehicle, HAA guns and mobile kitchens were involved. These exercises were essential to make sure the whole regiment could be mobilised as quickly as possible and operate in the field when required on active service.

We travelled considerable distances to Lunnaberg Heath, the Baltic Sea, Holland and other destinations. Due to my roots on Titterstone Clees I have always been interested in accent and dialect. The army was therefore a wonderful conglomeration. I took great pleasure in listening, deducing where individuals came from then asking them to see how near my guess had been. Every day we heard numerous accents including Scouse, Geordie, Yorkshire, Lancashire, Cockney, North Wales, South Wales, Birmingham, Cornish and the Shires. A dozen or so squaddies were journeying in the back of a lorry towards the Baltic. Tables and other requirements were stacked and some of us dozed. On waking the chap next to me was chatting away. I thought I was dreaming because the accent was so familiar. I asked him where he was from. He replied, "I da spect theist eard of a plaace called Ludlu ast?" Quite excitedly I said that I had. He continued, "Well I comes from Cleobury Mortimer." The name of that

SS Barracks behind wagon. Alf with organised Office HQ wagon ready for manoeuvres to the Baltic.

chap was Percy Smith and I had the good fortune to

Ready for deployment and camouflage:- RCO Alf with his jeep. I drove thousands of miles in BOAR then failed my test when demobbed in England.

meet him on a few occasions. Every vehicle was thoroughly inspected for cleanliness, wheels, inside, outside, top and underneath. Then when satisfied the CO (Commanding Officer) ordered each Battery onto the autobahn. Every heavy, towing, and matador vehicle had an armed soldier standing with his head up through the cab turret. This was usually my role with a driver pulling a HAA gun. After a few circuits around the barracks I was issued with a green ticket and told to drive a jeep. This I did on many manoeuvres. Smaller vehicles towed limbers and the last contingent in each Battery to leave was the Catering Corp attachment with all their requirements to feed us.

When driving a jeep I was accompanied by a guide, told to go ahead of the convoy and given a map reference to tell each vehicle where to stop. I then became an RCO, a road control orderly. My duty was to give each group of vehicles a deployment map reference a little way ahead. Our destinations were always densely wooded areas or heath land. My job was a responsible one and my mistakes could have had dire consequences. I had to make sure that the correct map reference was given to each driver and repeated to me before his vehicle could proceed. Soldiers were always trading and bartering, money being in very short supply for National Servicemen. If I was a little pushed for cash I would ask for a cigarette before supplying the map reference. Time was of the essence so drivers readily handed one over. By the time deployment was completed I had a large pile of fags. I didn't smoke so I traded them for chocolate or biscuits.

Lucky escape:- The damaged matador after hitting a tree. Note the turret on top of the cab.

Mile upon mile of Germany's roads were lined with trees planted very near to the road edges. When standing with my head through the cab turret I was very aware how little leeway there was for driver error with these huge vehicles. Of course the inevitable was bound to happen. The long straight stretches and the trees flashing by at very regular intervals were hypnotic. Suddenly our matador lurched towards a tree. I dived down into the cab. Too late! The driver had fallen asleep over the wheel and bang; we'd hit a trunk. Fortunately we were unhurt, the driver too relaxed to worry until he was jolted to life. He was severely reprimanded and the recovery of the Matador and HAA gun was quite a performance.

Deployment was followed by camouflaging, the digging of latrines, the erection of sleeping quarters and catering facilities. Finally we had an inspection to make sure that we were all as realistically concealed as possible. Food on manoeuvres was always superior

The crash:-Inquisition by the CO. My driver feeling rather sorry for himself and extremely contrite.

to barrack cooking but the outdoors and physical work gave us a keener appetite too. Fine weather made these exercises tolerable in spite of vehicle inspections and extremely cold nights. When conditions were suitable we were ordered to collect metal drums from the cook house, punch holes through their bases, erect scaffolding made from tree branches and mount the drums about seven feet from the ground. The scaffold had to be robust to support ladders leaning against it. Then in turn we had to strip off and stand beneath a drum while a comrade poured cold water into it.

The verdict – cool but refreshing and a feeling of comparative cleanliness. We had to clean every inch of our vehicles and equipment with cloths, brushes and anything available. Every wheel hub, petrol tank, headlamp etc had to be seen to be pristine enabling thorough examination to make sure everything was in perfect working order. Once again we were conditioned to accept that this drudgery was essential.

Night guard duty was an experience. The brief was to patrol in pairs, armed and space ourselves a few yards apart. When near the Baltic Sea in dense woodland I was stepping carefully along, my fellow guard being a few yards behind. It was pitch black and the enormous number of frogs croaking nearby made for an eerie atmosphere. This was compounded because as you neared the frogs their croaking ceased abruptly only to start again to our sides and behind.

Suddenly something hit me across my Adam's apple and threw me to the ground. I thought we'd been ambushed. My companion on hearing the thud and my yelp crawled up to me. We lay listening. Only the frogs and rustling leaves disturbed the blackness. I got to my knee; stood up slowly and ran my hand up the tree trunk I had fallen against. To my enormous relief I touched a camouflage net tie. I realised that I had walked into the guy rope and been knocked off balance.

When temperatures were icy cold, the rivers froze over or we had had rain for days. The ice, mud and damp conditions made me think of trench warfare during the first and second world wars; of scurvy, rats, flooded trenches and numerous fatalities. This bolstered me knowing that hopefully with luck two years would be my limit in the army.   Frost covered camp beds and sodden toilet paper made me vow I would never go on a camping holiday in civvy street.

It is quite extraordinary in retrospect to remember what a significant impact those two years made on my life and I am positive virtually every other National Serviceman would say the same.

Time passed but some impressions never fade. Our battery parked up for a short time on one occasion very near to Cologne Cathedral. That prominent, beautiful building was completely isolated. A huge area around it which was flattened by allied bombing had not been redeveloped and we discovered that only slight damage had been incurred on one wing of the cathedral. Our curiosity asked why this was. Apparently the cathedral had been a prominent marker for invading aircraft and remained as such throughout bombardments. During one weekend we had a chance to visit Hamburg and investigated the Red Light district. I had never experienced anything like the 'Reepabahn'. To see half naked prostitutes hanging out of windows or seductively reclining here, there and everywhere, trying to persuade all and sundry to enter their abodes was amusing but unnerving.

The gruelling Nimeagan marches were events at which the army prided themselves. To march as much as twenty five to thirty miles in full kit was an endurance feat. How on earth did we do that? Things in Cyprus were hotting up. I was ordered to see our Adjutant. By this time I was a B1 Clerk, the top grade. He told me a B1 Chief Clerk was required to take charge in Cyprus at a Regimental HQ: that I had the appropriate

Manoeuvres near Baltic Sea:- Alf second from Left

qualifications and time of service remaining to be sent there. I was instructed to pack my belongings and prepare to travel to the Hook next day. This I did, taking a similar route to the one when I first landed in Germany. I was waiting to embark with a group of soldiers when a dispatch rider approached and asked who was Bombardier 879 Jenkins. I acknowledged him to be told, "You're not going to Cyprus." On asking why the change of instruction he said, "HQ has discovered you have five months and two weeks to do. The ruling for the post is six months." I thought to myself that I could have told the stupid Adjutant that if I had been asked. So I made the long journey back to Oldenburg rather disappointed to be denied a new experience in another part of the world.

Back in Barracks from the Baltic Sea. Now counting the days towards demob.

Giving our room a wash out:-Trevor Nuttall Left, Alf 3rd from Left , Terry Joy with the bucket and ----Tyrell.

There was a huge fire tank in the camp in which at weekends we were allowed to swim. Weather was hot so like others I had a dip or two. A few days later I felt really poorly and boils erupted around my waist, on my neck and right arm. I went to the MO and was ordered to hospital. For the only time in my life I experienced delirium. I remember putting my arms around my body and grasping my arms but peculiarly I couldn't feel anything. However within a week or two I was back in office routine. I still have the boil scars. Like every other National Serviceman I had a calendar on my locker and assiduously crossed off each day and counted how many more I had to complete before release. At this time the new German Army was formed. I was involved in instructing and lecturing new recruits. There was not compulsory conscription but many were coerced to join up because it was one avenue of employment. Of those I was responsible for some suddenly became friendly and understanding, realising that many of us did not wish to be in the forces at all.

Having passed a number of examinations, being a B1 Clerk and an Acting Sergeant my wage was £5 a week. This truly was good money with food and clothing supplied. As was the army rule seven shillings per week was deducted from my pay and placed in 'credits'. This was retained to pay for any equipment lost or damaged. Time passed and demob week arrived at last. I had been fortunate not to have incurred any deductions so I collected my demob credits of £120. I was wealthy. I purchased a camera, of course a cuckoo clock and other presents to take home.

As was the custom we had a little celebration and a few demob drinks. Unfortunately I passed out.

Someone had spiked my lager. I was roused in my bed by Terry. The first thing I did was to search for my credits. They had disappeared. I was frantic and furious with myself. Of course the journey home would be free - but I hadn't got a penny for a snack, drink or emergency. In despair I went to the YMCA and the Salvation Army and explained my predicament. They kindly loaned me funding and I learned from them that mine was not an unusual occurrence. Thank God for the Sally Army. I have always supported them ever since.

After my eighth trip across the North Sea I reached Harwich, Woolwich then Birmingham with money in my pocket. Although I knew the bus journey would take two and a quarter hours to get to Clee Hill I was so relieved to get on the Midland Red 192. I was still in my army uniform of course and as we pulled away from Bewdley a lady crossed the bus and said, "I recognise the Regimental flash on your shoulder. My son Percy Smith is in that Regiment and he is coming home this week. Do you know him? Much to her surprise I replied that I did indeed know Percy; but; I didn't tell her Percy had some extra time to do. In my office duties I had dealt with a minor offence concerning Percy and I knew at least a fortnight had been added to his service time.

Within an hour I was getting off the 192 in Clee Hill village and walking along the railway track towards home. I was disappointed to see weeds growing up between the sleepers due to the railway line's obvious little use. Few trucks were in the sidings but at least the engine shed was still there. The huge drum house at the top of the Green had numerous windows smashed by vandals and many railway and quarry buildings had disappeared. It all looked so sad and desolate; not at all how my mind had remembered the locality. I thought to myself that these changes would undoubtedly have made a considerable difference to pub trade. This was September 1956. The previous two years had made a tremendous impact on me, but, the view from those hills was as incredible as ever and I hadn't seen anything to compare with it in my travels. I was home.

I had considerable difficulty in settling or sitting, even for a minute. It was so unusual to be able to make my own decisions again. Mum, Dad and Marina were delighted to see me and keen to chat about my experiences because both parents lived in an age when travel was a rarity, financial rewards minimal and neither had ever been abroad.

I realised life would never be the same for me again and it would not be possible for me to slip back into my former routine. As much as I would have liked and no matter how much I was steeped in the area, work was not available on the doorstep. Two years is a short episode in a life span but I had travelled, communicated with all and sundry, gained in confidence, been subjected to humiliation and hopefully was a little more tolerant.

However I was so happy to be back on my beloved Titterstone Clee Hill, able to have chats with the pub customers and a game of darts with them.

The quarry's work force had been depleted and sales of cider had dramatically dropped at Dhu Stone Inn. A few more ladies came in and the conversation of the male contingent was a little more courteous and muted. We still had cattle, pigs and poultry on the small holding and Dad continued his undertaking business.

Unfortunately I had little time to settle. I had to make preparations, buy clothes and earn some money as I realised my savings were meagre. The 18th of September came quickly and I was off to Worcester College of Education to begin another episode of my life – teacher training. Would I succeed?

Worcester Teacher Training College

I had known Worcester since early childhood. My Mother's sister, Aunty Gladys lived at Callow Farm, Martley Hill Side. Every summer holiday my sister Marina and I spent at least two or three weeks there. We loved it. Aunty Gladys was so kind and often took us with Uncle Fred to Worcester markets from which we invariably returned with a pet rabbit or something else special. The farm was surrounded by woods and the edges of all the arable fields were eaten bare by hundreds of rabbits. Quite often when cutting a field of corn a hundred or so rabbits were caught. Corn rabbits were the best to eat having beautiful, almost white flesh. It was a sight to remember seeing numerous dogs racing after bolting rabbits, occasionally a whippit tumbling head over heels over sheaves, men and boys whooping and waving their stout sticks and swiping, often unsuccessfully at approaching scared rabbits. There were two orchards of mature cherry trees, where during early spring cousin Mervyn had connected wire lines from tree to tree laced with tin cans. When the cherries ripened he was instructed by Uncle Fred to sleep in an old car. This was placed strategically in the middle of the orchards and those wire lines were all fixed and terminated on the car roof. As the dawn chorus broke, Mervyn had to rouse himself and yank on those wires with all his might. Birds were startled and the tremendous flapping of wings reminded me of the release of pigeons at the start of a Saturday pigeon race back home at the Dhu Stone Inn.

Callow was also blessed with many Worcester Pearmain trees, damsons and every variety of plum imaginable including Victoria, Purple Pershore and Egg plums. Every week in season we would help strip the trees and fill as many chips as possible. I would eat too many gorgeously looking, ripe ones and finish up with an upset tummy and lots of heat bumps. Aunty Gladys and Uncle Fred took the full 'chips' to Kidderminster market where plums sold for 2d per pound. This seems a paltry sum but the return was sufficient to pay the rent for Callow Farm. I have so many wonderful memories of that place; building dens in the woods and Mervyn creeping up and scaring the living daylights out of me as I sat contently and all alone inside my creation. Operating the binder when cutting corn created a grown up feeling. Raising and lowering its sails, tightening the canvases, re-connecting the unpredictable knotter and driving the wonderful Ferguson tractor when it came on the market for the first time – all special.

Aunty Gladys was a tireless worker. Her home was spotless and every item of furniture had a highly polished, antique patina. Her fruit cakes were delicious as were all her culinary creations. But! She loved flamboyant hats. Marina and I were subjected to long, tedious sessions in Worcester shops while milliners patiently flapped around providing numerous hat styles, hoping to secure a sale.

Cousin Mervyn had a younger sister Mabel who if I remember rightly was born when he was seventeen. She had very poor health when small and I remember clearly Aunt Gladys placing her over the arm of a settee and beating her back to try and release phlegm from her congested lungs. But I have to confess Mervyn was my real hero. As a youngster ten years or so his junior I felt there was nothing he could not achieve or do. He was an excellent horseman achieving considerable success at gymkhanas, a courageous point-to-point jockey who was always immaculately turned out when following the hunt.

He was an accomplished mechanic able to repair anything that came his way and get any old machine to work. He ran or hurried everywhere and worked furiously. I had considerable difficulty keeping up with him. His father, Uncle Fred was traditional and conservative in his farming methods. Mervyn, although paid a pittance – little more than pocket money and petrol, purchased fertilisers and applied them on parts of crops to try and update Uncle – all to no avail.

He treated Mervyn like a dog and I have seen him produce a horse whip and whip him round the fold yard. I found this a cruel enigma because he treated Marina and I with kindness. Mervyn always looked forward to me going to the Callow because as a result he was given more latitude in my presence.

Through thick and thin Mervyn and me remained solid. I loved to go with him and his beautiful horse Silverstone to gymkhanas, watch him play football or accompany him to taste the special ice cream at Martley Post office. He was prominent in tug-o-war and was known by Martley Young Farmers' Club as the Martley Hare.

All these thoughts came flooding back to me as I arrived at St. Johns and Worcester College of Education.

A week or so earlier I had received some written information telling me that I would reside in A Block. B Block was the administrative hub and lecture rooms and C Block was for Home Economics and ladies' accommodation. The buildings were all single storey and by the look of them had probably been used for forces' purposes during World War II.

I found my room. The door label read Mr Alfred Jenkins and Mr Don Walker. I went in to find it furnished with two lovely beds, desks, table lamps, curtains and wardrobes. What a contrast to an army environment!

I was greeted by Don a Bristonian. He was slightly taller than me, slim, wore spectacles and seemed affable enough. We chatted about hobbies and pastimes. Don asked me if I was interested in music. I expressed a love for brass bands and he said, "I play the piano a little."

He had unpacked and decided to have a walk round. I sorted out my belongings and placed them in my lovely wardrobe then wandered towards B Block. On entering I saw the assembly hall on the left and could hear someone playing very professionally. I pushed the door ajar to see a goodly number of people surrounding a grand piano. I walked towards it discreetly. Imagine my surprise to see my room mate Don; fingers flying across the keys holding this group of people entranced. I thought to myself that he was a modest chap and remembered that he had said, "I play the piano a little."Don was reliable, consistent and needless to say we became life-long friends.

The New Entrants' notice board in B Block gave details of meal service in the refectory and the Principal's introductory address the following morning.

My first evening meal was beautifully cooked, very civilised and unhurried. The rest of the day I wandered around to get my bearings, had coffee in the Common Room and after idle chat returned to our comfortable room.

We assembled at 9.00am to be addressed by Mr Pearson the Principal. Without being condescending he reminded us that we were all obligated to uphold the good name of the College. Mr Pearson had an easy manner which helped me relax. That likeable man was always in evidence and he had a photographic memory for faces and names.

I discovered that there were 360 students in the College; all looking better prepared, self assured and more able to tackle teacher training than I felt. Looking round the Hall about 50% were young ladies most of whom were straight from 6th form and continuing their academic studies. The men were older, virtually everyone having been in the forces, worked in industry or travelled the world in some cases via the Merchant Navy.

WorcesterCollege 1956; Now Worcester University:- On holiday with room- mate Don Walker and his family in Cornwall; 285 miles from Clee Hills. We became life long friends.

Principal Mr Pearson addressing some of Worcester students on their first day:- Alf 4 rows back, central. To the right of him friends Don Walker, Vic Hughes and Ron Hardwick.

Worcester University:- Alf Right and Tony Tomlinson left. We both broke ankles on the same day playing rugby for College. Tony had a BSA Bantam and learnt to ride it with his plastered leg over the handlebars and me holding the crutches as pillion. We practised round the outside of the rugby pitch until Tony felt confident to drive us to the refectory. It caused a few problems with officialdom.

Brief guidance of necessary procedure had been given to all prospective students before interview. Secondary students were asked to choose at least one academic subject. I chose geography with handicraft (now CDT). In addition we were expected to study Professional subjects which included child development and psychology, plus P.E. Primary students had to choose one specialist subject too.

After our first child psychology lecture we were given a suggested reading list and told it was a must to have certain copies of our own and not rely on the resources of the College library. After looking at the reading titles I had more self doubts. Could I absorb this academic information and write critical essays to the required standard having hardly pursued any serious reading and writing for so long?

The following day I met Mr Jim Wilson, Head of the Handicraft Department. He was a delightful gentleman, humorous and encouraging. I was so pleased to see the variety of timbers, tools and furniture being designed by students and run my hands across the pristine surfaces; but research and the place of craft in education required thought, design and a thesis.

Due to my parent's income I had secured the maximum grant, the princely sum of £30 per term.

Plenty I thought; but by the end of the first week I had to spend a term's allowance on essential books, tools and stationery.

The Rural Science Department had excellent staff. Lecturer Frank Saunders giving advice on poultry husbandry. Alf with the 'pullet' and David Thomas on the Left making relevant notes. I had made the purposely designed poultry cub in the background

Mr Wilson gave us a synopsis of what we should strive to achieve. This included progression in practical skills, design of individual projects and appropriate areas of research. Initially his aim was to assess our craft skills and potential so as to be able to advise on suitable projects depending on our "starting point".

Being a secondary specialist Mr Wilson did not impart any teaching techniques at this time because our first teaching practice was to be in primary schools. The primary tutors however gave us concentrated lectures on child psychology, child development and curriculum content. Our first essay titles were issued with reading sources and a dead line for submission.

My first geography session, as with handicraft, produced a handout of the expected 1st year syllabus, number of essays and essential reading. My room mate Don had also chosen geography, I found myself sitting by Cyril Bullock. He was ten years older than me, self assured and well equipped for the course having been in the Merchant Navy and visited many parts of the globe. The senior lecturer Mr Lovatt made it obvious that he was extremely biased towards secondary education selection and opposed the idea of comprehensive schools.

Only three weeks after arriving at Worcester we had our first teaching practice. It was compulsory for all secondary students to have experience in a primary school and I was assigned to Evesham. We travelled by special bus daily. I was accompanied by Ron Hardwick. He was a secondary student and we eventually became firm friends. For the first couple of days we observed an experienced class teacher, were encouraged to help individuals with tasks and at the end of the week take a full class lesson. I was not used to seven to eight year old children. They were to me like bees round a jam pot. No sooner had I set a task they were all around me – finished – before I was able to assess what was going on. I *was* exhausted after forty five minutes. However with encouragement, analysis of performance from my visiting tutor and support from the class teacher I was delighted to find by planning numerous appropriate tasks I was able to cope with thirty five pupils for a whole day by the end of the third week.

Of my first six weeks in the College I had spent half that time in a classroom. My personal tutor felt I had an affinity with children and would make the grade. Some students at that early stage were advised to leave the course. I was very relieved and pleased but could see that continuous, detailed preparation would be essential to be successful.

Teaching practice completed and buoyed with reasonable success we all had experiences to relate and the privilege of a short respite before lectures restarted.

I now had a concept of Worcester College of Education. The comfort of the furnishings, our own room and lovely food was still a real novelty and so much appreciated. Freedom to chat and organise oneself plus the perk of so many young ladies continually inviting us to coffee, all combined to make near utopia. What a contrast to forces life! Seeing and reading about modern students' experiences I ponder about the tremendous difference. Of the three hundred and sixty only one had a car. It was a gleaming, red sports model, the envy of us all and the affluent owner captured the best looking ladies there. One fellow, my friend Cyril Bullock had a motor cycle but of course as I have mentioned he was 32 and had saved a bob or two. Vic Hughes another good mate, previously in industry had a smart Lambretta and Tony Tomlinson a BSA Bantam. Numerous students had an assortment of old bicycles while the remainder's mode of transport was shank's pony. To my knowledge therefore there were only four vehicles in the college.

Money was very tight indeed. In a whole term I managed only two half pints of shandy. Most socialising was within the college with perhaps ten or a dozen friends congregating in one person's room for coffee. Drugs were unheard of and because cash was so scarce one spoonful of coffee only in a saucepan full of milk and water was boiled up to make drinks for the whole group. Very few of us went home during term time not because we didn't wish to, but because we couldn't afford bus fares.

Life was uncomplicated and affluence unnecessary to be able to enjoy the simple things of life such as relaxing on college lawns during warm, summer days. Many of us enjoyed participating in the variety of sports teams, drama, dancing lessons and putting these into practice at monthly college dances. In many cases the person we had been placed with at those dancing lessons became regular partners. We all became proficient at the quickstep, modern and old time waltzes and the foxtrot.

Computers were unheard of as were of course mobile phones. All lessons and theses had to be written in long hand but one or two students were lucky enough to have ancient typewriters, and in my second year my parents assisted me to buy a portable Olivetti typewriter. I still have it.

Worcester was an excellent place for concentrating on and applying tried and tested teaching techniques. Great emphasis was given to lesson planning and organisation. Continual appraisal of every individual student was evident. After only six weeks we all knew in no uncertain terms from tutors whether they felt we had a reasonable chance of making the grade in teaching. In our own minds too we had crystallized whether teaching was for us. With only one week's teaching practice under our belt we were instructed to find a blackboard in a lecture room and use it regularly before the next practice; make sure we could write legibly the full width of the board, in a straight line *and* with exemplary spelling.

Between my first and second teaching practice I became disillusioned with the geography tutor. In my humble opinion I felt that his lectures were poorly prepared, his notes being no more than a few scribbled on the back of an envelope. I needed clear guidance as to what information should be absorbed to enable me to teach effectively in secondary schools. This was not being conveyed. I was not clever enough to succeed unaided.

Mr Lovelace had however changed his attitude towards comprehensive education. We had been informed that his son had recently failed the 11+ therefore his parents' choices for him were reduced to either private education or the general melting pot. I decided to change my course, terminate geography and opt for rural science. I approached Mr Lovelace* saying I had discussed my course with Dr. Westgate my personal tutor. Mr Lovelace's response was, "Well Jenkins, if you want to stay with the pigs all your life so be it." I knew then I had made the correct choice.

The next phase of my college life was enjoyable. The Rural Science Department tutors were enthusiastic, enjoyed their work and their attitude rubbed off onto students. Lectures were informative and I participated fully. Frank Saunders was first class in animal husbandry. The farm facilities were good and Dickie Major's knowledge of plant propagation was superb. I thoroughly enjoyed absorbing knowledge of root stocks, aerial layering, budding, grafting, pruning and botany.

Dickie was a country man through and through. He was not an academic but superb at demonstrating the application of his practical knowledge. He had few teeth, continually smoked a pipe, had a beaming, weathered smile and a strong Worcestershire accent. His favourite expression when demonstrating pruning apple trees, raspberries etc was, "Cut 'um back 'ard."

Mr Jim Wilson the head of the handicraft Department was an astute, excellent tutor and teacher. We respected him because he could take over a class and inspire the pupils without humiliating students. He paid great detail to teaching technique.

My second teaching practice was at Halesowen Technical College. During my second and third weeks I was expected to take whole classes for eight lessons per day. Jim came in on three occasions, wrote copious

Some names have been changed.

constructive and critical appraisals in my lesson preparation book and followed these up with detailed discussions about my strengths, weaknesses and recommended, future strategies for me to adopt. At the end of the third week one thing he wrote was, "Good work Alf – but use your eyes to save your feet."

During our second year Jim expressed regularly that every member of staff should aim to be part of a cohesive team and not exist in isolated subject boxes. The College musical production for the summer term was Ruddigore. Jim gathered the 2nd year students together and said, " You will watch rehearsals, liaise with the producer and choreographers and construct the scenery so that it will do what they desire." This was a very worthwhile experience and paid dividends in later years. I particularly enjoyed the picture gallery scene where pivoted portraits revolved to allow live characters to step through the frames during a momentary blackout and replace portraits. The sets were given an extra unifying dimension when painted by the Art Department.

Most students of our day appreciated the sacrifice their parents had made to support them, felt privileged to have an opportunity to study for a career and realised that sort of opportunity was denied to many who were equally deserving. We therefore worked and played hard being determined to make the most of that opportunity.

I had the misfortune to break my left ankle while playing rugby and friend Tony Tomlinson broke his too in the same game. We hobbled around on crutches for weeks.

Finding that quite a portion of our lunch break was taken up getting to the refectory Tony decided to try and ride his BSA motor cycle. He sat on the machine having one foot on the ground and his plastered leg straight in front of him over the handlebars. A mate kick started the bike and off shot Tony leaving me watching and wondering how on earth he would stop safely. When I arrived I was relieved to see the BSA by the entrance and Tony inside enjoying his meal. He greeted me with, "I've got it off to a tee mate. I'll give you a lift back." I resisted that offer and suggested that we needed a place where we could have a soft landing if necessary. So after a bit of riding practice round the edge of the rugby pitch Tony felt confident to risk me as pillion on the College roads. We soon became a familiar sight careering along to evening meals, complete with crutches and plastered legs and every pedestrian giving us a wide berth. We were questioned by tutors about these antics. They emphasised this stunt was at our own risk so we successfully carried on for weeks. Marvellous fun and a memorable episode, but, looking back rather foolhardy perhaps?

Time passed as it must and our final teaching practice came all too soon. I was assigned to Bristnall Hall Boys School in West Bromwich. We travelled daily by college bus meaning an early start and a late arrival back. To take stock of how the day's lessons had gone, prepare details for the next day and often visit a tutor for appraisal meant a very late bed time.

The kindly Head of Department at Bristnall Hall was a very traditional, stern gentleman but extremely helpful and encouraging. Strong discipline during workshop lessons is absolutely essential considering sharp tools, fast revolving lathes, timber being moved around, band saws etc. But because the pupils knew their teacher was consistent, boundaries having been established, rules were not questioned and a happy, industrious atmosphere prevailed. The teacher's craft skills and demonstrations were first class but there was little opportunity for creativity and individual flair by pupils.

Having observed for one whole day, assessed, chatted with and helped individual pupils I was in charge the next day.

By the end of six weeks I had learned a great deal. With the help of wonderful Jim Wilson I acquired many constructive techniques and procedures and felt reasonably confident that I could make a success of handicraft teaching.

Our Rural Science experimental plots looked superb. Of the grown specimens some were used for lecture demonstrations and laboratory work, some for the Home Economics Department and any remaining produce we were allowed to use.

I had an excellent row of 'tender and true' parsnips so Don and I decided to make some parsnip wine. We obtained a recipe and a large cooking pot from a couple of young ladies in Home Economics. Having sliced up and boiled the parsnips we needed to press and strain them. What could we use? Ah! nylon stockings. We managed to borrow a pair on condition that if they were ruined we would have to fund a new pair.

Having added other necessary ingredients, the strained and cooled potion was funnelled into empty cider flagons, leaving the screw tops off. During each evening of the ensuing couple of weeks we watched our wine effervesce merrily. We felt drained having put a fair effort into the six week's TP and decided to have a day or two at home the following week-end. We placed our wine inside my wardrobe, put cotton wool loosely in each bottle neck and locked the doors.

Returning on the Sunday evening I was anxious to examine our brew, see if it had settled and if so put the screw tops in place. On entering the room the smell was stronger than a brewery. I opened the wardrobe doors. Catastrophe!!! Glutinous parsnip wine had spurted all over the wardrobe and most of my clothes were congealed into a mass. What a mess! Panic!! I pulled out the bottles. Only about two inches of wine remained in each one. I piled my clothes on the floor and looked in despair at my sticky, discoloured wardrobe interior. By this time Don had arrived. He began to laugh. Amid my gloom I could see the funny side of this predicament, sat on the edge of the bed and laughed with him until tears rolled down my face.

Sugar soap, again from the Home Economic's friends did a wonderful wardrobe cleaning job.

Everything which could be washed went into the ablution's basins and my one suit was taken with much garbled explanation about its condition to a dry cleaners in town, paid for by the last bit of my year's grant.

The last half term was pressurised due to so many deadlines which had to be adhered to. Mr Jim Wilson advised me to apply for a specialist third year at Loughborough giving me his full written support, convincing me I had the necessary ability and saying it would greatly enhance my career prospects.

Three weeks later I was delighted to hear I had been accepted at Loughborough. My parents thought I was becoming a perpetual student but I explained to them that it would mean an extra salary increment and better job prospects. They agreed I should accept the place but they and I knew some income would be essential to sustain me as well as a further grant if I was to be able to go ahead.

The end of my two memorable and happy years at Worcester College of Education arrived. There were some tearful good byes with some of the young ladies and my good friends, Don Walker, Vic Hughes, Cyril Bullock and Ron Hardwick promised to keep in touch.

During the summer vacation I was disappointed not to have time to roam the Clee Hills, visit work men on the railway incline at Dhu Stone and in the local quarries. Earning necessary cash for next year was priority and I did this via Post Office work and deliveries. As Mum and Dad had made many sacrifices for me I had to help them too.

Chores at home included hay making, early autumn muck spreading, working behind the pub bar and helping Dad to make farm gates, ladders, coffins and other carpentry requirements.

Mid-way through the break I was so proud and relieved to receive my examination's results; four credits for my specialist and 'professional subjects', child psychology and child development. Wow! This had exceeded my expectations. Under separate cover I received my teacher's qualification number, 564772. Dad was so, so pleased I had made the grade and reminded me that I was emulating his brother, Uncle Arthur Jenkins.

However being realistic it dawned on me that qualifications did not supply work or a secured vacation.

Loughborough College (now Loughborough University)

Leicestershire; flat with low lying mists and wide open spaces. What a contrast to the Welsh Marches with their small hedge lined paddocks, numerous wooded areas and rugged hills.

I arrived at Ling Hall, my home for the year. Ling was one of a group of quite attractive brick buildings three or four storeys high. Each Hall had a resident tutor. He was responsible for the day-to-day running, delegation of responsibilities, routine and discipline. Each Hall operated with a certain amount of autonomy.

All rooms were single and I was allocated to one on the third floor. The leaflet in my well furnished room informed me of the refectory location, times of meals and the instruction for every student to meet the Hall tutor at 9.00 am.

The next day meeting was quite an eye opener. I knew Loughborough was nationally noted for the athletic prowess of its P.E. students as well as its Handicraft students having to be second to none in technical design and craft execution. I felt honoured to be there. Our House tutor informed us there were two thousand at this male only institution, six times the size of Worcester and considered very large in those days. My mind has difficulty in realising that nowadays some universities have thirty five to forty thousand students.

Looking round the assembled company it was very obvious who were specialists in sport and P.E. Without exception they were athletic, generally tall and some extremely muscular. The Handicraft students were informed they would be permitted to use the swimming pools plus other P.E. facilities at selected times. General information ensued about the campus layout, instructions that females were not allowed in our rooms and that permission had to be granted to return after 10.00pm. Remember most of us were twenty plus and had travelled the world – but discipline was still very clearly defined.

Saturday afternoon followed and with new associates I found my way around. I was most impressed with the sports halls, extensive swimming pools, gymnasia and the serious training taking place although outside lecture time.

What a contrast to Worcester with its one rugby pitch! At least six matches were in progress. Athletes were practising sprint starts and hammer, discus and javelin specialists were honing their skills.

The next day I met Tony Tomlinson who had been accepted for a third year P.E. specialism. He was a Leicestershire lad and knew the area. We visited Loughborough town its carilion and surrounding countryside. It was a warm, autumn day and I was struck by the parched and cracked fields. Some cracks extended a hundred yards or more and were two or three inches wide in places. Allotment onions were dropping into the cracks. I had never seen those conditions in the Welsh Marches.

I was delighted with the Handicraft facilities. Every type of woodworking machinery was available but detailed safety procedures and one to one training on every machine was given before permission to use.

My workshop tutor was Mr Gough. How fortunate I was to have that privilege. He had formerly been a top man at Gordon Russell's furniture works Broadway and within a couple of weeks of our arrival we paid our first of many visits there. The quality of handmade furniture was absolutely beautiful; wonderful rose wood dining tables inlaid with intricate silver patterns; oak dressers, mahogany sideboards and beautifully proportioned chairs of Edward Barnsley designs. What an inspiration for us to emulate. Many of those special commissions were being exported to shahs and royalty in various parts of the world. We now knew Mr Gough's pedigree. He had gained our respect as a top craftsman.

In the next workshop were metalwork and blacksmith specialists and their head tutor was Mr Sandom. He was eminently known in the craft world having published numerous books which were in use in so many schools. During my CDT career teachers have asked "What was it like to be taught by such skilful craftsmen?" I was extremely fortunate and Mr Jim Wilson knew I would benefit from their expertise.

The staffing at Loughborough was of two kinds. Half the tutors were the best craft technicians, swimming and sports' coaches available. The other half were qualified in child development, child psychology and teaching techniques whereas all Worcester staff had been former practising teachers.

Forces life is an experience in being conditioned; a systematic ritual of being brain washed to conform for a reason i.e. to face death without question if needs be. University and College experience was the opposite and not an easy opposite for me initially. However after two years at Worcester I had trained myself once again to think logically, academically and also constructively in practical sequences. The academic requirements at Loughborough were continually more demanding but I now had the confidence to master them. A thesis based on child development, sociometric studies or educational psychology had to be chosen. The expected expertise in craft skills was in the superb league.

Mr Gough outlined practical areas in which we were obligated to succeed, namely metalwork and forging skills, engineering drawing, to make a high quality piece of furniture involving the sequence of a sketch, detailed working drawing, a scaled working model and a finished product. We were shown an array of beautifully proportioned furniture, chairs, dressers, sideboards and dressing tables, all made by previous students from exotic and traditional timbers.

Phew! Could I match these? Could I even afford to acquire the necessary, good quality, seasoned timber? We were given one week to produce a sketch of our intended project. This was followed by a detailed analysis, questioning and modifications of the design decided between student and Mr Gough.

To have a whole day in the workshop was excellent. There was time to think, experiment, re-assess, sometimes making great practical progress, other days experiencing dejection, discarding work and starting again. Mr Gough was always unhurried, calculating and unflappable in emergencies. I remember him saying to me "Alf it's not making a mistake that is the problem. It is knowing your materials well enough, plus having the necessary skill to enable you to overcome that mistake. That will come as you assimilate more and more experience." That has stayed with me ever since.

Within a couple of weeks we were each assigned to a school for teaching practice. This was a *real* practice, one of endurance and long term planning. It was to be for one day each week for the whole year with the same pupils.

For any Secondary school student teacher in training at this time three or six teaching practices were the norm. They produced differing reactions as the end of the practice was approaching from, "I shall be very sorry to leave those lovely children," to "Thank goodness I've only got to endure one more lesson with that lot."

I was assigned to a Secondary School Minver, Crescent in Nottingham. It had an industrious atmosphere. The pupils were generally responsive, conforming and polite.

I enjoyed my coach ride through Nottingham which appeared bustling and very clean. My abiding memory was the heavy brewery drays, loaded with beer and being drawn by handsome, huge, white shire horses; their gears and harnesses festooned with lovely brasses. I noticed the bulbous wooden hogsheads, barrels, kilderkins and firkins. To see those familiar shapes made me think of home the Dhu Stone Inn. No doubt both horses and drays have long disappeared.

My regret was that due to my timetable I never had time to 'discover' the city. I observed three classes during my first day from 9.30am to 11.00, 11.15 to 1.00pm and 2.00 till 3.45 ; discussed the year's syllabus for each age group then the following week I taught the full day with pupils ranging from eleven to fourteen years of age. Fortunately the Handicraft teacher converted and prepared necessary materials for me and made sure tools were in first class condition. For the remainder of the whole year I was on my own, so to speak teaching sixty plus pupils of differing abilities. Weekly I had to modify and adapt tasks to match ability. Fortunately I was closely monitored and supported by the Handicraft teacher and visiting tutors.

As well as honing practical skills in college, researching and writing copiously, student life had special memories too. Tony Tomlinson my P.E. mate from Worcester and I met up often and he suggested I travel home with him one week-end to meet his lovely mum.

There was the old BSA of Worcester fame. Off we started on the eleven mile journey with me as pillion passenger. There were no stars, just thick fog and fortunately no broken limbs. We made good progress for a few miles when we came to a halt. Tony bellowed a few expletives explaining vociferously that the throttle cable had broken. No torch only a cigarette lighter which was little more than useless. What could we do? It would be a long, daunting prospect to push the motor bike. Tony decided I would have to wrap the throttle cable round my gloved hand, pull it when he instructed me and maintain the revs. Then when he shouted I had to pull on the cable to increase the revs to allow him to change gear. Each time I pulled we wobbled and seven miles seemed an eternity. However practice makes perfect and by the time we reached his home we were synchronising really well.

After a warm welcome and good food we were able to repair the cable by aid of the garage light. Apart from continued fog we eventually arrived safely back at Ling Hall. Fond memories!

I was privileged to be with so many athletes who already were and others who became of national and international acclaim. Alan Paske, the British hammer throwing champion was a giant of a man; a superb athlete and he astounded me by the quantity he devoured at a meal.

In the same corridor was Tony Waiters. He could pick me up under his one arm and carry me along the corridor. He later became Blackpool and England's goalkeeper. I marvelled being so tall how swiftly he could drop on a ball.

Brian (Winkie) Whiteman of England and Moseley rugby fame was another very likeable chap we met frequently. Being social secretary of our Hall I was lucky to enjoy many whose company I would not have had the privilege of knowing.

Loughborough had a superb 'sevens' side which competed in the Middlesex Sevens and Welsh tournaments. One team member Graham Tregiden knew I had an interest in Narberth, Pembrokeshire from my Worcester days and asked me if I would like to make use of a car for a week-end and pay a petrol 'whack'. This I did. The journey was 250 miles each way. They say that love is blind. I certainly must have been. What a journey when financial resources were so tight, just to see a young lady.

My abiding memory of the trip was dense fog, not the young lady. I did not have the responsibility of driving and the journey down to Pembroke was uneventful. However, the fog persisted and became more and more dense. On our return trip a pea souper was an apt description. We were forced to stop for a break and soon after resuming our travels there was a terrific bump. We were thrown about like peas in a pod. The car scratched through bushes – another bump. Our driver pulled up. We all piled out rather confused and discovered we had driven straight across a large, shrubberied road island, out the other side and into a gateway. Shaken but laughing with relief we pushed the car back on to the road and eventually arrived 'home' safely. How dare I occasionally criticise the irresponsible behaviour of young folk of today!

I began to understand the importance of child psychology and the phrase, "every child is an individual". As my teaching practice continued I had to pit my wits against diverse personalities and attitudes. There was no saying only one more week. The value of that protracted teaching practice was to make a student realise that in order to succeed and benefit pupils, individual empathy was essential. I was bolstered by the gradual improvement of pupils' practical results due entirely to me having expert advice on how to modify my demonstrations and impart my knowledge and skills. A frustration was the restriction on creativity. The school of thinking was still mainly 'manual dexterity' and this assured a strait jacket system.

Staff who taught academic subjects and sciences assumed Handicraft teachers and students were of a lower order. A little while after arriving at Minver Crescent the Handicraft teacher suggested I go into the staffroom at morning break time. I was wearing my brown 'open all hours' overall whereas many staff were wearing their academic dress. I sat down in one of the inviting chairs, so pleased to have a little respite. I was soon asked to stand up having been told the chairs were reserved for other individuals.

I was somewhat miffed, not thinking to expect that attitude in teaching. When we returned to the workshop I felt I now knew the Handicraft teacher well enough to sound him out about the incident. He said that other staff treated him with respect because of his experience and the fact that his assistance was often required especially to overcome problems with truculent pupils. Apparently when staff could not control unruly individuals they were sent to the Woodwork room to be sorted out.

He suggested I bring my academic dress the following week and he would invite me to sit by him in the staffroom. How fortunate I was to have an understanding, experienced handicraft teacher in charge of me. Thereafter I was not made to feel a lesser being in that staffroom.

I was concerned about the cost of and obtaining necessary first class quality oak for my intended dressing table. I spoke to Dad about this and he suggested I paid a visit home and inspected his stock of timber. We came across some beautiful, dry, quartered oak, coffin boards. They were just what I wanted. Dad offered to transport them to Loughborough. I asked what I owed him and he replied, "You can pay me when you start work next year." How do you repay parents?

My dressing table design included secret mitre dovetails, stopped and through dovetails and a secret compartment for jewellery. I was keen to get started on the carcase construction and endeavour to produce my best standard of craftsmanship.

Each week sped by and there was little time left after having to include two workshop days, another for educational psychology and thesis planning, one for research and the fifth for teaching practice.

But! it is said all work and no play makes Jack a dull boy and I was obligated to find time for my social secretary's responsibilities. This involved me assisting with organising regular Saturday evening dances. Correspondence as a routine was sent to all the ladies' colleges for miles around. Including Coventry, Matlock, Derby and many others, inviting them to bring a bus load each.

At Worcester lectures, meals and a major part of each day was shared time with young ladies and this produced a healthy, respectful etiquette and atmosphere. Loughborough was so different. The only time most of us encountered female company was at these occasional Saturday evening dances.

Those evenings began with masses of males milling around the Hall, turned out as best we could to impress, eagerly awaiting the arrival of a fleet of coaches and with luck female company. I spotted an attractive lady and made a bee line to ask her, "May I have the pleasure of this dance?" It was still the age of chivalry when it was the norm to go to a lady, request a dance and return her to her place afterwards. On this occasion I noticed the young lady was hesitant. No wonder! When she stood up she was a good seven or eight inches taller than my five feet six and a half inches. I battled on; holding her left arm aloft and peering past her arm pit to see where I was leading her. We must have made a funny spectacle but she had been too polite to refuse me and gave me an engaging smile when I returned her to her seat. I was ribbed quite a bit but at least the tall fellows knew she was a possibility.

My ego and pride being a little dented I wandered around with Tony and others. Most men smoked in those days. It was the norm and the lights traced beams of thick smoke haze drifting aloft.

Suddenly our chat was disturbed by a large fellow pushing against us as he swayed about. None of us knew him and he was obviously as drunk as a coot. This was unusual because we just did not have the spare cash to drink much. A nameless mate from South Wales who wore glasses and regularly borrowed the new A30 from home, became exasperated. He took a deep draw on his woodbine until it glowed supremely and quickly pushed it against the seat of the offending fellow's backside. He took off like a rocket, squealing like a stuck pig. We made a hasty retreat to another part of the very large Hall and merged with the crowd. I wonder if he's still got a burn mark?

Other dances came and went at which we always had pleasant evenings but one much later that term evokes something very special. As a contingent from Coventry Ladies' College came in I noticed someone I had seen on more than one occasion. I racked my mind and realised this was the young lady I had conducted around Worcester College a year previously. I approached her before she had even settled, asked her for a dance and she recognised me. We both immediately felt at ease. That incident proved to be by far the most important in my lucky life.

The year moved on rapidly. My little Olivetti typewriter was put to constant use helping me to bring my thesis and Sociometric Studies work to a conclusion. Teaching practice at Minver Crescent proved a most valuable experience, nurturing my confidence, giving me an affinity and genuine affection for the pupils and bringing rewarding critiques from visiting tutors. My dressing table neared completion. I eyed it with smug satisfaction when comparing it with the excellent quality of creations materialising around me. An enduring memory was encouragement shared and given by all my workshop companions especially Ken Almond who proved to be a special friend and excellent craftsman.

I had found time to visit all the workshops including those of first and second year students. On the third floor a group were assembling a large greenhouse designated for a local school. I forgot about it until I saw sections of it being lowered gradually on ropes. I am sure it would have been more expedient to assemble all the components at ground level but who knows; perhaps the tutors had let those first year students carry on to see how they would solve a problem which could have been avoided.

The summer term of 1959 brought an additional pressure. As well as the necessary completion of all written and practical work we needed to find a teaching post for the following September.

I scanned the Times Educational Supplement regularly hoping to spot a post in Shropshire area but no such luck. Reluctantly I abandoned the prospect of returning to Titterstone Clee for the time being.

I had visited Warwickshire, liked the area and noted numerous posts on the eastern side of the Birmingham conurbation. The accepted policy in those days was to submit a CV to an Authority and I did so to Warwickshire. After a successful interview I was given the choice of a post at Bishop Vesey Grammar School or Fairfax High School, a new comprehensive. Both schools were in the Royal Borough of Sutton Coldfield. Thinking of my past Headmaster Mr Beeby and the encouragement and opportunity he had given me I had no hesitation in opting for the comprehensive.

My Dad came to help me wrap up and protect my oak dressing table and other possessions to transport home. He was so impressed to see what had been created from those oak coffin boards.

My first real job

I had to find somewhere to live. I contacted Don Walker my Worcester room mate, told him of my appointment and said I needed digs in Sutton Coldfield. He reminded me that a student colleague had an uncle who was an insurance agent in Sutton Coldfield and that it certainly was worth a try to see if he could recommend anyone. Enquiries were made. To my surprise he sent an address, 44 Riland Road, saying that an elderly couple Mr and Mrs Risbridger had three married daughters and now felt a little on their own. They needed company and would consider "a young, tidy person, possibly a schoolmaster." Would I fit the bill I wondered?

Within a few days of my interview I was asked to visit Fairfax, meet other staff, be briefed on my responsibilities and prepare for term opening. I arranged to meet Mr and Mrs R at Riland Road on the same day.

The new, two storey building on the Falcon Estate was prominently placed at the top of Rectory Park Road. I was very pleased to find that Number 44 was less than half a mile from the school, a convenient distance to cycle every day.

What excitement and apprehension! My first job. A teacher at last. A position and profession I had doubted I would ever be able to aspire to.

I arrived at 11.00am and other staff were arriving too. Some were older than me but generally they were a young bunch. We were met by the Headmaster Mr Philpott. He was an imposing gentleman with a pleasant manner and of course wore his academic dress. He ushered us into the staffroom to meet his Deputy Mr Bott, fresh faced, tall and slim; and the Senior Mistress Miss Mahady. She had a strong Irish accent, held a cigarette in a nicotine stained holder, had highly painted nails and was extremely thin.

Mr Philpott began by saying, "You are my twelve apostles. I have chosen you. You are well qualified for your particular responsibilities and if you work hard there is no reason why, as the school grows you could not become Head of Department in your relevant subjects."

Mr Philpott continued by introducing each of the twelve assistant staff. Seated next to me was an experienced science teacher Dave Mitchell. I was informed that in addition to teaching Engineering Drawing and Handicrafts I would assist Dave with Rural Science. We were to become friends for life.

The school was opened with just eleven and twelve year olds numbering about two hundred. I was instructed that a wood lathe and circular saw would be installed as standard but that I was responsible for equipping the workshop to teach twenty pupils at any one time. I was asked to order all hand tools and anything else necessary for the Autumn term. I was given permission to spend ten days in the workshop to assimilate everything, sharpen all planes and chisels and convert timber ready for my new classes. This was a wonderful career opportunity, not an experience afforded to many long term professionals much less a probationer.

I was to be given considerable autonomy, be able to organise myself, make everything to do with my Department fall into place, teach my pupils, write syllabi to 'O' Level but be prepared to be inspected by Mr Philpott before Half Term.

I left the school and my new colleagues at lunch time; very excited and with a whirling mind.

I was off to meet the Risbridgers at No 44 Riland Road. Mr Risbridger tall, slim, a heavy smoker with a sallow, creased complexion greeted me with a warm handshake and lovely smile. He said little initially leaving questions to Mrs R. She was a diminutive, slim, dark haired lady with hair pinned tightly back in traditional style and wore an all round apron. I assessed both of them to be in their mid sixties. She shook my hand, eyed me up and down; asked me about my family home and if I was a finicky eater.

After a moment of silence she asked Mr R what he thought and he replied that he would go along with what she decided. With a smile on her face she said, "Very well! I will give you a week's trial and if you don't fit in I'll send you packing."

So I knew precisely where I stood. I was shown my bedroom, a space where I could write, mark work, study and relax. I was told I would be welcome to join them at any time plus dine with them. Finally I was told that unfortunately I could not stay with them for the first few weeks of term but that they had arranged a stop gap for me at Whyle Green about a mile away.

On leaving Mr R gave me a reassuring slap on the back and I felt Mrs R was warming to me a little. From my point of view I was delighted to hopefully have the opportunity to live in this small, beautifully clean, terraced home with its well organised and productive garden which opened on to Rectory Park.

Most teachers when transferring posts or even beginning in a school for their first post, walk into a ready established system. My first post situation was unusual. Its success or failure would depend on my planning and preparation. I looked on it as a special opportunity.

There was so little time to help Mum and Dad, visit my favourite haunts or communicate with the locals. One thing was obvious though. Trade in the pub had declined alarmingly resulting in only two or three barrels of beer and cider being sold per week as compared to at least eight barrels of each when I had left for the forces. A combination of more mechanisation in the quarries; fewer men being employed; reduced use of the nearby Dhu Stone railway incline because of more stone being delivered by road, had contributed to this.

Here I was in Fairfax High School, in my own workshop, wearing my new 'open all hours overall' with the first group of pupils whose future expertise and success depended on me. This was quite a sobering thought.

For my class of eleven year olds this was a very apprehensive day, an enormous change of routine from the security of a primary school to their first lesson experience in a specialist classroom. I *could* not let them see that I was nervous and apprehensive too. I was organised. The tools were in tip top condition. The boys enjoyed their morning and so did I. What a relief!

The afternoon with twelve year olds passed well too. With no one breathing over my shoulder I felt content at the end of my first day. I went to my temporary digs at Whyle Green. My room and food were reasonable but the couple made little attempt to communicate. The gentleman of the house spent all evening studying his pools. Still I had plenty to do and my mind was completely pre-occupied with the rest of the school week ahead. Next morning break I found myself on playground patrol and corridor duty with Dave Mitchell. We were two ordinary people who found it easy to communicate with each other. The caretaker came by and we naturally passed the time of day with him and began to chat. We did not however forget our responsibilities and kept an eagle eye on the pupils. Miss Mahady came down the corridor and glanced a number of times in our direction.

End of break bell rang. Miss Mahady appeared and called Dave and I to her office. We soon discovered why. With some unexpected vehemence she said, " Mr Jenkins and Mr Mitchell I saw you talking to the caretaker. I do not accept that as being in order. I don't expect to see you talking to the caretaker again whilst on duty. Thank you." We were absolutely taken aback. Pupils were making their way to our classrooms and we knew Mr Philpott *expected* us to be there to receive them, therefore it was lunch time before Dave and I had a minute or two to chat. He said that in his previous post he had never encountered anything of

(Early days in the Handicraft Room at Fairfax). Note the old fashioned wooden Jack planes which were cumbersome and difficult for young pupils to control. I am wearing my "open all hours overall."

that nature and as an ordinary chap it was his inclination to speak to everyone. He concluded that in any case the caretaker was the most important person in school with whom to have a good relationship and he intended to continue to chat to Mr Oliver. I expressed my dismay too but as a probationer had to play things

Fairfax High. Mr Philpott (gowned), Alf second from left with 10 of the 'Twelve Apostles'

a little more tactfully than Dave and he concurred with that. Mr Oliver looked after all the gardening and Rural Science equipment therefore it was necessary for Dave and me to meet him to prepare for our first practical lesson. Dave knew of my precarious position and he recounted the 'Mahady' incident and expressed why Alf may initially be cautious about chatting while on duty. Mr Oliver laughed, shook my hand and remarked that Miss Mahady was obviously a force to be reckoned with. At this stage we agreed to refer to Mr Philpott and his Deputies as "Holy Trinity". Mr Philpott gave his staff freedom, expected them to be diligent, made sure they carried out their responsibilities, expected us to consult and alert him about problems and left us with a clear understanding that consequences would be dire if we let him down.

Many, many out of school hours meetings took place during that first term when Mr P explained his aspirations and planned ethos for Fairfax. Extra curricular activities and clubs were to be a required ingredient within every department. Four Houses were to be established, Kenilworth, Warwick, Stratford and Coventry and eight staff would be selected as Housemasters and Assistants. A pupil's code of conduct was spelt out and an acceptable dress code for staff. Healthy competition between Houses was to be the main channel for creating pupil achievements and incentives. Each House would develop a Duke of Edinburgh programme aiming at Gold Award. House teachers were to encourage talent competitions in art, crafts, public speaking, debating, reading and other avenues.

Fairfax High Sutton Coldfield:- 1961. Camping with Fairfax lads. Cannot believe these fellows are now in their 60's

Fairfax High School 1961:- Group of pupils in a sunny tent camping.

All this was to culminate in an inter House Eisteddfod at the end of the academic year.

By the time the first half term arrived we all had a clear concept of the aims and objectives in this new Comprehensive and our expected role in it.

I was pleased my stay at Whyle Green soon expired and I was optimistic I would be able to happily establish myself at Number 44 Riland Rd..

At the beginning of the following week I was invited to bring my belongings and my bicycle to 44 and join Mr and Mrs R for tea. They were so much more relaxed, welcomed me to their warm, comfortable home and I sampled Mrs R's cooking – a lovely roast and apple pie and cream. Delicious! I put my belongings in my room, told I was absolutely free to stay in my room, work or join them for a chat.

I joined them. Mrs R asked if I was prepared to pay £5 per week including week-ends; if the light and space in my room was adequate and to let them know what I felt about the the the bed. Two of their married daughters Joyce and Rene lived at Four Oaks and the third, Barbara lived and ran a Post Office at Erdington. They had one grandson, Christopher who would be starting at Fairfax next year. He was the son of Joyce and Bert. Mr R worked at Dunlop in the experimental department and his work was mainly to set up looms for weaving the inside of tyres.

I retired to bed quietly confident that I was going to be happy at Number 44 and have a homely relationship with Mr and Mrs R.

I rode my Elswick bicycle to school next day, tacking Rectory Hill quite easily. I propped my bicycle against the staffroom wall, took my bicycle clips off and walked towards the entrance. As I approached a lad asked me politely in a broad Midlands accent, "Please sir, kaw yow afford to buy a car?" I replied that I was afraid

Fairfax High School 1961, Camping. I wonder how many of these lads recognise themselves?

I couldn't. Thinking about my far from new bicycle I realised my Dad had purchased it for me when I had passed my eleven plus. It was not surprising that it did not appear pristine.

When I paid Mrs R £20 at the end of the month Mr R who by now asked me to call him 'Pop' said, "Excuse me asking but what is your take home pay?" I was able to tell him it was £32 per month. He said, "Mum, did you hear that. Alf has had to wait for a month to be paid. He's got £32 to bring home and he's given you £20. That leaves him £12 for a whole month before his next pay. I have to say that's a great deal less than I expected you to be getting." Having ascertained that I had been paid £21 per month three years earlier in the army he asked if I felt it had been worth sacrificing so much time to obtain necessary teaching qualifications. I felt it had and said I was sure finances would improve over the years and I hoped that my job was secure.

Within the next few days all three daughters called in at tea-time to see Mom and Pop but I suspect it was also to have a look at me and assess what they thought. Barbara always came on a Wednesday, her half day off from the post office. She was a different build from her sisters, much slighter, smoked heavily like her father and enjoyed a bit of leg pulling. She said, "You'll be alright here Alf. You'll love Mom's apple pie and cream." How right she was I was beginning to feel I had truly fallen on my feet.

I wasn't able to travel home at week-ends initially because the bus fare was too expensive. Discovering I could drive, Pop R said he had a Ford Prefect which he kept in a garage round the corner. He said that he felt he was past driving in heavy traffic and would I be prepared to drive them to see Joyce, Bert and Christopher at Four Oaks. I agreed saying that I admired his trust in me. After a little practice around Riland Road I drove to 37 Knighton Road, Four Oaks.

The Ford Prefect had had very little use. It was immaculate but I found the vision through the rear window difficult. It was pouring with rain and as we ascended the hill to Mere Green the wipers got slower and slower until they were little more than useless. Apparently this was a well known feature of that model.

As I approached the area I thought the houses beautiful and extremely palatial. Pop remarked that the area was very affluent being a dormitory for successful Birmingham business people. I was pleased to see Joyce again and be introduced to Bert and son Christopher. Their home was beautiful, spacious but homely. At the bottom of their garden the new Sutton Coldfield TV mast was being erected and it would eventually relay programmes to my home area of Titterstone Clees.

Bert was a lovely, easy going personality and we were to become genuine friends for the rest of his life. His hobby was maintaining cars and he had a pristine, red Jaguar. I enjoyed many a ride in that prestigious limousine. Unfortunately he suffered from rampant eczema which at times made his life a misery. I have seen him remove vast amounts of flaked skin from his clothes. And I have always had great sympathy for pupils who have had to endure this problem.

Many an evening when I was at a loose end I cycled to Four Oaks knowing full well I would be welcomed by my 'adopted sister' Joyce and her hubby Bert, a real friend. We would discuss the latest 78s while he introduced me to ribena and lemonade and I well remember him persuading me to buy my first record player.

I developed a canoe club at school. Boys were keen to join, work in a group and make those sleek craft. As Spring arrived we were able to use them on Birmingham canals and individuals submitted them for the Duke of Edinburgh Award Scheme. This was when I realised how valuable extra curricular activities are. Boys were there because they wanted to be, worked with tremendous enthusiasm; those hours were more relaxed than lesson times and pupils got to know their teachers as human beings. This led to better co-operation in lesson time too.

Our first Duke of Edinburgh Canoe being tested on Birmingham Canal

I was appointed Kenilworth House Master and as mentioned earlier this meant co-ordinating entries for the Summer Eisteddfod Kenilworth House, holding regular House meetings, briefing myself about Kenilworth, its ancient castle, conducting House visits there and taking part in camping expeditions.

Mr Philpott knew to what he wanted his pupils to aspire and I felt very privileged to be in such a vibrant, generally happy place with friendly, hardworking colleagues. I owe a great deal to that Head for giving me so many opportunities, the best start I could possibly have had to my career with considerable autonomy. There were not many aspects of current educational practices we did not experience in that school.

By now I journeyed home occasionally at week-ends. After travelling to New Street I caught the 192 Midland Red, which seemed to take an eternity to get to Clee Hill via Halesowen, Bewdley and every village diversion that could be found. That was in days before the by passes were built.

As always it was lovely to see Mum and Dad and later Marina, have a game of darts and meet the locals. The pub had its dart team competing in the local league. I was pretty good in those days so was often invited to fill in if there was a vacancy. I was pleased to visit the Rose and Crown at Tenbury. The Dhu Stone had reached the final of a cup competition. I was the last in the last pair to play and was so thrilled to get out on double three and so win the match and a cup. I still have it.

I was also developing a special relationship with Ann Edwards, the young lady I had shown round Worcester College and looked forward to borrowing Dad's car and visiting her at Inchmoor Farm, eleven miles from Clee Hill at Orleton.

Each time I returned on a Sunday evening to Number 44 I took my belongings to my bedroom to find a new pair of pyjamas, a leather brief case, socks or a tie on my pillow. I tried my hardest to persuade Mom R to let me pay her but Pop would say, "She charges you plenty. It's just a little bit of something back." End of conversation.

Luck can play a significant part in one's life. How had I been so lucky to find myself lodging with this lovely family who had virtually adopted me as a son? Sister Rene and husband Len lived at Four Oaks too and were great people. Unfortunately they had no children but a beautiful home. Rene had a very responsible post at Lucas's and Len held a senior position at Cincinatti. Sister Barbara was shorter and slimmer than her sisters. Again she and her husband Frank had no family. Both worked very hard, smoked like chimneys and Frank was always fooling about. On one occasion I was ill in bed when Frank called by. I heard him shout, "I'll liven him up." The next thing I knew he bounded into my bedroom, had put a lampshade on a concrete fence post and pushed it in bed by me saying, "There you are. Put your arm round that."

I was anxious to earn a little more. If Dave or other staff asked me to go out for a drink I could not afford to and I wanted to buy a small vehicle to be a little more independent. I asked Mr Philpott if I would be allowed to conduct evening classes. Having established a few ground rules such as students buying their own materials so as not to deplete school stocks he agreed that I apply to WEA. My Evening Institute classes were advertised in the Birmingham Post and I looked forward to enrolment.

When the evening arrived I was thrilled to see more than enough enthusiasts for a class. I took the names of the first half dozen, gave them note paper, asked them to give certain personal details and if possible make a sketch of what they wished to construct or repair.

The next gentleman said, "My name is Ken Jones and this is a friend from Tarmac". I proceeded to put down his details. Ken put his hand on my shoulder and said, "You don't remember me do you?" He said " We'll have a chat when you have time and enrolled the rest." I did not remember Ken but as soon as he reminded me that he was a Clee Hill boy I knew who he was. What a pleasant surprise to see him after so many years!

When I was a small boy Owen Jones was a quarry man who lived in the hamlet of Bedlam and worked in Titterstone Quarry. He had three sons. Due to mechanisation, a smaller workforce was needed in the three local stone quarries and with redundancies imminent some decided to obtain security by moving away. This is never an easy decision to make when one has lived in a close knit community, has known everyone and had such freedom of movement and panoramic views from one's doorstep. Mr and Mrs Owen Jones and their three boys moved to Kidderminster where Owen secured work in a carpet factory. The three sons all gained entry to King's Charles Grammar School and went on to obtain excellent degrees. This was seen as an exceptional achievement for Clee Hill lads and a proud accolade for the parents.

Ken was holding a senior post at ICI, saw my evening class advert and came along. From that day on we met, visited the theatre and kept in touch.

As preparation for my handicraft lessons I illustrated work in hand by perspective, coloured sketches on the blackboard. These illustrations remained on display during the week to enable interested pupils to copy them and relevant notes. During one evening class Ken's friend asked, "Who produces the blackboard sketches?" I explained that I did and the reason for doing so. He proceeded to give lavish praise, enthusing that he thought they were exceptional. He said he could do with someone with this particular ability and concluded, "Would you consider coming to work for me at Tarmac? I'll start you on a £1,000 a year and pretty well guarantee you a successful future. Think about it." My goodness! My salary at that time gross was £450 annually. I cogitated during the week, knew I had only just started my career and dearly wanted to make a success of it. Reluctantly the following week I declined his gracious offer. I have often thought what that change could have meant. Life as I have said is one of choice, chances and opportunities. I never regretted not pursuing that choice.

The Evening Institute income was very welcome indeed and the hourly rate better than my day time salary. I went to the local bank to see if I could make a hire purchase arrangement to buy a Mini Van. The new price in the local showroom was £360. After further discussion I decided that I could make a down payment of £40 and pay off the rest at £8 per month if I continued the evening work.

Fairfax began to hold social functions and I was given the opportunity to invite a guest. I was keen to invite Ann but I needed somewhere for her to stay overnight. I asked for advice from Mom and Pop R. Her response was, "I knew there was someone you had your eye on otherwise you wouldn't nip off at a week-end; *and* you thinking about getting a vehicle too. You tell your young lady we would be very pleased to meet her and she can stop here."

The week-end event arrived and so did Ann. Mom and Pop R made her so welcome and on the Monday Pop said, "That young lady is OK Alf. You could do worse than stick with her you know." Of course I was tickled pink, thanked them profusely for their hospitality and began to think that I would wish our relationship to flourish too.

I did not go home the next week-end so Pop asked me to get the Ford and take him to the Cup on the Parade for a drink. I walked under the railway bridge and turned left into a quiet suburban road. I looked behind me and reversed the car out of the drive. Crash! What had I done! I jumped out to see that I had backed into the front of a spanking new Mini car. Oh dear! I paced up and down that road for ages, knocking on doors. Eventually I found the owner. To say the least he was not best pleased. I apologised profusely and said that I would pay for all the damage because it was entirely my fault. That however did not appease the gentleman. I am sure that I would have felt the same. Having given him all relevant details I retreated, leaving the victim holding his head whilst examining the damage.

I walked back to Number 44. Pop asked where the Ford was. I hesitatingly explained what had happened. He took a deep 'drag' on his cigarette and said, "Don't worry. We'll go round and sort it out. I'm well insured." I was riven with guilt and I kept repeating , "How *do* you repay such a magnanimous family?"

Mr Philpott continued to encourage us all but held an inquisition regularly. Opportunities were continuous and all the staff felt obligated to take them. One day he came into the staffroom and said, "I have a wonderful experience opportunity for our pupils – an Educational Cruise on a ship called the Dunera to the Mediterranean. Nine hundred pupils from around Britain will be required to fill the ship. They will have proper lessons in classrooms daily. They will use a number of currencies when on shore excursions and have meaningful running commentaries when passing eminent spots like Cape Trafalgar. It will cost each pupil £34 for fourteen days. I need one male and one female to take them. Who's game? Let me know tomorrow".

That evening I rode on my trusty Elswick to see Dave Mitchell and his wife Joy. They had small children and were paying dearly for pretty basic accommodation. I helped bath their little ones and Dave said, "You should volunteer for that cruise. You've no ties. Get cracking. Mr Philpott will cater for your pupils in school." That was it. I volunteered on the proviso it would not cost me dearly. Mr Philpott reported I would have to pay £17 – nearly the cost of another month's digs. I had my doubts but he just said that I should do another month's evening classes and that this was an exercise which should not be missed. Deal done. The following day I was told that Miss C.... would be accompanying me. The cruise was announced in assembly and older boys and girls given a letter to invite parents to take up the opportunity. In no time there were twenty boys and twenty girls on the list. I collected £1 from them each week.

Not enough schools had taken up the offer. In lieu our school was offered a cruise around the coastline of Britain calling at major ports. Staff thought this an excellent idea because it was applicable to the syllabus but parents refused saying they had paid for a cruise to Gibraltar and back.

The British India Company arranged a substitute cruise for October and due to inconvenience caused reduced the cost to £17 per head. That may not sound a great deal to pay but it was the equivalent to two weeks wages for a teacher.

The week before the cruise a parent visited me to say he had been made redundant. There was no way he could see that his son could now go and asked if I would explain the dilemma to his son. In the nicest possible way I said that I felt it was his responsibility. All to no avail. I did the explaining to a very disappointed pupil, who was confronted with embarrassing questions from his classmates.

Excursions with pupils are not taken lightly by a teacher. You are in loco parentis, ground rules have to be established and parents have to agree at an open meeting that these have to be adhered to.

The 14,000 ton Dunera was extremely well fitted out and equipped. It had a series of classrooms, a first class operating theatre, pleasant sleeping quarters for pupils, individual cabins for staff, a swimming pool and very good food. The itinerary included calling at Coruna, Lisbon and Gibraltar. We had ample time for classroom instruction. A number of currencies were used by the pupils. Deck hockey, netball and PE were part of each day but the most meaningful and exciting aspect was evocative commentaries such as "This is where the battle of Trafalgar took place. Can you imagine the noise, the smoke, the huge galleons etc etc....?" The experienced, trained staff were very capably led by an excellent Education Officer.

As a result of this meaningful, experience the pupils produced excellent creative descriptions. A reporter from The Birmingham Post met us in Gibraltar and on our return a report and photographs occupied the paper's front page headed, "Fairfax pupils on pioneer voyage." There was so much constructive benefit gained but a few experiences stick with me. On passing through the Bay of Biscay the pupils saw an awesome water spout which they were told could capsize a small craft. The pupils really enjoyed inter-school deck hockey competitions with an enthusiastic, tall, slim, dark haired Scotsman. His name was Tam Dalyell who I realised many years later was an elder statesman of the House of Commons and "a thorn in the flesh of Margaret Thatcher". One pupil suddenly developed acute tummy pains and had to have an operation for appendicitis. This was an anxious time for us all but fortunately had a successful outcome. Of course we did not have the means of instant communication via mobile phones etc in those days. In Gibraltar the pupils were intrigued by the Rock apes, had their first glimpse of the Mediterranean Sea and I had permission to visit a local lad and schoolmate from Clee Hill, Basil Brown who was in the forces at that time. That was a special pleasure.

My teaching companion carried out her duties but on every occasion possible donned her bikini and had ample personal attributes to flaunt effectively in front of me and young, impressionable crew members.

Recently I had the pleasure of being invited to the 50th Anniversary of Fairfax High School. My wife Ann and I had a joyous time with old friends Dave Mitchell and Julie but a moving, nostalgic experience was to be emotionally welcomed by a group of sixty two year old men and women who I had taken on that cruise. They shook my hand and hugged me, impressing on me that they would never forget going with, "Old man Jenkins on that cruise." I was a mere 25 years of age at that time.

Pop R loved his home at Number 44. From the street side it appeared a run of the mill terraced cottage, but inside the family had created a cosy home of welcome. Its narrow, attractively laid out back garden stretched down to Rectory Park, an oasis clad with a variety of trees and extensive recreation space. He enjoyed the regular visits of a Collie dog which would position itself in a goalmouth and bark incessantly until his owner fired the ball. The agile animal then sprang into the air in an attempt to stop the shot. Wonderful! The Erica covered rockery concealed the roof of an air- raid shelter to which Mom, Pop and family had scarpered many times to spend a night during World War II until the wailing siren gave the All Clear.

My extended family were so kind and generous and in spite of my misfortune with the Ford had the trust to ask me to drive them to see relatives at Leamington Spa on numerous occasions.

Neither had been abroad. The daughters encouraged them to take a 'dramatic' decision and book a week's holiday in Switzerland. I was assured that I would be well catered for by staying with Joyce's family at Four Oaks. I was delighted knowing that I could easily cycle daily to school but Pop concluded, "And you will take the Ford to use daily. So don't try to protest." I remarked to Bert that I would never be able to re-pay such trust and kindness but he retorted that I should forget that as I was great company to them. He mentioned that Mom R had said that I was good to have around and they looked on me as an adopted son.

By now I was well established at Fairfax. I was really enjoying my work. I had hardworking, knowledgeable colleagues many of whom were conducting WEA Evening Institute classes like me. The school was growing rapidly bringing additional responsibilities. One of my favourite extra curricular activities was taking pupils with their finished canoes to try them on the Birmingham canals. That gave them and me a considerable sense of achievement, proved good craftsmanship by being water worthy and was a major step towards a Duke of Edinburgh's Award for those boys and girls.

In 1962 I became concerned about my Dad's health, his state of mind and Mum's concern for him. The situation continued to deteriorate and came to a head when she rang to say Dad had got bowel cancer. The prognosis was that he could have six weeks to live. He was admitted to Kidderminster General Hospital. I was able to visit him and Mom and Pop R came too. Dad's was a pioneering operation in those days and within two days two others who had had a similar operation on the same day had died. By now I had obtained my new Mini van. This made visiting to hospital and home much easier.

The Times Educational Supplement was advertising a post at Ludlow Secondary Modern School and I felt in the circumstances I should apply. Mum desperately needed support with the public house and smallholding. It was a worrying situation to see customers off the premises at night time closing and Dad was not physically able to prepare beer and look after animals. Neighbours were very helpful but I felt this was a time when I was needed and able to re-pay my parents for the sacrifices they had made for me. Also my relationship with Ann was blossoming too and I knew that she would never relish city life. I presented my predicament to Mr Philpott. In his thoughtful way he commended my achievements at Fairfax, said he would not like to lose me and emphasised my career benefits by remaining there. He concluded, "I really sympathise with your family problems. Many of us have been through similar ones. I do not want to appear callous but in life it is necessary to always try to look beyond the immediate." I thanked him for his support and thoughts.

The following week I applied for the post as Head of Handicraft and Engineering Drawing at Ludlow Secondary School. I was successful. My Dad went home, fixed up with a colostomy and was extremely depressed. He was convinced that every person could see what his problem was and as a result was extremely embarrassed.

It was with mixed feelings and much sorrow I said goodbye to Fairfax, its pupils, my colleagues and the lovely family who had virtually adopted me. However the thought of returning to Titterstone Clees after eight years was a real thrill. How had it changed? Would I be lucky enough to find a stable relationship with Ann? What did the future hold?

Cleeton St Mary's School Clee Hill

In school we are given historical dates of important events which in many cases changed the course of history. Some dates are definite such as the Great Fire of London 1666 and the Great Plague of 1665. However The Agricultural Revolution was given as 1725 and Industrial Revolution as 1745 but these dates were only the beginning of great change which probably took a century to percolate through the whole of Britain. Education has been the same and its standards and progress having depended on teachers, teachers' leaders, Acts and local environmental variations.

As recently as 1947 when I began at Ludlow Grammar School, boys and girls from "The Bonk" were ridiculed due to their mode of dress, dialect and upbringing. We were as I have written before considered a race apart. Cleeton St Mary's School has had considerable academic successes and 11+passes as many people of my age will testify but prior to the 1960s things had slipped a little. Social history represents the nuts and bolts of our society and experiences of Mrs Daisy Passman (nee Price) and Mrs Ann Jenkins (nee Edwards) deserve to be remembered as a significant episode. When Daisy was appointed as Head she stated that many of the children were pale and looked as though a good meal would be welcome. On her first day she heard a noise at the door. Colin said, "Don't worry Miss. It's only Daisy." She thought that a little ironical but of course none of the pupils knew that was the name of their new Head teacher. She opened the door to find a large sheep pushing against it and given half a chance she would have been in the classroom. According to the children she had indeed been used to doing this, hence the pet name for the sheep was 'Daisy' .

Cleeton St Mary School, Clee Hills 1961:-Back Left Ann Jenkins (nee Edwards) and extreme Right Mrs Daisy Passman (Nee Price). Pupils L to R Back Row:- Tessa Lewis, Susan Breakwell, Carole Broome, Heather Crowther, ..Jordan, Doreen Price, Jean Pearce, Hazel Broome, Glenys Jordan; Mid Row Trevor Pearce, Keith Broome, Colin Crowther, David Price, Alan Broome, Geoffrey Dolphin, Jim Howells, Ernest Lewis, Christopher Lewis, Patsy Broome. Front Sidney Lewis, William Worrall, Steven Broome, Derek Jordan, Roger Broome, Jonathan Skidmore, Joe Howells. Andrew Lewis.

Teacher Daisy desperately wanted a cup of tea. The tap outside was frozen. Jean one of the pupils told Daisy to put some snow in the saucepan, boil it and pour it over the tap. She carried the hot water outside and began to pour it over the tap but quickly Jean said, " No you start at the bottom of the pipe and work up

Cleeton School, Clee Hill 1961:- Back Left Ann Jenkins, Right Daisy Price (Head). Back row children, L to R Vera Bradley, Elizabeth Broome, Doreen Price, Jean Pearce. Middle Row, L to R Linda Wellings, Roy Price, Geoff Dolphin, Derek Wellings, Heather Crowther, Jim Howells, Colin Crowther, Ernest Lewis, Hazel Wellings. Front Row L to r Trevor Pearce, Roger Broome Sidney Lewis, Alan Price, Andrew Lewis, Joe Howells, Christopher Lewis, David Price.

it." This Daisy did and it worked. Soon the water began to flow and Daisy made her tea. This was the first lesson of many she received from Cleeton children. They were very hard but happy days. Those children had not had anyone with any system or real control to teach them for a while. They were however happy, willing children and after operating a system and them getting used to it, it was a real pleasure for anyone to visit.

One day Mr Broome knocked on the classroom door and said, "This new fangled invention they've put in has stopped working. Can you help me?" Daisy asked Ann the Infant teacher to keep an eye on the big ones and went after Mr Broome to a nearby cottage. Electricity had just been installed in a number of the alms houses. Daisy turned the switch off, inserted a new bulb, turned on the switch and the cottage lit up. Mr Broome thought it a miracle. On her arrival Daisy was alarmed to find there was little or no equipment in the school at all. No mathematics equipment and hardly any books, paper or pencils. Mr Bob Keyse the new Head of Clee Hill Village school paid a visit, was very surprised and gave Daisy *six* pencils. But despite the lack of equipment Daisy said the children were so pleasant, responsive and manageable. She devised a system of concentrated skills including arithmetic and writing, then as an incentive choices of activities such as weighing, measuring and educational games which pupils could pursue on completion of the skill's work. The pupils loved this and worked really hard to be 'free' to choose activities.

Cleeton School 1961/2:- Patchwork blanket for OAPs. Back Row, L to R Geoffrey Dolphin, Jean Pearce, Alan Price, Keith Broome, Colin Crowther, Doreen Price, ----Jordan. Middle Row, L to R David Price, Trevor Pearce, Heather Crowther, Hazel Broome, Jonathan Skidmore, Ernest Lewis, Joe Howells, Christopher Lewis, Andrew Lewis Jim Howells. Next Row, L to R Tessa Lewis, Gary Crowther, Susan Breakwell, Carole Broome Jill Price, Patsy Broome, William Worrall. Front L to R Steven Broome, Roger Broome, Derek and Glenys Jordan, Sidney Lewis.

They had no reading scheme and teachers had to use their professional expertise to devise one. However as Shropshire Education Authority appreciated the predicament, a continual flow of visitors ensued and some help did materialise.

Of course Cleeton was an idyllic place to visit from April to September but no one ventured there from The Authority during winter time.

Daisy and Ann spent a great deal of their own money and on one occasion purchased a set of rose patterned cups and saucers from Ludlow Town Hall market in which to provide a cup of tea for influential visitors.

Cleeton School 1961/2:- Cleeton Common Road in the background. Back Row L to R:- Carol Broome, Jill Price, Tessa Lewis, Steven Broome, Sidney Lewis, Roger Broome, Glenys Jordan, William Worrall. Front Row:- Gary Crowther, Derek Jordan, Patsy Broome, Susan Breakwell.

Colin Crowther, who was a lovely boy always made the tea and brought it in. This of course impressed the guests.

Cleeton School 1961:-Old school building in the background. Back, L to R Heather Crowther, Sidney Lewis, Trevor Pearce, Joe Howells, Glenys Jordan. Front L to R, Derek Jordan, Roger Broome, Steven Broome.

Mr Charlie Jordan the postman was a small, elderly man, much liked and always welcome at the school. On delivering the mail he would say, "Here you are. They don't need any replies." He obviously had made a thorough inspection. The teachers found that if a postcard was received Mr Jordan really knew the content.

In wintry conditions he would say, "Ladies it's the devil's snow. You wants to shut up shop and make for wum." That really was the sensible thing to do and he knew from experience that in wintry conditions and darkness children would have difficulty finding their way home safely and the teachers would be blocked in by snow too.

Mr Webb the paper man said that Daisy's predecessor had had a daily newspaper therefore there was no questioning. Daisy was expected to have one too. When the Authority decided to supply school meals an inspector came from County Hall and said, "My goodness this is like Wuthering Heights up here." As a result of this new facility Mr Davies drove the meal's delivery van and picked up Florrie Webb from the Glass House on the way. She served the meals with the help of the teachers and they all did the washing up in the porch sink. Old Mr Davies was a huge, gorilla of a man with a glint in his eye and a fancy for the women. In fact he took the advantage of kissing Daisy on one occasion much to her surprise. The coal house was full of slack coal and Daisy had permission to sell it all to Mr Ernie Yapp. In its place Daisy secured a delivery of grade 1 coal for the two school fires and maintained the same quality of supply from then on.

One day Daisy was stoking the fire in her room when suddenly she was hit in the chest with boiling water. The back boiler wall had worn so thin she penetrated it with a poker. Nurse Hoskins had just left the school having carried out a nit inspection. Luckily however Daisy wasn't badly scalded, experienced considerable discomfort but was lucky the spurt of water had missed her face. As a result of that problem central heating pipes running from the back boiler were useless for some time.

As a stopgap eleven oil filled radiators were delivered but Edie the lady who acted as caretaker was extremely apprehensive about connecting and switching them on so the school remained very cold for most of that time unless the teachers found time to do this work. It was 27degrees Fahrenheit in the classrooms.

Like every local house the school had bucket toilets. Fortunately they were emptied occasionally by "Flaxer", Mr Bradley; but much of the time they were full to overflowing. In winter time they were frozen too. With that and the cold conditions both pupils and teachers only used them if desperate.

There was no telephone in the school. The Authority till that time thought the public telephone in the hamlet quite adequate for the teachers' needs. Sometimes when a member of staff went to use the box she would find the door half open and a couple of sheep sitting inside. When she had cleared them out she usually stepped in something unsavoury to carry back into the classroom. There was no clerical help. Teachers would often write correspondence at home and use their own telephones at their own expense when time was of the essence.

The staff were always trying to improve the school structure and fabric. After complaints they were informed that the main chimney was near to collapse. Mr Higgins from Ludlow came but the low mist was so thick they couldn't see him on the roof. During one of her first days Daisy could hear a constant clinking sound. At break time she went out to investigate and discovered that the thick icicles on the telephone wires were clanging together.

Teachers very seldom saw parents. It was a different culture in those days. They seemed to allow teachers to "get on with it". However it was obvious the children had very few luxuries at home. Most pupils wore boots because this was sensible for the rough terrain. Their clothes were basic, well repaired and clean and undoubtedly they had loving and caring homes. The children were tough and although it was often very cold in school as stated they were determined not to leave their coats on.

A new road had just been made from Cleeton St Mary down to Bromdon and beyond where a sect called the Bruderhof farmed and lived.

The snow in 1963 was very deep and up to the road side finger posts. The teachers remember that little Joe Howells fell into the snow and disappeared. His tiny red hat was left on the top and bigger brother Jim had to struggle to pull him out.

The hamlet practically owes its existence to a Mr Pardoe who built the church, almshouses and the school. He also built the shooting lodge where parties came every year.

Daisy taught children from aged five to twelve. A number of boys should have transferred to Lacon Childe School at Cleobury Mortimer the year before and it was not clear why that had not happened. It was a mammoth and almost impossible task to try and teach nearly thirty children of that age range adequately and give them all a fair, stimulating opportunity. Daisy did her best for the older ones initially and gradually worked down the age range; but she was absolutely delighted when Ann joined her to take responsibility for the younger element. Their experiences, of not that long ago were an incredible contrast to a classroom and society of today. Now there are numerous methods of instant communication, secretarial help, teaching assistants, teacher's contracts, computers wonderful equipment and first class, ready-made reading schemes to name but a few assets.

At Caynham on her way to Cleeton School, Daisy picked up Mrs Jones who was the Headteacher of Hopton Wafers. The roads never seemed to be gritted and they were like driving on "the dodgems". Mrs Jones, who was of a nervy disposition would be screeching in the back with apprehension.

On one occasion Daisy was summoned to Farlow because there was trouble in the school. Miss E....., the Headmistress had got a carving knife out to someone. On arrival she found Miss E... as drunk as a lord. She shouted to Daisy asking why she had come and she replied, "I've come for a cup of tea." Someone brought her a cup and keeping an eye on this large carving knife Daisy said, "What are you doing with that?" The reply was, "I keep it handy in case they don't behave." Thankfully after a while and some considerable patience Daisy managed to remove the knife and took Miss E... home. What would be the reaction nowadays?

There was concerted pressure at the time for the Farlow children to be moved to Cleeton but there was naturally considerable resistance because as it was said, "The Devil you know is better than the one you don't."

After Daisy had been there a while the Authority was impressed with the impact she had made. The Chief Inspector of Nicaragua was visiting Shropshire and he was sent to Cleeton to see what had been achieved in a comparatively isolated community school with very few resources. Of course that gentleman was "as black as the ace of spades." For the pupils he was the first coloured person they had ever seen.

Daisy recalled that on her first day at break time most of the pupils had disappeared. One child who was near said, "Miss, when you wants us you as to ring the bell." Sure enough they all came running. They had been used to doing their own thing, spending very long sessions on the hill sides among the fern and gorse bushes playing hide and seek. So to re-establish a structured routine took some time. When Ann joined Daisy she said, "It was wonderful. Here was another professional. It was like Stanley meeting Livingstone."

The school was given a roller type blackboard and the teachers thought it a revelation. More written help and instructions could remain on various sections for older pupils to refer to. The old pegged easel blackboard remained in the infants' room.

At the end of their first and second years Ann and Daisy organised and paid for a Christmas party. They co-opted friends in Brimfield, Miss Griffiths and Mrs Penfold to cook cakes, make sandwiches and transport them to the school.

In the spring Daisy borrowed Reggie Webb's mini bus and drove all the older pupils to Brimfield to Miss Griffiths' where they played in the fields and had tea. The response of one child was, "This is better than the Hill Miss because you don't scratch your legs." By that she meant that there was no gorse and heather.

Daisy tried to enhance the place and interest the pupils by planting spring daffodils bulbs. Of course she didn't take 'Daisy' and other sheep into account. The new green shoots were all eaten off before they had a chance to come to fruition. Colin said, "We knowed that would happen Miss."

Daisy made a birthday cake. It was a number of layers of plaster of Paris covering a round tin with twelve holes in the top. A number of candles would be inserted into the holes to correspond to a child's age and the school gave a rendition of Happy Birthday. This type of recognition of a pupil's birthday in schools is commonplace now but a real novelty to Cleeton's children. She also made them all a cup of cocoa on their arrival at school in the morning. Again this was paid for out of the teachers' pockets including necessary milk and sugar. Teachers continually emphasised that the pupils were extremely polite and respectful and that it was a joy to take them anywhere.

Some of the buses were a little ropey. As Daisy said, "You knew that you were on the road because there were holes in the floor through which you could see it". Mr Poulter at Hopton Garage was the first one to wave to them while travelling to school in the morning and the last one in the evening. This was a practice they consistently adhered to. Everyone they saw had to have a wave because Daisy and Ann said, "We might need a push in the winter."

The teachers were occasionally invited to visit a grandma. Furnishings in general were sparse. There was the usual scrubbed topped, pine table and flag stones. As one grandma said, "I annu got many cups only a few cracked uns." However the welcome was always warm, homely and hospitable; a trait for which Clee Hill people have been renowned. A school photograph was taken and I know from records and old pupils that earlier ones had been taken too. However the twelve year olds of Daisy's time could not remember a previous one. It is recalled that when a wedding took place all the pupils were allowed to go out and enjoy the spectacle.

Cleeton St Mary's Church; almshouses rear left. When a wedding occurred pupils would be allowed to go out and watch.

In 1959/60 Daisy was asked to go on a P.E. (physical Education) course. The lady sitting next to her was from the Bruderhof. Over the weeks they became friendly and she invited Daisy to visit the sect at Bromdon. She said that her experience was an intimidating one and although she is not of a nervous disposition she felt almost "absorbed". She had never been so frightened.

At the time Daisy had a little red Hillman Imp. On parking it, her new found friend Jenny, greeted and took her in. There was a woman sitting in a chair with her legs covered; was obviously crippled and very formidable.

Daisy was invited to tea and went via the crèche where she was introduced to a little lad named Tobias. The dining room had a long refectory table. Daisy was positioned on one side, Jenny opposite and the formidable lady at the end. The door opened and some big fellows came in. The meal placed before them was rye bread with cheese served on wooden platters. By now Daisy's only thoughts were how to escape from there. She was introduced to the fellows and after eating, the formidable one beckoned the men and they all left. Jenny was asked to leave too. In came a mountain of a man, black haired, beard and very swarthy. She noticed all the men wore cords which made a creaking noise as they walked.

The formidable lady proceeded to tell Daisy things she would have to give up in life because they assumed she wished to join them. She was informed that she would co-habit with them.

By now she really was on edge and was thinking about Miss Griffiths, her landlady who had warned her not to visit the Bruderhof. But! Daisy had been curious because this sect from Germany made lovely wooden toys, farmed the land, were self sufficient and lived frugally.

Daisy was *so* relieved to "escape". It had been common knowledge that the "mouths of the locals had been shut" and no one therefore would converse about the Bruderhof. Daisy confronted one or two and said, "You could have told me about them," but the reply in each case was one of non-committal. It remained an enigma as to why the sect appeared to have such a hold on some locals.

Bruderhof Communities were known in Germany as Place of Brothers. They were Christian religious communities and had branches in New York, Florida, Pennsylvania, Germany, Australia as well as the UK and may still have. They were primarily called The Society of Brothers and the Hutterian Brethren.

The Bruderhof's foundation is faith in Jesus and "Love your neighbour as yourself." They followed the Book of Acts of "one heart and mind and shared all things in common."

Bruderhof shared everything and did not hold private property. No member received a salary or had a bank account. Income from self sustained businesses was all pooled and used to care for all its members and for various outreach efforts.

The entrance to the Bruderhof private Graveyard:-The group known locally as The Brethren settled on a farm at Bromdon quite near Cleeton St Mary, Clee Hills. This graveyard is still beautifully preserved although the sect left Clee Hills some years ago.

The Graveyard of the Bruderhof:- Most of the small gravestones and plaques are surrounded by heathers and the whole of the area beautifully maintained. Ann Jenkins outside the gate.

They did not serve in the Armed Forces of any country and they claimed to a model way of life that removed social and economic divisions that bring war. The Bruderhof claimed to draw inspiration from a number of sources including the German Youth Movement. It was founded in Germany in 1920 by Eberhard Arnold an intellectual speaker.

They outgrew their house in Sannerz and moved to Rhon Mountains nearby. With the rise of Adolf Hitler and Nazism the Rhon Community moved its draft aged men and children to Liechtenstein in 1934 because they were conscientious objectors, refusing to serve in the armed forces. With continuing pressures from the Nazi Government they moved to England and became known as Alm Bruderhof in 1936. Their property was confiscated by the Nazis in 1937 and the remaining members given forty eight hours to flee. By 1938 they had re-assembled in England.

When in England the population grew to 350 largely through the addition of young English people. The Communities and their stance against pacifism attracted deep suspicion resulting in boycotts. When confronted with all German members being interned or leaving England as a group the Bruderhof chose the latter and sought refuge in Paraguay and USA. I have not discovered why or how some remained in England and settled for a number of years at Bromdon.

The grave of Maria Ecroyd, 1883 – 1962. One of the well maintained graves in the Bruderhof Graveyard.

Grave of a one year old infant:- A small child Stephen Lord of the 'Brethren', The Bruderhof; the sect who had lived at Bromdon, Clee Hills for many years after World War II.

The Bruderhof came to Bromdon when I was six years old in 1942. My Dad being an undertaker and conducting funerals far and wide knew of their cemetery. In fact he said that he had been told that some ground had been consecrated before the cemetery was established because an infant who died soon after their arrival was buried in the corner of a field, a fact that I thought very strange at the time. You can imagine it would be a topic of conversation in Dhustone Inn. This has however been established by JV Hinton, quoting, "an infant boy who they decided to inter in the corner of Egerton Meadow outside the house platforms."

As a young boy at Dhustone Inn I often heard my Dad and customers talking about the Bruderhof. Due to their self contained method of living they isolated themselves. Their unfamiliar life style and different language did not help. Their doctrine was a simple one and the welfare of their companions was of paramount importance; very commendable.

They farmed well and diligently. Their animal and crop husbandry was of a good standard considering the difficult terrain and climate. Their children were expected to take part in all husbandry tasks. It was an integral part of their daily chores in order to become proficient in adulthood. Their future depended on it. This is not unusual to me. My sister Marina and I were brought up to think like that as were all Clee Hill children who lived on holdings and farms..

We Clee Hill people have always been and still tend to have a suspicious nature. It is what Clee Hill native friends and I call the "who wants to know" syndrome. Sometimes what is not apparent is made up to make pub talk a little more interesting so intrigue may have led us to incorrect and unfair assessment of this sect. However those in touch with Bromdon's "Brethren" had considerable respect for them.

Their crèche and school life was spartan and strict but there was a caring nature. Remember many of the children were originally orphans, displaced and lost children some of whom had survived concentration camps. What Heaven to discover the solitude and tranquillity of Bromdon; but that countryside can be harsh and unforgiving. They continued to farm three establishments namely Upper Bromdon, Lower Bromdon and Cleeton Court, in all nearly 600 acres.

As stated in Wheathill 1086 – 1986 by JV Hinton, "The Brotherhood must have by necessity the means to everything for themselves in death as in life." I wonder if their cemetery is still cared for?

With the appointment of Ann, Daisy hoped that their combined professionalism would make a difference to Cleeton children. She was also able to put her Bruderhof experience in the back of her mind.

Ann had had an interview at Worcester College of Education. When I saw her name on the interviewee notice board I realised that she was from near my home area. Students who experienced this were asked to offer to conduct such interviewees around. This is how I met Ann Edwards for the first time. Unfortunately she was not accepted at Worcester but was "sent to Coventry", Coventry Teachers' Training College in 1957.

On attaining her teaching certificate in 1959 she applied for a post in Shropshire. Two places cropped up in the South of the County namely at Stottesdon and Cleeton St. Mary. Both places were rural situations but Cleeton in the shadow of Titterstone Clee was the more appealing to Ann.

Ann's application to Cleeton St Mary's resulted in a surprise interview. She had not passed her driving test so her parents dutifully transported her from Inchmoor Farm in North Herefordshire to Clee Hill, some eighteen miles. That was considered quite a distance in the 1950s.

True to form sheeting rain and low cloud obliterated the splendid views, making the journey hazardous and depressing for a low land farmer's daughter.

On arriving in Cleeton St Mary the little school seemed to be in the middle of nowhere. The building was half sheet iron and situated on the edge of Titterstone's common land; alongside a row of almshouses, a church and a few small cottages and could hardly be seen for fog.

"Where did all the children come from and how did they get to school?" she thought.

On entering a classroom she was greeted by the Headteacher Miss Daisy Price who introduced her to the unusual interviewing panel. On reflection it reminded Ann of a scene from the Vicar of Dibley or 'Miss Reid, the village school.'

Recent visit to Cleeton School. This was Ann's classroom. The entrance to the playground was to the left of the picture. The iron gate is still there and the classroom house is called 'Classroom Cottage'.

Having nervously seated herself Ann reviewed the assembled group. Firstly was the tall vicar, Reverend Hewins, clad in black with highly polished gaiters.   Next to him was a jovial, rotund, ruddy-faced farmer with a profusion of whiskers emanating from his nostrils and ears and the third person   a very short, grey haired gentleman with a rather timid disposition.

The batting was opened by the Headmistress. She said that due to the fact that the magical number of 27 pupils had been reached an assistant teacher was permissible. She continued that she desperately needed an infant specialist and proceeded to ask Ann about her experience of infant reading schemes which completely befuddled the governors present.

The vicar was keen to ask about Ann's religion and attendance at chapel or church. The timid governor was concerned about transport and travel in inclement conditions during the regular notorious Clee Hill winters while the whiskery gentleman kept piping up, "Have you got a certificate?"

After this brief encounter Ann returned home hoping for success. Some weeks later she was absolutely exhilarated to be accepted for the post. This news was however tempered when she discovered there had been only one other interviewee and she was so near to retirement age it would have been a waste of time to accept her.

A new adventure was about to begin.

Cleeton St Mary's redundant school as it appears today. The entrance to the school 'playground' is new for vehicular access to properties. Note the cattle grid to keep out Common sheep. Ann's classroom on the right had a sheet iron roof. The brick building was the junior school and the white building behind, the school house. The only phone available was the kiosk seen on the left, outside the school boundary.

Further numerous discussions took place between Miss Daisy Price and Ann to ascertain her precise responsibilities   and   timetable content for a group of 13 pupils aged from 4 to 8 years. Ann's greatest surprise and concern was that there was virtually no specialist infant teaching equipment and no reading scheme. She exclaimed that in all her training she had never seen a school so lacking in pupils' necessities.

Summer holiday was spent planning, visiting the school, preparing lessons and making the all important equipment.   She was extremely concerned about not having basic necessities to enable her to teach to an accepted standard.

A farm worker at Ann's home was pretty handy at construction and he was commandeered to make a folding Wendy House with shelves which would double as a make believe shop too. Ann made curtains and from a flour and water mix made imitation cakes, sandwiches, buns and loaves – all for the shop.

After making seasonal jam at home the plum stones were boiled, dried and varnished. They with horse chestnut conkers baked hard, were to act as counters. There was literally no acceptable, commercial equipment in the school. Every piece of teaching apparatus and visual aid had to be made by the classroom teacher. Pictures were cut out of magazines and backed with flannel to enable them to adhere to a board covered with flannel, known as a flannel graph. This was used extensively to aid reading and number exercises.

Painted orange boxes with curtains draped over their front made good cupboards for the Wendy House. A large, glass, commercial battery holder became an aquarium and home for two goldfish, Orange and Lemon which had been May Fair prizes.

She constructed a Ten Box for number bonds. This consisted of wooden strips graduated from one to ten so that all number combinations up to ten could be visually practiced. No maths books were in stock so every number bond card was made by Ann as was every exercise book for each child's recording. These books were made by stitching pages of kitchen paper with sugar paper covers together. Their daily news books were made in the same way.

With no duplicator, typewriters, secretarial help or teaching assistants everything had to be made and written out long hand by Ann. So! although the number of pupils was small it was a formidable task for two teachers to stimulate the age range from 4 to 12 and cover every desirable and required aspect of the timetable.

Each morning was for 3Rs while afternoon was choosing and activity time. This included painting, sewing and knitting tables. Surprisingly the boys loved knitting. Equally they opted for the Wendy House and dressing up too. The Science table included old clocks, a phone, meccano and other things to take apart and assemble. The Nature table had beans in jars between blotting paper and glass, sticky buds, cress on damp muslin, wild flowers plus anything of interest collected on weekly walks . This included sheep's wool, bird's feathers and skulls.

Regular story time was a late afternoon activity and games depended entirely on weather as did many other things. In addition there were drawing, cutting, gluing and colouring activities.

Special days in the calendar were noted; for instance in November the classroom walls were adorned with photographs and information about Bonfire Night, Remembrance Day, Prince Charles's birthday etc.

In spite of being in charge of pupils at lunch time the teachers still had to pay for lunches. Ann chose to take sandwiches to save a little.

Bucket toilets were fifty yards away at the end of the playground. The same facility was used by staff and children alike. As mentioned the big room had central heating pipes running from a back boiler but they were continually freezing up and occasionally burst. The problem was eventually remedied by adding antifreeze. The small room was perpetually cold in winter time and the little ones were encouraged to wear many layers.

On one occasion when Ann opened the door Orange and Lemon were frozen solid in their tank. So ended their short existence.

Oil lamps were fitted in the junior classroom but no lighting at all in the infant's room. So on dark, winter days classes often finished early and stories were told in the dusk. Electricity did not arrive in this hamlet until the early 1960s and as mentioned the inhabitants were most apprehensive about using it.

The telephone box was used only in emergencies. Then teacher's help was required to insert coins, 'get through'; or when the caller had been unable to get an answer show her how to press button B and get money back.'

The postman, Mr Jordan did an extremely arduous round over the Hills. When he eventually arrived at the school he was always invited in for a cup of tea and to thaw out. Invariably he would say when the wind was howling and the snow whiffling, "It's the Devil's snow ladies. You'd better pack up or you wunna get across the common."

The Infant fireplace had a wooden mantelpiece which had badly warped from the heat and had caught fire on a number of occasions. Fires were laid and lit before school opened and had to really be stoked up to produce any heat. In fact Ann said that they began to have some benefit just about the time children were going home. Both fires had heavy guards around and like most country schools these had wet clothes hanging and steaming from them most of the day.

Radio programmes were much valued.   Pupils thoroughly enjoyed the variety of voices and joining in themselves too but the youngest pupils were most enthusiastic about a nature programme which was accompanied by colourful, printed pamphlets.

Ann brightened the classroom and created additional interest by making homemade visual aids for Days of the Week, Colours, Numbers and a Weather Chart. Here pupils chose an appropriate card and symbol to display and depict that day's weather.

Ann has taught at many schools over 40 years but maintains that there was something very special about her experience at Cleeton St Mary.

As very many have heard me say that in 1947 I did not find the transfer from Clee Hill Primary School to the "city" of Ludlow Grammar School an easy or particularly happy transition. You may recall due to dress, rural background, dialect and generalisation made by folk about Clee Hill children we were considered to be a "race apart."

The apprehension and experiences of Cleeton children whose lives were even more remote and their school a very small unit, the shock was much greater than mine when eventually they transferred to Ludlow Grammar School or Lacon Childe at Cleobury Mortimer.

I had the blessing of a simple early life with freedom to roam but little influence from city life and the outside world. Cleeton pupils were not tainted either and Ann felt their naivety completely honest.

Initially Ann was embarrassed but quickly realised their candid and open responses were an integral part of their natural makeup.

The following illustrates this wonderfully. One morning a young lad came to school bursting with great news. He said, "Our Mum put a loaf on the table last night and it fell apart. Er didnu ave to cut it. It was all in pieces." This of course was his first experience of seeing a sliced loaf and his expression conveyed that he thought it was really magic.

There was often talk about going to bed early. They were told that having a good night's sleep and so being ready for school, wide awake and ready to learn was sensible. One little lad said, "Our Dad dunna bother to wear any jamas. E gets into bed ooth just is shirt and tucks the tail between his legs." There are few secrets about home life not known to teachers of young children.

Having a natural love and affection for children Ann and I would have difficulty in operating nowadays in this over protected, politically correct world.

One reception child shouted, "I wants a pee pee Edwards." She contrasted this with a much later incident at another school when a well spoken, sophisticated infant enquired, "Miss could you show me to the bathroom?" And, a little later asked, "Miss, could you wipe my bottom please?"

Pets were often discussed in class including the value of one as a real friend, the fact that they never answer back and the need for us to care for and feed them. Most dogs were loved and cherished on Clee Hill but they were working animals and had to earn their keep. Children were very fond of them, would put their arms around and hug them. They were however never allowed into the home but more often than not kept in a kennel during all weathers and restricted by a chain. This was not at all cruel in our minds but just how animals we loved should be kept. There were no little jackets specially made for them. Cats were allowed in but were expected as part of their diet to catch vermin.

A sad little face greeted Ann one morning as she arrived. She asked the little chap what was the worry. He said, "We inna gwan to ave any more kittens at our plaac Mrs Jenkins." "Oh dear" said Ann. "Why is that?" "Well our Mum took our cat to the vet last night and ad er ole stitched up." "Oh I see," concluded Ann and continued with the lesson, hardly daring to bat an eyelid.

Ann opened a child's desk to help her get out her books. She immediately tried to restrain Ann from doing this and said, "Dunna do that Miss, you'll let my rabbit out. Ann exclaimed, "What rabbit?" The child continued, "He's mine. I brings im ooth me to school every day." Obviously the child did not have a rabbit at all and this was her imaginary consolation.

Ann and Daisy tried to give pupils experiences beyond their immediate environment by organising educational outings. The families were given due notice and true to form, as I have often done, the pupils came along with sandwiches and usually a bottle of cold tea or cocoa wrapped in a sock.

The first trip was to Dudley Zoo. Excitement mounted. The bus arrived and when everyone was seated, off they set along Cleeton road. These children were just not used to travel and Ann recalled that two thirds of them were sick before they reached the top of Hopton Bank not more than a mile or so from the school. Luckily the teachers were well prepared with buckets, newspapers and bags.

On a recent visit taking some of our grandchildren to see where Nanny Ann used to teach we were so pleased to see that the old school hadn't been neglected. The sheet iron roof had been removed, the school made into accommodation and Ann's Classroom aptly named "Classroom Cottage."

God bless Cleeton and all who have been taught there over the years.

Cleeton School Clee Hill 1963/4:- Miss Freda Pugh, (Headteacher) back left.Back row Left to Right:-Christine Broome, Angela Broome, Eula Bowen, Michael Broome, Dawn Bate, Gillian Worrall, Michael Worrall. Middle Row L to R Martin Woodhouse, Trevor Howells, Sandra Broome, Linda Worrall, Kevin Breakwell, Jackie Bate, Ian Broome, Jenny Howells, Gillian Broome, Norman Dolphin. Front Row L to R Joanne Lewis, Keith Bowen, Kevin Woodhouse, Jonathan Pearce, Luke Wilson, Anthony Groves?,(Little) Sandra Broome, Mandy Broome.

Daisy Price left to be replaced by Miss Freda Pugh as Headteacher. Both have remained our firm friends ever since.

About this time Mr Thomas Hall became the postman for the Hopton/Cleeton area. He like Mr Jordan his predecessor and Mr Maund of Clee Village walked a round each day which was in excess of twelve miles. At 6 am he tended his small holding then made his way to Hopton Wafers Post Office to collect letters and parcels before beginning his daily journey.

Mr Thomas Hall the postman:- (Taken from a local Newspaper photograph). By calling at Cleeton School he became a welcome friend to the children. Here he is being greeted by Head teacher Miss Freda Pugh and Mrs Ann Jenkins (assistant teacher) seated on the left. The school was built in 1872 when most of the dads of the pupils were employed in the stone quarries or nearby coal pits. Thomas was always provided with a warm cup of tea and had time to 'thaw out' before continuing his round of twelve miles.

1943/44:-Hopton Bank Garage:- Teachers of Cleeton School recall Hopton Bank Garage with considerable affection. On wintry days they were often extremely grateful for the help they received from the proprietor. This illustration in front of the garage in 1944 shows well known bus driver Mr Wilfred Crowther. Garaged is one of six 29 seater buses belonging to Charles Motors, later to become M & M. Petrol pumps were wind up because electricity had not come to Clee Hills.

His round was very arduous taking him up to Watsall Cottages 1,750 feet above sea level. Here the grass was often frozen, tinkled like glass and it was quite common for him to have to navigate considerable snow drifts. He was always relieved to get to Cleeton School meet Head teacher Miss Freda Pugh and her assistant Mrs Ann Jenkins. A cup of tea and time to warm through was very welcome before continuing his journey. By the time he reached home it was evening, still leaving his small holding to attend to.

Memories of the Bruderhof by Clifford Pearce

Clifford has for many years lived at Cleeton Court, Cleeton St Mary, near Titterstone Clee Hills.

He is one of the very few people who had direct contact with the Society of Brethren, knew them and was employed by them. We are therefore most privileged that he has made a contribution to this record.

Clifford:- "They were known to me as The Society of Brothers, otherwise known as The Huttaereuns.

They purchased Lower Bromdon which had 223 acres in 1942. In 1943 they purchased Upper Bromdon which was 215 acres and in 1943 the 193 acres of Cleeton Court.

Their set up was farming. They had very little machinery and the whole group used to help out. They would plough a field, work it down with hand tools and break it down further with their feet. All was very primitive but they made progress.

I went to work for them in 1953 when they had a Ferguson Tractor and the Ferguson System. (For those of you not familiar with farming methods, tractors previous to this time had no mechanical means by which to connect implements to them. Harry Ferguson revolutionised farming by making 'the Fergie'. This wonderful tractor had mechanics which allowed an operator to back up to trailers and other implements, lift and operate them so much easier).

I was asked to work in their carpenter's shop; then went out onto the farm working with their carthorses on the land. Finally I ended up as their main tractor driver.

They were very hard working and devoted to their beliefs. No matter what the weather they always seemed to be happy and singing.

After a few years they became self supporting. They had thousands of poultry, a milking herd and probably the best flock of Clun Forest sheep in Shropshire.   There were at one time 21 nationalities in the commune from all walks of life.   There were judges, solicitors, carpenters, mechanics and even people who used to 'walk the roads'. Everyone was treated the same whether millionaires or penniless.

Having 600 acres they were quite scattered while at work making gates, repairing fences and other farm maintenance.

I have been to their weddings where the couple would spend days sitting on a bench in their burial ground – very serious. At their funerals they were very different; sending their deceased off on a very cheerful note.

They started moving out in 1957 when my Father purchased Cleeton Court. In 1961 they sold both Upper and Lower Bromdon and moved to Bulslrode in Buckinghamshire. They moved on to Darvel in Sussex where I have visited many times. They had developed the making of wooden toys in a big way and were exporting them all over Europe. Some had become multi-millionaires."

Ludlow 1962 – 1970

Initially my thoughts were much pre-occupied in finding a new home for Mum and Dad. My sister Marina and I discovered that property in Ludlow was beyond their resources resulting in them having to decide on Leominster. We were relieved to find they had lovely neighbours.

Dad improved psychologically, became stronger and was determined to help others cope with the inconvenience of a colostomy. He visited people many far and wide encouraging and giving support. He soon felt confident enough to use his skills again, applied for a post of general factotum at Moor Park School and was appointed. He enjoyed the variety of tasks, repairing windows, glazing, painting, decorating, repairing school furniture and developing a friendship with the new Head teacher, Mr Watt.

It was fortunate in hindsight that my parents had moved from the Dhu Stone at that time because so much happened quickly there. Trade dropped dramatically due to a depleted workforce; re-organisation of the stone quarrying industry and the closure of Mr Clarke's Railway. They would have been so dejected to have seen this all happen.

Ludlow Comprehensive School was at a transition stage. Most of it had moved from Lower Galdeford in Ludlow to splendid accommodation at Burway, very near to my old Grammar School sports fields. However the Handicraft, Home Economics and Needlework Departments remained at Lower Galdeford until their new premises were built.

My colleagues were a splendid bunch and we developed an excellent, happy working relationship. Pam Snead was in charge of home economics and Jenny Hewins (nee Powell) needlework. Both were extremely competent, talented ladies, loved a bit of fun and got on really well with me and Bill Smith. Bill, the metalwork teacher was a lovely North country fellow. He was so easy going and when at break was able to fill his pipe with Saint Julian tobacco, light up and puff away everything in the world was serene in his eyes.

Pupils came directly to us for all morning sessions, walked to Burway for afternoon lessons whilst Burway pupils walked to us at lunch time.

Our team had considerable autonomy at Galdeford where the Head left it mainly to our professional discretion. We immediately began launching pupils on appropriate courses for GCSE examinations and I established an engineering drawing course for first year pupils at Burway too.

Wigmore High School building was underway during my first year at Ludlow and so Ludlow saw its last intake from Orleton Village. Those boys and girls were a lovely bunch. I knew them and their families and felt a special affinity with them. It has been considerably gratifying to watch them grow up, have families, contribute to our communities and become without exception good citizens – but I cannot believe that they are in or near their 60s.

I missed the wonderful facilities at Fairfax and the excellent workshop I had established but I was looking forward to eventually repeating the exercise at Burway.

The now nationally famous Ludlow Festival had just been established and it was an exciting challenge to be asked to coordinate with the Art Department and Miss Thelma Carter to produce appropriate artefacts to advertise Ludlow Castle's Shakespearian play and fringe activities.

One great plus and pleasure was to be back hearing the familiar Ludlow accent and the dialect of Clee Hill and Wheathill boys and girls too. It made me feel at home.

Discipline was no problem at Galdeford. However some of the fifteen year old boys in their last term didn't always see the necessity to buckle down and give of their best. Like most other areas Ludlow had its long established families who had not always seen eye to eye and as a result of tension it was not a happy sight to see one girl dragging another along the playground by her hair.

Colleague Bill Smith had a wonderfully, dry wit and would often make some comment to create a laugh. Due to his pipe he soon became known as "Whiffy" by the boys. He was also known as "Buff it" because if a metal article needed polishing Bill in his north country accent would say, "Aye lad, buff it up.".

As the date for moving approached Bill and I had a couple of week-ends and a few week days preparing all the machines and equipment for loading. We were aided by a few fifteen year olds. They were lovely, willing lads, respectful and helpful but not of the top flight; therefore they did not suffer too greatly by missing a few academic lessons.

We were labouring away taking rag bolts out of the floor to release lathes and really needed a drink. We asked Mervyn to pop to the next room and make a cup of tea. He returned a few minutes later to say it was ready – but we were at a crucial stage of levering a lathe off the floor so I asked him to keep the tea warm. A couple of minutes later I shouted to Mervyn but he didn't reply. I went to investigate as he came rushing out of the door. He was quite distressed and blurted, "I was keeping the teapot hot but I've had an accident. It's blown to pieces." I followed him in. The china teapot was in smithereens and tea leaves were splattered up the wall. The poor, agitated lad had put the teapot on a hot ring with disastrous consequences. Fortunately Mervyn was not injured and in hindsight that was an amusing episode.

About this time Bill's wife Norma secured a post at Bitterley school as cook. Bill had managed to buy a semi-detached cottage in the village. The family was very pleased. Bill could travel the three miles to school easily and Norma could walk the few hundred yards with their small son Michael to school daily.

Previously Bill had been renting a property at Wheat Common near Richards Castle and on the day of the move he was most anxious about Sandy their beautiful golden retriever. Sandy found it very difficult to settle and during the week-end had tried to find her way back to Wheat Common.

When leaving school on the Monday Bill told me this story and asked me to keep an eye out for Sandy in case she had slipped away again. I was still living with Mum and Dad prior to leaving the Dhu Stone Inn and I had offered a lift to a colleague Phyllis Edwards who wanted to visit her parents in the hamlet.

I proceeded from Ludlow up and over Angel Bank. As I neared Dhustone Lane turn, low and behold there was Sandy trotting along quite unconcerned. I asked Phyllis if she would mind walking the short, remaining distance home while I captured Sandy and returned her to Bitterley.

I called "Sandy, Sandy". She bounded up to my mini-van. I held the door open and she eagerly jumped into the back. As I drove off talking to her she put her paws over the back seat, tongue lolling out and happily looking out of the windscreen. I retraced my route down Angel bank, turned off to Bitterley and arrived at Bill's cottage. I knocked on the door. Bill appeared, contentedly puffing that pipe of his. I said, "I've picked Sandy up and brought her home. I found her at the top of Angel Bank." In his North Country accent Bill said, "Eeh, that's funny. She were sitting on t'carpet in front of t'fire a few minutes since."

I called Sandy from the van. Bill held the cottage door open and in bounded Sandy with us both following closely behind. Imagine my profound shock and hilarity to see two Golden Retrievers in front of the sitting room fire. I soon ascertained mine was not Sandy a bitch but a dog.

There was nothing for it but to return the dog to where I had discovered it. My new found friend readily jumped back into the van and I let him out at Dhu Stone Lane, gave him a gentle pat and said, "Go home."

A couple of days later I discovered my new friend was called Brandy and was owned by the proprietor of the Royal Oak public house situated two hundred yards from Dhu Stone Lane.

Lucky me!!. Summer holidays of 1964 were very special for me. On August the 8th I married my fiancé Ann. This proved to be the luckiest day of my life.

Ann's home, Inchmoor Farm was near Orleton Village in North Herefordshire just five miles from Ludlow School. After much hunting we found a property in Orleton. Bower House was a three bedroom, semi-detached house; and although condemned we were convinced we could make it into our home. It was for sale by Russell Baldwin and Bright at auction. The property was in a deplorable state and my Dad thought it was too run down to tackle and said, "Don't forget Ann will be your wife and it is your responsibility to look after her and make this a decent place to live in."

Neither Ann nor I had any experience of bidding at an auction. We discussed this with John Crofts, a relative who worked as a fine art specialist at RB&B and he decided to bid £1,000. My salary was £420 annually and we were concerned about what was needed to make Bower House habitable.

We were unable to attend the auction because I was teaching at Ludlow and Ann at Cleeton St. Mary. We anxiously waited for the end of the day. Ann collected me and we dashed to see John. His expression gave nothing away and he said, "I don't know what you will both think, but I had to pay £1,020 for Bower House. We were euphoric. We knew we were a little short of the 10% deposit and the extra £20 would be a large chunk out of my monthly wage. However we were determined to look ahead. It became our precious and happy home for 42 years.

This was 1962. Ann and I had do doubts what so ever that we wanted to marry and make a home together. We searched the whole area, came across Bower House and luckily purchased it. I was still at my parents' new home in Ryeland Road, Leominster and Ann was at Inchmoor Farm. We visited our future home the next day after school. We were more than excited but my Dad's words began to ring in my ears because there was a mammoth task ahead of us.

The property could not be seen from Tunnel Lane because of trees and hedges. On Rock Lane bank there was a very large elm tree which had grown through the road side wall of the house, cracked it from top to bottom and its roots had penetrated through the dining room into the hall way. The bare kitchen housed a copper and a dead, disintegrating hedgehog lying near by. We walked round the whole property. We liked the size of the rooms. Downstairs there was quite a large dining room, lounge and a kitchen of similar size. There were two entrance doors one which led to the kitchen sheltered by a rusty, holey sheet iron roof. To the right there was the usual bucket toilet and to the left the front door which led into a light hall from which led the stairs and doorways to the three downstairs rooms. Next to the outside toilet was a large baking oven which butted onto the kitchen.

The garden was quite extensive and I could see the potential for a good, family vegetable area. At the top of the garden was a dilapidated shed used for coal but had obviously been a pigsty and probably a cow shed. Could this be made into a workshop? To the right of the house was a lime stone cottage, Bower Cottage, the home of a charming, elderly lady Mrs Rose Manning.

Upstairs there were three substantial bedrooms. The whole house was in a very rundown, dilapidated, damp condition but it was ours. Water was carried via a garden wicket gate from a well at two cottages above, now The Bower. Both Ann and I were capable of hard work and were itching to get started.

We visited the local Council to try to arrange a mortgage. Conditions were stringent. Due to the fact that Bower House was condemned the Council would not allow us a mortgage unless we agreed to proper plans being drawn up, basic facilities being installed i.e. mains water, a bathroom, the house to be rewired and many other conditions. On top of all these we would be obligated to employ a registered builder to assist with the programme and the mortgage had to be arranged with the Council at the then extortionate rate of 5%; this was considerably higher than obtainable from other sources. It was assessed we needed to borrow £2,500. That on top of the purchase price was frightening. However the Council was prepared to allow all the aforesaid because I had a secure job "with reasonable prospects". They also agreed that the appointed builder could use us to do necessary labouring work.

The following week end we began to excavate all the ground floor. We worked like slaves, not knowing our own strength and endurance. After the first long day's work Ann and I sat on two empty beer bottle crates in what was to be our dining room looking at frozen condensation which had trickled down the walls. What a tremendous task there was ahead of us; but we were happy. Mains water was about to be piped through Orleton Village. We agreed to be connected but there was a frightening charge of £8 which many locals refused to pay. Remember that was a week's wages for me, my monthly salary being £32.

I considered myself fortunate because many local cottagers were renting their homes for 2/6d (12 and a half p) or half a crown per week . The gate way to our new home was very narrow; secured by two six foot high ex railway gates anchored into the remains of cider press stones.

All our labour was done with wheelbarrow, pick and shovel and ultimately we dug out over 30 tons of earth from the floors. This exposed the tremendous elm roots which we sawed into manageable lengths to remove. Ann's Dad Kenny loaned us his tractor and trailer to remove this considerable mound.

Ann's Dad loved to come up the village and see 'life'. Our next project was to excavate a trench in which to install a main's water pipe. Kenny gave us invaluable help especially assisting us to crow bar out tremendous boulders which more than spanned the trench. When completed the water board laid the pipe into the house and builders Caldicotts from Tenbury began installations.

For every spare moment during the next two years Ann and I worked to prepare our future home including having numerous bonfires and removing 22 damson trees from the garden. Nothing was purchased until we could afford it. Uncle Reg Worthing got us a cooker for £60, a considerable outlay but at the same time he asked me to be Clerk of Orleton Parish Council for the princely sum of £5 per annum. I remained a Parish Councillor for the next 37 years. Previous to our marriage we both had a mini-van. We could not afford to retain the two so sold one for much needed cash.

In ensuing years we made and renewed every window and door; built our own kitchen units and even made bunk beds. That is how we developed Bower House. In 1965 son Graham was born at home. It was a long delivery session for dear Ann, in the region of 26 hours. We had used mountains of old bricks removed from the house to lay a foundation for a drive from the road to the old coal shed ready for Mr Watkins of Leintwardine to provide a layer of tarmacadam. The thought of the cost of £40 kept me awake at night. I saw our first child Graham being born. I was thrilled. I could not believe such a miracle was possible. Those little toe and finger nails were so perfect. He was our boy and it strengthened our faith enormously. I looked out of the bedroom. It was 5.30am and I said, "I am looking forward to him riding his tricycle on that beautiful tarmac.". One day he rode his bicycle up Manor Lane and saw a neighbour Sid Edwards 's bike propped against a gate. Over the gate in the field lay Sid. Graham rushed home to say that he had seen a dead man. After an alarmed description to Ann she told him to go back in a couple of hours and have another look and she was sure the 'dead' man would have gone. Sure enough inebriated Sid had.

Helen our older daughter was born at home the next year so dear Ann had a very demanding time for a while. Helen's birth was just the opposite, taking little more than half an hour. Top of the Pops programme had just begun when Ann became uncomfortable and by the end of the programme little Helen was with us, six weeks premature. Old Doctor Vaughan came to see Ann. He assessed Helen and weighed her. She was a little under 5 pounds. He stood rubbing his chin then put a large pair of scissors on the scales beside her. "There you are. She's just over five pounds. So, I think she can stay at home and not go to hospital," he said. He returned home and brought his own heater to keep her warm and said that she was to be confined to the bedroom for six weeks.

Our family was completed by the birth of Karen in 1972. By that time we had developed a large vegetable garden, productive enough to supply vegetables for the five of us for most of the year. Being true country folk we gathered blackberries and other fruits in season . Ann made jams, preserved much and even made her own clothes.

We never had the desire to become rich. Ann's main wishes were to be married, have a happy home and family. She enabled me to pursue my teaching career and as long as we were happy, she was. We were so lucky to have three healthy, able children. Graham was very much the older brother to whom his sisters looked for support and help. He made so much for them being practical and creative. His tiny garden plot had a notice which read, "Keep off". All of them experienced tremendous freedom in our lovely village.

When Helen was about two years old she was very keen to help her Mummy with household chores. One morning Ann was hoovering but popped up stairs to get a bundle of washing. While away little Helen decided to take the plug out from the mains. She was not strong enough to pull it out so went to the kitchen and got an all metal knife from the cutlery drawer. Ann suddenly heard a loud crack and scurried down stairs to see what was amiss. She could not see Helen. She was cowering behind an easy chair. Ann discovered the all metal knife wedged behind the three point plug. She pulled it out of the socket and saw that the knife blade had melted in two places where it had crossed the terminals. Luckily the new wiring for the house had saved little Helen's life. How distressed we were but at the same time so relieved. We still have the knife. In 1972 after a long labour in Hereford Hospital Karen came along to complete our lovely family. Graham was ingenious and because we did not buy him cycles he made up his own from scrap bits he collected from here and there. We decided to have some bantam hens. It was one of his jobs to let them out; but like his Uncle Roger of Portway who he thought was special, he would devise an easy way of doing a difficult chore. Within a short time Graham had made an attachment for the chicken house 'pop hole' and ran a string up to his bedroom window so that he could let the poultry out as soon as he got out of bed. He was wonderful to his two sisters and helped them make all sorts of things with which to play. He even made a lever mechanism to lift and lower their doll's washing line. When Karen was a toddler Dr Snape came to visit us to bring a very ancient map of our village. We rolled it out on the lounge floor and intently examined it. We were all intrigued with its content and completely absorbed. Suddenly Ann asked where Karen was. We rushed through the open front door. On entering Dr Snape had inadvertently left the garden gate open. We searched everywhere. Karen was nowhere to be seen. Helen went off across Church Lane on her tricycle crying, "I have lost my little sister." Graham went on his bicycle up Manor Lane and we went down into the village. A few minutes later we saw Mrs Kitty Collings walking up Millbrook Way holding the hand of a small child. It was Karen. Kitty had found her by the side of Mill Brook. We hugged Kitty we were so relieved. Such is life! No matter how careful parents endeavour to be, worries occur with

Bower House. Our new home

The elm tree which had grown into the wall of the House:- The roots had penetrated into the middle of the dining room and had cracked the house from top to bottom

Our Kitchen:- Just a copper in the corner and an earthenware sink. We had removed a decomposing hedgehog that had crawled in through an open pipe and had just begun removing 30 tons of earth from the floors. Happy days!

The old coal shed and pigsty; Alf starting work to develop it into a workshop and garage. In the foreground are the hundreds of bricks Ann and Alf took out of Bower House and laid them to make a foundation to the tarmacadam drive.

Bower House:- When our children grew, we purchased the cottage next door and assimilated it as part of our home. A far cry from the condemned home we purchased.

little ones. However nothing made us happier than to be at home, our children helping us to attempt the many projects required to make our home the place we all loved.

Move to Burway

The move to Burway was a mixture of sadness and excitement. Our autonomy ceased but the new premises were as impressive as those at Fairfax had been.

The suite of Handicraft rooms consisted of woodwork and metalwork rooms. A large central lobby for ambitious projects and access to the outside; engineering drawing room, pottery and craft room, a specialist art room and a long corridor/display area plus excellent offices for storage, privacy and security.

I was eager to organise the department and make a mark with the technical/engineering drawing. A great plus was once again to have a staff room, meet other colleagues, swop ideas and co-operate with other departments. Next door to me was the art room with Miss Thelma Carter. She was an outstanding artist who produced the best and most ambitious art from pupils I ever experienced in my career; this in spite of the fact she professed to dislike children.

One colleague, Jim Price was in charge of the PE Department. He had an excellent rapport with the lads, was down to earth with no airs and graces. Not surprisingly we became very good friends.

Jim started at Ludlow on the same day as me, or at least he was supposed to. However for some reason there had been a misunderstanding. Jim's starting date had been given a day later than mine. He had in fact driven past the school into Ludlow and could not understand why there appeared to be so much activity. He soon found out the next day when confronted by the Headteacher.

School life has changed dramatically during the last fifty years. Autonomy of teachers and discipline procedures are unrecognisable to me. The following amusing episode illustrates this so well.

I was taking a woodwork lesson with a group of twelve years old pupils when one or two began to audibly complain about an obnoxious smell. I queried what the problem was and they pointed to Freddy who was looking rather sheepish. I took him into my office while those around him held their noses and contorted their faces. Poor Freddy said, "Sorry Sir. I've made a mistake." It was certainly obvious what that was. I told Freddy not to worry and phoned Jim. He always had a stock of shorts and tops for PE emergencies and games sessions.

I stopped all the machines, gave the pupils a theoretical exercise, asked Bill next door to look after my class and took Freddy down the long corridor. Jim said, "Strip off Freddy and get under that shower." This he did – no arguing. Jim produced a towel, top and shorts and said, "Give yourself a good wash round."

At this moment we noticed that Freddy had a considerable operation scar on his chest. Jim queried, "What's that scar from Freddy?" He replied, "Oh, our muvver took us to the 'ospital when I was a little un and'er said it was to have my tonsils out. Well they took my bl....y 'eart out didn't they."

Jim and I both convulsed into laughter so innocent and unexpected was Freddy's response. Would we be able to handle such an incident in the same way nowadays? I suspect not.

The Head was a man with some good ideas but as soon as I was established at Burway I could not help comparing his qualities with Mr Philpotts. This Head had some excellent staff but seemed unsure of himself and continually created emergencies to "keep us all on our toes."

One novel idea was his inter-com system. There was a loud speaker in each classroom coupled to his office. When the bell rang three times the classroom speaker switched on. This was the teacher's signal to instruct the pupils to stop work, sit up, and listen. This was followed by a few testing puffs by Willy. The communication was an excellent idea but once the novelty wore off pupils openly began to sigh and ridicule and this was extremely difficult to suppress. From the teacher's point of view it interrupted the flow of work too. However discipline at Burway was good and in general pupils conducted themselves around the building acceptably.

The Deputy Head at Burway was Don Keyse He took an annual group camping to Arthog near Fairbourne in Wales. He asked me if I would be willing to go with him. I did this for a number of years and so formed a sound friendship. Don was a big, fit, agile teacher; an excellent swimmer and one who commanded tremendous respect from the pupils. He had a lovely, easy manner with the pupils but they knew their boundaries and he was an excellent colleague. Unfortunately there was continual friction between him and the Head.

Miss Waite the Ladies' Deputy ran an excellent Young Farmers' Club and they produced memorable displays for annual Harvest Thanksgiving celebrations. This remarkable, placid even tempered lady was a great example to everyone. The pupils loved her and this was well deserved too. Don's bit of sound advice to pupils was, "Don't try to grow up too quickly." How important that is!

Camping at Arthog Ludlow Sec School 1965/6.Friends Don Keyse (Dep Head) at back and Pam Snead (Home Economics)back left; with a group of older school pupils. Do they now recognise themselves?

Arthog had tented accommodation. The usual four staff accompanying the pupils were Angela Pearce, Pam Snead, Don and myself. The week always included a shoreline project on flora and fauna identification and preservation; long walks to the summit of Snowdon, camping on Cader Idris, pony trekking and craft projects.

Arthog site was on sloping ground below extinct slate mines and quarries. When we were checking round the tents at night it was an unusual thrill for us to see glow worms all along the bank. I have only seen them once since and that was in New Zealand. I was still fit and very slim from army days but the long hikes were not easy with youngsters. It was a real struggle to cajole and push them along the final mile to Snowdon's summit. I remember on one occasion going to the summit cafe and a pupil raced back to give Graham Owen a can of drink as he encouraged a few stragglers to complete the journey. The joy on Graham's face is a lasting memory.

Part of the programme was to camp above Glynn Cai. One evening I was showing some lads how to pump up and light primus stoves when suddenly the tail of one lad's shirt ignited. I rushed across and in the emergency had to rip it off his back. He spun round, fists in the air *but* fortunately for me he realised the problem and subsided.

Ludlow Secondary School. Graham Owen History teaching colleague. Near the summit of Snowdon with some of our campers:-Graham a great colleague; good disciplinarian and lovely humour. 1965/6

Before one such visit to Arthog the Head decided a worthwhile project would be for me to instruct a group

Ludlow School 1965/6:- Trek to Cader Idris. Pam Snead (colleague) back left and Alf Jenkins seated in front. I recognise a couple of Orleton lads here.

Ludlow School Arthog week 1964. Colleagues Pam Snead middle left and Angela Pearce mid right. Clive Everall an Orleton lad sitting in the front.

of boys to plot a profile of the bed of Cader Idris lake and direct the pupils to make a model from this information.

How was this to be executed? The Head asked Mr Keyse the approximate depth of the lake and a group of boys were instructed to make a depth gauge from rope, knotted at one foot intervals. How were we to obtain the measurements? The canoes which had been made in my department would be transported to Arthog for this purpose and sheets of plywood to make the model. I expressed my reservations about the possible dangers to pupils to no avail.

I was asked to convert the sheets into two feet strips for ease of transportation and also produce 24 sturdy slats each 4 feet long. I assumed these were for some other classroom project.

Transport was arranged for the canoes and I assumed also for the plywood .

On the day of departure we checked all details, loaded all bags, cases and requirements onto buses and lastly the boys and girls.

We were just about ready to leave on the Shropshire County Council utility buses when the Head came running up the path with a group of lads carrying sheets of plywood. He got onto a bus, opened the back emergency door, called me and instructed that the slats be evenly placed from one rack to the other above the pupils' heads across the aisle. He then instructed the boys to push the plywood through the emergency door.

Don and I were speechless. The bus driver appeared extremely agitated and demanded what was going on. The Head explained that the ply was to be slid over the slats above the heads of the sitting pupils. Not surprisingly due to the driver's fear that swinging round sharp corners in Wales could lead to heavy boards collapsing onto pupils' heads, he bitterly complained. This led to an unseemly altercation. Don supported the driver who flatly refused to allow the plywood to be placed as planned. Don pointed out the dangers to pupils and his responsibility as Project leader. To our enormous relief this reckless scheme was quashed and the plywood transported by trailer. This was my first experience of the Head's technique of executing an idea without formal consultation.

About an hour after our arrival two canoes and plywood also arrived, safely. Midweek we set off to plot a depth profile of Cader Idris Lake. Llyn Cau had open access from one side but three quarters of the lake was surrounded by menacing, quarry-like cliffs which towered above and disappeared vertically into the black waters below.

Arthog week 1964 from Ludlow Secondary School:- Don Keyse and Angela Pearce on the beach at Fairbourne resting, when doing a Beach Study with part of our camping group.

We unloaded the canoes, put on life jackets and with notebook, paddles and depth gauge, rowed a little from the shore and tried to remain static while lowering the depth gauge. This had to be repeated regularly at similar intervals. This was by no means easy. Depth measurements were relayed to the nearby second canoe.

When we reached the scarp face the boys were jittery to see the ominous vertical cliffs. We had to turn around and row again to the open side. Don and I were more than a little relieved to reach land safely with our cargo. I did not sleep easily that night realising what we had done was risky and foolhardy. I refused to carry out similar undertakings on future excursions because I assessed the risk to pupils was too great. My stance created tension with the Head.

During that same week we had just completed a long hike and as usual the energy expelled to keep some youngsters going was considerable. What exasperated teachers was that as soon as we had reached our destination the youngsters were full of energy and wanted to play football.

Arthog week 1964:- Ludlow Secondary School. A horse trek which Alf Jenkins (centre) organised. Mawddach Estuary in the background. Alf had the previous day broken a rib and was in considerable discomfort.

Feeling rather tired the teachers sat down for a break. I had my back against a large rock and tilted my hat over my eyes to shield the sun. A young lady called Katrina Albrecht crept up and stuffed grass down my shirt. I got up and chased her across the heath land. She stumbled and fell suddenly. I collided with her and in so doing caught my chest on her raised knee. I experienced an acute pain in my ribs but it subsided after a time.

The next day I was scheduled to take a group pony trekking. Only then did I discover that I had broken three ribs.

I reflect on many happy incidents at Arthog with Ludlow pupils. In general they were responsive, polite and willing. In later life it has been so gratifying to see many of them mature into good, capable citizens, playing a valuable role in our communities; having stable families and still being unexpectedly respectful when we meet. More out of fashion with this modern, familiar society is the,"Hello Mr Jenkins" and not the expected "Hiya."

Arthog School Centre 1964. Alf Jenkins front right:- Having a breather near the summit of Snowdon with a group of our pupils.

I was the form teacher of this 5th Year class at Ludlow Secondary School. A really lovely bunch of pupils. Having a leaving lunch organised by Pam Snead and the Home Economics Department.

Due to excellent colleagues and responsive pupils I obtained much satisfaction from progress and examination results, but it was sad to see the rapid turnover of staff. I well remember one teacher remaining only for half a day – a great contrast to Fairfax.

Like every other teacher I did my regular lunch time and break duties. At the end of one morning break Graham Owen and I were watching pupils moving along corridors and up and down stairs.

George came our way as a buxom fifteen year old young lady came down the stairs. She was extremely well blessed and flaunted herself unashamedly. As she got to the bottom tread George rushed forward, put his arms around her and kissed her quite blatantly. Graham is his strong welsh accent said, "George you mustn't do that. You must treat our young ladies with respect." George's immediate response was, "But sir, I likes 'um." There was really no answer to that.

An educational report released at that time was The Newsome Report. It was one of the most sensible and productive reports during my Secondary teaching career and in my opinion it is a great shame its effects are nor practised today. It aimed at giving less able and non academic pupils a better deal by insisting that appropriate syllabi were constructed according to individual's needs.

Our extensive indoor facilities enabled me to construct walls, partitions, roof,guttering etc to reflect every aspect of a house. I devised a meaningful, beneficial course which required accurate measuring to make cutting lists and quantities for wall papering, decorating and construction work. It was most enjoyable and satisfying because the majority of pupils in this category enjoyed the stimulus and could see the necessity for the mathematics and written work involved.

I equally enjoyed encouraging able pupils too. Through my system many produced work of a very high standard and more than a few aiming for GCSE in fact displayed work to Advance Level standard.

I devised what I thought was a meaningful progression for examination pupils. They were encouraged to tackle a project according to their ability. These ranged from tables with inlay, cabinets, rocking chairs, tambour fronted doors, kitchen units etc. Each pupil was encouraged to produce an initial sketch in my engineering drawing lessons of their intended project; make a working balsa wood model of it; after much discussion produce a working orthographic projection, sectional drawings and exploded views of joints and finally a detailed cutting list of required materials. The practical application followed for most of the following year. After a three hours practical test and written examination each pupil was required to display all written and practical course work. The whole school was invited to visit the exhibition over a fortnight period. This gave the examinees real kudos and proved to be a worthwhile stimulus to younger students. Remember this was the early 1960s, well before the emergence of CDT (Craft Design and Technology).

Bill and I produced some fine craftsmen and women, non greater than Malcolm, the most meticulous young craftsman I encountered in my career. He loved the work, was so enthusiastic and would have lived in the Department if it had been permitted. He proved an invaluable help to me and made superb examples of every woodworking joint to put on display, including stopped, mitred and secret dovetails, for the benefit of other students. So amid the continual, contrived 'emergencies' and difficulties there was much satisfaction and creativity in my Department. This was enhanced by new blood in the name of David Weston, a really talented young man who managed the most rewarding earthenware totem poles and other unexpected feats with 'C' stream pupils. Sadly he did not stay long, eventually left teaching and became a most successful and accomplished potter and artist running a rewarding gallery in Cornwall's Mevagissey. David was followed by Janet Fletcher (nee Milner), a wonderfully enthusiastic and able person. She loved the youngsters, produced imaginative results and was a pleasure to teach with. Another considerable acquisition was David Lomas. He assisted me in Woodwork giving me more time to concentrate on Engineering Drawing. Dave left for Lacon Childe's School in Cleobury. I was sincerely shocked by his early death.

Unfortunately every piece of broken school furniture was sent to my department. This was a good idea of the Head's in theory but not possible to keep abreast of without hampering the pupils' course work. This produced a quandary for me and occasionally led to a pile of broken chairs being stacked outside my workshop. A general inspection took place and I was complimented on the high standard of work and the industriousness of my Department. But! I was questioned about the unsightly pile of broken chairs. I was obligated to explain why they were there. I was told that it was justifiable to include such repairs provided they did not prove detrimental to pupil's progress in coursework. The inspectors reported their findings to the Head. After the inspection I was summoned to his office and asked, "Why was that pile of broken chairs left outside your workshop? I will go so far as to say that was provocation." I politely replied that I had raised the problem about excess broken items with him on a number of occasions and that it was impossible to hide a considerable number of broken chairs. To avoid disrupting pupils I decided to go in on Saturdays and repair the backlog myself. This pacified the situation.

Rob Pritchard the new Head of Rural Science arrived. Due to my experience in his subject and the necessity for our departments to communicate and build a large cedar greenhouse, we became close friends.

I felt completely at ease with Rob. He was a first class teacher with high standards and expectations, empathy with the country code and a wonderful family man. My wife Ann and I had two very young children and she was so pleased to meet Chris, Rob's wife who also had two small ones of a similar age. We soon found The Hope, Rob and Chris's rented home. What a lovely bolt hole! We always felt welcome there and could just turn up without ceremony – real friendship. Our family relationship has continued to this day becoming very special indeed.

My success with pupils sustained my enthusiasm amid the occasional blips. Ludlow Festival had recently begun and since has achieved national and international renown. Our art and handicraft syllabi embraced joint projects for the Festival. In the mid sixties Miss Carter the art specialist and I were asked to produce elaborate banners and knights in armour to be mounted at the Castle entrance. A group of lads designed and made an inverted pyramid to slot on a rugby pole in front of Ludlow's Butter Cross. The result was really impressive.

The day before the first performance I was told to prepare all our work and co-opt Mr Mear the grounds man to transport it to the castle and be on hand to help. We duly travelled to Castle Square and the Head arrived. I asked where we were to position our knights etc mounted on rugby posts. One was to be dug in by the ancient canon and the other lashed to the High School chimney. Mr Mear arrived with some lads and I began to dig up ancient cobbles by the canon, while Bill positioned ladders against the High School chimney and hauled another cut out knight aloft to lash round the chimney stack. No sooner had we removed a few cobbles than Mr Price the mayor of Ludlow appeared. We knew each other very well. He was more than a little agitated, called me to one side and in no uncertain terms asked me what the h--- I thought I was doing and who had given me permission. Of course I tried to explain. Once again the Head had not consulted. Our compromise was to put a banner above the castle entrance.

The mayor was still with us expressing his concern when simultaneously Miss Grayfoot, the Headmistress of the High School tackled colleague Bill about the chimney. Again to our great embarrassment the Head had not consulted and we were thrust into an invidious predicament.

Many other such incidents could be recounted by Jim Price, Rob and others but I wish to emphasise that there were so many constructive and positive aspects of the place too.

During this period I suffered from lack of sleep, hypertension and tummy ulcers. Dr Ovenden visited, gave me an injection and I slept for a week. This made Ann and I take stock.

Our two children Graham and Helen were six and five years of age. Ann being an infant teacher was so expert and able at encouraging them to read. I did my fair share of bed time stories too and really enjoyed watching my children's responses and appreciated their daily language development.

Friend Jim Price qualified for secondment and went to Aberystwyth University to retrain for Primary Education. Also another close friend Rob Pritchard left with his family, to teach in Ramsey Grammar School on the Isle of Man.

I became more and more intrigued and interested in how little children mastered the miracle of reading and I remember saying to Ann, "How do you teach children to read?" Her response was that she didn't really know; that she had been trained to use many techniques which in different combinations usually proved successful. She said, "If you are so interested why don't you re-train like Jim and teach Primary children?" My reaction was that I couldn't possibly cope with little ones because they reacted like bees round a jam pot.

However Jim contacted me, said that the Aberystwyth course was superb, that he was thoroughly enjoying it and because of my interest I should seriously think of giving it a go. I applied, was accepted and never regretted my decision. Thank you dear Jim!!

When dramatic decisions are made there are always positive and negative experiences. I left very good friends at Ludlow and I really disliked the idea of being away from my wife, home and family every week for the best part of a year. If I decided to go into Primary education my salary would initially drop dramatically. I decided to hedge my bets and as part of the course, qualified as a Secondary school counsellor just in case Primary education proved not for me.

A complete change of direction

In July 1971 aged 35 I completed my academic work at Aberystwyth University and was extremely happy and relieved to be well qualified in Modern Primary Methods and Counselling. I could now teach if I so wished any age from five to sixteen.

Having no intention of returning to Ludlow Comprehensive I began scanning the Times Educational Supplement again. Before I found any post, within a few days I had a phone call from Mr Taylor, Education Officer for Hereford and Worcester saying that Charles Hawkins, Head of Madley Primary School needed help for a couple of terms. He suggested it was a chance for me to feel my way in this field. He was convinced that I would get along well with Charlie Hawkins and concluded by saying, "Have a go." I did and a new exciting chapter opened up before me.

The distance to Madley was 27 miles each way. My wife and I had organised two cheap vehicles during my Aberystwyth episode, a Mini van and a Morris 1000. We sold both and purchased one reliable vehicle for my daily run. Would I cope with Primary Education for two months? I was not at all confident that I could.

The Dhu Stone Incline Railway 1970/71   Neighbours of Railway Terrace

I followed my dear friend Jim Price to Aberystwyth University in 1970. I found it both academically and emotionally taxing. I wanted a change but was I taking the right step?

I hated the thought of leaving my wife and young children Graham and Helen for the major part of every week. My home life was happy and settled and it was quite a challenge to confront constant and intense academic study after the regular and familiar routine of the classroom.

Before launching into Primary Education with my new qualifications in Modern Primary Methods and Secondary School Counselling I was delighted to find time to visit "The Holy Mountain", Titterstone Clee Hills and my home area Dhu Stone Hamlet in the summer of 1971.

Here I was at the top of the quarry railway incline about one hundred years after its completion, just a few yards from by home The Dhu Stone Inn. Dhu Stone hamlet with Railway Terrace to my left; ornate brick built Rouse Boughton Terrace in front of me and New Buildings to my right. This was my immediate environment during the 1930s, 40s and 50s. My home Dhu Stone Inn was a very busy, country public house. My Mum seemed to continually run everywhere from early morning till late at night, organising the home and serving quarrymen customers.

My Dad was continually stretched running a small holding, making wheels and farm wagons, gates, ladders and peoples' business requirements. In addition he always had household repairs of windows, other secondary fittings waiting and was the local undertaker too. On top of all that he had to make sure that there were supplies of cigarettes, beer and cider ready to be "pulled" for the thirsty, hard working customers. Late at night he and Mum washed all the dirty glasses by hand, mopped the floors and wiped the seating ready for next day. Work was endless. From an early age when Marina my sister and I were home from school we were continually at work too; carrying water, haymaking, cleaning the cow house or entertaining customers while Mum was preparing food. There was little time for leisure and no time for boredom. But! looking back we loved it all. Mum and Dad were devoted to each other, gave us security and life was uncomplicated.

I was experiencing an uncanny silence, my surroundings were like a lunar landscape with cotton wool clouds floating, effortlessly by on a gentle breeze.

Where was the railway incline, the signal box, the drum house, weigh bridge and tar macadam plant? Had I dreamt the incessant throb of crushers and tarmacadam plants; continual squeaking and clanging of railway trucks, the tremendous boom of quarry blasting and whistle and chug chug of George Price's railway engine? Of course it wasn't a dream. I may not have remembered what I had had for breakfast that day but my childhood memories were as clear as a bell. I **was** there.

My mind wandered. Mum signalled that I had a session of freedom before customers came in at opening time. I raced up the Green past Railway Terrace to the signal box on the brow of the incline. I was warmly welcomed by railway workers who were our trustworthy friends. Mum and Dad knew them all too and I felt completely relaxed, happy and secure in their company.

This was a snug cabin with a roaring fire. Mr Purslow, Mr Prince and others were protected from the cutting winds and inclement weather. They toasted their bread while cheese dripped from a long home- made wire fork. How appetising and tasty it was. The signal's wind up phone and other equipment was on the other side of the boarded cabin and a long storage box seat on the other.

I loved to look out of that window but couldn't unless I was allowed to stand on the box seat. How nostalgic it was to hear those men communicating in our local dialect. We were of course not encouraged to use it at Ludlow Grammar school when I was a little older. It was not considered to be socially acceptable. (*See Titterstone Clees and Up the Lane and Back again).

I looked to the left on Railway Terrace. Marina and I knew every one of the occupants in the six houses and all were employees at the coal pits, quarries and railway complex. Those hard working people were the salt of the earth and an integral part of my life.   Our home the Dhu Stone Inn was their social centre. They all visited the pub not only to have a drink but socialise, hear local news, play darts, sing, play cribbage, quoits or have a chat. We sold paraffin too so every local came to purchase a can full for their table lamps and in winter collect emergency supplies of bread. It was a real ordeal to get supplies to the pub from Clee Hill village a mile away in driving, blizzard winds and deep snow.

In the far end of the Terrace at Number One lived Mr and Mrs Purslow. They were a quiet , friendly couple especially to us children. Mr Purslow worked on the railway from the Dhu Stone to Clee Hill. He stored his tools in huts alongside the track. The huts were constructed of railway sleepers and the only light into them was from an open door. They were to me a little spooky but I often went in to help carry out plate layers' hammers, picks, shovels, tins of grease and oil.

Next door at Number Two was George (Tacker) Lloyd. It was a wonder that I knew his correct name because everyone seemed to have a nick name which most of them went by. However some resented their nick names because they were derogatory. Tacker was an affable man and always kind to Marina and me. He was one of the earliest I recall because when very small I was standing by the bar door and responded to him shyly. It was Christmas Eve and he said, "You'll have to be going to bed very soon Alfred otherwise Father Christmas may not call." Christmas presents were very meagre but how excited and grateful we were. Tacker's wife Lillian, a quiet, frail lady was confined to a wheelchair which was not easy to use around the cottages on slippery quarry setts and uneven terrain. Their children were Dorothy, Arthur and Freddy, he was very short and had deformed legs. However he was determined and clever , held down a good job and never failed to get to work. His family relatives reminded me that they had to push him all the way to and from Clee Hill School in the wheelchair. They were unable to make short cuts over stiles and down the Pit Ground but had to make a three miles round trip along the railway line path and through Clee Hill Village. Elsie Cleeton said it was an exhausting daily chore.

At Number Three were Ern Bradley, his wife May and daughters Ella and Ruth. In those days no one had main's water, indoor toilets or electricity. Like other coal miners in the locality Ern had a delivery of one ton of coal monthly. This was tipped on the roadside by Dhu Stone Lane railway bridge some distance from the cottages. In his trade as carpenter and undertaker Dad made many robust, farmyard style wheelbarrows. He always loaned Ern one and helped to bowl the coal to his coal house. As well as the ubiquitous pig sty; this was another essential store. In return for the loan, Ern loaded up Dad's barrow as full as possible when labour was finished, to take home as a very welcome perk. We always had to have a roaring, open fire for workmen to warm and dry themselves as well as to enable them to cook and make toast during their lunch break.

Weather was often very cold and windy with bitter storms. As a result quarry men always stood with their backs near to the fire when they came in before sitting down on benches and screens to consume their 'snappin'. Mum often jokingly remonstrated with them saying, "All you who stand before the fire, will you sit down is my desire; that other folk as well as you may see and feel the fire too."

By the time Ern arrived home from his 'shift' , complete with steel toe capped boots, corduroys and blackened, sweat streaked face and hands May would have carried many buckets of water from the Terrace communal tap, filled the copper in her back kitchen and with the help of a coal fire got the water steaming hot.

As all locals did, Ern brought in a long metal bath and deposited it in front of the kitchen fire. May bucketed the water into the bath so Ern could soak in front of the fire. She would wash his back and a little later he would appear unrecognisable from the man I had seen earlier walking along the railway line home. Ern was a very tidily dressed person when out but his hands and face bore tell tale marks of blue streaks embedded in his skin – so typical of our local miner's trademarks.

Ella being much the older girl soon left home but had grown up with us as a dear school friend and neighbour. She was strongly built with a happy countenance. Sadly Ruth was born with deformed feet; in fact I think they were turned round backwards. Her legs were encased in irons and her feet covered with special boots. What a trial Ruth had! Her considerable handicap meant she experienced great difficulty walking , was often carried or placed in a wheelchair. It seemed to Marina and me that Ruth's young life was monopolised by visits to hospital and operations. How did she endure it?   Her resilience was a great example to others.

After many, many operations Ruth's feet pointed in the correct direction and as a teenager she had the joyful thrill of wearing her first pair of fashionable shoes. How wonderful it must have been to look and feel normal in the company of her contemporaries. We admire her, think it special she has remained a friend and become a capable mum and grandma too.

Ern with his quiet, discreet manner was absolutely trusted by Dad. He often needed help to deliver a coffin to quite remote squatter's cottages around the Hill and across gorse strewn common land. This was before I was old enough to help Dad.   Many people died at home in those days. Travel was difficult. Hospitals were remote and country folk could not afford to be taken to a mortuary. The deceased, with coffin remained at home until funeral day. A goodly number of cottages had just one bedroom and a landing with a ladder for stairs.

Imagine the problems of removing a body from upstairs to be laid out in the 'parlour'. Dad would discuss necessities before hand with the family, and those who perhaps wished visited a neighbour, while Ern and Dad plus other helpers delivered the coffin; took off a door; strapped the corpse to the door and lowered it down the ladder to be placed in an open coffin for all to view until funeral day. Ern was a confidante and never known to discuss details of Dad's professional work in the pub.

How easy it is to instantaneously communicate with anywhere in the world nowadays. I marvel how Dad efficiently conducted his business. Clee Hill is a large, remote area and most people needing help came to him on foot or by bicycle. He had to cycle one and a half miles to Clee Hill Village to make all phone calls. Only quarry headquarters had telephone lines. What a godsend Dad found it when Dhu Stone Hamlet had a telephone box installed by Doris Hammond's shop, Rouse Boughton Terrace in 1952. It was only about four hundred yards away from home.

How excited we were to receive our daily post and be able to write long letters to reply to distant friends. Mobile phones are an amazing boom, but it is still foreign to me to see someone using one in a supermarket to ask someone at their home what they require. Planning it seems is not such an essential nowadays.   It is still unforgiveable to see a mum pushing a pram with one hand, mobile phone and cigarette in the other discussing something of what appears to be of vital importance – while their small child experiences no conversation.

Is the occasional silence, or observations of one's surroundings, or meaningful face to face conversation no longer appreciated? Do we have to be in continual touch with others via the mobile? What has happened to written communication we so enjoyed receiving?

May, Ern's wife was a member of the Hill Top Edwards family. They were all large, strong, robust people who visited our pub regularly. Many of their wedding festivities took place in Dhu Stone Inn, with lots of singing and copious amounts of beer being handed around in gallon enamel jugs. Receptions and after wedding parties were simple affairs, often held in a cleaned out and decorated tallit (a room near the roof where hay was often stored) and honeymoons hardly existed. Most newly married couples were back at work the next day because everyone was so short of cash. There were thirteen in May's family, all hardworking and such a happy, homely group to visit. Marina was bridesmaid for nearly all of them. We often ran up and over the old, disused quarry, known as the Rabbit Hole to receive a warm welcome. We loved it.

The youngest son Fred was about ten years my senior; a good friend who had an excellent voice. Local soldiers when coming home on leave often brought me a harmonica. I became quite proficient with my chromatic model. I played most week-ends in the bar because customers were always ready for a sing song.

Christmas was special, the pub wonderfully decorated with holly, mistletoe and streamers and crammed with customers. They knew every word of every carol in the book and singing was momentous. Fred persuaded me to play while he did the singing at every Dhu Stone Hamlet cottage. My idea was to earn some pocket money but it was in short supply and instead we were plied with copious varieties of home-made wine. My return home with red eyes and blurred speech did not amuse my stern Mum at all. As a

Pig and Whistle Butlins Holiday Camp:- Left to R, Bill Brown, Freddy Edwards(my carol singing friend), Alf Jenkins, Basil Broome. Obviously in good voice.

punishment she made me mop all the floors after the customers had left. I was not safe enough to wash and wipe the pint glasses. That was left to Marina, Dad and Mum. But! my giggly frame of mind was not much concerned even when I received a further reprimand for tripping over the mop bucket.

In Spite of these blips Mum liked Freddy and he persuaded her to allow me a week's holiday with him and other chaps when I was just fifteen, at Butlin's Holiday Camp Pwllheli. That truly was a rapid growing up experience.

Ern purchased the first television I had ever seen; a nine inch Bush. I was thrilled to be invited to watch a world heavyweight boxing championship . All curtains were drawn, no lights on; flickering black and white transmission but so wonderful. It really was exciting to see a live programme. My occasional treat was to visit the Clifton Cinema in Old Street, Ludlow or the Picture House in Castle Square to watch Pathe News and Sport which of course reported many happenings well after the actual events.

Those cottages all had their individual 'smell' due to the fat, cigarettes used or home made wine they brewed. All were homely in the one and only living room. Every cottage had a table lamp situated centrally on the table, by which to sew and patch, with a crochet mat beneath it. There was often a sampler on a wall and a biblical quote. There were very few pictures and reading books in evidence but always a large wooden cabinet radio from which it was possible to receive two channels, the Home Service and Light Programme. We all enjoyed the regular programmes of In Town Tonight, Itma, Workers' Playtime, Mrs Dale's Diary and Dick Barton – Special Agent which was my particular favourite. Most evenings we would be out playing on the 'Tips' but all rush home to be in time for the theme music at 6.45pm.

There was always a fire screen inside a fender, a hod of coal, sometimes a few logs and a container of coloured spills. A typical mantelpiece was adorned with a chiming clock and one or two china or earthenware ornaments. Many families had a caged budgie or canary and there was many a pigeon loft at the bottom of the kitchen garden.

Number Four was the home of Dick Beddoe and family of Barbara, Marjorie, Johnny and Nancy – all our friends and as always Marina and I felt at home there. Barbara often took me for a walk in the pram along by the railway line to try and get me to sleep while Mum was attending to her necessary chores and customers.

When she left school, being a hard working girl Barbara secured employment on Harry Green's farm at the bottom of Mill Street in Ludlow. She had to milk his cows by hand. Mill Street sloped very steeply down to the river Teme which was bordered by Harry's fertile flood plain fields. The lower part of the street contained part of Ludlow's ancient town wall and the eight hundred years old Grammar School. Higher up, the street was blessed with many elegant Georgian houses culminating at the top with the beautiful, Victorian Town Hall (now sadly long taken down. Why?) and very special Border Marches Castle. This ancient town with its traditional medieval street layout and fine examples of architecture spanning from Middle Ages to present day is, some claim the prettiest town in England.

When I walked down Mill Street each morning to school, Ebenezer King my Geography and Art teacher would glide by the edge of the pavement on his sit up and beg bicycle, scuffing one foot along to make sure he was able to stop at the school entrance.

Barbara would be doing her milk round. She often crossed the road, clad in her wellington boots, brown overall, head scarf concealing her curlers and give me a cheery greeting. Her faithful horse plodded on, pulling the milk float loaded with milk churns; stopping intermittently where required without commands; quite memorable. He would stand while she got on the float to take off a canister and ladle. She knocked at each door to be greeted by ladies in their all round aprons, holding their jugs to be filled with fresh, still warm milk.

Marjorie was our age, a good friend who walked to school with us daily. Nancy was a Downs Syndrome child with a lovely warm , happy smile and personality. She remained at home always, giving no respite to Mrs Beddoes.

Dick was a tall, strongly built man who worked in the quarry and loved his pint of beer. He said to me that Mum and Dad served each lunch time caller with two pints of beer or cider from trays as they arrived. This was to give them drinks as quickly as possible because lunch breaks were only half an hour. I asked him why they were given two pints at the same time. He replied, "We adna got much time fer snappin and we wun dry. So the fust un didnu touch the sides."

Dick was one of our local barbers. Mr Charlie Lucas from New Buildings was quiet, calm, slow but gentle. He like Dick was a quarry barber too. Dick by contrast was rapid. We had to sit on an empty beer case in Dad's workshop some distance from our house. He often placed a basin on the back of your head to get an even cut round the neck. The charge was six old pence a time and the experience was agony because his clippers were always blunt. I swear he tugged out more than he cut.

Number five was home to George, Sally Price, their daughter Gladys , son-in-law Arnold Crowther and grandson Derek. George a stocky, rotund man of about five feet five inches was never without his cap and boiler suit. He had a small Hitler style moustache. He was a dedicated engine driver on the Dhu Stone railway and therefore appeared different to quarrymen with their corduroys, hob nailed boots, muffler, yarks (knotted neckerchief, straps round trousers just below the knees)and calloused hands. George shunted empty trucks along the level top a mile or so to Craven Place near Clee Hill Village; picked up full trucks and brought them back to the brow of Dhu Stone incline. He was mustard at his work and could control the engine so precisely. Often I watched as he eased trucks gently towards the brake dummy to which the full trucks had to be linked. Too much push could nudge the trucks too far and send them careering down the incline prematurely. Constant shouts and signals ensured the huge links were hoisted to complete the connection.

George's oil rag was always in evidence especially when he put the engine to bed in the 'engine shed' nightly. Each morning he made sure the LMS Sentinal 7164 was loaded with ample coal and filled with water from the tower nearby. He occasionally replaced a piece of tarpaulin which he made and suspended in the front of the cab to reduce the sting of the biting wind.

Sally Price was typical of many locals with her all round apron, head scarf concealing her curlers replaced by a hair net "when tidy". She was profoundly deaf but like the other neighbours gave us a warm welcome. Gladys was more rounded; didn't seem to have her own opinion, repeating everything Sally said and nodded after every one of Sally's utterances. But! she ruled her husband Arnold with a rod of iron. He was a lovely, docile quarryman who was always tidy and reserved. He was restricted to routine and forced habits. Each evening he climbed over the sleeper railed boundary fence of Railway Terrace and knocked gently on the back door of the pub. When Mum opened it he stepped quickly inside. She knew Arnold's routine; took a pint bottle from him, went to the 'beer engine' and took a pint of mild ale back to him quickly. Then returning to the beer engine with payment in hand she poured a pint into the bottle with the aid of a tun-dish(funnel for pouring beer). Before she could make the few return steps Arnold had gulped down the pint, froth still clinging to its sides.

With full bottle in one hand and wiping his mouth with his other he dashed back home. He **must have** been given a set time to make the journey or perhaps it was to make Gladys think he hadn't dallied to have any drink at all. Poor Arnold! Many times since I reflected that it not only women in life who may experience cruelty in marriage.

Number six was the home of another Price family namely Bill, Mrs Price, Vera , Jean and Bertie. Bill, a small, slim man always tidily attired and his trade mark cap. He was a member of a long established Clee Hill family of Random Farm which was situated very near to the famous Three Farked Pole. They were hard working hill farmers who also delivered coal by horse and cart and cut most small holder's fields of hay grass with their horse drawn mowers. The sight and repetitive 'click click' of the mower's reciprocating blade evokes vivid memories. Stan and his father Ben took it in turns to fit spare blades on a special stand and with experienced skill sharpen gleaming teeth on one side only and rub the burr off on the other side. The sharpening took an hour of patience and care which could only be achieved after years of practise.

George Price engine driver (the one with the cap) standing outside the engine shed with photographer Mr W.A. Camwell. Note the tarpaulin at the front of Sentinal 7164 to minimise seering wind and the water tower. (No health and safety rails to the ladder).

The Engine shed showing clearly the buttresses. These were erected after the shed was built to prevent gale force winds blowing it over. In the distance on the right I can discern the position of a sign which said, "Trespassers will be prosecuted forty shillings."

Meanwhile the other continued round the field looking carefully all the time for any stone, branch or missile which may cause damage to the working blade. No blade of grass was wasted in those small hedged paddocks.

My Dad, like others would scythe the gate way entrance to each field and enough of an area to be able to open the gate and allow horses and machine to draw inside without flattening any precious grass. Not only was every bit precious but almost impossible to cut when bruised and flattened.

Ben and Stan carried on until darkness made work impossible. They retired to the pub bar, consumed copious quantities of cider and staggered, bleary eyed to sit on the shafts of their cart. Having rested, those sure footed horses transported Stan and Ben a distance of two or more miles over tracks and common land with just stars to light the way. With legs dangling over the sides of the shafts how did they balance themselves? To my surprise they would be back at daybreak as bright as buttons to continue their labours.

No wonder Bill Price was an equally conscientious railway man. He changed points, coupled trucks and did lengths man's maintenance. On the side of each truck was a very strong clip under which Bill would place a card with the weighed load, content and destination. His movements were jerky because he was unable to rotate his neck normally due to some abnormality. As a consequence his neck and shoulders moved at the same time. A gentleman who lived in nearby cottages at the Dhu Stone had a very unfortunate experience while abroad in the USA. This left him disturbed and demented. He was completely harmless and local people liked and pitied him. Most evenings he walked the short distance from his home to the railway track and systematically removed many of the truck tickets from their clips much to the exasperation of Bill.

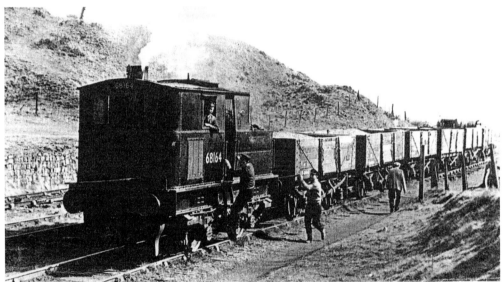

Sentinel 68164 returning from Craven Place to Dhu Stone. Mr Bill Price can be seen in the distance walking away. We walked this track everyday to go to primary school and on returning home New Buildings and Rouse Boughton children had to cross the railway line; this in spite of a large notice saying , "Trespassers will be fined 40 shillings."

Bill was a quiet, agreeable man who always greeted Marina and me with warmth. Mrs Price was considerably taller and slim. She was quietly spoken and in her younger days during World War I had worked on the Overhead Railway which transported 600 tons of stone daily from Magpie Quarry to Detton Ford where it joined the Ditton Priors to Cleobury branch. She recalled, "I earned the best money I ever had in my life; seven and six pence a week." (thirty seven and a half pence). (*see Titterstone Clees, Everyday Life for more photos and information).

Vera, a pleasant diminutive lady worked at a Tenbury factory, had the usual quiet welcoming nature greeting us with warmth as neighbours. Mrs Bill Price looked after younger daughter Jean. That lovely, gentle girl was slightly built with a pale complexion, spectacles and floral patterned dresses. She, perhaps because of her medical condition was always clean and tidy. She spent a great deal of time with my Mum, sitting with her on a high backed screen chatting to her and the quarry men. Always someone would ask while eating his half loaf of bread, cheese and onion, "What did you have for dinner today Jean?" The answer invariably was, "Boiled bacon and parsley sauce." Sadly Jean was whipped off to Queen Elizabeth Hospital Birmingham at the age of sixteen and to everyone's consternation did not survive a heart operation.

Jean's was the second death we experienced at school within a short time. The other one was that of John Thomas of Winthills Farm. He was a tough, typical boy who was always in the middle of a rough and tumble. The last person we expected to die. Deaths of two of our contemporaries was a real jolt to us, our small country school and community.

Everyday life of local people:- I consider myself extremely fortunate to have been born into this special, remote area with its conglomerate dialect. Ludlow just five miles away thought us a race apart and we were. Our speech was different and unusual, our lives simple and uncluttered. Folk walked everywhere and carried weekly shopping great distances. I marvelled that my Mum and other women had not got arms as long as apes, stretched by heavy loads.

No one had a telephone and telegrams frightened us beyond imagination because they always brought distressing news. I so clearly remember Mum opening one and bursting into convulsive tears on reading that her brother Tom from Erwood had died two days previously.

Lavish homes and rich furnishings were unknown. Money was hard earned by long hours of breaking stone in quarries and coal mining. As one local said, "We ad tu work tu live and get summat tu ate."

Holidays and honeymoons were very rare and non-existent to most. Every penny obtained was carefully utilised by the woman of the house. As the wonderful bard of Clee Hill, Dennis Crowther said, "We didnu av a oneymoon. We adnu got a klet. If we wun lucky ween goo down tu Fairy Glen and put our fit in the bruck. No sea-side trips only the dart outing."

People had little or nothing but even in dire circumstances meagre resources were shared when necessary. My Dad as a local undertaker experienced the organising of whist drives and dances to raise money in order to bury a person when a family had virtually nothing. It is thoughts of this nature that I hope have always kept my feet firmly on the ground.

No food was discarded. A sell by date was unheard of and if items in the wire mesh, fronted food safe appeared a little mouldy it was scraped off and consumed – and we survived.

Hospitals were miles away and not easily accessible and when illness struck there was no income. While in quarry work everyone was expected to put whatever weekly they could into a collecting box. So when we heard, "Oh, Charlie is on the box," we knew he was ill and receiving a meagre subsidy from it.

From my signal box position so many memories monopolised my mind. We knew so well every family in our thirty local houses, went to school with Dhu Stone children, played cricket and football on the Green and endless hours of fox and hounds in the Wallers.

Each cottage had a long garden where crops of vegetables of every kind were grown. These were all devoured and welcomed in homes. All peelings and household waste and 'frum taters' (small potatoes used for the pig) were put in swill tubs. At the top of most gardens was a pigsty constructed of obsolete railway sleepers, cadged and carted home by employees. The sty housed the ubiquitous large white. They were monstrous. Some were sixteen, seventeen or even twenty score or more. All pig swill was heated up, sometimes a little expensive pig meal added and fed to the precious pig. I often thought pigs had better treatment and more regular meals than some local people.

It was quite common to see blackened saucepans and pans suspended in a pig swill tub. When the contents effervesced they produced an acid reaction which cleaned pots and pans superbly.

We became quite fond and attached to our bacon pigs, watching them grow and thrive from piglets. Dad often fed ours a small shovel full of coal to crunch. He maintained it was a good medicine. All bacon pigs were killed when there was an 'r' in the month, much to the concern of us children looking on. We hated to hear the eerie, piercing sound of their squealing as they were forced by half a dozen sturdy men to a long, wide pig bench; knifed and killed by Sammy Goodman. But, that was the necessary cycle of a pig's life.

Once dead the animal was put into a barrel of boiling water, first the tail half then the head half and scraped clean. The sound of those scrapers and the glint of sharp knives stays with me and especially the memory of Sammy Goodman saying, "Come 'ere young un. I'll 'ave thee in the tub." I remember running panic stricken to hide behind Mum. The white, hairless pig was carried into the wash house to hang before a couple of days later being cut up and jointed. Hams and flitches were cured for weeks in salt then finally hung up from the kitchen ceiling to dry. The occasional maggot dropped on to the kitchen table but was hardly noticed. Pork joints were shared with neighbours who returned the compliment when their pig succumbed. Fresh meat had to be disposed of quickly because no one had a refrigerator or any means of keeping it fresh. Flitches and hams were so important and an essential part of a family's daily winter food. When Dad was slicing a few rashers for breakfast I would often persuade him to give me a small raw piece to chew.

To the modern super market generation this all may sound gory, unbearable and barbaric. To us it was essential to enable families to survive. It was expected for folk to work really hard to earn money for food. To enjoy the regular pint was considered part of a working man's existence too.

At a week-end many took their greyhounds tracking and wiring hares and rabbits; another essential staple part of our diet. Absolutely nothing was wasted. Even rabbit and mole skins were hung up to dry and sold for a few pence.

At the other end of most gardens and the furthest possible point away from the cottage was a lavatory. Some had two holes in the wooden seat, one much smaller for children. One row of twelve cottages nearby had six toilets only. Everyone knew what the long trek down the garden meant, often accompanied by a Park Drive, Woodbine or pipe full of St Julian.

All ashes from house fires were placed in large piles beyond the toilet and once weekly the toilet buckets were tipped and covered in the ashes. In turn most of this plus all pig manure was dug into gardens to help produce next year's crop of vegetables. I find it amusing nowadays when people think re-cycling and organic growing is something innovative when sixty years ago it was the only way to survive as a family and perpetuate crops.

Many local workers in squatters' cottages also had a cow which they tended and milked after a long day from dawn till dusk breaking stone with a 'boster'. I well remember asking one quarry man how he coped with this ceaseless action trap of work and sleep. He replied, "Surri Alf, when I picks up my spade it's like a spoon atter usin a boster all day." They even made time to visit my home Dhu Stone Inn at week-ends making their simple, community fun. Perhaps they would sing to Marina playing the piano; play their own concertinas, melodians, whistles or do a party piece. I would play my mouthorgan for them to sing popular songs. Everyone was occupied playing fives and threes, darts, cribbage and quoits. There was no such thing as a large, flat screen television or a juke box. My grandchildren often ask, "Grandad how on earth did you manage to survive without a mobile, ipod etc?" (* see Titterstone Clee, Everyday Life).

Women's work was not just a constant round of chores in the home. All locals who were able went hop and potato picking in season. They travelled miles in the back of a lorry or on Sid Smith's bus to share a crib or gather potatoes to make a little extra income to buy shoes for their children. After a day's work it was back home to carry every drop of required water from a communal tap. The weekly wash took a whole day and with Clee Hill's inclement weather garments were draped everywhere in the small cottages to dry. No wonder most of us had only one change of underclothes per week. No one found that unusual . We must have all smelled the same in school.

Repairing clothes was essential. Patches were inserted in trouser knees, buttons were sewn on and large well worn coats and trousers were cut down and made to fit children. Bed clothes and sheets were patched and repaired and those beyond that stage were cut up and used as dusters and dish clothes or 'rags' as they were referred to. I learnt many years later that ladies were not able to buy sanitary towels etc but made the best with nappies and oddments.. Old sacks were rolled up tightly and tied with string to make draught excluders and reduce snow drifts which whiffled in through ill fitting doors. Old clothes were cut up into strips of about four inches long. Then pulled through holes made with a bodkin in washed sacking. These made colourful, warm mats. Children helped make these. A dead lamb or sheep's skin was cut from the carcase, dried and made into beautiful bedside mats. I had one by my bed but I did not know till years later that is was from my pet lamb which Dad had sadly driven over.

Back to Industry

Dhu Stone had been the hub of Titterstone Clees' Industrial Revolution. Coal trade of the Middle Ages had continued to expand into the 1800s with a considerable work force. There were numerous deep coal pits at Random and Magpie Hill which is above and slightly beyond Clee Hill Village, many of them with shafts 100 yards deep. Hundreds of shallow bell pits operated at the slightly lower level of Catherton, Coreley, Knowbury and above Bedlam Village. In fact they formed a necklace round the Hill.

The canal system boom had transported some Clee Hill coal and Leominster had benefitted; but the rapid development of the railway system in the 1800s dramatically 'swamped' further canal development. Tunnel Lane canal at Orleton for instance was therefore not finished.

Coal had been transported and ironstone too by pack horse and horse and cart, in particular to Downton Forge.   Much coal had been taken for local consumption but was also delivered to Herefordshire, Worcestershire and Shropshire.

Although the industry was prosperous it was bitty, uncoordinated and run by many small groups and individuals.

The railway system had developed from South Wales to Hereford, Leominster, Ludlow and continued to Craven Arms, Shrewsbury and beyond. There were many local branch lines too including Tenbury Wells and Bromyard.

In 1862 The London North Western and West Midlands Railways took over Shrewsbury/Hereford stretch. A group of entrepreneurs had the dream of building a by line from Ludlow to Bitterley and an incline railway from there to Dhu Stone and Clee Hill to monopolise the coal trade. The main promoters were Sir Charles Henry Rouse Boughton BT, Andrew Boughton KT, The Honourable George Winsor Clive (Earl of Craven) and James Wicken.

The line received an Act of Parliament on 22nd July 1861 the share capital being £30,000 in £10 shares. A Mr Wylie the appointed engineer reported that the line was feasible for a locomotive from Ludlow to Bitterley but that an incline of 1 in 12 would also be necessary. In fact the last stretch to Dhu Stone was 1 in 6.

Mr Wylie, Engineer for Shrewsbury and Hereford, Tenbury and Bewdley was asked to go ahead and draw up plans. No wonder there was such a desire to embark on this project because it had been estimated by Joshua Richardson of Neath, South Wales that the Titterstone Clee mineral fields, about 3,000 acres of coal were sufficient to supply 500 tons daily for 150 years. Also a considerable quantity of ironstone was envisaged.

Construction went ahead rapidly and started near a bridge 400yards from Ludlow station in the parish of Stanton Lacy. The use of Ludlow station was rented for £10 per annum.

The track was to terminate in a field in the parish of Coreley, the property of Earl Craven.

The whole length would be 5 miles 7 furlongs. However David Wylie died in March 1863 but his partner and brother-in-law Mr William Clarke, who had until 1861 been engineer on the Punjab Railway in India, took over. He was paid £50 per annum for his services. By then it was established that "Jewstone", later known as Dhu stone, the well known Clee Hill dolerite had been tested and found suitable for building material and therefore a possible second use for the railway incline.

On March 30th 1864 Mr William Clarke reported that the line was more-or-less completed and that the rope, one and a half inches in diameter would be ready for installation on 1st June. The Railway was opened to Bitterley on 24th August 1864 but the incline was not fully operative until 1867.

Photograph by Hugh Davies 1950s. The Double Track approaching Bitterley

Photograph by Hugh Davies taken in the 1950s. Hugh can be seen walking away from us on the track while the trip is approaching Bitterley Yard. The engine driver obviously knows that his photograph is being taken.

Hugh Davies 1950's:- Passing under the road bridge at Bitterley Yard. Single track on the right leading into Bitterley's huge siding .

Initially the Clee Hill line was independent with its own locomotive, named after Sir Charles Rouse Boughton. From 1877 it was worked by the Great Western and London North Western and became part of those companies in 1893. Until 1877 horses had been used for shunting and hauling from Dhu Stone to Clee Hill Craven Place after which they were replaced by steam engines. (Keith Beddoes 1997).

A sum of £2,400 was to be left with the Court of Chancery of England to be forfeited to the Crown if the line was not opened to passenger traffic by the expiry date of four years. Some tolls specified are of interest. For use of the engines for propelling carriages the rate was a halfpenny per mile per passenger or animal or per ton of goods. For the use of the carriages the charges were up to two and a half (d) old pence for 1st class, one and three quarters d for second class and one and a quarter d for 3rd class. Beasts of burden up to 4d per mile, cattle 2d and small animals 1d per mile. Two mile rate for dung, one and a half d, coal, two and a half d as was sheet iron; 3d sugar, 4d for cotton and 5d for fish. An extra 1d per ton was to be charged for incline transport.

By 1870 the regular revenue accrued, ran at £2,880 per half year.

A single track line ran from Ludlow to Middleton siding, (now a small housing estate), then on for a total of about 4 miles. Here about half a mile from Bitterley the railway climbed at 1 in 20 into Bitterley Yard, a very extensive marshalling yard. Western Region 0-6-0 engines could maintain the movement of 20 trucks along this stretch at about 3 mph providing conditions were dry and not slippery. On the downhill 23 trucks were permitted on a trip. Bitterley siding construction necessitated a great deal of labour with tremendous removal of rock and soil having to be cut away from the hill side. The steep incline continued from Bitterley for one and three quarter miles rising from 650 feet above sea level to 1,250 feet. This necessitated a gradient of 1 in 12 and for the last 100 yards or so to Dhu Stone 1 in 6. The bottom of the incline started with a single track, bending gradually to the right then absolutely straight to the turnout.

Automatic points allowed entry of the tracks from below while full trucks from above descending changed the points over. The turn out had four rails and above the turn out proceeding to Dhu Stone were three,

The bend at the beginning of the incline bearing to the right from Bitterley. Note the vertical pulleys and the steel rope just discernible. Below is the Dummy truck at the front of a trip. Bitterley signal box is on the right. Photograph from Bylines manual produced in 1996 and taken by Hugh Davies in the 1950s.

Looking up the incline from Bitterley. Vertical pulleys on the right ,and track running by Bitterley signal Box off to the large marshalling yard. Photograph by Hugh Davies – late 1950s.

with a common central rail. This avoided the cost of a full length double track all the way to Dhu Stone. This compromise allowed the up and down rope to be kept apart on a different set of pulleys.

The 'endless' wire rope was one and a half inches diameter and treated with shellac to preserve it. From strain in use the rope did stretch and as a boy I recall engineers periodically cutting out a section, unwinding the component's strands on either side of the cut ends and re-weaving an overlap. This was intricate and

Photograph from Derek Crowther in 2012.This was taken in the 1930s. In front of the above mentioned Bitterley signal box. George Jones on the left. Next Tom Lloyd driver of the Loco at Bitterley who came from Leominster,The 'Boss man' is not known, next Mr Timmis and right Cliff King from Shrewsbury. Numerous railway men came from Shrewsbury area daily to carry out repairs.

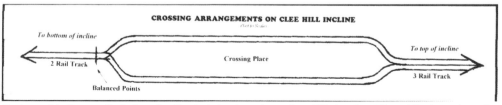

The turnout halfway up the incline. See the single track coming up from Bitterley; the 4 lines at the turnout crossing point and 3 rails on the upper side continuing to Dhu Stone.

clever work. The result was a short, joined length more bulbous than the remaining rope but with use and strain of weight soon reduced in thickness.

Occasionally the rope had to be replaced. The cost in 1952 was £3,000.

Dhu Stone Quarry being the first Hill quarry to open in 1864 developed Dhu Stone Hamlet as an area of habitation and the fulcrum of Clee Hill's Quarrying industry.

Blasted, crushed stone came down three feet gauge inclines in metal trucks. Their speed was regulated by a rope being wound round a wooden drum built and rotating between two brick pillars at the top of the hill near the quarry. Some of the stone continued in trucks along the high stone wharf to be tipped into wagons on the main railway.

They were shunted to the 'Glory Hole' weighbridge positioned to the right of the photograph on page 105, before joining the downhill trip to Bitterley.

An excellent photograph by Hugh Davies late 1950s. The three rails are well illustrated with the common central rail, the 'down' wagons in the background with the dummy at the back having 'collected' the rope. On the right of the picture the wire rope is running over the pulleys and connected to the 'up' trip which is out of the picture going down to Bitterley. The tops of Rouse Boughton can be seen background left and road bridge ahead.

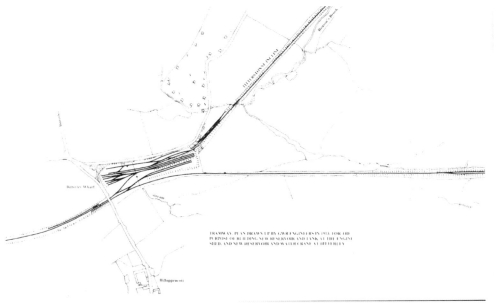

This drawing done in 1913 by a GWR engineer shows the railway line at Bitterley; the impressive Bitterley marshalling yard and the narrow gauge incline to Titterstone quarry which opened in 1881. Also the incline to the Dhu Stone with turn out transferring from single track to the "passing turn out" .

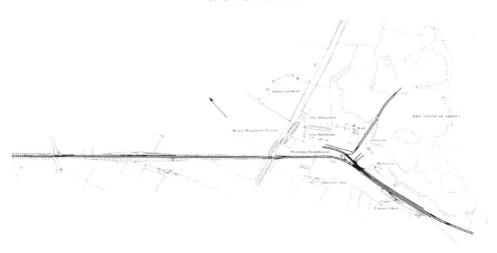

The top half of Dhu Stone Incline:- Above the turn out there were three rails, a common central rail with rollers for the wire rope on either side. This sketch shows the railway road bridge, Rouse Boughton Terrace, New Buildings, Railway Terrace, my home Dhu Stone Inn, Drum house, engine shed and Dhu Stone Quarries. Above Rouse Boughton Terrace was The Bungalow, our wooden "Village Hall" where we had the Coronation tea in 1953. The railway line is shown continuing to Craven Place, Clee Hill Village.

1922 Photograph of Dhu Stone Quarry fulcrum:-The drum at the top of the hill on brick pillars which regulated the speed of full trucks descending to the tar macadam plant, the top of which can be seen background left. In front of a Rouse Boughton chimney and roof can be seen trucks to be filled from the hopper, sheeted and shunted back onto the main line. The impressive 'sett' built wharf is evident and trucks to be shunted to the "Glory Hole" weighbridge just out of picture on right. On the wharf near the 'tarmac' plant is a modern metal truck beside an obsolete wooden one. Behind the buildings on the wharf was a reservoir which supplied the works with water (see sketch above). The large building to the left is the Drum House.

The Drum House:- This was a place I was often allowed to go into as a lad to see water constantly pouring onto large wooden brake blocks. Continual pressure by the wheel man on the right to slow the trip to 3 to 5 mph would have resulted in ignition had not copious amounts of cold water been used.

An early 1900's photograph of Dhu Stone wharf:- The building at the rear belching dust was the first stone crushing plant for Dhu Stone Quarry. It was dismantled and superseded in the 1930s. I remember the concrete base only. On the wharf is a wooden truck the type seen in Dhu Stone in the early 1900s. They were followed by triangular metal bodied tipping trucks. Main line trucks are on the railway below.

Photograph from Bylines taken by Hugh Davies in 1956. The downward empty trucks are descending from Dhu Stone. Both upward and downward continuous rope clearly visible, running over brightly worn pulleys. The road bridge with Dhu Stone Lane is in the background, the Kenhard family home far left, originally known as the Railway Boss's home. Immediately left is the end cottage of Railway Terrace. In front on the railway are large, wooden blocks which swung across the track at end of the working day and the lovely white gates closed.

Dhu Stone Wharf. Trucks in the siding:- This photo was taken a few years after the first photo was taken in the early 1900s. The stone crusher has been dismantled; the structure remains more or less as I remember it but the wharf was built higher with a layer of formed concrete placed on top of stone setts.

This 1950's snap shows the remains of Dhu Stone Crusher. In the far right the windows and entry to the "Glory Hole" weighbridge. It was so called because in the absence of workmen we went into its entrance, stamped our feet on the concrete steps which led up to the wharf. This generated trembling reverberations and echoes from our shouts.

1950s locomotive hauling trucks which have just appeared over the brow to begin their journey to Craven Place. The signal box is back left; the obsolete road weighbridge on the right. In front is a new asbestos garage purchased by my Dad. It was easier in snow fall to drive from here than home.

Other metal trucks went to the tar macadam plant where stone was mixed with bitumen automatically and a retarding agent applied to avoid the tarmacadam setting before it reached its destination. Trucks were shunted through a siding running behind the Drum House and positioned under the hoppers. Stone coated with tar, 'tarmac' was dropped into the trucks and shunted to others, weighed, hooked together to make up a 'trip' and descend to distant destinations.

On a large open space opposite the tarmac hopper was a road weighbridge operated by Sammy Thomas of Knowbury and Benny Warrington of Clee Hill during my childhood. As well as railway transport, lorries were loaded under the tarmac hopper, sheeted and weighed before driven by road down Dhu Stone lane to required destinations. Behind the Drum House to its right were New Buildings, a row of twelve houses and to its left Rouse Boughton Terrace. Above the wharf in the background right was a substantial property the home of Mr Lucas a quarry official.

1950s No 1142. Drawing trucks away from the incline top at Dhu Stone. Drum House looking the worse for wear in the background.

1950s. Just a few yards from my home at Dhu Stone Inn. No 47183 stationary. Drum House right. Quarry Manager's home behind. My dear pet dog in the foreground. Garage behind and left of the engine purchased by my Dad from the road weighbridge site.

Dhu Stone quarry when fully operative blasted stone at 9.am and 1.00pm daily. The explosions could be heard twenty miles away and was a signal used by many farmers when working in the fields that it was lunch time.

Upwards of 600 men were employed at Dhu Stone and I remember during working hours the sky was obliterated by clouds of crusher dust. The air was alive with crashes, bangs and squeaks from machinery

The reverse view of the previous photograph showing one of the many "eerie" equipment sheds with no windows.

1958 No 1142 hauling trucks from Craven Place to Dhu Stone, filled with road stone from Granite Quarry near Clee Hill Village. On the right are fitter's and sign writer's sheds now part of Clee Hill Plant Hire business. On the left is home of Mr Edwards an employee. The trucks at the rear of the trip are passing over level crossing leading from Clee Hill Village to Craven Arms Inn (The Kremlin). The track was being used for just three days per week. Evidence of grass growing round track.

1958/9. The 1142 near Dhu Stone incline. The railway beginning to be overgrown and nearing the end of its life.

Late 1950s. A deteriorating, sad site for many locals and me. The tarmac (right) dismantled. Weighbridge far right obsolete. The signal box still operating (front of Railway Terrace). Drum House left and my home Dhu Stone Inn background left. In the distance behind my home and to the right was the Pretty House so named because of its decorative brickwork.

View from the Incline top shortly before closure.

and blasted fragments flying like shrapnel, damaging property roofs. There was an obvious absence of birdlife and no sound of bird song. However on long, summer evenings some small birds and their song became evident; but I never recall seeing buzzards, ravens, kestrels, stone chats, wheat ears and many other species we see so many of today on the hills.

As a child when health and safety rules had not been heard of I often stood by the railway line watching the trips progressing, my parents and the workmen having no fear I would come to harm.

By this time my Dad was a very poorly man with bowel cancer and a prognosis of six weeks of life. His dejection was palpable and exacerbated by the decline of the industries so obvious around him. I tried to keep his spirits up by talking to him about the wonderful work he had done as a wheelwright and asking the reasons why he and Mum had come to the Dhu Stone Inn. Occasionally he would say, "Who wants to know about my work anyway?"   His skills were so precious that I retorted, "I do and lots of other folk too."

In hindsight I was so grateful for those chats I had had with Dad. I know they took his mind off things to come, inspired me to begin writing and collating notes about our exceptional area and kept Dad to the forefront of my mind; a wonderful craftsman, a fine Dad with an exceptional variety of rural skills at his fingertips. I did not however feel that I had the ability to produce a book. To me that sort of expertise was not in my makeup. However it did finally lead to the production of our first book, "Titterstone Clees, Everyday Life, Industrial History and Dialect" which remarkably to date has had five reprints and has been enjoyed in many countries .

Bringing myself back to reality the last photograph was the scene I saw from the top of Dhu Stone Incline. For some reason unknown to me a downhill trip had broken away in 1960 and crashed into the left hand side of the road bridge doing considerable damage and rendering it unsafe. Remains of wheels etc from cut up trucks are evident.

Government was keen to close many by lines to save money. This accident expedited Lord Beeching's policy. Henceforth all Clee Hill's quarried stone was transported direct to destinations via huge lorries. What a folly that has proved to be! It has exacerbated road congestion that need not have materialised. That photograph is a sad site. The present bridge has a large pipe beneath it. The railway was cut up for scrap a little later and so brought to an end over a century of Dhu Stone being a hive of industry.

Belfry Blacksmith's Shop. Johnny Cleeton (senior) strikes for Horace Key.

Miscellaneous Photos:-

Test Blacksmith's piece: Lock made for a test piece by Horace Key.
The top was screwed clockwise to open and close.

Retirement of some Clee Hill Quarry men with guests:- L to R back:- Teddy Broome, Secretary, Bill Wiltshire, Marina Clent MBE, Sam Lloyd, Leonard Davies, Ern Edwards. Front:- L to R Ken Butcher, Alec Evans, Donald Martin, David Cadwallader, Gordon Howells.

Quarrymen Retirement and guests:- Back L to R:- Phil Baulcombe, Ern Edwards, Marina Clent MBE, Sam Lloyd, Adrian Coles TD MBE, Pam Coles. Front Row L to R:- Ken Butcher, Alec Evans, Donald Martin, David Cadwallader, Douglas Beeston.

Aerial Ropeway 1930s (Magpie to Detton Ford):- Employees both men and boys at the beginning of the overhead ropeway which ran for three and three quarters miles from Magpie Quarry to Detton Ford. Ropeway carried 600 tons of stone daily in 256 buckets. Each bucket held half a ton.

Aerial Ropeway Repairs. Taken from near Magpie Quarry showing pylons going toward Catherton Common. Cottage near Cleeton Road in distance; ropeway buckets on ropeway. One of the workmen with 'reeks' (quarry rakes) spreading stone is Mr Cleeton the well known postman who covered the area of Doddington and Cleeton.

Granite Quarry:- One of 4 lorries which were 3 way tippers. Roof of the Craven Arms Inn (The Kremlin) in the background; John Hancocks in bed of lorry, Horace Key Blacksmith above right shovelling,

Clarice Dolphin, (Mother of Desmond Key) 1939.   This is of interest because it shows the 'gibbit' (water spout). This was situated up the common land about 100 yards from the Coreley Turn, above the present bus shelter. It supplied water for a cottage nearby (now demolished) and The Sheds further up where the RAF base was during World War II.

The Primary Field. Madley CP Herefordshire

Twenty seven miles to drive to work. Still, I was only going to have to endure it for two months.

I had been warned that Hereford was becoming a traffic bottleneck and that to avoid considerable delay it was necessary to negotiate the New River Bridge before 8.00am. This was in 1971 and the problem continues to increase dramatically.

I had developed a considerable degree of confidence in Secondary Education in the field of Handicrafts and Engineering Drawing, having organised two large departments from scratch, been in charge of nine staff and enabled pupils to acquire excellent external examination results.

I was at the gate of Madley Primary School – very unsure of my ability to succeed in this new field. I was greeted by Secretary Mrs Audrey Price, a rotund lady with a lovely smile and most relaxed countenance. She took me to meet Mr Charles Hawkins the Headmaster.

After a brief chat I was invited by this south 'Walean' to join him for school assembly. Immediately I discovered Charles had a superb voice and a wonderful relaxed but respectful attitude with the 230 infants and juniors. Rhian Morris could make the piano dance, playing with such aplomb and again she had a superb voice. I thought I was in the 'Land of Song' . After the Head's engaging assembly I was introduced and greeted by what proved to be a happy staff.

Most of the ensuing morning was spent with Mr Charles Hawkins telling me that due to an increase in pupil numbers he needed to have more time for administration and additional teaching help. The plan, if I proved suitable was for me to teach the top juniors by the integrated day system.   The Head of Hereford and Worcester Education Authority assigned me to Madley knowing I had received some training at Aberystwyth in that particular system.   I was to observe Mr Hawkins for the first week, help with groups and gradually assimilate the whole class of thirty two. I had a tour of the school; met Mrs Eva Millardship the Head of Infants and told I may find myself spending time in her class.

I liked the integrated day system and felt it was more akin to secondary school and handicraft teaching than the whole of every day being broken up into traditional rigid 'class' periods.

I observed how Mr Hawkins covered every aspect of the necessary curriculum including spelling, tables, mathematics, reading, writing and through project work history, geography and environmental science.

He set children according to ability in reading and mathematics. In project work all pupils were introduced to the same content but encouraged to produce written results to match their potential. The morning timetable existed of instruction to the whole class, and groups in all subjects apart from themed project work.   As each skill was taught summary notes were recorded on the blackboard with appropriate bold headings and left there for the whole week. Pupils were told they were expected and encouraged to work to those targets by the end of the week. Projects of such topics as, The anatomy of birds; The human body; Trees, wood and man; Local church architecture etc were afternoon work, an aspect being introduced weekly with occasional site visits. A flow chart of each project development produced by Charles remained on display during its execution. Afternoons also included games, PE, singing, musical productions and class assembly preparation each being responsible for producing a school assembly once every two months. The afternoon system enabled Charles to hear every child read regularly. There was no such thing as Classroom assistants.

Within a fortnight I was taking the whole class and being left on my own to cope. At this stage Mr Hawkins invited me to call him Charles – a step I appreciated.   At the end of each day I was exhausted but delighted to be able to control, occupy, beneficially interest and achieve moderate success with this "beehive."

My twenty seven mile journey home gave me the chance to unwind but the detailed continuous preparation was extremely demanding. In spite of my years of teaching experience it was just as exhausting as my very first teaching practice. Of course being a Dad of two inquisitive little ones, Graham and Helen I wished to participate in bath time, bedtime stories and try to share some of Ann's responsibility too. I realised there would be no let up in my new daily routine.

Did I really want to continue with it?

Visits and observations by Charles became less frequent but at the end of another week he spent the whole day with me, checked in detail not only my lesson management but marking and correcting methods. His verdict was, "I think you can do this job. I am happy to have you for the next two months. I agreed to stay. I knew Ann would be pleased. Charles gave me considerable autonomy. I began to relax, enjoy my work again and plan ahead.

A week before my two months was up Charlie said he was convinced I could be a success in Primary Education, that there could be an opportunity for a full time post at Madley and he would be pleased if I would apply for it.

Dear Ann was heavily pregnant, no longer able to continue peripatetic teaching. I discussed my possible future with her, pointed out that I did not command the income I had been accustomed to at Ludlow, that there would be another mouth to feed with luck; there was no likelihood of an imminent increase in pay and fifty four miles of travelling daily would prove expensive.

Being ever the optimist, an excellent manager and completely unselfish she said we could manage financially. The important thing she said was for me to be happy . I retorted my wish was for us all to remain a happy family. I was beginning to enjoy my new situation and I was captivated by my young charges mastering the skills of reading.

On the 30th November I rushed Ann to Hereford Hospital and next day our third bundle of Joy, Karen was born. Ann had quite a difficult time with the birth of Karen and although we had planned four children, two a gap and another two, with that birth experience and expenses increasing we decided our family had to now be complete.

By Christmas a permanent post materialised. I applied and was accepted. Charles Hawkins was a first class, thoughtful teacher. I was lucky to have such an example. He was good at everything, including cricket, running and all sports. Our relationship was excellent, my confidence blossomed and my responsibilities increased each week. Staff informed me that they thought Charles was taking advantage and imposing too much on my shoulders but I absorbed it all because it was from my point of view an excellent opportunity and I had not entered Primary Education at a young age as they had done.

Charles introduced me to anyone in educational circles who he thought mattered. Within a short time I was teaching the top class full time, organising inter school Junior school games, attending local football tournaments and taking weekly swimming sessions in Hereford. Incidentally this was at the time when the pool was sited where the present Courtyard Theatre stands. The water for the pool was heated from city waste which was fed into furnaces attached. That seemed to me to be a revolutionary idea.

After six months at Madley Charles asked, "Do you wish to make your future career in Primary Education because I think you should. I answered that I needed him to assess my prospects and he retorted that I needed to show competence in the infant field as well as junior if I wanted to ensure possible promotion. With this in mind he arranged to take my class while I joined Eva in Reception for sometime every week. This was a unique opportunity to be tutored first hand by such an expert as Eva Millardship in reading and number techniques. How many Head teachers would give a novice such an opportunity?

Encouragement and course opportunities ensued. Eva and her husband Tony became life- long friends. My practical skills enabled me to produce sets for school musicals and much to my surprise Charles encouraged me to submit an application for Madley's Deputy Headship. Unexpectedly I was shortlisted but when I met the other candidates plus one other existing member of Madley staff I said to myself, "Oh well this is practice, beneficial to my CV and good experience."

At interview I was questioned by County people intensively about infant reading schemes, my reasons for preference of integrated day systems as opposed to a traditional timetable and what I thought Madley lacked. I said it could be enhanced further by a more comprehensive and better equipped library. Charles

Hawkins cottoned on to this and asked if I was appointed would I take on this added responsibility. I responded positively.

Much to my surprise with only two years experience I became Madley's Deputy Head. The pay increase was more than welcome.

I became more involved in administration and was confident enough to deputise in Charles's absence.

By now I had been introduced to every senior person at the County Authority of Hereford and Worcester Education but my wish as well as being successful in Primary Education was to develop an idea Charles had had for sometime which I felt could be a most beneficial experience to every child. He asked me to pilot an Educational Exchange with a Coventry School. We needed to find a school in a completely urban environment whose pupils had experienced little of rural life and whose parents had very different occupations from those in Madley. From the Madley end my class of top juniors were to be guinea pigs.

Charles and I spent many hours planning what we wanted our pupils to experience and educational benefits our pupils should obtain from such an exchange. I sent a profile of each of my class pupils to my Coventry opposite member of staff, stating an individual's interests, characteristics, parents' occupations, allergies and a photograph. My opposite number had to find thirty plus pupils of a similar age and pair them as suitably as possible. I planned for pupils to leave Madley on a Monday morning, have a whole week in Coventry area and return the following Monday.

My proposed ideas were for a daily programme of educational visits to factories and places of historical interest; spend part of most days in school; take a traffic census outside the school, go home each evening with host children; live and sleep with the family and come to school each morning with their host acquaintances. In the same academic year the Coventry children would visit and stay with their 'new' found friends; live in their homes; have a similar programme but of course Herefordshire visits would be to cider factories, the Welsh countryside, churches and Marches castles.

Having put forward this concept we held parents' meetings to discuss the venture including many apprehensions written about and voiced by them.

We did not appreciate initially what a mammoth time consuming task this proved to be. However since the day I had been commandeered for National Service at the age of eighteen years and two weeks and suffered from acute home sickness I had vowed that if I became a teacher I would give young children appropriate experience to minimise the impact of this awful experience at as early an age as possible. An Educational Exchange would go some way towards this.

In parents' discussions we decided pocket money would be £1 per day, distributed by me each morning and there would be no extra. Parents solemnly agreed not to 'squirrel' more into suitcases and no one was to ring either way until the Friday evening before the following week-end to minimise home sickness. Host parents would have the opportunity to spend the whole week end with their guest children and organise a suitable programme for them.

Pupils were to show me a stamped addressed envelope/postcard which they would be told to write and post on arrival in Coventry. Time was to be allocated to encourage children to write a comprehensive diary of events. Life was so much more simple and manageable – no mobile phones or other modern methods of communication being available in the 1970s. Individual medication was recorded in detail. I promised I would visit every individual home during evenings and arranged that host parents would make a packed lunch for excursions. Staff fully acknowledged that if we worked closely together that much educational, social benefit and lasting friendships could be nurtured. It was arranged that when possible host children and their visitors would all participate in educational excursions. Staff were to be accommodated by host teachers.

This pilot exchange was to prove a great success and it worked because of the meticulous preparation, cooperation and dedication of staff of both schools. Parents' apprehensions turned to enthusiastic praise and I was convinced Educational Exchanges would feature in my future career.

By gaining the trust and confidence of parents I developed considerable autonomy from that pilot Exchange. In this age of mobile phones, computers etc, some achieved disciplines would be extremely difficult to demand nowadays.

One precious memory was of a brave parent who was prepared to take a boy into her home who was in care and had previously been a compulsive thief. She had four boys of her own and had confidence she could cope with every eventuality. However before the exchange week ended it was discovered this lad had pilfered numerous items from the family home. She sorted out the situation to her satisfaction, refused to prosecute and kept in touch with the lad for many years and even invited him to the farm for holidays. What a lady!!

One humorous but realistic comparison was the quarter of an hour traffic survey. In Coventry our pupils' graphs produced scores of every type of vehicle as expected. In Madley the Coventry pupils' survey was an amazing contrast to them producing a pack of fox hounds and a tractor.

Madley was a good school. Numbers increased as did Charles's reputation. My daily programme was packed and very enjoyable. Charles had been impressed by the lasting beneficial effects from the pilot scheme especially the quality and quantity of creative writing. However he felt that even more could be achieved by an Exchange with a London school.

Luckily Betty Watts was teaching with us and said she had a friend who was a Head teacher of Benhilton Cof E Primary School, Sutton, Surrey, just fifteen miles south of London's centre.

In my fourth year at Madley with Betty's help I went through a similar preparation as described for Coventry. Betty accompanied me to Sutton where I met Head teacher Peggy Taylor, a special person and her Deputy George Stanghan. This larger than life man was a one off; six feet three inches, over twenty stone and an incessant smoker.

Suffice to say that that Educational Exchange was a resounding success with our London programme including visits to Hampton Court, Westminster Abbey, St Pauls, Big Ben and a culminating tour of the Houses of Parliament organised by Leominster's MP. Some exceptional guides were delegated to us and pupils will never forget those wonderful visits. I taped the entire tour when one guide said to one young girl, "Now you come to me. Pretend you are the Queen and you young man are to be Prince Philip." The guide then proceeded to describe the Queen's entrance to her robing room and from there to the Long Gallery room and on to the Commons and Lords. It was a wonderful bit of theatre and the pupils were absolutely absorbed. What history lessons! Those guides were so gifted and well informed.

The unexpected always makes personal, special memories. George arranged for me to stay at the vicarage very near to the school. He informed me that the vicar was on holiday but everything, food, bed, telephone etc was in place for my stay and the vicar would return on my second evening.

Having seen all our pupils paired up, met their host parents and dispatched to their hosts' homes I was lucky to have a peaceful night and an enjoyable following busy day at Benhilton.

Having checked all was in place for day two excursion I visited a number of homes with George, was very pleased with my reception and to see pupils happily playing with hosts and so retired to the vicarage.

I settled to sleep quickly but was aroused by a loud banging. I stared at my watch. It was just past mid-night. I went in my dressing gown to the door to investigate. I was confronted by two men, one being supported by the other. Immediately the supporter in a thick cockney accent said," I'm the taxi driver. I've brought this chap from Heathrow Airport but he can't find any cash. I want twenty quid."

I was completely taken aback but reluctantly produced £20, a considerable sum in the 1970s. On paying, the supported chap was pushed though the doorway. He wobbled; glared at me and said in an inebriated slur, "Who the devil are you?" I tried in vain to explain but before I was able to do so the inebriated vicar slumped on to the settee and was away with the fairies. I left him in a deep slumber and returned to bed.

On rising I went to the kitchen to be met by a very contrite man who realised who I was; repeatedly apologised and asked me to faithfully recall the previous evening's events. I was considerably relieved to receive my £20, related my experience to a disbelieving George and tucked the experience tactfully away.

Staff of Madley C of E Primary School when I arrived there
From L to R: Back Row Mrs Audrey Price (secretary), Cilla---, Alf Jenkins, Eva Millardship. Miss--White. Front Row:- Betty Watts, Nora Mason, Charles Hawkins (Head teacher) Trixie, Mrs Gutteridge.

George lived eight miles away from Benhilton School near to Epsom race course. He felt it would be appropriate to take a school party to see where the famous Epsom Derby was held and tell the pupils about the tremendous gathering of gypsies selling horses and other annual contributors. As mentioned before the pupils were encouraged to write about their experiences and having been to Epsom one girl wrote, "Today we went to Ups and Downs where a famous annual race is held."

George's journey to school due to heavy traffic took approximately an hour. When he returned with his class to Madley it had been arranged for him to stay with my family. Having dispatched his pupils we made our way to my car. George asked how far we had to travel. On being told that it was twenty seven miles he was dumbfounded. He had never visited Herefordshire before, was astounded to find we arrived home in forty five minutes and he was welcomed warmly by my family. Herefordshire proved to be a very special place in George's heart and to my children he became "Uncle George" and a dear friend to Ann and me for the rest of his life.

Once it became known what a worthwhile experience an Educational Exchange could be, parents of younger pupils began asking if their children would have a similar opportunity when they reached top class. As a result the second Benhilton Exchange was oversubscribed.

Madley life was stimulating and the musicals we produced in Madley's beautiful church memorable especially Joseph and His Technicolour Dreamcoat.

George visited my home for summer holidays and my children loved him. He was an experienced child psychologist, an excellent teacher and knew how to encourage their response. On arrival at Bower House each of our offspring received an unexpected present. George would say, "Now then while I am here I want to do something with each of you. What would you like to do Graham?" "I would like to go fishing Uncle George." "You Helen?" "I would like to go to the Adventure Playground please." Karen being very young was always happy to have the security of Helen and go with her.

The excursions duly took place but no sooner had Graham departed with George than they returned. In his exuberance to make a catch Graham had fallen in the river. He was like a drowned rat but very happy.

George had raised five children by himself because his wife sadly died while they were still young. My daughter Helen was about nine years old at this time, sensitive and caring as she has always been. George loved a regular drink of whisky and each evening while we were preparing our three for bed he would say, "Oh well, I must go for my prescription." Helen would say, "Mummy why does Uncle George have to go for his prescription every night. Is he poorly?"   Readers will have deduced he visited The Boot Inn.

George like many in those days rolled his own cigarettes via his Rizla roller and papers. Before he departed for his journey home at the end of a stay he would sit at the kitchen table, roll thirty and and put them in three equal piles. He placed them on the dash board of his Mini-Estate. How did he manage to squeeze his bulk into that small vehicle?   Helen asked why he placed those piles of cigarettes like that. His reply in his broad cockney accent was, "Well Helen, this pile is for me to smoke between here and Swindon. This pile is for the M4 and this one through Worcester Park and home." What a character! A really dear friend.

Our children genuinely worried about George returning to his home thinking he would be looking after himself again. Helen's concern would manifest itself by saying, "Mum, let's make Uncle George a cake to take home."

In the spring of 1974 I felt I was sufficiently experienced to confidently apply for a Headship. On my second interview I was thrilled to be appointed to Canon Pyon Primary following the retirement of Mr Arthur England. There were just thirty nine pupils on roll but I can safely say it proved to be the most challenging post of my entire teaching career.

Madley Primary:-Early 1970s, Back L to R Cilla, Eva Millardship, ------------, David Barrett, Nora Mason, Edward Johnson. Front L to R Audrey Price, Betty Watts, Charles Hawkins (Head), Rhian Morris, Alf Jenkins.

Madley Primary School early 1970s:- Alf Jenkins on the extreme right with his first full time class in Primary Education. Soon after this was taken Mr Charles Hawkins persuaded him to stay in the Primary Field. He became his Deputy Head and never regretted the change of direction. He wonders if the pupils recognise themselves? They were indeed a lovely group and Alf received wonderful support from their parents.

Canon Pyon School 1974

Travelling fifty four miles daily had begun to add significantly to our family outgoings. We were counting the pennies carefully so halving the mileage to Canon Pyon was a great help. Fuel prices had rocketed. We were back to square one. We put Bower House on the market for £13,400 and looked at numerous properties at Upper Hill and Tillington area but Bower House did not sell.

Little Canon Pyon School was a Victorian, red bricked building with a lovely back drop of wooded Pyon Hill, wheeling, tumbling ravens and soaring buzzards. Herefordshire apple orchards with beautiful pink blossom co-existed alongside mature hardwood plantations. Small paddocks, red and white faced cattle and red Herefordshire soiled fields completed a beautiful village environment. A small playground with a well stocked fish pool created continual interest. A modern terrapin classroom placed at the far end housed the infants and parents had provided a learner swimming pool.

I had taught in city schools which had acres of playing fields but these children had no playing field at all, quite ridiculous for a country school.

Some Secondary school colleagues in particular assume that the smaller the school the easier the administration and teaching task. This is not so. I had been in schools with one thousand pupils but Canon Pyon proved initially to be my greatest career challenge.

Mrs Janet Weaver was the established Infant teacher. She was excellent, experienced, dedicated and a committed Christian. I was extremely lucky to have such a colleague who gave unstinting service and a wonderful start to all her pupils.

I was greeted by Secretary Mrs Pat Edworthy, experienced in the school admin and a most accommodating and supportive person – so lucky again. School meals were delivered daily from Hereford and served by a most cheerful group of village ladies and the food eaten in the classrooms. Resources were meagre. I was given a list of every sheet of art and craft paper in stock by the past Headteacher. It was completely inadequate as was the equipment and stationery. The reading scheme was not to my liking. With only me to consider in the Junior area minimum consultation was necessary and I was able to make changes quite quickly. My greatest challenge was to teach the whole range of junior pupils from seven to eleven. Although only twenty one pupils the range of reading skills and general development was enormous. Having Pat was a tremendous bolster. I could leave her to deal with most things which cropped up. She made everyone most welcome, but protected me from unnecessary interruptions. I had been hoping my move to Canon Pyon would give me plenty of time to develop my research about the Industrial and Social History of my beloved Clee Hills but that was not to be initially. However I was able to visit the area, begin to collate industrial photographs and sharpen my thoughts about their locations. I had a wonderful collection of photographs of quarrymen , miners and industrial plant which had kindly been given to me by customers who had visited my home, Dhu Stone Inn.

A fair proportion of the Juniors were itinerant romanies some of whom had very poor acquisition of language, sentence structure or written skills. Some gypsy families had settled in the area however.

The Integrated day system was of course very different from what pupils had experienced. Many pupils necessitated individual programmes so this system suited.

I wished to make an impact and make the small entrance warm and welcoming. Space was very limited. Shelves in the entrance foyer were stuffed full with outdated books and paper. The appearance was untidy. What could we do? Ann made bright curtains to cover the shelves and set up an attractive fish tank. We paid for these ourselves but the welcoming effect was transformed.

I had meetings with all the governing body very soon to expound my intending policies, seek their full support and stress that my pupils must be given the same opportunities as far as possible as those in larger schools. There were insufficient numbers to be able to have competitive football, netball and other team games at Canon Pyon. The Governors were enthusiastic about my ideas, especially the possibility of team games with other local schools and my enthusiasm was infectious. Miss Jay and Major Fowler were so supportive as were Lydia Davies and her hubby at Church Farm.

I promoted the idea of a new reading scheme by suggesting Janet and governors accompany me to look at One Two Three and Away being used at Madley school. I expressed my wish to introduce an Educational Exchange with a London school and invited a parent from Madley whose children had participated to explain what was involved and beneficial from such a venture. My wildest dream was to encourage the Governors to investigate the possibility of purchasing a school field. I had a parents' meeting and all twenty seven families attended.

Funding was an acute problem because so very little 'new' had been purchased for some time and capitation allowance from the Authority was completely inadequate for my wishes. I asked for a meeting with Authority advisors and was granted considerable extra funding.

Parents were daunted by costs especially the remote possibility of obtaining a school field. I suggested a school fete and with their help made a list of proposed stalls and activities. We ultimately listed twenty seven stalls. Parents thought this naive. "Who would be left to support and purchase? " Parents of the like of Ken Edworthy, Dennis Lewis and others worked so hard to prepare, publicise and promote the event.

We were tickled pink to see scores of people attend. The resultant profit was nearly £400, a great sum for such a small school in 1975. We were away. The community now knew Ann and me and Janet introduced us to everyone. Canon Pyon was on the map.

My mind was completely absorbed by my new challenge. Many of the romanies required a firm hand. Some were sullen, unpredictable and threatening to the local children. I would often find them up the neighbouring orchard trees, on the school flat roof area or sticking compasses in anyone who passed. The indigenous Canon Pyon children were model pupils, polite, pleasant and most co-operative; a pleasure to teach and encourage. Older pupils encouraged and protected smaller ones. One family of romanies was so shocking it was ostracised by their own kind. Our greatest disappointment and frustration was to have them suddenly up sticks and move away after working so hard to make progress with them.

One morning when admitting pupils at the beginning of the school day one itinerant girl was clutching one of her hands under her armpit. I asked her what was wrong but she continued to incline her head, refuse to look at or answer me. After numerous requests and the same stubborn response I deemed it necessary to catch hold of the girl's arm. This revealed a filthy, bloodied rag wrapped around her hand. I removed this carefully much to the protests and shouts of Sally*. I was horrified to discover the tip of one finger snipped off and the one next to it with a section nearly amputated too.   We had no classroom assistants but it was necessary for me to get Sally to Hereford Hospital as soon as possible. Poor Janet Weaver had to accommodate the lot. I knew that there was not a remote chance of contacting parents to transport and take responsibility.

I drove Sally to Hereford A and E. Her wounds were attended to and it was the end of the school day by the time I returned to Canon Pyon . I eventually found the home base on a local farm. It was a wooden hut with plastic sheeting at the window spaces and the whole family was housed in it. I knocked and the stable type door was opened. Initially the mother's response was to say the least not warm. Why was her daughter late home? Why was her arm and hand bound up? Why had no one contacted her? So the questions continued.

After giving her a chance to vent her feelings I asked why Sally had been sent to school in such a distressed state with a serious injury wrapped up in a dirty rag.   At this the mother informed me that she and her hubby had left early to work in the fields and their daughter and her small brother had been left to chop fire wood for the evening before going to school.   She was genuinely horrified by what had happened and ultimately grateful for our care. How can government expect children from such diverse environments to all have the same fair chance of success?

Many of our itinerant parents were very supportive in what we tried to do to help their children. On more than one occasion they would see me near the school gate alongside the road, would wave and throw out a sack shouting, "There you is Sir, give them to the kids." I would open up and examine the contents which could be fruit, nuts or cans of squash. Their kindness was no doubt genuine but I was always apprehensive of the origin therefore disposed of and never distributed the goodies.

One family the Johnsons had settled in the area and worked for Canon Pyon farms for years and was well respected. Billy was a freckled faced, sandy haired, likeable lad who tried and everyone took to him. Janet had seen that he had ability especially in number work.   This continued when he became a junior pupil and his performance was equal to many Canon Pyon children.   Suddenly he began to be absent on a Friday.   After a few recurrences I queried this habit. Apparently his parents were most pleased with his number progress and persuaded him to accompany them to market to assist with calculations and keep a record. Quite a feather in our caps! However later on Billy so enjoyed school he wouldn't go to Hereford despite his parents' protests.

Racing ahead, Ann and I were invited to centenary celebrations at Canon Pyon. Friends and a number of past staff plus Revd Elaine Goddard were enjoying the proceedings. During a break Elaine brought a little, sandy haired, freckled faced lad to us. She said that the boy wished to have a word with Mr Jenkins. I was absolutely and emotionally overwhelmed when he said, "My uncle Billy asked me to say a big thank you to Mr Jenkins."   I was so thrilled to receive such an accolade. Colleague Janet Weaver would have been so gratified.

I was anxious to organise an Educational Exchange to Benhilton School in Sutton Surrey from Canon Pyon. The major drawback was the number of ten and eleven year old pupils I had in the school. Parents knew of these exchanges. News had travelled so I invited a Madley parent to talk to those in Canon Pyon. Parents were keen and supportive for me to go ahead.

Benhilton was prepared to select half a class of top juniors. This was a difficult decision for a school to take. I could only muster twelve pupils; asked permission for two of my family to make up a number to fill a

*(name changed)

My first Headship:- the staff of Canon Pyon (1974-1976)
Back row from L to R:- Dennis Lewis (Groundsman), Janet Weaver (Infant Teacher), Liz Jenkins (Lower Juniors), Alf Jenkins (Headmaster), Front Row:- Val Preece (Dinner Lady), Pat Edworthy (Secretary), Freda Bounds (Children's Supervisor), Mary Hall (nee Evans) (Dinner Lady).

mini-bus; had a few refresher lessons driving one and consequently was confident to drive to and through London.

The Canon Pyon pupils were exemplary, extremely well mannered and untouched by city life. A similar programme to previous ones was organised. One child had a dilemma – she didn't like the host parent's packed lunch saying that the fillings "gave her the belly ache" and asked Ann what to do. She suggested we swapped some sandwiches to avoid embarrassment but the child retorted thoughtfully that she would have more of the same the next day if it was assumed she had heartily eaten them. Ann tactfully had a chat with the host mum who asked the child to choose a filling. Problem solved.

Just before we were due to leave Canon Pyon for London, TV News was jolted by MP Airey Neave being blown up by an IRA bomb and killed in a car park very near the Houses of Parliament. This made parents jittery but they agreed I should still go ahead with the exchange. The next day I was due to meet MP Temple Morris who had arranged a conducted tour of both Houses of Parliament. I was not sure of the route so George asked Father Philip if he would accompany me. I knew Philip well and all the children had heard him deliver a sermon in Benhilton Church the previous day. We duly left for Westminster. Father Philip sat in the front seat next to me. All went well until we got to a large roundabout which had a number of exits. I was relying on Philip to point out the appropriate exit. I approached the roundabout in a number of lanes of traffic. I looked furtively at Philip, went all the way round the island but no command came. Round the island I drove again becoming slightly agitated. There was still no command, but I could see Philip mouthing and realised that he was stuttering but unable to speak. On the third circuit he shot his arm forward as we approached the next exit. Great relief. I was off the island safely. On return to Benhilton I related the incident to George. He would not believe Father Philip stuttered saying that he never faltered in the pulpit and was absolutely lucid. Another memory for the archives.

Carrying on to Westminster we were directed to an underground car park area. This turned out to be none other than the actual one in which Airey Neave MP had been assassinated. What would the parents think?

Ann and I unloaded the bus, noted the Henry Moore sculptures and crossed the lawn to the road which passes the Houses of Parliament.

Peter Temple-Morris, MP for Leominster pictured on the Terrace of the House of Commons with Mr A.E.Jenkins, Headmaster of Canon Pyon School with Mrs Jenkins and pupils. I wonder if the pupils recognise themselves? The party were on a two week visit to London as part of a primary exchange with Benhilton School, Sutton Surrey. Peter Temple-Morris said, "I think Mr and Mrs Jenkins are to be commended for organising this visit to London which involves as it does the exchange of London and country children which is an excellent idea and I hope will be emulated by other schools."

I needed to safely see the pupils across and my method was to cross the road myself, leaving the pupils in the care of responsible adults. When I felt a crossing was possible I emitted my piercing whistle which my pupils well knew and beckoned them across. I looked around and soon saw the white, distinctive hair style of MP Temple-Morris. He signalled the group towards him. He spoke to me asking if we were the expected group from Herefordshire. I answered in the affirmative. He said with a wry smile, "I thought so by the way you crossed the road."

George had some unconventional methods but the pupils clearly knew their boundaries and there was a lovely atmosphere in his classroom. He knew the British Isles intimately, was a great football fan and as I have mentioned liked a drink. As a result he knew the emblem of most football teams and many public house signs which had an historical significance. Much of the class's attractive art was inspired by this. George then tactfully broadened the work having captured their interest, into meaningful historical and environmental projects.

If a child stepped out of line, which I am told was very seldom, George would say, "Well my boy you'll have to meet Sidney." This was a size thirteen flexible plimsoll. George would produce it from his desk drawer, bend the pupil over and give him one whack across the posterior. Very effective. No more trouble and boys and girls continued to laugh, enjoy themselves, work hard and learn from Big George.

At the conclusion of this exchange our numbers on role increased and I was delighted to welcome Miss Elizabeth Jenkins. What an enormous difference it was to be able to teach a two year span only. Ann and I had the fortunate pleasure to attend Liz's wedding a little later.

Canon Pyon Juniors:- The whole group I drove to London on a mini-bus for our Educational Exchange; on the terrace of the Houses of Parliament with MP Temple Morris. To fill the small bus I had permission to include our own three children, Helen 3rd from the left in front of Ann; Graham in front of Mr Temple Morris and Karen in the front.

To have a game of football I had to take the boys across a busy road to a cow patted field; but it was better than nothing and the boys were so elated to don football boots, tops and shorts. However I was truly thrilled to come to an agreement with a local farmer and secure a playing field continuing from the playground. It was a wonderful addition not only for sports and games but space for fetes, relaxation for the pupils and other functions. Our recognised Harvest Thanksgivings encouraged by Revd William Tavernor with fruit and vegetables being donated to a local Nursing Home brought us much pleasure.

One should accept advice and opportunities when they arise. At this stage two County Advisors alerted me to the possibility that Canon Pyon under the current policy was likely to close; surprised me by saying they would like to keep me in Hereford and Worcester and would I apply for other schools. I did and was extremely fortunate to be appointed to a beautifully built, modern building, Leintwardine Endowed Primary with one hundred pupils.

Mileage was reduced so we had no need to sell Bower House. I was saddened to leave Canon Pyon and even more so when I learnt that it did not close but continued to thrive.

I am so pleased to report that this lovely school is thriving; the numbers are continuing to increase and in 2013 became an Academy.

Canon Pyon School Football Team 1976:- after we had acquired a small field for the school. Back Row L to R:- Ian Edworthy, Andrew Roberts, Ian Watkins, Robert Bufton. Front Row:- Kevin Rosser, Gary Southall, Kenneth Bird, Mark Rawlings.

Canon Pyon School 1974 (No romanies):-Back row L to R:- Robert Bufton, Ian Walker, Gary Southall, -Kevin Rosser, Andrew Roberts, Kenneth Bird, Ian Edworthy, Jacqueline Woodhouse, Gillian James, Andrea Bufton, Tracey Lewis. Middle Row:- Anita Evans, ---Bowkett, Ruth Lloyd, Katie Watkins, Mark Rawlings, Lynne Preece, Peter Roberts, Andrew James, Lesley Lewis, Susan Lewis, Janet James, Alison Chandler. Front Row:- Jamie Wilson, --- Bowkett, Virginia Harris, Tracey Bowkett, Tracey Rawlings, Andrea Bird, Gillian Evans, Sarah James, Richard Holden, Kevin Rosser, Ian Green, Andrew McLoed, Richard Rumsey, Neil Lloyd.

School Pool:- Built and funded by parents in 1971/72 for a cost of about £2,000. Those who helped included Ken Edworthy and Dennis Lewis.

Leintwardine Endowed School

Summer 1976 brought two opportunities of Headships at larger schools, Fownhope and Leintwardine. I was shortlisted for the former then within a few days Leintwardine.

I have to admit I did not pull out all the stops at Fownhope because it was twenty seven miles from home and was somewhat relieved not to be appointed. My strategy had been a calculated risk but Ann and me were thrilled I was appointed at Leintwardine Endowed School.

I consider myself to have been more than fortunate in my teaching career. I have chosen to be in C of E schools because of my philosophy and the added opportunity of inculcating a particular code. Luck has played a special part because I have had the good fortune to meet so many genuine, able people and colleagues, many who have become lifelong friends to Ann and me.

Each school has a special place in my heart and life's patchwork but to be appointed to Leintwardine was a dream come true. To be able to drive unimpeded by town traffic through most beautiful countryside was a daily joy and of course the distance was reasonable. Our children were settled, attended excellent local schools and both sets of our parents were quite near. We had ample space, able to grow sufficient vegetables year round and I had a workshop where I could maintain my craft expertise and had no need to sell Bower House.

I visited Leintwardine very regularly to assess and prepare my own classroom area as teacher of top juniors. I swelled with pride when I took in details of that purpose built, well designed building.

I met my three teaching staff, spent time talking to them and assessing their classroom strategies. All were well established, competent and experienced so I decided to leave well alone and gradually deduce what changes if any would be necessary.

In that light airy building there were four well designed classrooms with ample storage drawers and work top space. Each had a 'quiet' annexe, toilets, cloakroom and access to the playground and large playing field. A comprehensive library area could be reached from each classroom without disturbing others. A well equipped gymnasium/ assembly room/lunch hall was accessible from classrooms and library and beyond was a well equipped kitchen. In addition there was a staffroom (what luxury) a separate administrative office, stock storage room and an adequate car park.

By the end of my first week I felt exhausted, happy and optimistic about our future. My predecessors had done an excellent job of developing the school. Audrey Turner and her assistants Em Murdoch and Mrs Dodd ran the kitchen like clockwork. Nearly every one of the 80+ pupils had school cooked lunches and more than usual shelving around the kitchen was filled with local, preserved fruits which had been collected and bottled by Audrey and her ladies. They did that free of charge in their own time because their efforts were so appreciated. My secretary Mrs Josie Adams was experienced, worked hard and made everyone welcome.

Again as at Canon Pyon there were no teaching assistants but there was a wonderful library volunteer Tess Baller who gave a tremendous amount of time, researched books for all ages and was as capable as any teacher.

Mrs Jukes, a village lady came in virtually every day to hear pupils read. She was patient, kind, had very commendable reading skills and was willing to learn more.

Our caretaker was wonderful, jolly Barbara Cook, whose cleaning was excellent, did far more than was officially required, had a tremendous sense of fun and humour and was a pleasure to have around. Our crossing patrol gentleman was affable, elderly Mr Tonks and Father Richard Smith who lived next door in the new vicarage proved an excellent pianist and a great school support. The enigma we were faced with at school was our catchment area included many parishes ranging from high to low church but with the help of Father Richard we were able to accommodate everyone in our school assemblies with no objections from parents.

Due to the fact my staff were competent I was determined to assess the standards of my pupils especially their achievement in mathematics and language. I introduced environmental projects to encourage ample written work, creative writing and develop an appreciation of the communities. I began by inviting local business people to talk to the pupils . They were so enthusiastic and helpful and welcomed our class visits too. This excellent village included a butcher, librarian, post office master, local bank manager, fish and chip proprietor, garage owner, local farmers, Mr Martin whose very traditional store was an Aladdin's cave, the veterinary surgeon, vicar, police constable and others.

I used a tape recorder to remind pupils of our experiences which led to copious written work, art and practical mathematics. Of course the more written work my pupils produced the more there was for me to correct. Even the least able made valiant efforts and I was able to analyse written and language deficits, plan appropriate testing, categorise those who needed particular help, stretch high fliers and plan constructive changes. The children learnt an enormous amount about those who contributed daily to the vibrancy of the village and how they all were important, intricate parts of the whole. The children began to feel they knew these people, acknowledged them and welcomed the village policeman as a friend.

There was no respite from my classroom teaching; no free and preparation periods so all administration, preparation and planning was done before school, every evening and at week-ends. I valued assemblies as a time when all the school could gather together daily and we could inform each other of events. But! I was able to lead by example, show I could obtain good results and inspired others to display work attractively. I had very few worries because it was obvious that my staff worked well and efficiently and they were pleased to see that I capitalised on their excellent groundwork. Our Education Authority and inspectors were continually encouraging me to be forward looking especially with regard to pupils' comprehensive progress, relevant reports, reading schemes and analytical testing. I persuaded each class teacher to write detailed reports along similar lines for every pupil and pass them on as children progressed. This developed trust between my staff and me. We knew our pupils.

I was indeed fortunate to inherit three excellent staff. Tall Victoria Ball in Reception, was sophisticated, well spoken and very able. Although very experienced all three were willing to adapt and try new ideas especially when they could see that by example I was making pupils work and obtained positive results. Vicky had a good sense of humour and was intrigued by the Herefordshire accent and dialect. I was amused to hear our pupils trying to emulate Vicki's phraseology and intonation. She made a very positive contribution to the school and much to my delight became Head of neighbouring Wigmore School.

Beti Lloyd, a cheerful, bright eyed lady taught the next class. Again she was an excellent, experienced teacher , very industrious who demanded high standards. She had a warm personality, a wonderful wicked sense of humour and spoke Welsh fluently. Beti was a real country person and could empathise with the pupils' environment and knew where every one of them lived. She played the piano for assemblies and my goodness how she could enthuse the children to sing. She helped produce first class entertainment to which parents were eager to come, also senior citizen's parties in school annually. Beti maintained that if we were able to laugh and have fun together we could overcome whatever came our way. She was absolutely right. She was extremely loyal to school and me. She said to me some time later, " Knew you would be OK Alf Jenkins by you greeting me with a warm smile and a firm handshake." She was married to farmer Sid who managed the Downton Estate. He was a joy to be with, to hear and see his profound knowledge of wildlife. He was one of seven brothers all of whom were keen on horses and loved pony trotting races. Sid could get money out of everyone. At our school fetes he insisted on being on the gate and even managed to make the teachers pay. Sid, Beti and family of Robert, Denise and Di later became life long friends. We spent many happy evenings at Gravel Farm, Downton. Eventually they went to the Lodge by Downton Church and we helped them to move. There was a problem getting a bed upstairs. Firstly we cut a large notch out of a beam but that did not give enough clearance. Ultimately our son Graham cut the bed in half, much to the amusement of Beti. It took some time to rebuild it but all ended well. Sid's boss was Mr Dennis Lennox, a lovely gentleman. Sadly he developed cancer and died young. The extraordinary coincidence was that Sid developed the same problem a year or two later and left us prematurely too.

Isobel Davis was a Tibetan lady who had married an English Army Officer. Isobel was about four feet ten inches tall and was as rotund as she was high. She was full of life, had an infectious laugh and loved her pupils. As a child she had to ride a yak many miles from the Himalayas to her boarding school and experience the same process on her return home at term end.   She often used the word "Darling". She said that while riding on those long journeys in spite of the incredible scenery she became bored and studied the movements and flight of flies around the yak's head. Although flies have amazing eye sight she discovered she could catch them in her fingers by following them. She demonstrated this numerous times in school . Her first cousin was Sherpa Tensing, the celebrated man who conquered Everest with Sir Edmund Hillary in 1953. She was most distressed when her parents passed away because she was not allowed to bring any family possessions out of Tibet.

This amazing lady was one of the most interesting people to talk to I have ever met. Tony, her husband was so proud of her but even though her English was very good she often used words incorrectly such as "these polystyrene dresses." She loved her garden and found it easier to kneel down when working in a flower bed. Being very big breasted she would say, "These things get in the way Darling."

She loved her pupils and they reciprocated having tremendous faith in her every word. She always felt her pupils could do better. When I introduced Neale Analysis reading tests to the school I marked every pupil's results. On seeing one child's results Isobel said, "Oh! she can do far better than that. Can she do the test again?" Of course that was not permitted.

Isobel was outstanding at netball and could produce a piercing whistle using her thumb and middle finger. Due to her enthusiasm and ability our girls in spite of their smaller numbers compared with other schools, occasionally won the area tournament and always performed well. She lived at the bottom of Watling Street on the old Roman road which had passed through the village. She rode her bicycle to school but seemed unable to take her hands off the handlebars to signal that she wished to cross the road and enter the school car park. Instead much to the amusement of parents and pupils she would stick out her right leg.

We all encouraged pupils to bring articles of interest and wildlife to school. As a result Isobel's classroom housed a most interesting museum to which we all had regular access. Our Chief Inspector Jack Tempest was an imposing, very tall gentleman who sported a head of red hair and a goatie beard.

Jack was a great encourager and his vast experience readily earned him respect. We looked forward to his visits. Isobel always said it made her neck ache when she looked up to speak to him. She readily appreciated his advice and on one occasion she looked at him and said, "I never thought that a young dog could teach an old dog new tricks."

Further along Dark Lane there was a Commune. Most of the adults were very capable, professional people. In their wisdom they decided to withdraw their children and teach them themselves, much to the concern of the children. They really enjoyed playing and communicating with others. Soon after this decision the Commune parents asked me is they could borrow a supply of our maths and reading books for their use. I contacted Jack to obtain a ruling and express that I was not happy to deplete our precious stocks. He wholeheartedly agreed with me and stated that he would be obligated to visit the Commune, assess if they had established an acceptable timetable and review the work being produced to see if it was of a reasonable standard. As far as he was concerned they would have to buy their own resources.

On his next visit he went to the Commune and called to see me on his return journey. His complexion matched his red hair. He sat down in my office and said, "Life is full of surprises. I knocked on the door. After a short while a lady came and to my astonishment she was naked. She didn't seem terribly surprised to see me and asked me to wait just a minute while she went to put something on. She returned in just a pair of wellington boots." I asked if he had managed to collect his thoughts and inspect the timetable etc but he replied that he had left instructions that he would call and do that on a specific date.

Some years later I was invited to Jack's retirement. Giving a synopsis of his career and thanks to all my fellow Heads he said, "There is one Head teacher sitting here who will remember one extremely embarrassing experience I had." He proceeded to recount the above story much to the hilarity of Head teacher colleagues.

Again I organised an Educational Exchange with Benhilton. On having preliminary discussions with George he said, " You wouldn't believe it Alf but there is a young teacher here who is pestering me to marry her. I'm too old for that but I'm flattered ." When the Exchange materialised Mrs Eileen Baker one of the top junior teachers came along with George and helpers to Leintwardine. Eileen was the lady George had been referring to. Not so long after George succumbed and Eileen became Mrs Stanghan. They spent their honeymoon in Orleton and subsequently had a very happy marriage. Eileen idolised George and loved his sense of humour. He used to make play of keeping a diary about her and would say, "Well Graham I only gave her seven out of ten today." When asked why he would recall that she hadn't been too helpful in the green house that morning or some such incident. Eileen chuckled about it all knowing that it was harmless fun. But! whenever our children saw George they would eagerly enquire what mark Aunty Eileen had been given that day.

About this time I was invited to go to Pebble Mill studios in Birmingham to meet the producer of Woman's Hour, Peter Windows. He had been told that I knew quite a bit about the Clee Hill Dialect. I duly went and as is the usual practice was not allowed to have notes but to answer questions off the cuff. Peter said that he could not believe that people from Clee Hills, could not be understood in Ludlow which was just five miles away and he asked how I could substantiate that. I told him that on my second day at Ludlow Grammar School I had been asked a question by the history master who seemed unable to comprehend my answer. Mr Fred Reeves said, "Jenkins were you born in a cave?" As a sensitive, rural lad my already inadequate confidence was further dented. I continued the programme by giving many examples of Clee Hill dialect words and explaining how the conglomeration had come about. That programme initiated a particular path that has become an integral part of my life.

Many parents and all my staff heard the programme and suddenly I was asked to lecture to organisations far and wide about my beloved Titterstone Clee Hills and its dialect. On leaving the studio I regretted mentioning the incident with my History Master Fred Reeves, but I need not have fretted. Within a few days

I received a nine page letter from him. As I digested its content I began to glow with gratitude. Fred was an eminent and respected historian. He said that he remembered well that I had not enjoyed his lessons but was thrilled to discover I had a considerable knowledge of Clee Hill's industrial and social past. He said, "Some good must have come from my teaching." He concluded by saying that he wished me to terminate my research for the time being, asked me to write down the information I possessed, publish a book and let him have a copy, "before I pass on."

Teaching was not only my job, but with my family, my life. But requests from various historical societies came my way, so, being a compulsive worker I began to collate more photographs and notes and give lectures around South Shropshire, Worcestershire and Herefordshire. Thus my first broadcast unexpectedly rebalanced my life somewhat. Teaching was the bread and butter and as I have said more than a job but with my love of growing vegetables for my precious family, renovating repairing and improving my home every moment of my time was filled.

The Educational Exchanges continued partly because of success and parents wanting their children to benefit from such an experience. One of our visits was to Elan Valley to see how dams had been built to collect water from the considerable water shed and supply the cities of Coventry, and Birmingham and many villages en route with a regular water supply.   We had the privilege of being conducted under one dam by a friend of teacher Beti Lloyd. I, as well as the pupils found that extremely interesting especially the method of construction and transportation and usage of thousands of tons of materials.

Lion Pottery was a thriving business in Rhayader and we made a number of visits there. Pupils were able to see the complete manufacturing process and purchase small dishes, condiments etc. The business folded some years ago so the unique striped pattern and logo is no longer available. Ann and I have a collection of over sixty pieces which we really enjoy. I wonder if any of those past pupils have kept some as a momento? On one of our visits we went to a border castle which had a narrow, winding staircase to its turret. George led the party but two thirds of the way up found it too much and too narrow for his considerable bulk. So he straddled three steps and every one continued to the top by passing under his legs. This incident was graphically recorded in the pupils' diaries.

Our pupil number increased considerably with pupils coming from as far as Lingen. The area often experienced inclement weather and considerable snowfall blocked roads and country lanes. Our regular school transport was Mrs Griffiths and her mini-bus. What a lovely lady! She was so caring, knew everyone of the families, looked after the little ones as if they were her own and made sure they were safely delivered. She also brought relevant notes and details from parents making sure the information was handed in. During such spells many more tractors were evident outside the school gates than cars.

The boys loved their football. I was helped by able parents and was delighted when one of the Priday family was selected for trials as Hereford United goalkeeper.

When refereeing one match my right heel went into a depression created by a rabbit. I collapsed in considerable pain, unable to stand. Adults carried me into school from where I was transported to Dr Simon Snape at Orleton Surgery. He helped me to my feet and placed my right knee on a chair. I could see I had no control over my right foot. It just dangled uselessly.

"You have severed your Achilles tendon, Ann must take you to Hereford Hospital. Take some nightclothes with you because this will need an operation. I will ring the Hospital and inform them of the requirements." During the evening I returned home, right leg duly plastered. Dr Snape rang to speak to Ann and check the situation. He was distressed to hear I had been sent home. He informed Ann that I must be taken back to Hereford because unless I had an operation I would never walk well and one leg would be slightly shorter than the other. He intended to inform the Hospital to x-ray the ankle and operate. I was fortunate that Dr Snape was experienced, had worked at Hereford Hospital was known there and was insistent.

Back to the Hospital. The X-rays showed the tendon had severed completely by the bone and had to be sewn to the ankle. I lay in bed next day feeling sorry for myself when a nurse arrived carrying a large box and a tape recorder. I opened the box to find a huge papier mache egg, in two halves tied by a bow of yellow ribbon. I parted the egg. It was filled with lovely notes from the pupils and beneath a tape recording. On reading the contents I was emotional.

This wonderfully accurate caricature: With the pupil's notes I found this lovely caricature of my three staff and me. I think it was drawn by Beti Lloyd's son Robert. Had readers had the good fortune to know us all, it is very apt. The author on the left (spectacles and trimmed beard); next from L to R is Beti then tall, dramatic Victoria Ball and lastly rotund Isobel Davis.

The nurse returned reminding me to play the tape. I sat back and listened. It began with Beti playing the piano and pupils singing well known songs which I particularly liked. The singing stopped and I was almost in tears. Then in turn the teachers wished me well and a speedy return to school. I was about to turn off the machine when voices continued. I recognised Isobel saying, "Now he's away let's order a few foot stools for the staffroom. Our new secretary Pauline will order them for us on requisition." Vicki piped up, "A good idea and let's have an extra five minutes break. No one will be the wiser." All agreed and Beti followed by saying, "He's got a bottle of sherry in the cupboard . I don't know why he's keeping that. We'll have a tot of that at afternoon break."

I realised it was a wind up and thought how lucky I was to have a staff who knew I would enjoy it.

Sadly on leaving hospital my foot was set with toes pointing in the same direction as my leg. This resulted in the leg plaster having to be replaced every few weeks, the shortened

An assembly of staff, past, present and future Head teacher:- Back Row Left to right, Mrs Bonniwell (Curate's wife), Mrs Mary Williams (Supply teacher), Mrs Galliers, Mrs Parker, Mr Parker (future Head), Mr John Ley (former Head teacher), Mrs Audrey Turner (Kitchen supervisor), Alf Jenkins (present Head teacher). Second Row:- Mrs Victoria Ball (Teacher) Mrs Ley, Mr Tony Davis, Mrs Valerie Jukes (Reading helper), Mrs Emily Murdock (Kitchen Assistant). Front Row:- Mr Tonks (Crossing Patrol) Mrs Ann Jenkins, Mrs Pauline Oliver (Secretary) Mrs Prosser, Mrs Isobel Davis (Teacher), Beti Lloyd (Teacher), Revd Richard Smith, Mrs Dodd (Kitchen Assistant), Mrs Barbara Cook (Caretaker).

Staff at Leintwardine Endowed School 1970s:-L to R back row:- Mrs Morgan (Kitchen); Beti Lloyd (Teacher); Barbara Cook (Caretaker); Mrs Dodd (Kitchen); Vicki Ball (Teacher); Front Row L to R:- Mrs Dukes (Voluntary Helper); Mrs Turner (Kitchen Supervisor). Alf Jenkins (Head); Isabel Davis (Teacher); Josie Adams (Secretary).

Achilles tendon gradually being stretched and the foot progressively bent into its normal position. This took months. I was occasionally driven to Leintwardine and my home phone frequently rang with some query.

I was extremely frustrated because for the first time in my life I was unable to go to work. Summer Time came; the garden needed digging and so many jobs were waiting to be done. There was no possibility of me returning to school . I was not a happy bunny.

1970s- Police Force Poster Competition:- L to R:- David Spencer; Ruth Oliver; Matthew Reece.

Graham and Ann decided to dig the garden to keep me happy and begin planting it. I was extremely grateful but critical when they were not about. I even crawled across the garden to straighten a row of onions. How ridiculous was that? I have never been allowed to forget it.

With no prospect of being able to stand in my workshop or return to Leintwardine soon I decided to concentrate on my notes and photographs concerning the Titterstone Clee Hills. I looked at what aspects I had and decided on a pattern for a possible publication. I doubted very much whether I would ever be able to produce anything which would be acceptable. My tolerant wife suggested I used

1970s Leintwardine:- Newspaper photograph of some of the Leintwardine Pupils participating in Map Making. Do you recognise yourselves?

Leomister Exchange with Tengeru, Tanzania. With the help of School Secretary Pauling Oliver, Alf Jenkins arranged for Abel Sheshengale to spend time on the Harley Estate, where he saw "puggins".

the dining room table to spread out the various categories. I became absolutely absorbed in my research and writing. To the pleasure of my lovely family it gave me direction and purpose again.

I returned to Leintwardine as soon as I was able to walk but I was curtailed. Fortunately supportive parents came to help with boys' games and football practices and take them to tournaments.

Having been away from school for such a long time I had itchy feet and knew friend Roy Conod was planning to leave Tenbury C of E Primary School. I fancied the opportunity to assist teachers and organise a school without the additional responsibility of a full time class as well. I applied to Tenbury Wells and was appointed. I did not want to leave lovely Leintwardine but I thought my age would soon begin to dictate any further career opportunities.

I was to leave Leintwardine Endowed C of E School its wonderful staff and community with very mixed feelings, apprehension and knowing it had been an extremely happy episode of my life. In a term's time I would be off to Tenbury, follow a man who had an excellent reputation and to be in charge of a school with four times as many pupils; quite a challenge.

Sutton Educational Exchange:- Just about to board Mr Griffith's bus to take the school party on an Educational Exchange to Benhilton C of E School, Sutton Surrey. Alf is on the left, Ann, Isobel and our daughter Karen are on the right of the group. Those lovely pupils were so polite that they shocked parents in London. Now all grown up they will undoubtedly recognise themselves. Mr Griffiths from Leintwardine garage is driving the bus. On the extreme right stands Revd Richard Smith, Mrs Griffiths who taxied many pupils in from the countryside, Mrs Gibbs and Mrs Fanning.

*Leintwardine:-*Mrs Turner (Kitchen) Beti Lloyd and Victoria Ball with pupils waving us "God Speed"

The Ancient Camp on Titterstone Clee Summit

The Camp:- **Titterstone Clee Hill** lies some five miles east of Ludlow and is "crowned" by a camp which covers the whole of Titterstone's comparatively flat top. Inside the Camp wall it measures about a half a mile long and a third of a mile wide. The area is about 71 acres and is 1,749 feet at its summit.

In addition to the information given to me by my Dad in the late 1940s early 50s, I have been able to substantiate and broaden his facts by a booklet given to him many years ago entitled, "Excavations of Titterstone Clee Hill Camp Shropshire 1932, published by The Antiquaries Journal, January 1934."

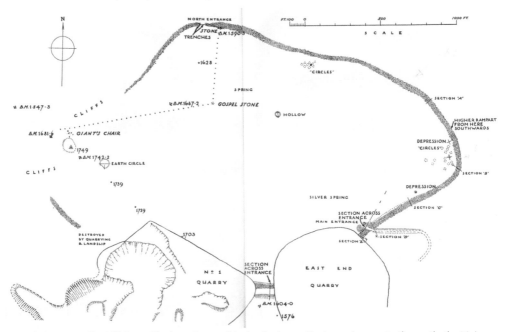

Map of Titterstone Clee Hill Camp. The boundary wall is clearly shown; the two entrances to the south, the Main one which is to the south east, a further entrance in the north and the damage done to the complete Camp circle by quarry workings in the south. Note the stone circles, the Gospel stone, the Giant's chair and the spot height of 1,749 ft.

There was an important connection between the Camps on Brown Clee and this one on Titterstone because an ancient East/West track way which passes under a rampart. "The two main branches of this track to the west are well attended for the prehistoric period". (Miss LF Litty, local Secretary for Shropshire Arch, 1926,pp233, 1927 1nd 1929) and Titterstone was placed to command their point of Junction. The defence of such a camp is normally a single rampart without a ditch but as can be seen from the above plan between No 1 Quarry which opened in 1881 and the horseshoe, East End quarry which opened late, there are two ramparts.

My Dad pointed out to me the damage on the south side to the camp enclosure caused by quarrying. At that time I was saddened by the closure of Titterstone quarries because of the centralisation of the operation to Dhu Stone/ Granite side of the hill. It meant many Dhu Stone men would have to walk further to work, there would be a reduced work force due to more mechanisation and therefore less trade probably at my home the Dhu Stone Inn. However I was very pleased in hindsight otherwise further damage would have been done to the Camp enclosure. The Rouseboughton family too felt that the quarrying in No 1 quarry was getting too near to Titterstone summit and if allowed to continue the wonderful, well known skyline would be altered; hence the initial move to East End, Horseshoe quarry. There remains a Bronze Age cairn referred to as Earth Circle near the spot height of 1,749 and the western Giant's Chair. From here looking south I have always had a tremendous feeling of exhilaration. It is such a commanding spot over the surrounding countryside and a precious childhood memory shared with Dad. As I have said many times, to me it is the best view in the world. To the North of the Camp are more stone circles and a North Entrance. These circles were excavated and found to be natural.

There is a considerable stretch of scree both in front of the South and Main entrance and although not a real obstacle nowadays it is thought it could have been useful in slowing down attackers. The question the excavators asked themselves was why only on the East and South West positions were there real defences? They said it may have been because of the enormous size of the Camp and the magnitude of the task of erecting defences. They did however make use of natural defences. The attack was most likely on the South East, gentle slope side. In historic times the North and North East was covered with dense forest and therefore attack was not expected. Brown Clee was generally considered friendly on the Northern side. Only on the South side were attacks likely hence the strong defensive work. The general plan shows depression circles in the East of the Camp, more circles to the north, the North entrance, a Gospel stone as well as those already mentioned. The plan of the Main Entrance shows many discovered post holes, two hearths and stone facing.

Twenty six post holes in all are illustrated, some were three feet in diameter and eighteen inches deep while in front of the rampart the line of circular holes was smaller and about 5 feet 3 inches apart. They were bottle shaped, dug through old top soil into hard yellow sandstone. The diameter at the top was 18 inches and the bottom 21 inches and depths usually 20 inches. Posts were therefore wider at the base to give them greater stability. No traces of wood was found but a thin layer of 1 inch grey clay was placed at the bottom of each hole to act as a bedding and preserve the wood. The posts were whole trees with roots which were roughly pruned but not entirely removed to give a 'spread' at the base. No metalling was applied to the road entrance. The top of hard yellow carboniferous sandstone was considered a sufficiently good surface. Of the Main Entrance, within it, four periods were indentified during excavations. (1) period of original construction, (11) a time of neglect and probably disuse, (111) a period of re- construction, (1V) when the Camp was still in use but defences were partially dismantled. It was suggested that the full width of the entrance was 37 feet and there may have been two lines of post holes for upright posts flanking a central roadway 8 to 9 feet wide. Apparently this was not the appearance of a normal pre-historic gateway. It is thought these 'fences' were more likely to be a support for a wooden bridge which carried a pathway from rampart to rampart. "Such a bridge would give a more extensive command over hostile forces approaching the gate and passages blocked in time of war to provide an added barrier.

The bridge projected some distance past its supports to give a broad sweep and commanding view. On the south side some of the post holes were 4 feet deep because of possible slippage and slope of the land.

There is evidence that in a period when danger passed there was indeed a slippage of ground, supports of the bridge uprooted and

Map:- Showing relative position of Camp compared with surrounding area. Note how Limer's Lane could have begun at least at Caynham Camp and beyond; also continuing to Oreton Lime Works.

holes were filled with debris. In period (111) it is suggested there was a renewed threat of war causing re-construction of the defences and a final era (1V) when the Camp was still in use but defences were partially dismantled.

It is suggested that there was a double gate at the Main Entrance; the western one being the smaller, seven and a half feet, and the eastern one nine and a half feet. Gates were hanged it is thought on the upper and lower posts and closed to a central one.

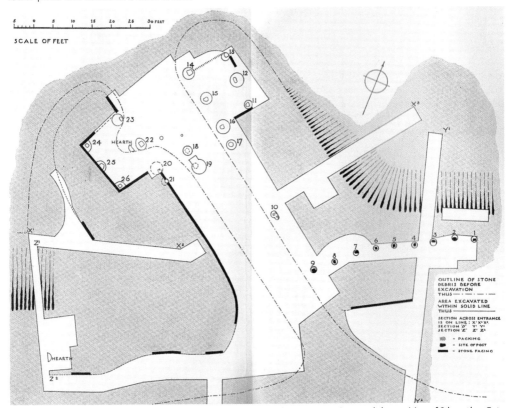

Plan of Main East Gate. This shows the 26 post holes discovered during excavations and the position of 2 hearths. Gate posts Nos 16 and 20 served also as connection to the Guardhouses. It is thought the Guardhouses were erected in period (1). The post holes around the Guardhouses are similar to those at the gate and different from the palisade holes 9 and 10. The Guardhouses both East and West are trapezoidal and identical in shape and size. The Guard post holes are 3 feet and 3 feet 6 inches deep.

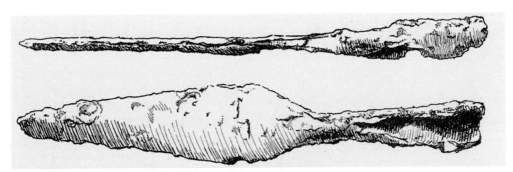

Saxon Spearhead; Found in 1928 by an employee at Titterstone Quarry

Palisade holes:- No 3: Left shows hole before clearance. Right shows after partial clearance with packing intact (ruler measures 1 foot)

Section of a dry stone wall. This is through the Main East Gateway

The West Guardhouse. During excavation.

Main East Guardhouse:- Post holes positions. See the plan of The Main East Gate.

A section through the rampart. This is just above and very near to the Main East Gate

Section across Entrance – western portion; Looking East showing walls of period (1) and (111)

View from the Camp Wall. 2010 Granddaughters Alice and Emily with my wife Ann. I am showing them the Camp in relation to Cleeton St Mary's village and school where Ann taught in 1962.

The outside diameter of holes could not always be assessed accurately. The circle shown on plan of Main East Gate is the size at the top, with all the larger packing stones removed; the inside line represents the size and position of the actual post, ascertained from the packing.. In some holes traces of wood remained; some was very decomposed, resembling red jelly but the rest was brown still showing grain.

The East Guard house floor sloped down to the entrance roadway and the Western one was flat. On this floor 7 feet from the back wall a very small flake of flint was found. The central portion of this area was covered with a thin layer of burnt wood fragments which increased in thickness until close to hole No 22 where it is marked Hearth. There was a semi-circular patch of red earth mixed with burnt wood. It clearly indicated the site of successive fires, separated by intervals of time. Ash was found also covering the surrounding floor.

In peaceful period (1V) the gate was dismantled and what remains is a thick layer of road metal of "River Gravel" across the entrance. This was laid over the whole width of the fairway in the Entrance from the upper end of the Guardhouse down to a distance of 70 feet to the line of the stone revetment of the rampart. The material had a buff, sandy nature and the presence in it of very small quartz pebbles. It had been carried from Cornbrook but another likely source is Shirley Brook where such material could be seen in 1932.

The system is certainly at least of Early Iron Age and falls into line with similar discoveries. There is implication too that after defences were disused the Hill was still used "in time intended to be one of lasting peace."

The summit with its firm and good grazing land and copious springs would form an excellent animal pen in time of war and peace. In its original state the encircling wall would have been quite sufficient to prevent stock from straying. "The climate on the Hill even in summer is far from genial. Rain and cold NE winds are frequent and the summit well down below the level on the rampart is commonly enveloped in cloud. ". Nothing has changed certainly not in my life time and as my old friend Dennis Crowther, now sadly passed on, would say when the Hill was foggy, "We'n add tu goo down tu Ludlu to see the daa light."

Snippets of Interest   Extract from Woolhope Naturalists' Field Club, May 25th 1893:-

A paper on "The Clee Forest and the Clee Hills" was read at the Titterstone meeting of the Severn Valley Field Club, June 25th, 1868 by William Purton, Esq.   He stated that according to a document at Faintree (which purported to be the minutes of proceedings of a Court Swaincote for the Forest of Clee in the fifteenth year of James I) the meaning of the word *clees* is open downs, or the common of the hill above the woods and enclosures and townships and parishes. The forest therin is called *Les Clives*, alias Clee, sometimes *Les Clives.* Clive is an old English word for hills, from the Latin *Clivus.* It had been contracted into *Clee* before the Conquest. Eyton says in his account of Cleobury North, that "the Clee Hill is so called from the Saxon word for Clay."

Extracts from Country Rambles written in the Kidderminster Shuttle – July 8, 1911:-by Mr G Thompson, Headmaster of St Mary's School, Kidderminster.

What a delightful ride it is to Cleobury whether by road or rail. If one goes by road it is difficult and slow, especially if a west wind is blowing, but most enjoyable and ever varying. If you are a lover of woodlands ask the stationmaster at Cleobury to direct you to a footpath through Mawley Woods from the platform. Claiberie, Cleburi, or Cleobury Mortimer the borough near the Clees is the Home of the Mortimers, was a royal desmesne previous to the Norman Conquest.................. The old road may be traced through the fields below, to the ford across the Rea. The mills here probably occupied the same position as the predecessor mentioned in Domesday. The paper mills provided employment both at Cleobury and Hopton but the cost of conveyance so increased the selling of goods that one by one they were closed.......Much of the lack of business (of Cleobury) is traceable to the fact that the railway – and that only a single track with no Sunday trains – is two miles from the tiny town...........Now we are out for the day, riding carefully or walking down the steep pitch to Hopton Wafers, climb the mile to Doddington Church, ask for the path to the "Forked Stick" and enjoy the long walk over the common, past the coal pits until you reach the Dhu Stone Quarries and railway......Titterstone consists of basalt or dhu-stone which may be best understood as cooled lava. This basalt has in its upward thrust overturned and tilted the stratified layers and then spread itself over them. It appears to be of no great thickness for it has been pierced through here and there by coal measures which have been sunk through to coal measures below; hence we have the curious spectacle of mounds, engine house etc at an elevation of 1,500 feet. This coal is conveyed by diminutive tram lines and wagons to the Great Western line a little north of Ludlow. What a bleak, unfruitful table-land this is over which it runs to Ludlow – its course obscured by snow in winter and marked by 'hoar' or boundary stones on either side..........Squatters have settled here and there, cleared the surrounding area of stones with which they constructed their rude dwellings and so cleared the ground into crofts, in which a few hardy animals find scanty food.

At length we shall see before us an encircling mound of loose stones of the same material, formed by clearing the internal area, and piling the blocks around the summit. This mound of loose stones is very difficult to traverse; entrances are carefully arranged for defence; and once inside find a space measuring about 900 by 600 yards, and at an elevation of over 1,700 feet. According to tradition, this hill was constructed by Caradoc, who in his struggle against the Romans fortified various hills.

What an extensive bird's eye prospect reveals itself from the cairn 1.749 feet high. Radnor Hills stands silhouetted against the western horizon, the many hills of Shropshire and Montgomery stand out to the north west, the Cotswolds, Malverns and as far as the Black Mountains and the Sugar Loaf form the boundary to the south. But the shadows are lengthening to warn us to begin our return journey. It is about 18 miles from Kidderminster to the summit of Titterstone and the whole round may well be taken on a August Bank Holiday.

Tenbury Wells C of E Primary School.
(The culmination of My Teaching Career)

When the new term of September 1980 was fast approaching I realised how fond I had grown of Leintwardine Endowed School and its community. I was excited but apprehensive when I began to think seriously about the future. Leintwardine school numbers had increased significantly to one hundred pupils and the beautiful, well designed, cohesive building was easy to manage, a great contrast to Tenbury C of E. Primary.

I began with 238 pupils on roll and during my time there was to rise to just under 400. Situated on the Bromyard side of Tenbury Wells it had a split site. Infants and lower Juniors were in a flat roofed, modern building with admin block, an Infant playground and an extensive playing field. Middle Juniors were in a lovely Victorian brick building with a steeply pitched roof and a Junior playground alongside it. To complete this part of the school was a part time SLU (Slow Learner Unit) as it was termed in those days, in a terrapin classroom.

On the opposite side of Bromyard Road, "Up the Steps" was another brick building which housed two Top Junior classes.

The Infant block had a very spacious hall equipped for PE and at its end a well resourced kitchen, conveniently able to serve meals direct into the hall. Continuing from the Infant's playground was a very adequate playing field. But! Bromyard Road was dangerous. Teachers accepted the additional responsibility of making sure pupils crossed safely and because pupils were widely spread , cohesion and timing of lessons was not easy.

By the end of my first week I had talked to every member of teaching, kitchen, caretaking, ground staff and the only Teaching Assistant Hilary Aston. I had a good idea of their apportioned responsibilities and knew I would grow to like and be happy at Tenbury. After all Tenbury Wells had been known to me since I was a very small boy when Dad frequently took me to the stock, mistletoe and holly, poultry and produce sales in the Round Market. The "Town in the Orchard" still retained its small country town flavour with an interesting variety of shops, courteous proprietors and employees.

Uncannily looking at many pupils' faces I recognised their features and it was a pleasant shock to realise that I had taught their parents at Ludlow and to be warmly greeted by them.

A substantial bus bay had been constructed on Bromyard Road purposely for school buses. I was surprised to see that eight buses came each day to deliver and collect our pupils in addition to the substantial number who walked from town and came by private vehicles.

I knew from my interviews that the catchment area was extensive and incorporated a number of villages whose small schools had closed in recent years.

I was more than fortunate once again to have a wonderful Secretary, Mrs Jean Picton who made every visitor, parent and child very welcome, was an excellent short hand typist who prepared and organised my correspondence very efficiently. At this stage with the Reception Teacher Mrs Aileen Jordan she ascertained all playgroups and villages from where our possible future pupils would hopefully come.

Having the option to be a full time administrator for the first time in my career I opted to do as much planning and research before spending regular time with all classes. I soon had a comprehensive map of all villages, drove to Yarranton's Bus Depot at Eardiston and with their help travelled with my pupils to all the centres where they came from. This gave me a comprehensive knowledge of geographical and transport problems experienced; met parents at the end of lanes where their children were dropped and made notes of the distance they had to walk ; and more poignantly appreciated the importance of making sure they were dispatched safely each evening from school. When some missed buses and arrived late very little explanation was usually needed. Parents really appreciated my time and research.

When small cohesive schools closed, parents especially those who had reception aged children found it unexpectedly difficult to travel up long, narrow, unlit lanes; place their precious little ones on buses and leave them in the care of a bus driver to deliver them many miles and return them on time to lane junctions, still some distance from home. My heart has missed a beat when on more than one occasion I have received a fretful call from a Mum at perhaps 5.30pm to say her child had not been on the bus – absolutely alarming!

Tenbury had a band of excellent, experienced staff with a vast knowledge of the area and families. Deputy Head was Paul Gregory, Aileen Jordan (Reception), Marion Bassett, Phyllis Jones, Lyle Brookes (Infants), Pat Grainger, Joyce Griffiths, Drew Shepherd and Sandra Franklin (Juniors). Fiona McLullick was in charge of our part time SLU. They all appeared confident with their particular responsibilities and had experienced two past Head Teachers at least. All were prepared to be adaptable and had the interests of the pupils and school at heart.

Some tried and tested pre-school strategies were already in place but there was room for adjustments. Aileen and Lyle assisted me to produce comprehensive guidance booklets which contained elementary pre-writing, reading skill techniques and essential preparation details for all new entrants. In addition to holding pre-entrance parent's meetings I arranged with my reception teacher to visit all "play groups" in the catchment area. Nursery classes and pre-reception groups were in early stages of development and Tenbury having a very scattered rural area, none were familiar with their future school.

Those visits proved so beneficial and mums felt more relaxed having received a warm handshake from Aileen and myself. Parents were truly surprised to see me sitting on the floor with their little ones and getting many to respond to us. The 'tour' broke the ice, especially where village schools had closed. I hoped parents could see that when their children began at Tenbury we would do our best to help them feel happy, secure and make progress.

However in spite of our excellent groundwork numbers fell to 220. I was well aware that it would take some time to turn this around.

The Authority pointed out, quite rightly that Tenbury C of E was now over staffed. I therefore had the unhappy but necessary responsibility to identify staff who could on sound educational and organisational grounds be dispensed with. This was one of the most unhappy and difficult Headship necessities. But! I was in charge. It was my responsibility to sort it.

My identifications led to National Association of Head Teachers, National Union of Teachers and National Association of School Masters opposing each other vehemently. Nowadays mediators are materialising who are not affiliated to any of these professional trade unions who can objectively advise, counsel and listen to all parties. My goodness how I wish I had had such a resource available.

Tenbury C of E Primary:- *Soon after my appointment. The photograph contains all the teaching staff secretary, grounds man, caretakers, kitchen staff, teaching assistant, 'pink ladies' & crossing patrol.*

None the less the NAHT was extremely supportive and professional. They approved my decisions and I felt vindicated when one identification led almost immediately to a Headship.

I read School Log books of records a decade previously when the Head was distressed and appalled to find he had three broken homes in his small town school with such idyllic rural surroundings. With staff help in 1982 I ascertained there were an average of eight broken homes in each class. How sad! Society had dramatically changed. School meals at that time were £30 a term.

Always looking for improvement in work and encouraging governor participation I initiated holiday illustrated diaries and asked governors to mark them. This gave them some idea of time taken by staff to mark. Many parents encouraged their charges to write and illustrate copiously everyday occurrences and visits.

Always humorous reports arose. One child had been lucky enough to visit both Ludlow and Warwick Castles. As a result he wrote, "I liked Warwick Castle much better than Ludlow because *Ludlow wasn't finished.*" He obviously felt that those magnificent medieval ruins had been left prematurely. So much for a child's interpretation of history. Teachers learn all the time.

That year brought improvements. I persuaded the Authority to sell "Up the steps" house and supply two large terrapin classrooms for upper juniors on the junior playground. This helped provide more teaching time, less interruptions and no danger of continually crossing Bromyard Road.

A larger PTA than I had previously experienced worked extremely hard and at the end of my first year handed over £1,400 to school funds. It turned out fortunately that I would be at Tenbury longer than any of my previous schools. Parents and staff organised many excellent fund raising functions and fetes.

My willing, conscientious caretaker Les Grice was a one off; a wonderful chap. His wife Em was a conscientious school cleaner too. A lovely couple.

Les Grice and his wife Em. Les the caretaker and his wife.
He was a one off (this photograph and many others of Tenbury Primary were loaned by Mrs Marion Bassett who always seemed to have her camera on hand).

On one fete day Les was assisting organising stalls for a fete and Owain Picton, the husband of Jean our secretary offered to help me carry some very long trestle table tops to the field. Owain was a lovely, genial chap and extremely tall. We were carrying one top down the corridor Owain having placed himself at the front. Les had stopped for a breather and to stoke up his precious pipe. As Owain passed him he said, "I didn't think you could carry a table top on your own Owain." Hidden from view, little me was following behind holding the back end. As I appeared by Les he said in surprise, " Oh Sorry gaffer I didnu see you there," much to my amusement.

Occasionally Les would find himself slightly under pressure because of his many duties and tight schedule. I had an easy relationship with him. One morning he knocked on my door and said, "I'm in a bit of a fix Gaffer; the little 'uns are coming to the learner pool in ten minutes and I can't drop on anyone to help remove the cover. Could you find a minute to help me please?" I put on my 'open all hours' overall which I kept in a locker and quickly helped Les. I walked back round the building via the car park where I bumped into a couple of visiting parents. The gentleman thinking I was the caretaker said, "Could you show me to the Headmaster's office please?" I gave him directions and nipped through the hall. When Jean announced I had two new parents to see me and showed them in, I was sitting at my desk, minus my overall. I will never forget the look of astonishment on the gentleman's face.

My philosophy has always been to participate as much as possible with parents and staff on informal occasions. Thereby they could see me to be fallible and able to enjoy everyday situations. This I felt resulted in difficult situations often being more manageable and communication easier.

R to L:- Paul Gregory : Deputy Head who became Head of Cookley Seabright school, Alf Jenkins in the middle and replacement Deputy Head on the left Mrs Phyllis Jones.

Mr Edwards a rotund, jovial chap had a local fuel business. He was an active PTA member and suggested we had a sponsored cycle ride, said he expected me to join in and helped to map out a twenty mile route. I rode very little but still had my trusty Elswick which Dad had purchased for me.

To make sure that I was able to finish the course I dusted off the old bicycle and began cycling in the evening, gradually extending my runs from Orleton as far as Wigmore and returning via steep Kill Horse Lane and the Goggin. On one such trip I stopped for a rest, put my bicycle down and sat on a small grassy island in the middle of the road. As I rested, red faced, the vicar of Leintwardine Revd Richard Smith drove past. As he did so he looked back and waved. A week later a report came back to me that Alf Jenkins had been sitting at the bottom of Kill Horse Lane, very red faced with an old rusty bike; and, that he had, "obviously gone down -hill rapidly since he had left Leintwardine". Eventually the sponsored cycle ride arrived. A motley collection began from Bromyard Road, the police having been alerted to the intended route. The return journey came via the notorious Raddle Bank a mile or two outside Tenbury. Just before we were due to descend I heard some anxious shouting. The handlebars of one lady's cycle had come adrift and she careered into a nearby hedge resulting in minor scratches and bruises. How incredibly fortunate the incident had not occurred a few hundred yards later on, on the bank itself.

Staff tradition was to have an end of term Rounders match against pupils and we all entered fully into the spirit by dressing up. In addition we had numerous staff visits including Stourbridge Glass, Kidderminster Carpets and Jesus Christ Superstar.

1983 saw my first major inspection. Our numbers on roll were increasing necessitating more staff and classroom space. From over 130 applicants we appointed Mrs Jenny Rodgers as a transition teacher from

Staff v School Rounders Team:- *Third from left is Mrs Brooks who became SLU teacher and sixth from the left Mr Bill Sutton who joined us when Knighton on Teme school closed. Yours sincerely has the turban and blacked face .*

Staff Hockey Match 1984:- Children amused by Alf's appearance.

Visit to the Safari Park 1980s:- Hillary Aston at the back, Alf at the front. Do you recognise yourself with James Phillips, Stuart Morris, Clare Bows and Cassandra Jordan?

1982. Cycle ride for Fund Raising:- Alf at the front with his trusty, rusty bike about to lead off a section of the participants.

The Guy:- *Mrs Hillary Aston (Teaching Assistant) back left with some of Mrs Marion Bassett's class and The Guy. Each year Hillary made a guy with pupils and the craft flair of Marion. This particular year it was chosen to go to Birmingham Pebble Mill TV Studies.*

infants to juniors. She proved outstanding and carried on the well inculcated skills experienced from existing staff. I was thrilled by the inspection which said, "Only one pupil in the 3rd year floundering in reading. Success is due to excellent teaching. The SLU is to be commended and the teaching assistant too."

Mrs Hillary Aston our only teaching assistant was loved by everyone. My decision was for her to spend a large proportion of her time in the SLU because she had the patience of Job, persistence and determination. Fiona McClullock, Head of the SLU valued Hillary because she was as good as any qualified teacher. An individual programme was devised for every pupil by astute Fiona and because some were disruptive and unable to concentrate I made individual cubicles. These worked wonders.

Hillary could spread herself so thinly to be at all nine class teachers' beck and call; preparing materials for them; assisting in all classes, helping with our extraordinary Christmas Hat Parades when every child was

Old Wembley Stadium:- *Hillary and my wife Ann on an Educational Exchange standing on the hallowed turf.*
Below:-Sutton and Tenbury pupils in front of the Old Tower at Wembley Stadium

Amazing Christmas Hat Parades:- Every child was encouraged to produce a Christmas hat at home and persuade parents to assist. This annual display produced such unusual and exciting designs.

Teddy Bears Picnic; We had lovely times on the Common. Below: Again with our new School Uniform, designed by the pupils with its badge of St Mary's Church and apple trees of "The Town in the Orchard."

encouraged to make a hat at home, while teachers got on with essential classroom work. Hillary displayed wonderful classroom Christmas decorations each year in the school hall and always rustled up a hat for any child who seemed unable to produce one. With Mrs Marion Bassett she also produced enormous Guys for Bonfire Night one of which was chosen to go to TV Pebble Mill Studios. Marion was clever at display as well as photography.

Tenbury Primary Stamps Trophy:- The school had had a long tradition of collecting stamps which The independent Order of Foresters gave to Save the Children. This photo shows when the school had 80,000 stamps still to come in. After three consecutive years of winning the Cup, a presentation of a special plaque was made by Hereford Technical College (1980s). Back L to R Mr Alf Jenkins, Mr S Davies. Front:- Julie Element, Melissa Taylor, Jenny Gough, Roger Bemand, Andrew Hughes, Mrs B Hodges.

All staff were extremely generous with their time. Aileen, Sandra, Lyle, Joyce, Marion, Hillary, wife Ann, other staff and parents helped organise excursions to York, Bath, and I.O.W during the alternate years of our Educational Exchanges. By this time I was expected to include these in pupils' experiences. Hillary Aston and Sandra Franklin class 9 teacher were very loyal, always came on these, were excellent with home visits and comforting homesick victims. Lasting friendships developed both for staff and pupils and I know many still keep in touch.

The College of Perceptors thought these Exchanges were of great educational value and I was persuaded to write a thesis to encourage other schools to attempt similar ventures. I was delighted to become an Associate of the College of Perceptors.

My school was developing from strength to strength and because of demand our SLU became an all day unit, taking in pupils from Burford and liaising with Leominster Westfield Walk Special School. Unfortunately Fiona moved but I was fortunate to replace her with Enid Brooks. Numbers continued to increase. Knighton on Teme school closed and I felt very concerned for the parents whose charges were obligated to transfer from a small, cohesive, rural school to one eight times its size. Fortunately their Head teacher Bill Sutton was sent with them and that helped. He was a lovely natured gentleman, extremely knowledgeable of country life and a very good teacher. I felt it wrong for him to be demoted. So, after much cajoling I

Weighing In:- Some of the Staff of Tenbury Primary School being weighed on the Cattle weighbridge for A Fete competition. Back Row L to R:- Lyle Brookes (Head of Infants), Phyllis Jones (Retiring Deputy Head). Front L to R:- Alf Jenkins, Jean Picton (Secretary), Aileen Jordan (Reception), Marion Bassett (Infants), Joyce Griffiths (Deputy Head), Sandra Franklin (Top Juniors). Below:- Centre, Bill Sutton with Les Grice left and Marion Bassett right. (Birthday Celebration)

persuaded the Authority for him to be appointed as an emergency peripatetic Head for other schools and remain as a fill in at Tenbury when not required. He was versatile and could fit in from Infants to top juniors. We all enjoyed his company.

Musical productions were a great strength in Tenbury, giving concerts for OAPs and visits to entertain local villages too. I was very proud of the school's contribution to Hereford Musical Festivals due to the expertise of Mrs Pat Grainger. To me music is one of the most effective means of promoting a school.

Music hath Charms:- Our music teacher Mrs Pat Grainger with some pupils in the School Hall. I was always very proud of their contribution to Hereford Music Festivals and of giving so much pleasure to OAPs.

Publishing of our first Book 1983:- It was an incredibly proud moment for Ann and me having done years of research to see the first print of our first book rolling off the presses; "Titterstone Clee Hill, Everyday Life, Industrial History and Dialect." It has become a best seller of local history. Above, one of the first copies being presented to Mrs Gillard, Tenbury PTA.

Amid my heavy educational commitments I was thrilled in 1983 to publish my first book about local Industrial and Social History, entitled, "Titterstone Clee Hills, Everyday Life, Industrial History and Dialect." Ann and I were ecstatic by its popularity and over the Christmas period sold one thousand copies and got most of our outlay of £10,000 back. To our great surprise and satisfaction it has had five reprints and in 2013 was still the most popular local history book on sale. Copies have been sent to Europe, Canada, USA, Australia, New Zealand and Africa. School was becoming cramped for space and forecasts showed numbers would increase further. With help of my Chairman of Governors we arranged discussions with the Authority to look at accommodation options and a larger resource area. The Victorian building was of a sound construction and my practical aptitude could see the roof space being utilised. The Authority agreed I could discuss possibilities with architect Mr John Wheatley to see if there were practical possibilities of making an upper floor into additional classrooms with skylights. Preliminary drawings were produced and the Authority agreed to allow detailed working drawings and costing. When

I was shown these I was truly elated but felt costs were so prohibitive the scheme would never get off the ground. With considerable disruption to staff and pupil's work continued for the next three years resulting in my Deputy Head Mrs Joyce Griffiths and others working during holidays to clear and reinstate temporary teaching areas, and be continually shunted around .

Getting to know teacher's families and concerns has always been extremely important to me. I consider it is of great benefit to understand individual's anxieties and life outside school. Many of their husbands and wives became over the years more than just acquaintances. My staff never took advantage of this but were able to divide their professional responsibilities from their private lives.

However I always felt it a privilege to be a teacher and hours put in by me, no matter how long my work took me to do I considered it part of my professional salary. I therefore felt uneasy when teachers' contracts stipulated their number of professional teaching hours. It became necessary for Heads to be prepared to ask for help at galas, tournaments, drama productions etc. This thankfully was never necessary at Tenbury with dedicated people like Sandra Franklin and Drew Shepherd who were responsible for such Junior extra curricular activities. As mentioned already most of the staff readily went along on educational excursions to help pupils during holidays.

Teaching is an all consuming occupation and on numerous occasions I have been so pleased to see members of staff returning to school after the loss of a loved one and unbeknown I would observe discreetly how they were coping in their classes. It was a great comfort for me to see all of them without exception absolutely being 'taken over' by the children and able to be normal during lesson time. A year or two earlier Aileen had lost her hubby Tom, my Deputy Phyllis her husband David, Lyle her husband Bob; Joyce husband Geoff and Caretaker Les his wife Em.

With such a loss it is impossible to continue life in the same vein; therefore it is essential for a Head to appreciate that. Losing Mrs Grice brought in another exceptionally loyal, hard working person Mrs Lloyd.

1980s photograph of most of the staff:- Back L to R: Helen Earl (Crossing Patrol), Marion Bassett, Pat Grainger, Enid Brooks, Mrs Bill Sutton. Middle Row:- Drew Shepherd, Hillary Aston (Teaching Assistant), Jenny Rogers, Aileen Jordan, Sandra Franklin, Les Grice (Caretaker). Front:- Sue Passey (Pink Lady), Lyle Brookes, Jean Picton (School Secretary), Alf Jenkins, Joyce Griffiths, Mrs Lloyd (Assistant Caretaker), Mrs Terry (Pink Lady).

Ann and I have been involved for a number of years with a Church project between an agricultural Institute near Arusha in Tanzania, and Leominster. We have had the pleasure of visiting Tengeru Institute and inviting our African friends here. I had the responsibility of placing visitors with a variety of people and professions from auctioneers, schools, milk round lady and other situations. We so enjoyed a school visit to Mr Mick Oliver the Harley Estate gamekeeper to see his pheasant chicks, that I decided it would be ideal to send an African friend Abel Shashengale to spend time with him.

Mr Mike Oliver of Brampton Bryan with one of his faithful dogs. Mick was a natural with school children and really enjoyed explaining to them all that was involved in breeding and raising pheasant chicks.

Abele was used to Game Reserves so was very surprised not to see large, wild animals roaming about the estate. But he loved to see the sheep dogs working , signs of predators, and "pudgins".

Inspector Jack Tempest felt I should share my experience and expertise with training graduate students. In 1986 he therefore encouraged me to take a Head teacher Fellowship at Birmingham University. I certainly did not enjoy the daily journeys to Birmingham in inclement weather. However, the experience of genuine clamour of aspiring graduates to want to know intimately from practising teachers, the details of proven teaching techniques which would enable them to cope with thirty plus pupils, was quite a shock. It was analytical for me to be questioned as to why I advocated certain strategies and techniques. It was constructive in making me question my approach anew. The sobering conclusion was for me to appreciate how my generation in teacher training was obligated to be taught, questioned and corrected from a very early stage by excellent tutors; even to the extent of writing in a straight line across a blackboard and spelling accurately too. These students in Birmingham were encouraged more in academic expertise than in essentials they themselves thought necessary. Did those Fellowships cause a re-think?

When I began at Leintwardine in 1976 our Authority Inspectors and Head teacher seminars began in earnest to stress a Head's role of developing a school's accountability, not only to the Authority but to parents, society and government. No longer were Inspectors satisfied with a school being successful in isolation. In Primary Education every school was expected to have a well structured reading scheme with an adequate resources area; structured mathematics schemes and every aspect of an expected curriculum to be structured to give an "all rounded education". Pupil's records were to be kept in a similar format throughout every school and for those records to be available to parents, passed on from class to class and every teacher. No matter how competent an individual teacher he/she had to be encouraged to fit into their school and its philosophy. Testing at crucial stages was expected to become the norm and results forwarded with pupils when transferring from class to class and Secondary Education.

Computers were being introduced – a complete enigma to me. Most teachers thought it may be possible to ignore them. Thank goodness we did not.

Sex education with explicit slide films were to be compulsory. This was an aspect of Primary Education I never felt at ease with or felt necessary to be presented to such young minds. I have never been convinced of the wisdom of it ever since. It may have done some good but I am sure it has added to promiscuity and experimentation that is so prevalent.

The role and responsibility of a Head teacher had suddenly changed. I was determined to inform my staff what the future would soon require and equip them voluntarily to be confident and capable teachers ready for legislation.

The new School Badge:- Being displayed by Mrs Marion Bassett and parent--------------------.

From my first day at Leintwardine and for the rest of my teaching career my aims were based on what I have just expounded with other excellent researched pointers. In general staff appreciated my motives with the standardisation of records and reports although I have to admit there was intransigence in isolated cases with some determined not to conform. Most could see that my preparation would give them a good standing in their teaching future. It would prove to be impossible to ignore this impending metamorphosis.

A reading test I much liked was Neale Analysis Reading Test. Its results gave a clear picture of problems being experienced by a pupil in reading, letter recognition, blends, terminal sounds, initial sounds and ascertained a reading age. Most teachers liked it and had a clear strategy for each pupil. In April 1988 the Bishop of Hereford came to open the wonderful new and re-furbished facilities in the Victorian Block. It was one of the proudest moments of my teaching career – honestly a dream come true. The facilities had four spacious classrooms, the SLU, a Head teacher's office on the ground floor and a lovely library/resources area and two top junior classrooms upstairs with views across the school playing field. At last Tenbury Primary School pupils were all on one site in suitable accommodation, able to access the Hall undercover. No more terrapins. People wanted to bring their children to Tenbury and the school was near to increasing to another group category. I was pleased to appoint another teacher Mrs Gill Evans.

When I first taught in Primary Education I was not in favour of a school uniform. I liked the variety of pupil's clothing and as long as children were presented tidily preferred parents to choose what they could reasonably afford. As time progressed however I became aware that many pupils, girls in particular seemed to relish wearing a different dress every day which quite overtly caused resentment from others.

I consulted my Deputy and Head of Infants, Joyce and Lyle. They were in favour and after consultation with the staff and governors we were given an overwhelming approval. Pupils were asked to submit designs. The one chosen contained a roundel with St Mary's Church in the back ground, trees with apples reminding us "The Town in the Orchard" and Tenbury C.of.E School printed around the edge. The uniform colour was to be dark blue. It became so helpful to be able to recognise our pupils anywhere. It was a great leveller; pupils were proud to wear it and it made it a closer, cohesive unit when visiting sports events and exchanges.

To help transition to Secondary Education all top juniors took annual tests during their last term. Writing tables were spaced out in the hall and I helped Sandra Franklin to administer. On one such occasion I was

Our Lovely Kitchen Staff:- L to R Mrs Queenie Giles, Mrs Joan Burden, Mrs Caldicott, Mrs Pauline Green and pupil Melanie Jinks.

handing out papers when I suddenly experienced a most excruciating itch in a very sensitive area. I explained to Sandra that I would have to leave. I dashed to my cloakroom for a swift examination. I could not see a significant problem but the irritation became unbearable. I informed secretary Jean I would have to leave and make tracks to our dermatologist, Doctor Penny Ovenden. After an embarrassing examination I was told to go home; bath and apply ointment but the tremendous irritation did not subside.

Next morning wife Ann was suffering the same intense discomfort. We both went to see Dr Penny. When she had examined Ann straight away she said, "I know what the problem is. It travels like wildfire in a warm bed – its scabies." We were almost traumatised and asked how this could be. Ann was upset saying that we were clean and careful washing hands, beds etc. Dr Penny said that she had experienced more teachers with scabies than most professional sections of society and asked if I had had a jumble sale and had I handled the goods. The answer to both was that we had had a sale the previous Saturday and I hadn't felt it necessary to wear gloves.

We were sent home with instructions for all the family members to bath and apply ointment to every part of our bodies including the soles of the feet and palms of hands and to change all bed clothes every night.

Thank goodness the scabies subsided and my hair no longer stood on end. I called all my staff together. They were highly amused but shocked by my story. We never had another jumble sale during my time at Tenbury.

Soon after David Jones passed away his wife Phyllis, my very experienced Deputy retired. This created a shuffling of staff and I appointed Lyle Brookes as Head of Infants and Joyce Griffiths as my Deputy. Their loyalty and close co-operation in my career has never been surpassed by anyone.

Often at end of term assembly as we were about to file out of the Hall, on more than one occasion Joyce would stop everyone, ask them to sit down and listen. Then she would say, "Mr Jenkins always says 'Thank You' to everyone. He is our Dad and he looks after us all. I want you to say Thank you to him and give an enormous clap". That would bring tears to my eyes. What a lady!

In the summer of 1988 I experienced regular ear irritation, went to the doctor and had syringing. The irritation subsided and hearing improved. However the problem occurred more and more frequently and I mentioned to Joyce that at times I could not hear, especially the younger children's voices. After a number of syringing appointments my hearing did not improve and I was alarmed.

My Doctor tested my hearing and advised me to go to hospital. In January 1989 I had a further hearing test to be told I had a considerable hearing loss in both ears. I returned to school and explained my predicament to Joyce and Lyle. Joyce said that she should have mentioned to me that some staff had said they were sure I had not heard what they had said recently and it had caused confusion. Joyce and Lyle felt I should contact our Education Officer. This I did and he promptly sent me to see Dr Hanna at Nuffield Hospital. Ann came with me. His diagnosis distressed me and I asked him to repeat it. He told me I had a severe hearing loss in both ears throughout the whole range and he could not understand how I had coped in school. His verdict was that he would advocate to the Education Officer that I should have leave forthwith.

Ann and I drove home in tears. I was not looking forward to going to school. Haltingly I told Lyle and Joyce I was being advised to take two months leave; gave the reasons why and said I was obligated to have more tests the following month. In a disconsolate frame of mind I explained the situation to my staff. There was much consternation. I left school with a heavy heart but I was not the only one.

Again I visited Dr Hanna. More Tests. He stated that he hoped that without pressure and anxiety my problem would improve but unfortunately the tests showed further deterioration. He continued, "You are at the top of a very successful career. I recommend you listen to me. You have a severe, deteriorating hearing problem. Give up while you are at the top. If you don't, pressure could exacerbate the problem. You could possibly be stone deaf within a year". Oh dear! What a bombshell.

I reported to Mr Turnbull our Authority Education Officer and had an interview with him. He said, that he did not want to happen to me what he had experienced with a past friend and colleague. His illness led him to go from a pinnacle to being hounded out by parents. "That will not happen to you. I am going to recommend that you resign forthwith on health grounds."

On February 16th 1989 I had a letter from Darlington informing me I would be retiring at the end of Spring term.

I had been working with the Authority for a long time to encourage easier access and continuity for pre-school children's education in Tenbury. At last the Authority had agreed to assist special provision to position a classroom near the infants department and later a covered way. This good news lifted my spirits somewhat. The press reported, "The headmaster was tremendously proud of the efforts of Nursery Class teachers Pat Hadley and Linda Armishaw and their Committee. When the future was bleak for them they had courage to forge ahead, raise funds and acquire a building." He wondered how many of the general public would have taken the same gamble for someone else's children. Mr Jenkins's one regret was that he would not be able to see the Nursery become a permanent part of the school's education provision. Councillor Olwyn Barnett at the opening ceremony said, "Tenbury Primary School has been very fortunate in having such a remarkable headmaster. I thank him for all his contribution to education. He has done a marvellous job."

The New Nursery Unit Opening:- A proud moment for Retiring Head Alf Jenkins, watching Councillor Olwyn Barnett unveil a plague with members of the Pre-school, hardworking Committee ---------Mrs Armishaw and Mrs Hadley.

I could not appreciate the end of my teaching career was becoming a reality. Many of my lovely staff visited me at home. Joyce and Lyle were frequent visitors seeking guidance and assurance about admin matters and Hillary and Tony Aston's optimism often made Ann and me smile.

How pleased I was to have been to Birmingham for a Fellowship. This had given my senior staff experience of managing the school for most of each day.

On February 24th I met my staff and informed them at the age of 53 I was having to give up my career.

March 23rd 1989 my personal Diary read:- A day I dreaded. I went like the school boy as Shakespeare said, unwillingly to school. I was conducted into the Hall to be met by hundreds of former Primary school pupils. They were so genuine with their polite" Goodbyes". I was emotional and overwhelmed. My last assembly – the silence was uncanny. Joyce summarised by saying that pupils' Mums and Dads would say their farewell to Mr Jenkins that evening and concluded, "Now on your behalf I want to thank him again and wish him a happy new chapter in his life."

At 7.00pm my wife and family accompanied me to the school Hall to an occasion I will never forget. The preparation by staff was mind boggling. The evening passed in a whirl. I had found some old timber in the school garden shed and made it into a large cross for the Hall. Presenting that was the only aspect my mind absorbed clearly apart from the continual good wishes and handshakes. During the following week I settled and Ann persuaded me to read my scores of tributes and press reports. Were they honestly about me? If so the experience was extremely humbling.

In the local press extracts from what Deputy Head Mrs Joyce Griffiths said were, "Many changes have taken place under the excellent leadership of Mr Alf Jenkins. He has seen the school installed on one site, introduced a school uniform and the SLU became a full time unit to name but a few."

Presenting the Cross:- Alf Jenkins at his retirement presenting a cross to Deputy Head Mrs Joyce Griffiths, which he had made from old scrap timber found in the school garden shed.. L to R:- Mrs Ann Jenkins, Alf Jenkins, Mr Turnbull (Head of Hereford and Worcester Education Authority) and Mrs Joyce Griffiths.

County Councillor Mr Pip Jones said, "Mr Jenkins has made Tenbury Primary a show piece among primary schools. He has been a splendid Headmaster, highly respected by staff, parents and governors. It is such a tragedy after such a successful period having achieved the set up he wanted to be forced to leave. It is a great shame."

Chairman of the Governors said that the Education Officer Mr John Turnbull was in charge of over 400 schools and 5,000 teachers. It was a mark of his high esteem for Mr Jenkins that he came to his retirement presentation.

In his press release Mr John Turnbull said, "Friends, parents and colleagues have gathered in force to pay tribute to a fine man and a very special kind of Headmaster. He leaves behind a good name and many of us would aspire to no better epitaph. It is my privilege to make this tribute. I

PTA Presentation:- Members of the PTA make a presentation of a specially commissioned sketch of Tenbury Primary School and a cheque. L to R Mrs Boucher, Mrs Currier, Mrs Sylvia Muncaster, Mrs Aileen Jordan, (Reception Teacher) and Alf Jenkins.

would like to extend the thanks of the Education Committee for the excellent service Mr Jenkins has given to the Authority."

What did the future hold for me? My career taken from under my feet; but Ann my wife ever the optimist said that I had a multitude of skills. I would have other opportunities and she would encourage me to utilise them. What a lady!

Deafness Accepted

Life is a mixture of highs and lows. Deafness was a low blow and depressing experience. I had been completely steeped in my teaching. I had been respected, in charge, enjoyed it and could not visualise another existence. In fact neither Ann nor I ever thought of being rich. It was the satisfaction of pursuing something worthwhile that mattered to both of us. This is still an important motive in our lives.

Suddenly at the age of 53 I felt isolated, unable to communicate and my confidence was destroyed. The Education Authority said I should approach the Employment Exchange. I did. My deafness was assessed and my possible skills listed. It was suggested I should pursue my crafts skills and work on my own. This it was thought by the deaf specialist was sensible and would lead to less stress because my energy would not be exhausted by having to continually listen and watch. Mr Hanna said that if I continued to experience unnecessary stress I would be stone deaf within a year.

I enlisted for a business course at Hereford and arrived for my first day. I explained to the tutor that I was extremely deaf. However by the end of the first morning I was floundering; found I could not cope with the confusing cacophony so drove home dejected at lunch time.

I found using the phone impossible. Ann phoned the Employment Agency and they asked if she would be prepared to go with me to the business course. She was more than pleased to do this. The next Monday brought my second attempt to cope.

Craft Fair at Ludlow College:- This was taken by the Ludlow Advertiser.

On arrival Ann explained to the tutor why she was with me. She was invited to introduce us both to the group. She said, "I am Ann Jenkins, wife of Alf who is very deaf. So, I am the ears and he is the mouth." Her humour broke the ice.

From that moment on with Ann's help, better understanding from the tutor and the group I managed to enjoy the course. We met aspiring artists, painters and decorators, mechanics and so many more from all walks of life. We tackled such business essentials as cash flow, what was a reasonable hourly rate our woodworking skills could command, how to develop a relationship with our community, what finances we could muster and how much initial financial support was available.

Son Graham assisted me to choose and purchase equipment and took me to a national machinery exhibition in London. There I found what I had in mind, a Hegner jig saw and an automatic five function 'Combi' machine with spindle moulder, circular saw, thickness and surface planer and a morticing device. I purchased other machinery from Tewkesbury Saw Company including a band saw, large belt sander and stand drill. We saw a small second hand van for

Victorian Festival:- Granddaughter Alice on left dressed in keeping, helping serve on our craft stall, plus Ann and Alf with visiting friends the Nottinghams.

In Victorian Dress at Llandrindod Wells:- We attended this 9 day Victorian Festival for a number of years with our crafts. Alf is wearing cap, ganzi and muffler in the Clee Hill working men's fashion

sale outside a shop in Leominster. I purchased it and wrote our names and business details on the sides.

After much time setting up benches in my existing hobby workshop and positioning machines I was ready with Ann to begin advertising "Combi Crafts" – a name thought of by Helen our older daughter.

Our well loved Van:- Alf's sign writing helped us to be recognised where ever we were working.

My balance was not good but I was soon fitted with two hearing aids and in time they cured my unsteadiness. I was instructed to put the aids in for an hour initially and walk down our local Tunnel Lane. The experience was unnerving and extraordinary. I could suddenly hear much I hadn't heard for so long. Birds were singing all around me; but I could not make out an unusual rubbing sound. What was it? I eventually discovered that it was my shirt collar rubbing on my neck – unbelievable. Cheering up somewhat I ventured on down the lane. Suddenly there was a tremendous roar and I thought that the world was falling about my shoulders. Round the corner came a tractor which made me realise that I would have to be extremely careful at all times, keep on the lane side and that hearing aids amplified sounds more than I appreciated. My silent world was broken. Thank God for hearing aids. I persevered, got used to them and they restored my balance but realised they created some difficulties as well as alleviating others.

In October 1989 Ann and I as partners launched our little business. We thought if lucky it would last a few weeks but it continued for twenty years enabling us to complete our home mortgage.   We did anything and everything from decorating, repairing doors and windows and minor brick work. Producing a variety of over ninety wooden crafts we participated in about fifteen Craft Fairs yearly. We created Nativity Sets which still have an appeal to churches, grand parents and schools. Sign writing has been a great satisfaction as has renovating antique furniture.   All in all the new venture brought us in touch with such a lot of local people, enabling us to help and be trusted by them even to the extent of them going off to town leaving us tea making facilities and cake for elevenses.

I thank Ann wholeheartedly for working with me, making our business a success, pleasurable and fulfilling. In that unexpected chapter I regained confidence, attended lip reading classes and began to lecture to various groups from all over the Midlands about Industrial and Social history.

Nativity Set created by Ann and Alf: Following a visit to the Holy Land and being disappointed with the quality of Nativity sets there Ann and Alf decided to design their own. Their 11 piece Set made from selected Swedish Pine has proved and is still popular with schools, grandparents and churches. Prototypes of each figure appeared many times on their breakfast table before a satisfactory result was created. A 3D effect is enhanced by sanding components of each figure and animal to differing thicknesses so that as light strikes them the natural grain of the wood is highlighted.

An 8 foot by 4 foot sign; Made for Farmer's produce shop in Mill Street, Ludlow, Shropshire. This well known, hardworking firm from Orleton was established in 1960. As well as their well stocked shop they display in Ludlow market several days each week.

Ann & Alf's workshop:- Ann making sign for the Boot Inn, Orleton, Nr Ludlow, Shropshire.

The Boot Inn sign in its rightful place hanging outside the ancient pub in Orleton Herefordshire:- No matter how hard Alf tried he could not avoid the reflection on the right hand side.

Removal of Coal 1989/90

It is thirty years since we published "Titterstone Clee Hills, Everyday Life, Industrial History and Dialect", an occasion we recall with such great pride having been researching its content for over ten years. It was unbelievable to finally see the fruition of our work rolling off the presses. One local person had said with assuredness, "It will not get off the ground." We are delighted to have proved him wrong. Due to the fact it is an oral testimony to the thousands of local, hardworking quarrymen and miners we knew so well; who had little and were caught in an inescapable action trap, we are proud it has had five reprints and enlightened thousands in many parts of the world about this special part of England.

I refer readers to my section on Clee Hill Coal mining in "Titterstone Clee Hills..." where I explain at length working conditions of men of my childhood and those of many generations before. That information would however prove helpful if seen in conjunction with the following photographs taken in the late 1980s, early 1990s of the removal of a vast amount of Clee Hill coal.

Coal has been mined on Titterstone Clee Hills since the Middle Ages. On the tops of the hills near Clee Hill village there were over thirty deep pits producing good quality household coal. All those shafts were laboriously sunk to a depth of a hundred yards through incredibly hard dolerite. I have reproduced two line drawings from "Titterstone Clees..." to assist readers. The continual problems of working coal in the area with gas explosions, constant water seepage and a maximum height in many tunnels less than a metre must have been horrendous. However like many other primitive and unsophisticated domestic situations those miners knew of no other existence and assumed their lot was common to all.

My life and that of my wife was forced to dramatically change by my deafness. Bills had not yet started to descend on us but without my guaranteed salary we were extremely apprehensive because we still had a large mortgage .

In the first few days at home I spent most of the time in my hobbies workshop, got absorbed in repairing furniture and forgot about my predicament because I did not have to concentrate on listening to anyone. Ann was as patient and understanding as ever and managed to make me respond by blowing an ARP whistle which had belonged to my Dad.

However at the end of the week Ann had a phone call from Marina my sister at Clee Hill Quarries saying that Manager Mr Greg Gregory would like to see me. I was aware of mounting problems with stone production due to faulting which was resulting in less solid columns of dolerite and a worrying amount of 'muck'. Mr Gregory explained that there was danger of the last stone quarry closing because of the considerable extra cost of washing dirty stone and disposing of thousands of tons of clay and non saleable rubbish. It was becoming increasingly difficult to maintain full employment for the workforce.

On the Hill above Cornbrook a few hundred metres past Clee Hill village going towards Hopton there are numerous large spoil tips very near to the closed deep coal pit shafts. I have drawn the attention of those mounds and the bare patches on their sides caused by sheep sheltering from prevailing winds, to many groups while taking them on tours of the Clees. Those patches expose the mounds' content – coal. Most of it is poor quality and mainly slack dumped by miners from Barn Pit, Bottom and Top Trout Pit, Kilkenny and others in that immediate area because it was considered not of commercial value.

However in the 1980s Mr Mole from Mamble sought permission to make use of that 'open cast', easily accessible coal. Mr Gregory directed a number of experienced stone quarry personnel to work for Mr Mole. Consequently my friend Derek Crowther and others toiled with picks and shovels for some considerable time loading coal onto lorries.

The site of the World War II RAF camp is well known, again referred to in 'Titterstone Clees'. Directly opposite this camp site on the south side is where a considerable amount of coal was removed.

In the 1990s one of the Magpie deep pit shafts collapsed and quarry manager David Edwards contacted me to see it. The hole was huge and the danger obvious. David asked me how deep I thought that collapsed shaft was. I knew many were as much as one hundred yards. I could not hear but I could see as David lobbed a large stone into the abyss and counted slowly. After seven seconds he heard the boulder hit the bottom so one can gauge how deep that shaft was. Such collapses occur from time to time caused by prolonged wet or dry periods. A recurring problem is that Land agents responsible for mineral rights are not keen to accept responsibility for such incidents. Hence dangerous holes are left unfenced. David did not allow this to happen.

Collapsed shaft:- *This photograph shows the enormous hole. We estimated it to be 16 feet diameter*

We were intrigued to see locally made bricks positioned at ground level and continuing down to where solid rock was encountered. This was to prevent the top of the shaft collapsing.

Collapsed shaft protected:-This shows the fence erected by Quarry Manager Mr David Edwards and employees to avoid off roaders, motor cyclists and four by four enthusiasts disappearing from sight.

In 'Titterstone Clees', pages 9 to 26 inclusive I describe in some detail working conditions of men I knew well who had been Clee Hill miners. George Broome told me that none of the tunnels he worked in was more than thirty inches (75 cm) high; making it necessary for boys and men to crawl on hands and knees without being able to stand upright for six to eight hours a day. Water was always trickling into the tunnels and trousers were sodden by the end of a shift. Carver boys walking home across the hills in inclement weather contracted pneumonia and their life working in those pits was often a short one.

Over the centuries miners had discovered significant faulting, terminating working seams and mining, abruptly. This created much hard work to re-locate the seams. They told me too that seams were tilted upwards by ancient earth movements and so ran very near to the surface at Hoar Edge and Catherton. This is where hundreds of shallow Bell Pits had been worked and discovered.

In the middle of the Clees in the Magpie area some thirty plus pits were developed which had entailed making shafts through solid dolerite, locally known as granite, to a depth of one hundred yards. I described the daunting, arduous process of sinking such shafts in 'Titterstone Clees'. However those men persisting in lifting six inches of rock at a time with horses and lifting tackle beggars belief.

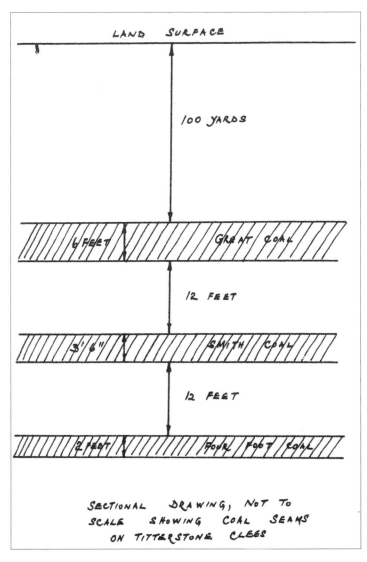

None of those miners had ever seen a geological map of the area or any sectional published Information, but what they described to me has proved to be absolutely accurate.

The sectional sketch shown on this page appeared in Titterstone Clees and shows a not to scale section of Barn Pit above Corn Brook in the Magpie/Watsill area. It illustrated the Great Coal Seam six feet thick one hundred yards below the surface. Twelve feet deeper the three feet six inches Smith's Coal Seam and twelve feet further down the Four Foot Coal which in fact was only two feet thick. These deep mines were worked for hundreds of years from the Middle Ages until 1926.

Again in Titterstone Clees I describe a particularly hair raising story of a young George Broome and his brother being trapped in eerie blackness and flood water; quite horrendous.

When I had the phone call from Mr Gregory he said he had been looking at my book again and was amazed

Left Mr Greg Gregory quarry manager; describing to Rev Vic Roberts on the right with foreman Mr Bill Jordan behind and myself the intended programme to save the Dhu Stone Quarry and sustain stone production for the foreseeable future.

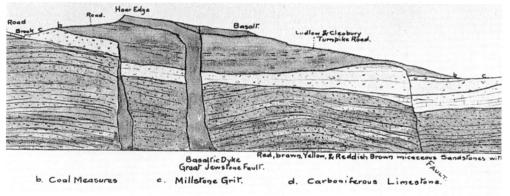

The sectional map of faulting, coal measures, Millstone Grit and carboniferous limestone strata is produced to illustrate the outcrop of coal at Hoar Edge and Catherton.

how accurate the assessment of former miners had been compared with the information of modern maps he had at his disposal.

In 1989 and 1990 a Scottish firm was contacted. They had to ascertain the thickness of good quality coal, how far it was from the surface, remove the overburden near Hoar Edge and expose the coal. It may be a misquote but I understand at the time that the Scottish firm was to be given any coal removed as part of the deal to hopefully enable quality stone quarrying to continue.

My first visit in 1989 saw huge diggers removing the considerable overburden of rubbish and clay beginning to expose coal in places.

The Dumper lorries:- Used to transport overburden and coal from Clee Hill Quarry area in 1989

Overburden: Overburden of clay, earth and rubbish being removed near Hoar Edge to expose the coal seen below. Due to faulting to the left of the picture at Hoar Edge itself the coal ran out to the surface.

Loading Overburden:- 1989 a digger loading overburden into a dumper lorry below it. I have watched 5o tons being loaded in two and a half minutes and seen those huge lorries sink into the ground under the great weight.

Exposed Floor of Granite:- In the foreground is the exposed "floor" of possible stone for production.

In the last photograph in front of the diggers and lorries is the impressive six feet seam of coal; above which is the overburden of soil, rubble and clay. The further East one goes the deeper the overburden. Some of this collection of photographs was given to me by Joyce and Tony Sloan of Milson.   They have certainly enhanced my own collection of this important episode of Clee Hill industrial history. A massive quantity of clay was removed in the operation and placed in an old quarry with the anticipation that in some king's reign it may be sold to industry as a raw material for the brick industry.

(Above) Hoar Edge Coal. Overburden removed. (Below) Lower coal seams. Huge pile of coal on left

It was unbelievably exciting for me to actually see the 6 feet "Great Coal Seam" exposed. It had been described so accurately many years previously to me by "carver boys" of the 1920s. Their working conditions were appalling, having to crawl on hands and knees along narrow passages, two feet six inches high with only a candle pushed into the side walls to light their way.

Foreman Bill Jordan 1989, Standing on a considerable seam of good quality, bright coal.

The lack of air made hard work even more difficult. Their trousers were continually sodden from dripping wet and the muggy atmosphere made them sweat profusely. In the cold air above ground their journey home cooled them dramatically frequently leading to pneumonia and a short life in the coal pits.

Management did not appreciate the demands made on boys or the efforts they made. Their wages were awarded reluctantly and often as soon as they qualified for adult wages having given some years of service, they were dismissed.

It has to be realised that on Clee Hills as in other industrial areas little other employment was available. Families were large and with numerous mouths to feed mothers were anxious to get able bodied boys into work as soon as possible to help put food on the table. I was interested to read the thinking of Quarrying Manager R.E. Jones by extracts from his lecture in 1921. He said, "Boys don't pay. If you have a boy now-a-days he may cost you as much as 60 shillings (£3) a week. A boy is one of the most unprofitable things in the world to employ. They are made to work and they know it. They want to be playing and get plenty of fun......You will not make money out of these workers".

How literal is this? "If a man thinks that his knowledge is complete and that he does not want to gain any other knowledge, then he will remain forever an individual in the dark." Mr Jones continued, "If a lawyer makes a mistake he gets the case over again. If a judge makes a mistake it is the law. If a doctor makes a mistake he buries his patient; if a plumber makes a mistake he puts it on the bill; if a bishop makes a mistake nobody knows the difference; BUT if a quarryman or a miner makes mistakes there is a commodity spoilt and that means £ s d through his mistakes".

Having a sincere empathy with Clee Hill people I never begrudged them carrying a disused rusty piece of sheet iron or a half rotten railway sleeper home to use as valuable kindling wood or make part of a precious pigsty. Families had so little moneywise so a 'glat' in a hedge would not be sealed with stakes and proper fencing but a mish-mash of old bedsteads and whatever was at hand. I illustrated good examples of this in my DVD "Up the Lane and Back again".

The 6 feet seam of Coal exposed.

I wonder what miners I talked to in the Dhu Stone Inn in the 1940s would have thought if they could have seen these sites. Unfortunately the colouring of this photograph does not portray the excellent quality and brightness of the Deep Pit Clee Hill coal.

The two thousand plus shallow bell pits around the Hill gave coal which was in comparison very poor quality due to the fact it was not more than thirty to forty feet below the surface. This resulted in wet from above penetrating coal and making it of a "slacky" nature.

The tunnel exposed was typical of those described to me by 'carver boys' who had worked them. They were just two feet six inches high (760 mm) making it impossible for even boys to stand up. No wonder during my childhood I saw many elderly Clee Hill men with permanent stoops.

Foreman and Friend Bill Jordan holding a piece of Thick Seam Coal. It demonstrates its brightness and quality. It burnt extremely well and justified why miners were persuaded to persevere with hammers and crow bars to make shafts through one hundred yards of Dolerite to reach the seam.

"What we've been aiming at." Coal seam in background. Bill Jordan Foreman standing at last on exposed Clee Hill Dolerite.

Loading coal. Patrick Sloan in 1989; having a breather. Note well used shovel on left.

For the previous ten years I had visited WIs, Historical Groups and other societies describing to them in detail how boys crawled along such tunnels with straps over their shoulders connected to a chain; which in

A Rat Hole:- 1989. Mr Bill Jordan drawing my attention to a coal pit tunnel (a Rat Hole). The coal seam thickness is illustrated by Bill stretching from his feet position to his horizontal arm holding a stout staff.

Looking inside a 'Rat Hole'. Just looking at this photograph makes me wonder how men and boys tolerated such conditions.   Dolerite wall on the left; skimpy roof supports held up by locally grown larch props and typical water through which men and carvers had to crawl to excavate coal.

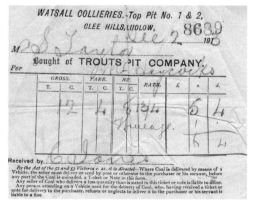

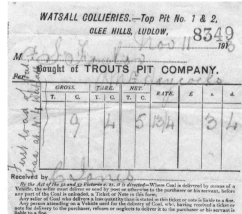

Two purchase tickets from Trouts Pit Company:- I was indeed lucky to see these. One is dated Nov 11th 1913 and the second Dec 2nd 2013; just a century ago. The weights of coal being purchased are 9 cwt and 12 cwt (hundredweights) respectively for 3 shilling and 4 pence (about 16p) and 5 shillings and 4 pence (about 26p) to a collector S Taylor and signed by Mr Haycocks for C Jones. These are all names I was familiar with on Titterstone Clee Hill .

By 1991 five hundred thousand tons of coal, plus thousands of tons of over burden of clay and soil had been removed to enable Clee Hill quarrying of road stone to begin in earnest again.

The Quarry's reputation was restored and much new machinery installed for the small remaining workforce to produce vast quantities.

The spoil of Trout pit can still be clearly seen in the Watsill area above Clee Hill Village; its scars of slack coal exposed by the constant sheltering of Common sheep.

'Rat Hole' removed:- Bill Jordan showing the route of the removed tunnel with remains of pit props

turn was connected to a box with skids under it known as a 'carve' hence carver boys. What a horrendous experience!! They only had a candle as a light and endured sodden clothes continuously for their six to eight hour shifts.

Bill's work was often very hard quarry graft but he was honestly grateful that he had not had to endure such a life in Clee Hill Coal pits.

Inchmoor and Kenny

This special place, the home of my wife Ann, has since the late 1950's been a second home not only to me but my children and grandchildren too. How many wish to stress the importance and influence of their in-law's home? I certainly do. Relationships depend on a two way process, give and take. We have received an enormous amount of 'give' from Inchmoor and its environment.

At the time of writing we experienced Nan Edwards, Ann's Mum returning home after a spell in hospital due to an unconscious fall and severe cut to her head. It has made us reflect about someone who is such an invaluable part of our life.

Again I stress it is good people, a willingness to greet others with a smile, make them welcome and accept them warts and all that is meaningful and treasured in life – not wealth and keeping up with The Jones's. That is not at all important to us. We have experienced much arrogance and selfishness from many of the 'new rich'. As a result we continually stress to our grandchildren that to be lucky enough to enjoy a career, find a good partner, be content and contribute to society will enhance life beyond measure.

But! I am jumping ahead because this 'must' section is a tribute to Kenny, Ann's Dad, countryman through and through. This short episode will have to suffice but many books would not do justice to Kenny.

My rural background surrounded by animals and pets contributed considerably to my makeup. Therefore when I had borrowed Dad's Austin and took Ann home from a dance in Tenbury to a remote farmhouse across fields in the late 1950s, I felt at home immediately because the environment was familiar.

Like many of my era I loved to whistle melodious tunes and so it was reported to me that Kenny would often ask, "When is the Clee Hill warbler coming again Annie?" Inchmoor was in those days a mixed farm. Eggs were sold but as was the norm there were always cracked ones. These had to be consumed at home. To Nan Inchmoor being an excellent, versatile cook this was no problem. However whenever I visited on a Saturday evening cracked eggs on toast, fried, scrambled or poached was always part of the evening's ritual.

Kenny, pipe filled with Saint Julien would be sitting watching television with a continual sparkle in his devilish eyes. Occasionally the television picture of 'Juke Box Jury' would fade and Kenny on demand rushed out to the engine shed, refuelled the generator, got it up to full power and the picture much to everyone's relief returned to normal.

Everyone was welcome at Inchmoor and without exception everyone wanted to visit. But! Kenny was a terrible teaser. One nephew arrived with girlfriend as usual, for Kenny to say, "Mike that's not the same girl that you brought last week." "Oh it is uncle Ken," retorted Mike, followed by, "No it isn't. That one had red hair." This of course produced a crimson complexion from both Mike and girlfriend but we all grew to expect such ribbing as part of Kenny's lovely character.

It was natural for me to participate in all the farming activities at Inchmoor but Kenny knew that at the time I was a Handicraft teacher, now known as CDT. The baler behind the tractor threw out special , small hay and straw bales because much of the handling was done by daughters Ann, Gill and Pat; hence the special packaging. The bales however landed in a higgledy piggledy, scattered manner. Kenny remarked, "You do a bit of woodwork they tell me. Could you make me a bale slave (sledge)? I want it to be fixed behind the baler and funnel collector to enable us to collect them in piles of six or eight and so push them off the slave gently to make it easier and more orderly to pick them up with the tractor."

He produced a bit of a sketch. I agreed to make a bale slave and said I would go to the sawmills at Woofferton and get some timber. Kenny said that wasn't necessary adding, "I've got just the thing." He took me into the dairy and there we were, looking at a beautiful mahogany dining table. I said that I could not possibly mutilate that. It would be sacrilege. He responded that the table would never again be used. So much against my cabinet maker's inclination I proceeded to demolish that beautiful table. Eventually the bale slave was produced and the polished surface enabled us to push off the piles of bales quite easily. We often slipped off as well but with a slight modification and non-slip footwear all worked according to plan. I did manage to rescue one small leaf from which I made a coffee table. This treasure remains in daughter Helen's home as a reminder of Inchmoor.

Harvesting has changed dramatically during my life time and an early combine harvester was a miracle to behold. To see such a machine combining the cutting of grain, thresh it, funnel ready for bagging and throw out waste chaff in one operation was unbelievable. What a change and time saving process this machine created compared with my childhood. Then I would sit on a binder with its sails revolving as the mower blades cut the corn and the rolling canvasses moved the stalks into the machine where it was knotted automatically and thrown out as sheaves. Depending on humidity the canvasses had to be regularly tightened and slackened and the sails raised and lowered to accommodate the length of the grain stalks. The knotter frequently malfunctioned too causing great annoyance and delays.

Kenny feeding some tiddling lambs:- One of our few and precious photos of Grandad Kenneth Edwards of Inchmoor, feeding two orphan lambs a powdered milk mixture. Note the pipe which was always a part of Kenny. By the time this was taken his left hip was badly worn and muscles of the leg greatly affected. He was a very contented man who I never heard complain about his own physical condition We tried to persuade him to have an operation but the TV series 'Your life in their hands' put him off completely.

Provided the weather held, the sheaves were stacked in 'stooks' of six or eight. Later those stooks would be loaded by pikles (pitch forks or pikes) on to thripled wagons and transported to barns to be threshed by a threshing box much later in the autumn. So the combine harvester condensed many days work into one.

When I first married I would dash home from school in late summer evenings, change and cycle along Tunnel Lane to Inchmoor to see combining of wheat, barley and oats. To experience the excitement of seeing scores of rabbits bolting in every direction as the stalks were toppled and watch excited people with dogs and sticks trying to catch a meal was really exhilarating. The downside was that I knew I would have to return home and work late to prepare for next day's lessons and mark books. On one such beautiful evening I approached Inchmoor gate and could see the combine over the hedge by the lane side. Whistling away I turned my bicycle into Inchmoor drive and craned my neck to see more of the machine. As I did so the bicycle hit a stone and flew off one way and I flew off in the opposite direction. Lying there battered and bruised and feeling sorry for myself, a wicked grinning face complete with pipe peered over the hedge shouting, "You alright Alfie?" I had to break into a smile in spite of my predicament.

I had driven a tractor since the age of eleven and before Harry Ferguson produced his revolutionary 'Fergie'. But! machinery and farms are dangerous places and even with experience accidents and deaths occur frequently. When transporting bales after harvest it is always a race to beat inclement weather. It is all hands to the pump so to speak. I was taking a load with other drivers down the 'damson' lane to the barn. The rule was to halt the tractor at the top of the hill and put it in bottom gear before descending. For some silly reason I did not stop completely but with over confidence knocked the tractor out of gear and attempted to engage bottom. I could not. The tremendous weight of the loaded trailer pushed me over the brow and before I knew it I was careering out of gear down hill. Brakes would not hold the tremendous weight and family watched on in horror. Somehow I avoided the trailer jack knifing, part of the load was jolted off and I arrived near Inchmoor in one piece very shaken but enormously relieved and NO reprimand from Kenny.

With the help of Ann's common sense I became trusted by Kenny and Nan Inchmoor. I very much enjoyed going into the cowshed and watching the cows being milked. Kenny always had radio music playing as it seemed to help the animals relax and be content.

Ann's Mum and Dad had talked of going to Cyprus but didn't think it possible to leave their many daily responsibilities. However we said we could do the milking and after practice proved we could. The in-laws were anxious as to how we could milk, get to our relative schools and fulfil all our own responsibilities. However Ann and I persuaded them to go.

After a couple of days we were so pleased to be able to complete the milking, put it through the cooler, place it in churns and transport it to the milk stand in Tunnel Lane ready to be collected by Cadbury's transporters all before a breakfast. Then we travelled to Ludlow School where Ann dropped me and went on to Cleeton School a distance of twelve miles all in ample time to be ready for assembly and classes.

However we were more than delighted to welcome Nan and Kenny back home to find all the stock alive and well and for the milk cheque to arrive a few days later. The holiday had been very much appreciated and although tired Ann and I were more than pleased too.

Kenny with some of his grandchildren:- Everyone was made welcome by Kenny especially the grandchildren. Back L to R, Malcolm Morgan (son-in-law) Duncan; Alf the author; Front L to R: Paul; Granddad Kenny; Graham and Helen.

The hardest traditional job still necessary was carrying bagged corn up a wooden staircase to the tallut (loft store room). I have never been a robust Atlas but reasonably fit after army service and an active life. However it was a killer for me to put those heavy sacks on my back and struggle up those steps. Matters were made worse when Kenny gallously (devilishly) suggested to the girls to give me a push making me stagger sideways and them laugh their heads off.

There was a profusion of damsons at Inchmoor and one lane and many hedgerow trees were a delight to see in full bloom during spring. Sometimes frost would destroy the blossom and the expected crop in autumn. It was always the case that a heavy crop commanded a low price and few damsons high returns.

However when we were newly-wed Kenny would say, "If you pick the damsons you can have the money". So every autumn we spent many evenings sawing logs for Inchmoor and in return picked and had the damsons. Damson boughs are notoriously brittle and well known for resulting in serious falls and injuries.

Kenny loved to join us, drove a trailer beneath each tree enabling us to pick most of them from that height. Even so arms and legs were always scratched profusely but I often remarked that I prepared many school lessons in my mind while up damson trees.

All full forty eight pound boxes were taken to Mr Tom Apperley of Temple House Ashley Moor Lane and in a good season we have been thrilled to purchase as much as a tea pot, hot water jug and tray from the proceeds.

Later when our children came along, in spite of Kenny being a terrible teaser, they loved him to bits. They asked Nan Inchmoor why she had married Granddad Kenny. She said that at school he was very naughty. She was ashamed of him but thought that if she married him she could make him a better person but remarked that she hadn't succeeded. Nan was obviously very bright and jumped two classes at Leominster Grammar school to find herself in his class. She said that whenever there was a problem he was to blame. She recalled seeing him wetting rolled up blotting paper and throwing it to stick on the classroom ceiling. As soon as Mr Pinder entered he would look up and say, "Come here Edwards." On another occasion the class was growing broad beans which were being encouraged to climb through a container hole towards the light. Kenny climbed up and broke the leading shoots off much to Nan's embarrassment. When leaving on his last day at school Nan's greatest humiliation was to see Kenny burn his class books in the playground. Our children loved to hear such stories but thank goodness they didn't emulate this aspect of his personality to my knowledge.

Our children were taught to understand that when Granddad Kenny was at home his horseplay, teasing and naughty antics was purely domestic. When he was in society he could be very well presented and his etiquette impeccable; touching his hat to ladies while riding his horse with the hounds etc. Our children learned that home allowed different responses from when they were in company. When at the dining table Kenny would purposely avert Helen's attention by saying, "Oh, look at that robin," and while saying so would remove some tit bit from her plate. Graham being a little older would quickly cover his plate before being distracted.

Kenny inherited Inchmoor Farm at a very young age, worked incredibly hard, never had much in the way of luxuries for himself or his family; but he paid off the mortgage by the end of his life and had the most precious gift he wanted, a happy home and a happy family.

Kenny the loveable, sincere clown continued to be the person we all wished to visit. What would he say this time? What would he do? Mr Pritchard the chimney sweep paid a regular visit to prevent Granddad clearing the chimney by setting fire to a bundle of binder twine to clear soot and cause a red hot chimney stack as he did on one occasion. Mr Pritchard charged very little but benefitted from generosity and a good meal. He wore long, gauntlet rubber gloves and I remember on one occasion he asked Nan if he could use the toilet. She directed him where to go and as soon as he had left the room and was out of earshot Kenny said with a chortle, "I hope he takes those dirty gloves off, " followed by ,"I don't know why he comes in to ask that, I always go round the back of the shed."

Stock transporters such as Tony Wright and Harry Wragg were always pleased to visit Inchmoor because the required stock was always ready. Early morning in ample time Kenny would say, "Come on; we'd better get those cattle sorted and ready. Ragged Harry will be here soon."

Daughter Helen was sensitive and alarmed when Kenny used an expletive. She mentioned to her Mum that she would make a swear box for Granddad and of course she told him. Kenny played on this, winding Helen up and gleefully saying, "If you think that will b------stop me b------swearing, it will not." Poor Helen was appalled and immediately told him that he had two fines already.

Scrabble and Lexicon were favourite pastimes resulting in all the girls being excellent spellers. Of course Kenny loved to break the rules and produce words no one had ever heard of. They would explode and tell him that that was not a word and he would respond but saying that it was a Russian sausage or some such in a confident manner.

There were so many occasions when hard work chores were made fun by Kenny and all family and friends wished to take part. These included chain sawing fallen trees for winter fuel or driving a flock of sheep miles to be dipped at Grosvenor's.

How was it he was able to make a fool of anyone on April Fools' Day. Year after year the family fell for his convincing tricks.

Kenny was an excellent farm craftsman. His pleaching of a hedge was a joy to watch and the girls loved to join him to have a fire and burn the trous (brushings taken from an overgrown hedge before laying it).

Turkey plucking and dressing at Christmas was very hard work but such a fun gathering. Each farm including Inchmoor, Portway, The Broad, Beech House and others each had a large number of turkeys which were reared for the Christmas market. I found it really hard work because of my comparatively tender hands. Pulling large turkey feathers is a real knack. Up to our knees in feathers the banter was continuous and sometimes unrepeatable. Different people were assigned to different jobs; some catching the birds, some killing, others feathering and a group of ladies dressing. Children were always with us playing and helping too where possible. I remember one episode when we were at Portway Farm when the children were told that Father Christmas was going to pay a visit. Just before he was due to arrive, Bill The Broad, one of Nan Inchmoor's brothers was just as big a teaser as Kenny. Bill called all the little children to him and said, "Oh dear. Father Christmas will not be coming. Someone has shot him outside Woolworths in Leominster." Most of the children began to cry but Nanny Portway, Jessie saved the day by saying that that was impossible because no one could shoot Father Christmas and that he certainly would be here. Shortly afterwards snow was gently falling and we all heard and saw a small tractor. Father Christmas (John Crofts) in all his finery came round the corner, ringing a large bell with an enormous sack tied to the back of the vehicle. What a scene! Ann and I almost believed in him ourselves. It is an occasion we will never forget.

Kenny was often joined by an experienced local farm worker Bill Pugh to hoe and harvest beet. It was essential to thin rows of beet by hoeing so allowing remaining plants to achieve a reasonable size. Both Bill and Kenny had tremendous skill and could hoe at slow walking pace. It was wonderful to see such a task being made to look like child's play. When harvesting beet both men could pull, chop and throw beet into a cart in one continuous, flowing movement. That was a great skill indeed.

During World War II many German POWs worked on local farms and many married and settled in Britain. Heinz Shroeder and his wife Iris was one such couple who worked for Orleton Manor and lived at Line Cottage very near to Inchmoor farm. Nan Inchmoor got to know Iris well and even delivered at least one of her children. Heinz amused and intrigued Kenny because of his resiliance and determination to survive. He managed to keep a few chickens and ducks and to make sure his little children were safe from the nearby railway line they were often penned in the poultry run with the birds. I can assure you they never came to any harm. Like their Dad they were survivors and Carol and William grew up to be lovely people.

Heinz's English vocabulary was limited. It never seemed to improve so every sentence was supplemented by expletives. His accent and manner amused us all but we considered him a real friend. Often we would hear Heinz shouting, "How's the bl...y kids Ken?" How's the bl...y Mrs Ken?" How's the bl...y milking Ken?" I never recall Heinz to be disconsolate and he often said, "You've got to make zee bl...y joke Ken." Heinz was always ready to tackle any problem but we never asked him where his ample supply of chicken feed came from.

In my early days of visiting Inchmoor I could not afford my own vehicle and borrowed Dad's. It was a beautiful, large Austin 16, made in 1936. It had been mothballed during the War and was a great pride of Dad's. He had purchased it from Mr Price of Castle Garage Ludlow, a gentleman Dad trusted explicitly. It had running boards, curtains and seats which could be removed for Dad to use it either as a hearse or for passenger work. I remember Ann being quite alarmed when I was giving her a lift and the seat tipped. I told her not to worry because Dad had just forgotten to secure it due to the fact he often took the seats out to put a coffin in. This really alarmed her whereas being used to the undertaking at home I took it for granted.

Having come home for the week-end from Sutton Coldfield I wished to see Ann, borrowed the car and drove off to Inchmoor. The usual route was to turn off the A49 Ludlow to Leominster road at The Salwey Arms Hotel. As I made the turn there was a disturbing clatter. I put my foot on the accelerator but there was no response. The car rolled to a halt. I got out to see, much to my distress bits of engine were strewn back along the road. I unscrewed the bonnet and lifted it up. Horror of horrors! There was a large hole through the side of the cylinder head . The con-rod had come adrift and smashed through the side.

Feeling very disconsolate I went into the Salwey and asked for Mr Harold Moulton who was a friend of Dad's and asked if I could phone home. With considerable trepidation I spoke to Dad and explained what had happened. He was fantastic; said it could have happened while he was driving and calmly said he would send someone to pick me up.

Again in those early days I was paying a visit to see Ann. When I left Dhu Stone Inn the sun was setting on a pleasant evening. I was greeted as usual and after a couple of hours had passed there was a phone call. Ann's Mum answered; came in and said, "Alf your Dad says the snow is so deep you will not get home." I could not believe the sudden change in circumstances.

Nan Inchmoor said, " Oh! Not to worry. I will go and sleep with the girls and you can sleep with Kenny. However there is something I must tell you and that is that he sleep walks. If he attempts to get out of bed, just grab him by the tail of his shirt and pull him back."

Well first of all I was not enamoured at the thought of sleeping with my future father-in-law but soon we retired to bed. Inchmoor Farm is about 150 yards from the Ludlow to Hereford railway line and in those days trains passed at very regular intervals.

So! what with noisy , intermittent trains and the apprehension that Kenny was likely to jump out I had very little sleep indeed.

These pages recall just a few episodes of my happy reflections of Inchmoor. Sadly Kenny developed a hip problem and a pronounced limp. He refused the opportunity to have a hip operation having seen surgeons sawing through the bones on "Your Life in their Hands". The result from walking over rough land was a strain on his heart leading to an early death at the age of 64. He had just completed paying for the farm.

Throughout his life all his efforts and money went into that so he and Nan had very few luxuries. But he possessed wonderful attributes, generosity and contentment.   When I recall Kenny the memories never evoke sadness but happiness and a smile to my face.

Bitterley Hydro Scheme (The Resevoy)

My parents worked very long hours and did numerous jobs to create a living in the mining and quarrying area of Titterstone Clee Hills, South Shropshire. I never recall my Dad having a holiday but just the occasional day with local friends at Ludlow Races where I remember him taking me too. He was shocked to discover that a cheese and onion sandwich was two shillings (10p) and jellied eels although he thought them a delicacy too expensive to contemplate. For us it was a sandwich from home to minimise expense. Dad also enjoyed a day point-to-pointing with Cyril Yapp or a very special treat to travel to Aintree for the Grand National, a yearly event eagerly awaited by the pub customers for the sweep.

Mum was however made to have short breaks and took us as far as Swansea at the end of World War II to visit relatives the Merrimans. Swansea was still a disaster area after considerable Nazi air raids. We often wondered how Dad managed because he was certainly no cook but no doubt he had plenty of fat bacon, butter, milk, eggs and cheese.

The long hours of pub work, wheel wrighting and undertaking were ceaseless but on Sundays the pub closed at 2pm and there was a break until 7pm before opening again.   This was a time when Mum and very often Dad too took us for walks to visit friends and when Dad was keen to show me places of importance contributing or having contributed to the area's industrial success.

Quite frequently Marina, Mum, Dad and I would set off up The Green from Dhu Stone Inn, over the railway bridge; up past Rouse Boughton Terrace and turn left across the Wallers bumpy track. All was amazingly quiet with often fantastic views towards Ludlow; so different from the constant throb, noise and swirling dust from the crushers on week days. At the end of the lane a gateway led down a steep hill to Ernie Bates' farm at Nine Springs. He was a lovely, elderly man with Dennis Healey eyebrows. He knew Dad well because there was often a cart repair to be done when he brought it to Dad's workshop with the help of his beautiful roan shire horse.

We passed through a gateway beyond the farm house to a path which ran past Walter Breeze's cottage on the right. His son Gordon, younger brother of Lucy and Dennis was a best pal at school. He used to run the two miles to our village school daily and continued with me on Midland Red Bus 192 to Ludlow Grammar School. He became school cross country champion, was a mathematics wizard but sadly died in his early fifties.

The path continued to and over Benson's Brook a considerable stream which had gouged out quite a deep channel and begins beneath Titterstone itself (see Discover South Shropshire's Titterstone Clee Hills DVD).

Just before the brook we veered left down a well worn path to the home of Mr and Mrs Ern Coates, their daughter Rita and son Clive. As in homes of other locals we were always warmly welcomed to their snug abode. It was a typical squatter's stone cottage; very small but as Dennis Crowther would say, "'Omely."

Ern worked at Bitterley Court, was a typical country man with numerous skills useful to the estate. Dad no doubt became friendly with him while carrying out gate making and wheel wrighting repairs there.

Without any persuasion needed Dad and I would leave Marina and Mum and take my cane fishing rod down to the adjoining field to the "Resevoy" as it was known locally, hidden among the trees. This was an unexpected site. He would walk me along the long, curved dam wall, sit me down in the middle, my legs dangling over nearly touching the water and ask to sit quietly. He said fish could hear vibrations from ones voice and also were wary of shadows on the water.

In front of me was an expanse of water curving round to my right which was probably 50 yards long. Beautiful reeds and bull rushes grew around its edges. The trees cast shadows over the water helping me because the jumping fish trying to catch flies seemed to ignore my presence. What excitement it was to have my first bite. I was hooked too and asked to go there often.

I could hear rushing water further to my left. Dad took me on across the dam wall to see my first ever water-fall. What a splendid sight! A torrent was pouring into the brook at least twenty five feet below, churning up a pool and continuing down the meandering stream.

Rod packed up, my trout wrapped in some dock leaves and feeling so proud, Dad took me down through some wonderful beech trees below the dam wall. The soft rotting leaves made a spongy carpet. Dad asked me to look up into the branches and said I would get a better view if I lay on my back. This we both did and he pointed out to me the natural whorl of beech branches. They were like spokes of a farm cart wheel each pair below allowing the one above to be placed in the middle of them and so allow light to penetrate through . I thought those smooth barked trees were elegant and a wonder of nature. Dad said that beech grew best where they had access to plenty of water and that a mature tree could absorb as much as four hundred gallons a day. Phew! But the exciting thrill was to see agile red squirrels jumping nimbly from one branch to another.

Our visits to Coates' cottage continued and of course the reservoir as well. It was a popular place for local lads especially during hot spells but Dad warned me that there was an accumulation of mud beneath the surface and the weeds formed a tangled mass. That, with the icy water from the Hill made a dangerous combination . This proved so because not that much later we heard that 'Watt' Davidson, of the well known local family and brother of Harley had drowned in the reservoir.

A railway line ran nearby. The wire rope connected to the empty trucks ascending and the full ones descending echoed through the trees and seemed to make a continuous whining sound. Dad explained to me that Messrs Field and Mackay had opened Titterstone quarry in 1881 and before it became fully operative the incline had to be constructed to transport crushed and sett stone produced to a wharf at Bitterley siding. There was already a siding there for Dhu Stone and Granite quarry trucks; but the hillside had to be excavated considerably more to create siding space for Titterstone trucks. At Bitterley the crushed stone was coated with tarmacadam and transported far afield.

Coal was plentiful at Dhu Stone and Granite Quarries to drive their machinery; but Field and Mackay for their own reasons declined to purchase coal and built the reservoir to power their machinery. It did not of course register with me at the time what a wonderful project it had been. It was years later I realised what fantastic pioneers Field and Mackay and later Mackay Junior had been to establish what must have been one of the earliest hydro schemes in Britain. Dad told me that locals had said that the reservoir not only produced power for driving Bitterley crusher but also produced electricity for Titterstone works but recent research has cast some doubt on that. However I write elsewhere that just a very few years after the reservoir was built, at the Golden Jubilee of Queen Victoria on the 11 June 1887, MP Offley Wakeman's office reported that in addition to bonfires on beacons of Shropshire a 'wonderful electric light shone on Titterstone Clee Hill'. I wonder what generated that power.? Was it the Bitterley reservoir? Perhaps Dad's comments were right after all. I would like to believe so. More research please.

The Coates', cottage was adjoining land to Park Farm. Dad visited that farm too and when Mr Hughie Huffer, his wife Mavis and family came in 1948 Dad became friendly with them through work. Mr Huffer was a very pleasant gentleman and I have fond memories of those days. The farm had originally been part of the Plymouth Estate and was sold off at the time of the Ist World War to Askeys of Knowbury, the famous local brick makers. I still have some of their bricks with the name imprinted.

At the same time Ernie Bate of Nine Springs passed on and a young man called Roy Guest came there. He was a bachelor, often visited the Dhu Stone Inn and I learned that his father was a headmaster in Wolverhampton. I became very fond of Roy and spent many summer days helping him with haymaking. He worked incredibly hard reclaiming poor, rush and bracken covered fields, was a great neighbour to the Huffers and Dad absolutely trusted Roy.

Plan of Reservoir at Bitterley as I remember it (cross hatched No 729).

A:- Titterstone Quarry Incline. B:- Reservoir as I remember it.
C:- Flow of Benson's Brook.

Because of his bachelorhood his meals were always rushed and I remember being so ravenously hungry but delighted to share his many tins of tomatoes and copious amounts of bread. Roy had a rotund friend John who often visited and gave a hand. He arrived late one evening but could not rouse Roy. He noticed a bedroom window open, got a ladder from the barn, climbed up and through. Unfortunately he misjudged its size and got wedged half way. This led to hollering and shouting for what seemed an eternity. Roy in a semi-daze came to the noise and tried to push John back onto the ladder. This failed. Outside he went and up the ladder and after much pushing and twisting freed an exhausted John. The problem had been his waist belt hooked on to the opening fastener. What a caper!

My occasional visits to the reservoir continued and I obtained a number of verbal reports about its origin from Dhu Stone quarrymen. Army service soon arrived and whipped me off to various parts of Europe. Teacher training followed and a teaching post in Warwickshire. It was 1962 before I was able to return to my home area, pick up the industrial threads and continue research in earnest. My oldest Grandson Sam, mentioned in the introduction has like all our family been encouraged to take an interest in Titterstone Clees. Being inquisitive he asked us to take him to see the Hydro Scheme and the old reservoir. Firstly I asked Richard Huffer, Hughie's son permission to locate Ernie Coates' cottage. I was shattered, after having related so many stories about my past visits to see that just one small corner of it remained.

The sad remains of Ernie Coates' Squatter's Cottage:- This photo is so reminiscent of the fate of numerous similar cottages around the Titterstone Clee Hills.

Sam sitting on the "Resevoy" wall where I had 60+ years previously:- He noted the prominent curve.

Other squatters' cottages remain intact further up on the other side of Benson's Brook; one in particular is 'Tommy Oxo's', the home of Mr and Mrs Davies and their son Tommy. Mrs Davies was a rotund lady and used to sit in their squatter's holding garden by their beautiful rockery. This extended right down into the brook gorge. Tommy and his Dad were responsible for placing the rockery stones in strategic positions but she tended it and it was something unusual; a real show for Clee Hill. Of a summer's evening she would sit in full view of everyone walking up towards Titterstone, was not at all discreet, legs wide open and Tommy would often be heard shouting to her, "For----- sake mother shut thy legs." Both Tommy and his father tended their small holding, cut bracken from the hillside for cattle bedding and worked long hours in Titterstone quarry. Tommy never got married and saved every penny he earned. It was so well known in my youth that he went down to Mr Parsonage's garage in Corve Street, Ludlow and paid for a new Humber Super Snipe in £1 notes. My goodness that made the locals stare. Moreover he also purchased one of the first models of Harry Ferguson's little grey revolutionary tractors.

Sam noted the pronounced curve on the stout retaining dam wall. I pointed out how it spanned from one side of the brook cutting to the other; that the curve was intentional to enable the two feet plus thick wall to withstand the considerable pressure of the body of water as I had remembered it.

Sam standing on the lower side of the Dam wall on Mr Huffer's bank. Note the splay and thickness of the wall. The inside of the wall is lined with quarry stone setts. These are sadly breaking away and will need attention in the near future to preserve the structure and avoid wet pouring in creating more damage .

I persuaded Sam to pace across the top of the wall he was surprised to find it was 50+ metres. He could hear water rushing over the far end and was captivated to see a twenty five feet water fall.

Standing on built up silt with no sign of water was difficult for me to accept thinking about the scene I had been used to in my young life. Could this area be cleared and a dam re-instated? Perhaps more realistically a small section could be excavated and shored up to illustrate the original depth of the inside of the Dam.

A view taken from the inside of the Dam showing the inner lining of stone setts:-

The original water area of the Reservoir, now silted up:- Grandson Sam sitting on the retaining wall.

Summer scene showing lush vegetation growing in the bed of the dry Reservoir:-Ann looking at the variety of rushes, reeds and plants.

Summer Time just below the Reservoir:- Gentle gurgling Benson's Brook in the background. Some of those ancient beech trees which I lay beneath to ponder about the symmetry of their branches and the long gone site of agile red squirrels.

The Titterstone Clee Hydro Scheme water fall. The sluice near the base obvious.

We walked below the Reservoir and crossed the brook to obtain a decent view of the water fall. We both agreed that the damming of Benson's Brook to produce such a structure must have been very time consuming and expensive. The fall of the water was really impressive.

The force of water pounding down into the brook was considerable even though there had not been rain for some days. I pointed out that this continual force would cause considerable erosion. This had been minimised by walling both banks and stoning the base of the brook too.

Looking towards the water fall on the left bank is a small brick construction within which is a sluice valve to regulate the flow all the way to Bitterley.

Sluice Valve housed in a brick surround; situated just below the water fall on the left bank of Benson's Brook.

Sam standing on Titterstone Incline Railway base. It ran just a few yards away and more or less parallel to Benson's Brook down to Bitterley Yard wharf and all the way up to Titterstone Quarry.

While looking at the railway incline base we found a section of the railway line, a length of incline wire rope and considerable ballast of the old railway base just below the surface.

The meandering of the brook continues to cause bank erosion and to prevent unnecessary damage, a little distance below the water fall a considerable stone sett wall was constructed probably at the time of the project.

The water pipe conducting water is eight or nine inches in diameter and can be seen clearly much lower down the brook where it crosses from the 'railway' side over two support walls to the turbine area just above a row of cottages at the foot of Bedlam bank. A channel or pipe to a millwheel or turbines is called a penstock.

The penstock crossing from the railway incline side to what was the turbine area. Sadly there is damage to the support pillars as a result of setts being removed and pilfered (see left of photo).

The pipe line to convey a powerful flow of water had been laid beneath ground level at the dam and travelled a considerable distance until it appeared above ground and crossed on two stone pillars to the turbine area (see photograph).

A most impressive stone sett wall was constructed just above Bedlam Cottages to retain soil and house a turbine and generator. Many of the base stone setts are of a considerable size, and I think of the effort to put them in place.

So much of the Hydro scheme is still in an excellent state of repair. I told Sam that Titterstone Clee Heritage Trust had been formed four years earlier with a main aim to preserve, enhance and renovate important Titterstone Clee artefacts. I told him we had been thinking since TCHT's inception that the Hydro Scheme was a must to register, preserve and renovate; but most of TCHT's energy had been taken of late in obtaining the only woodland area remaining on Clee Hill, namely The Nuvvers at Knowle. It is an area of some 30 acres and contains also the infra structure of an important ancient lime industry. That site had been secured and I was thrilled it was already being cared for, numerous educational courses held there; forest management and planting of selected trees.

The substantial stone sett wall by the side of Benson's Brook just above Bitterley Cottages. Sam was most impressed to think men with just the aid of small hammers had shaped all those setts. The wall which retained the turbines is still in excellent condition even after 130+ years.

Derek Crowther, a life long friend, ex quarry man and a former resident of Bitterley Cottages told me that reservoir water had been used until recently as a general supply but not as drinking water. A piped supply had been available from a small shed on top of the sett retaining wall. The following photograph shows a local family standing in that area.

The Flat area above the impressive sett wall above Bitterley Cottages. Building on the right housed a general water supply from the Reservoir Hydro scheme for use by the cottages. L to R Derek Massey, Mrs Clark, Lucy Massey, Mrs Massey, Mrs Taylor

Three friends who have lived in the area since my childhood, namely Derek Crowther, Tom Massey and Ian Montieth know well of my interest in our wonderful area and wished to share some of their information about the hydro scheme.   Well above where the penstock crosses the brook to the turbine area on the opposite side, is a concrete structure. This encloses a spring. Water from this point was piped to the row of houses at the bottom of Bedlam bank to give them all clean drinking water. A long length of the conducting pipe still remains in the brook alongside the impressive sett wall.

An   earlier   black   and   white photograph shows a group standing on the flat area above the stone sett wall some 60 years ago when the area was comparatively clear. In 2014 it is a different story. A great deal of the space is overgrown with

Bitterley Yard:-In the siding Field and Mackay trucks; behind is the blacksmith's shop & Bitterley Row. What the author believed was the Bitterley crusher is seen in the background right. When enlarged this photo shows a truck appearing at the base.

The 'spring' housing unit:- This small enclosure is about 50 metres up the brook above the stone sett wall. From here a supply was piped to Bitterley Row to give each house clean, Titterstone, drinking water.

brambles but with the help of the trio of friends they showed me the exact position where a generator had been positioned. It was mounted on a stone sett structure some seven or so feet high.

Ian stood by this structure while Tom and Derek showed me the end of the penstock pipe and the position of the turbine which they knew had been there during their early childhood. It had been only about ten yards from the generator stack. From this position a drain conveyed the used water from the penstock pipe to an outlet drain at the base of the stone sett retaining wall.

A generator powered from the reservoir was mounted on the top of this seven feet high stone sett structure. Many of the stone setts from the far side of the structure have been removed by individuals and used for numerous purposes.

Tom and Derek told me that the generator produced electricity for the offices by the Bitterley Row long before other electricity was in Bitterley area. They also stated that the stone delivered to Bitterley crusher came down on the Titterstone railway already crushed to a three inch size. This meant that lower power than normal would be necessary to enable the crusher to reduce the size of the stone to an acceptable size for the tar plant to make tarmacadam. They had been told that it was easier to maintain electric power from the generator than it was from the fluctuating force of the water from the reservoir. I tend to believe this was the case and that indeed electricity was produced from the hydro scheme. It is in the hands of future researchers to disprove this.

The photograph on the previous page shows a bridge crossing Titterstone incline railway. In the background to the right of the cottages where the incline begins to ascend to Titterstone there is a white building. It is positioned right by the side of the track. This is believed to be the Bitterley crusher.

As I mentioned elsewhere Mr Millichamp had worked in the quarry during my childhood but had a severe accident resulting in the loss of a leg. However he was a resilient man, persevered with a wooden leg and was

Ian Montieth standing by the generator stack. A few yards nearer the camera Tom Massey and Derek Crowther are clearing brambles to show me the position of the turbine.

Approximate position of the turbine. From about this point Tom remembers the drain which was open during his childhood and flowed into the brook at the base of the impressive stone sett wall.

retained to look after the quarry horses. He fed them in Titterstone quarry stables during inclement weather when it was not possible to take them to lower fields to graze at night, before being brought back for work at 6.30am next day. He also hobbled all the way to Dhu Stone Inn to collect and carry cigarettes back to the bungalow shop where he sold them to quarrymen. When friend Derek Crowther brought this photograph to me I was really thrilled to see that my memory had not played tricks.

The reinforced base of the crusher still stands proudly, almost as sound as the day it was built over a hundred years ago. (See photographs on page 201 and 202).

The drain opening into the brook. This ran from the position of the turbine positioned on the built up area above. During the childhood days of Tom Massey the whole elevated area retained by the massive sett wall was covered with quarry scalpings and a wicket gateway led from the cottages' side to the turbine and generator area.

An early 1900s photograph of Titterstone quarry area:-In the foreground is the 'bungalow'. Part of it was used for storage, office and an outside toilet. This is not the one which became the home of Mr Millichamp an 'ostler', that is the one where the foundation is outlined lower down on the flat very near the top of the railway incline. Background right shows three crushing machines progressing down the hill which then transported the stone to the sifting plant, behind and to the left of the 'bungalow'. There the stone vibrated over meshes and dropped down into bins. I do remember seeing the lower bungalow as a child but not this one.

Above and below remains of the bases of Titterstone crushers. The crushed stone went over these stone bases then, vibrated by varying sized sieves dropped into bins below.

View from Top of Titterstone Incline during the author's childhood (taken from 'Titterstone Clee Hills, Industrial History, Everyday life and Dialect').

Dr McGrannon while trudging up to the quarry to attend an injured quarryman ; head down in inclement weather was struck by a descending truck and killed. I understand from my Dad it was near the position of the wooden structure on the left side of the photograph.

This picture was taken very near the top of Titterstone Incline. Note the width of the railway pulleys. These allowed sideways movement of the rope where the rails divided as they approached the quarry. The ascending truck is clearly visible while the descending one is out of sight near to Bitterley Yard.

The dust belching from the tarmacadam plant on Bitterley Yard siding can be seen in the far distance.

Taken by the authors in 2013:-This shot extracted from 'Titterstone Clees, Industrial History' is at nearly the same spot as the one showing the working incline from Titterstone . The fence posts are still in position but all trace of the incline rails have been removed. Trees in the background near Bedlam village are much larger nowadays. The telephone posts carrying the line from Bitterley yard to Titterstone offices have been removed too.

A Ruston RB 4 (Ruston Burcyrus); At Titterstone Quarry:- This was the first machine of this kind they had made in 1929. Here it is in use at Titterstone Quarry soon afterwards removing a tremendous amount of overburden to enable stone quarrying to continue. The digger is swinging the overburden in to a truck on this side. It was a front load machine. A number of Ruston machines came to Clee Hill Quarries but later models had the number before RB. The first one was driven by Horace Key; later by Donald Martin then in the 1950s by Derek Crowther.

Clay and Brick making on Titterstone Clee Hills

I have stated in some of our other publications clay of the 'Clay', Clee Hills is found all around its lower regions including Knowbury, Coreley and Oreton. It has been recorded as being as much as sixty feet thick and fourteen different colours. It has been proved suitable for land drains, roof tiles, ridge tiles, bricks and even gravestones.

Askey's of Knowbury was a large concern in the eighteenth and nineteenth centuries, as was Davis's. I have examples of their bricks with names imprinted on them. Large brickworks were known at Coreley and other places around the Hills.

Most people of my childhood would have pronounced Clee as Clay; and it is recorded in Woolhope Society records that in the Middle Ages the area was called 'The Clay Hills'.

For years the coal and clay brick industries ran in conjunction with each other; bricks being made locally to reinforce the upper parts of coal pit shafts and lime kilns to stop them collapsing.

In our DVDs 'Up the Lane and Back again' and 'Discover South Shropshire's Titterstone Clee Hills' my friend John Hughes helped me tell the illustrated story of Clee Hill's clay industry and its special bricks. Also in our hard back book 'Titterstone Clee Hills, Everyday life, Industrial History and Dialect' more information can be found.

When making bricks the normal releasing agent of sand is used to line brick moulds but I discovered many years ago that on Titterstone Clee Hills coal dust was often used instead. This meant that when the bricks were fired tell tale black specks can be seen all around them. John and I had seen this evidence on Nuvvers bricks and at Sutton's of Oreton.

As a result of our earlier publications Colin Richards the then Environment Officer for South Shropshire encouraged me to continue my research in the area and introduced me in the early 1990s to a very special place the home of the Sutton Family at Oreton.

I immediately felt at home there because that magical place had evidence of a feast of traditional country crafts; including blacksmithing, wheelwrighting, timber conversion and cider making all of which I had been familiar with at home in my childhood. But! there was a very special addition, a wonderful beehive brick kiln; probably the only one of its kind remaining in the Midlands.

At a much later date Neil Sutton, son of Ann and Trevor informed me that the Sutton family had moved to Little Stocking, Oreton in 1861 when the yard was owned by Southams of Shrewsbury. This was at a time when the local coal industry was thriving and the start and tremendous development of Clee Hill stone quarrying began.

It was John Sutton who came in 1861 with his father William. John had two sons John and William, Neil's Great Grandfather. William saw and provoked the transition from just a brickyard to include the other crafts I have mentioned.

William had two sons, another William and George. As Neil said, "Thank goodness my Dad was named Trevor."

I know the problem experienced because when my family met together when I was young there were so many Alfreds it was confusing to know which one was being referred to; hence our first born being named Graham.

Colin Richards introduced me to George Sutton, Neil's great uncle. He was in his late eighties and I understood from him that he was the last person to fire the kiln still standing in the yard.

George described to me the process of brick making he had been familiar with. There were two kilns on the go more-or-less continuously. Clay supply was near at hand above the wheelwright's shop and dug from the hillside. Air was 'knocked' out of it by feeding it through a pug mill. It was then placed into a two

The Kiln as I first saw it:- It was in a very dilapidated state and small trees were growing out of its roof.

handled mould which had an internal size of a brick; an open top and a loose, 'frogged ' bottom. The clay was beaten firmly into the mould with a fist and cut off flush with the top of the mould with the aid of a wire similar to a cheese cutter.

The two handles on the ends enabled the operator to rotate them and push the loose base to remove the brick shape. This could not be done with ease without first lining the mould with a releasing agent of coal dust or sand. A steady continuous push with both hands on the loose base revealed an ideal brick shape.

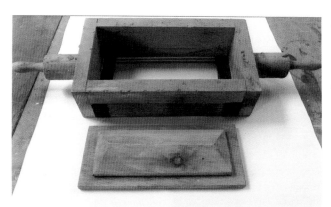

Bricks produced like this were allowed to dry for a period of six weeks in an open sided shed. It was essential to allow a free flow of air around the strategically stacked bricks.

The raw bricks were stacked carefully in the bee hive kiln via the doorway. The stacking was a real art only learned by experience. There had to be plenty of space between and around the bricks to enable air and heat circulation and avoid a large welded blob of unusable bricks.

A brick mould for Clee Hill bricks:- The 'frogged' bottom is held in place with strong elastic strips. The mould filled with clay after being lined with a releasing agent of coal dust or sand; knocked down firmly with the fist and cut off level with the top with a 'cheese' cutter. With the help of the handles the mould is inverted and the loose base pushed out in a continuous movement with both thumbs.

George told me that he stacked about 5,000 bricks at a time for firing and pointed out a small opening at the dome of the kiln which enabled heat to be regulated within.

Close up of one of the kiln's hearths:- A few of the kiln's seven hearths can be seen in the photograph.

The Kiln Door:- Dried bricks are loaded through the door; systematically stacked to allow heat and air circulation.

When all raw bricks were in place the door was bricked up with loose bricks as thoroughly as possible. Then raw clay was thrown at the bricks to plaster them all over and completely seal the doorway.

There are seven hearths around the kiln and three of them can be seen in photograph I. Dry sticks are placed in all seven and lit. Coal is piled on top. Each hearth was constantly fed to gradually build up heat within the kiln. The aim was to reach and maintain a temperature of 900 degrees centigrade. This took a great deal of skill and hard work too. It was necessary to maintain this heat for three days and nights – no mean feat. It was only the considerable experience of people like George who had a good chance of perfecting the finished product.

After three days the kiln was allowed to cool of its own volition.

When it was deemed to be cool enough the doorway seal was broken; the doorway bricks removed to hopefully reveal 5,000 cured bricks. While one kiln was cooling a second one could be stacked to enable continuous production.

I hit it off with dear George immediately because when I first met him he said with a twinkle in his eye, "Is your cousin Joan still alive Alf? By gom 'er wus a good looking 'ooman. When I was eighteen and 'er was about the same I took a real shine to 'er." I was able to tell him then that Joan Pitt whose parents had for many years lived at the Golden Lion public house at Lion Lane, Knowle, Clee Hill, was well and living in Hereford.

I talked a great deal from time to time with Trevor, Neil's Dad who was steeped in country life, the skills of timber conversion, wheel wrighting and carpentry. He never lost the interest in brick making and around the yard he found examples of drainage pipes, ridge tiles and even gravestones which had been made by his predecessors at Oreton. One oddity found he was convinced was a clay pattern for a very early railway line.

Trevor and author outside the beehive brick kiln:- Trevor showing me what he was convinced is a mould for a section of a railway line made in Oreton kiln.

Colin Richards the then Environmental Officer for South Shropshire worked very hard with me and others to make Authorities realise the historical value of Oreton's beehive kiln; probably the only one of its kind remaining in the whole of the Midlands.

With the help of Bridgnorth Council and Shropshire Council and the magnanimous efforts of the Sutton family he secured grant money to avoid the kiln's collapse and have it rebuilt. The procedure was monitored by archaeologist Glynn Barratt a friend, colleague and Trustee of TCHT (Titterstone Clee Heritage Trust).

Around the upper part of the kiln was a linked chain. This was very important because as the kiln was heated up it expanded and this chain avoided any likelihood of the walls collapsing. Trevor told me that this chain had not been designed for this job but had formerly been used in the local coal industry.

Neil has aspirations of firing this only remaining Bee-Hive kiln one day. I do hope this is possible.

Uncle George Sutton was encouraged by Colin Richards to relate his expertise to Acton Scott Historical Working Farm (recently televised in a series The Victorian Farm 2012) and enable it to construct a slightly smaller replica of Sutton's Bee Hive Kiln. This was successfully done and for the benefit of many observers has been fired on more than one occasion producing bricks made and fired to the traditional Clee Hill method. (see author's DVD Up the Lane and Back Again).

Neil took the trouble to measure Oreton's kiln and supply me with the following statistics:- It is about 12 feet high inside to the dome of the roof; is 11 feet inside diameter and the straight inside walls 8 feet. He made a calculation 14,000 bricks could be stacked inside but with adequate gaps about 10,000 could be fired.

Most of the tree growth removed from the Bee Hive kiln:- The safety chain around the top part of the vertical walls has been revealed. When the kiln was heated up during the brick baking process this chain avoided any possibility of expanding walls collapsing. (Cider equipment on left).

All tree growth has been carefully removed:- When doing so it was found that the roof was in a near state of collapse.

Discussing the art of making Clee Hill bricks:- Colin Richards (Right) the then Environmental officer for South Shropshire discussing the manufacture of Clee Hill bricks outside Oreton's Bee Hive kiln with Trevor Sutton.

Oreton's Bee-Hive brick kiln completely rebuilt:-Looking similar to what it must have done when originally made. Note clear hearths .Safety chain missing. Project monitored by Glynn Barratt..

In Titterstone Clee Hills, Industrial History, Everyday Life and Dialect I describe in detail the construction of a farm cart wheel and how to apply a metal band. When I first saw Oreton's Bee Hive kiln not only were cider barrels stored inside it but I noticed a pair of blacksmith's "dogs".

Just outside the kiln is a blacksmith's wheel, metal mounting plate and a ready supply of running water beside it. From my boyhood experiences at home of Dad being a wheelwright I knew how these dogs were used. An assembled cart wheel was positioned on the mounting plate and two people carried a heated, expanded metal hoop with the aid of the dogs.

The metal hoop was carefully positioned over the wheel, knocked into position onto the ash felloed rim with hammers and quickly cooled by pouring cold water onto it from the nearby supply. This made the rim contract, so pulling the wheel felloes and spokes tightly into position and prevented the wheel burning. The fixing of the rim was a real art. It had to be made ' cut and shut'(welded) to be not more than a quarter of an inch longer than the wheel circumference when heated. This enabled easy fitting and adequate shrinkage. Alf cannot thank Neil, Trevor and all the family enough for their help with this special project.

Neil and mother Ann, Wife of Trevor:- Standing outside the Bee Hive kiln at Oreton in 2009. Note the barrels. Of late the kiln has been used to store cider still made by the Sutton Family at Oreton

Blacksmith's wheel mounting plate to enable a metal rim to be fitted:- There is a supply of running water very nearby. Note the lifting metal "dog" being held by Trevor.

Clee Hill Clay Smoking Pipes

Mr and Mrs Harry Parker have been friends for many years, have been on tours with me around the Hills and taken an interest in my lectures and publications.   Imagine my delight when Harold produced the following for me:-

Dr David Higgins is a Honorary Research Fellow at University of Liverpool; a member of the Institute of Field Archaeologies.

David had received many fragments of smoking pipes from Harold and these are the results:-

" Mr and Mrs Harold Parker moved to 7 The Hollies, Clee Hill, Nr Ludlow in 1968 and collected pipes between then and 1980. When examined the group was made up of 43 fragments, comprising 24 bowl fragments (most of which are substantially complete), 18 stems and a mouthpiece. In broad terms almost all of the pipe fragments date from the middle of the seventeenth century with only a few later fragments being present. Three of the bowls have fired to a pale buff colour and another has fired clay adhering all over its surface, which almost certainly indicates that it once formed part of a muffle kiln. A muffle kiln was used by pipe makers to fire their wares and it was constructed of white clay reinforced with previously fired waste pipes. This fragment is important since it indicated that pipes were probably being made on or near this site around 1640 – 1660. There are 13 heel bowls represented, 12 of which date from c 1640 – 1660. One of these has fired into a buff colour and has a crude heart- shaped maker's stamp on the heel.   This has a serrated edge but no clear design, apart from a dot, is visible within the mark itself; others are plain. The rims are generally three quarters or fully milled but none of the bowls are burnished. They exhibit a wide variety of different forms and may well all have been produced in different moulds.. They seem likely to represent a number of different manufacturers operating in or near the Clee Hills at this time and are useful in that they characterise their products. The one later heel date is from 1660 – 1680 and has a circular maker's mark on the bowl facing the smoker.   This reads TG with 2 stars above and one below. The style of this mark is typical of South Shropshire or North Herefordshire and so it must have been produced in this area but the maker is yet unidentified. There are ten spur bowls seven of which also date c 1640 – 1660 including two that have fired to a buff colour.   This is interesting since spur bowls are not generally found over most of Shropshire until the 17th Century.   These seven include the one mentioned above with fired clay adhering, which probably represents a kiln near the site. This example has a particularly small spur and was probably made in the same mould as one of the other examples in the group as with the heel bowl. These pipes are characterised by generally having fully or three quartered milled rims and they are not burnished. None of them is marked. There is one slightly later bowl c 1680 – 1710 and another two fragments of nineteenth century date.   The final bowl is spurless and has a lozenge shaped stem. The bowl has a carination with a band of rose and thistle decoration. The design is produced by William Southorn and Co of Broseley and

Mr and Mrs Harold Parker:-moved to No 7 The Hollies Clee Hill in 1968 from West Bromwich. By wonderful coincidence they found numerous clay pipes in their garden; a most wonderful discovery. I had the pleasure of visiting them in 2014. The old Clee Hill all age school, which the author and his sister attended is on the left hand side when approaching Clee Hill Village from Ludlow direction. Fifty metres above the old school on the right hand side is The Hollies Lane. In the author's day it was known as Andrew's Lane. This was so well known by the pupils because if there was a disagreement between boys during school time they would say, "Right we will settle it across Andrew's Lane after school." We would all congregate and watch the scrap until a winner was declared.

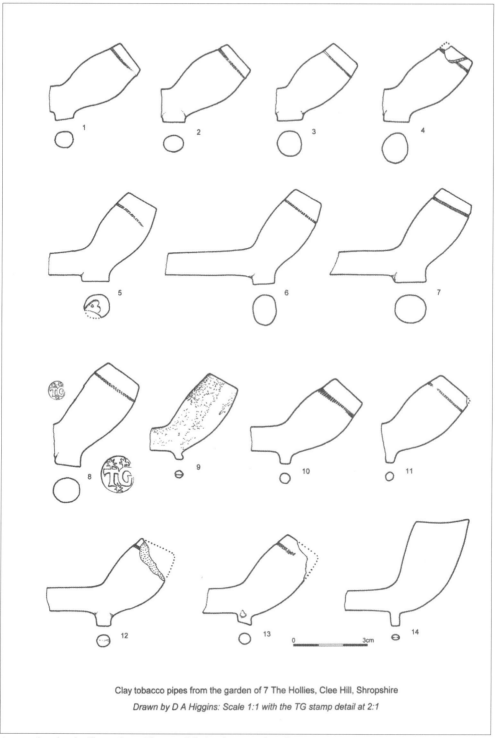

Clay tobacco pipes from the garden of 7 The Hollies, Clee Hill, Shropshire

Drawn by D A Higgins: Scale 1:1 with the TG stamp detail at 2:1

As stated under the illustrations:- They are full size drawings done by D A Higgins as a result of finds in The Hollies Garden Clee Hill. These are a very valuable addition to the industrial history Of Titterstone Clee Hill.

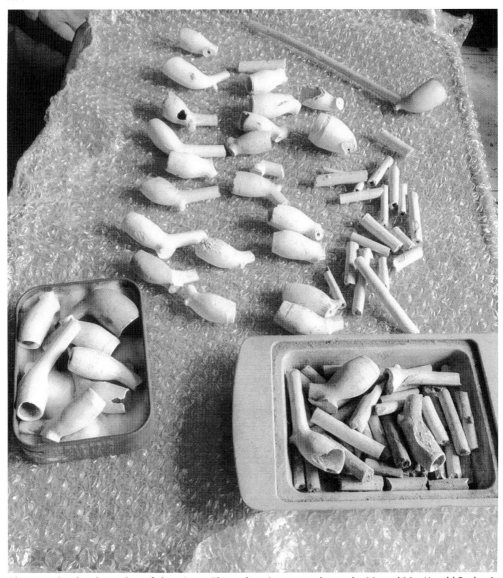

Photograph taken by author of clay pipes:- These clay pipes were dug up by Mr and Mrs Harold Parker in their garden at No 7 The Hollies, Clee Hill. From these Dr David Higgins made his full size sketches. He said there must have been a pipe kiln very near by. They were an invaluable find. The author remembers such pipes being sold in Dhu Stone Inn when he was a boy. They were in cardboard boxes and wrapped in tissue. They had a red tip at the end of the stem. His Dad Mr Richard Jenkins gave the pipes free of charge to customers who purchased twist and pipe tobacco.

dates from the late nineteenth and twentieth century (the firm closed in 1960). The stems are mainly of c17th as is the mouthpiece, which has a simple cut end. All of the stems are plain apart from two, which have milled decoration on them, both of which could have been applied at points where the stems have been mended during manufacture. One has quite a loose spiral of milling while the other is much tighter and acutely angled. This is an interesting assemblage that clearly suggests an intensive period of site use during the middle of the seventeenth century (19 out of 24 bowls). The mid seventeenth century pipes are characterised by plain, un-burnished bowls but milling that extends most of the way round the rim. Spur bowls account for almost of half of this group – a very high proportion for Shropshire. Only one of the mid-seventeenth century examples is marked but all are likely to have been made locally. Fired clay on one of the bowls suggests production on or near this site and these pipes might well provide the first indications of the character of pipe production on the Clee Hills at this time.

Clee Hill Cider

The sudden death of Trevor Sutton from Oreton in 2009 was a great sadness to me personally and an irreplaceable loss to our communities.

Trevor's knowledge of a multitude of rural skills including blacksmithing, wheelwrighting, brick making and hedge pleaching were all passed on to him by his uncle and other family members; all very common in the time of my childhood but what made *him* very special nowadays. In addition he was, with his brother John an excellent cider maker.

For years local farmers brought apples to the Sutton's yard to be processed. They have a mobile press still which the family formerly transported to different farms and carried out the cider making on site.

As a tribute to Trevor the family kindly agreed I could write about and illustrate their truly Shropshire itinerant method of cider making.

A petrol motor is connected by belt drive to a cogged cylinder called a 'hedgehog'. Apples are tipped into a box container above the hedgehog and as this revolves the apples are pushed onto the hedgehog with a specially shaped prod.   As soon as they revolve to the sides of the hedgehog the apples are pulped.

Trevor on the left and brother John on the right:- Trevor has tipped the apples and John is encouraging them to revolve to the sides of the hedgehog. In the background the petrol engine driving the hedgehog pulley is evident.

John pulling the lever operating below the hedgehog:- This makes it engage and crush the apples.

The apple container tilted to expose the hedgehog:- Hedgehog can be seen crushing apples.

A new hedgehog on the right made by Trevor's son Neil in 2011.

Apples crushed, fall through on to a flat shelf:- This is known as pulp. This is when the smell of cider becomes evident.

The pulp is shovelled out and put into a half barrel.

The half barrel being filled with pulp.

When the half barrel has been filled with pulp a strongly woven sack called a 'hair' is placed onto the base of the mobile press. The hairs are specially shaped to fold like an envelope and fit the press base. This is constructed to allow juice to run out through a spout.

Illustrating the cider press:- One hair ready to receive pulp and the press beam held aloft by two vertical strips of timber.

Knowledgeable country folk will recognise that the bed is mounted on reciprocal mowing machine wheels and axle. The wheels of course were essential to allow the press to be towed to any destination.

Trevor placing pulp on the first hair:- Levelling it out ready to fold the hair to position the next one.

Trevor is seen puffing contentedly at his pipe, absorbed in this annual ritual.

Folding the hair:- John and Trevor folding the first hair to enclose pulp; in preparation for the next one.

More apples are pulped by the hedgehog and placed into a number of hairs, each one being carefully folded exactly the same and carefully positioned.

Folding the top hair.

The 'Sutton' cider making process is different from other rural methods in the area. I have made hundreds of ash slats for Mr Jim Franklin, a well known cider maker from Little Hereford. He placed them between each hair; but Trevor and John's method worked well without them.

Props removed and heavy strengthened board with four cross supports is placed on the hairs:-
Bucket and half barrel in place in front of the spout to receive cider juice.

The weight of the board on the hairs begins to make juice ooze from the hairs. Good shot in the photograph of the former reciprocal mower machine wheel beneath the framework.

The first packing piece of timber is placed on top of the special re-inforced board:-Juice beginning to run from the hairs without much compression.

A number of suitable packing pieces of timber are placed on top of the special board:- A sturdy pole is used to rotate each screw on the right and left in turn. Trevor and John are careful to apply the same number of clockwise rotations to each screw to obtain even pressure.

John looking on in satisfaction as the juice begins to pour from the spout as pressure increases.

Between John and Trevor in the background is a barrel waiting to be filled. Far right background is the beautiful , old Bee Hive brick kiln before renovation.

Pressure has been applied:- Copious quantity of apple juice pouring from the hairs.

Author truly surprised to see so much juice being extracted from the hairs.

The reason for positioning a bucket within a half barrel is obvious.

Trevor tipping full bucket into an awaiting cask. This was stored in Bee Hive kiln to mature cider.

When the casks were full they were housed in the old beehive brick kiln. A porous peg was inserted into the vent hole to allow the 'cider' to work and ferment. When the contents settled a solid vent was inserted. This was the same practice that Dad did when all barrels at home in Dhu Stone Inn had been placed on the stillage. When barrels had been jolted about during transportation and heaved onto the stillage their contents was disturbed and created further temporary fermentation.

The engine and belt drive:- John with his back to us is feeding apples into the hedgehog while Trevor is shovelling out the pulp into the half barrel.

Life-long friend, Clee hill 'boy' John Hughes could not resist sampling the "nectar"

The photograph of John Hughes sampling the cider is to me the epitome of contentment. I can really smell the brew when I see that snap.

When all the juice has been extracted the pressure on the hairs is released. Dry pulp is barrowed into a container. Dried pulp mixed with other ingredients makes an excellent animal feed – but care has to be taken. Animals can become completely drunk if they are allowed to consume too much.

Bruce Asbury, whose home used to be the Lady's Finger public house on the Catherton side of Clee Hill often told the amusing story of drunken pigs falling about as a result of eating too many over ripe apples.

I consider myself extremely privileged to have been able to photographTrevor before his passing away,with his brother John to illustrate this particular historical method of producing Clee Hill cider.

At the end of the cider making season the hairs were opened up and spread on a hawthorn hedge. Then as Trevor said, "When frost bites, it reacts on the hairs breaking up the fine residue of pulp within the weaves and with a good shake completely cleans the hairs making them ready for next season's use.

Friend John's expression says it all, "Surri boy; this is klinkin".

Apple pulp removed from the hairs.

John Sutton on the right.Behind on right a barrel being filled. On left general view of cider making equipment and Left background is saw mill, housing a circular saw and timber conversion table.

Neil and his mother Anne, widow of Trevor. This shows the pair making cider for their first time, continuing a wonderful tradition. Neil has successfully run the sawmill engine and another of his aims is to get the timber conversion equipment usable again. Alf is so pleased there is now a good chance of yet another Clee Hill craft being continued.

The Lime Industry / Tours of Titterstone Clee Hills

In early 1960s when I returned to Clee Hills I was disheartened to see an area which during my childhood had been a hive of industry now looking like a lunar landscape. There was desolation; an eerie quietness; no dust and so many discarded remains of industrial past.

Titterstone Clee had an industrial heritage and resources equal to that of Ironbridge – the main difference being Titterstone is a prominent hill seen from miles in every direction whilst Ironbridge is now a gorge. It contained all that made Ironbridge famous. Why not similar fame for Titterstone Clee Hills? It undoubtedly warrants it. I decided to take steps to publicise, promote and enhance my precious home area. They are the only hills in England mentioned on the world famous Mappa Mundi; had been famous for its wide variety of minerals for centuries and in 2013 still well known for dhu stone, one of the best road stones available in Britain.

My Dad knew that Alf Reynolds from The Knowle had worked as a boy in one of our most ancient industries, limestone quarrying and burning. I persuaded local, well known bard and comedian Dennis Crowther to accompany Alf and me, record memories of the industry and Clee Hill's precious dialect (see "Titterstone Clee...." and DVD "Up the Lane and Back again").

Alf told me, like other seams of our "big Mac sandwich", lime had outcrops on various parts of the Hill, some of which had had extensive workings at Oreton and Knowle on the B4214 south of Clee Hill village where he had worked. There were lesser ones at Cornbrook, Gorstley (a play area for us as children known as the Gorsty because of its gorse bushes) and other areas too.

From what he had been told Alf said that Oreton like the Nuvvers at Knowle had existed for at least three centuries. As well as lime burning Oreton had quarried limestone blocks some of which had been used to construct St Mary's Roman Catholic Church on Henley Road, Ludlow(see "Titterstone Clee Hill Everyday Life....." for more information and photographs). It had many small lime burning kilns which I had visited the remains of in recent years, all of which were three day kilns.

Alf knew the Nuvvers area since the age of eleven and reported with pride the association his Reynolds family ancestry connected with that industry.

We approached the Nuvvers area from its north side, immediately below Knowle hamlet, south of Clee Hill village. Here the land suddenly dropped away and as I recorded in "Titterstone Clee Hills..." Alf remembered that in this vicinity there had been a large ash tree nearby which had been sunk a shaft. Attached to the shaft wall there was a metal ladder down which lime workers descended to get to the underground quarry.

He took us down into the wood where he pointed out that his ancestors had quarried limestone in a number of sites. Like the old Titterstone quarries overburden had slipped, overgrown and completely obliterated the quarry faces but the excavations were plainly there for all to see.

Copy taken from my book "Titterstone Clee Hills.....". Alf Reynolds showing me an obsolete lime, charging kiln completely filled with rubble and trees to avoid further animals falling into it and being killed.

Obviously faulting to the north terminated work at that level and Alf took us lower down and deeper into the woodland to show a beautifully constructed arch which he said led into a long tunnel opening up into an underground quarry which enabled the industry to continue.

The industry had its hiccups terminating occasionally and finally finishing in the 1920s. However I recorded in "Titterstone Clees...." that Alf had begun work there at the age of eleven as an errand boy and odd job lad. His main work was scything nettles and thistles to keep areas open and presentable. But; his overriding memory was taking lunch to his father and having to walk through the arch in front of us along the eerie tunnel to the underground quarry faces.

There the tunnel opened out into a considerable working area where the afore mentioned shaft and ladder descended to.

Alf's father spent most of his time taking empty trucks to the faces and returning with full ones. Alf recalled that the tunnel track was railed, uneven between the sleepers and narrow. When he walked along it alone carrying lunch (his father's snappin) he often heard the rumbling of an approaching truck. This frightened the life out of him when he stumbled and fell. Fortunately there were frequent 'escape' recesses which enabled him to pop in and allow trucks to pass.

Nowadays the tunnel has collapsed making entry impossible beyond a few metres. Turning south he took us along a level track which had been man -made to enable quarried lime stone rock to be transported through the woodland on its route to the lime burning kilns.

Tunnel entrance; Note the beautifully constructed arch; probably three hundred years old.

At the end of this truck line Alf brought us to a steep slope. This he said had been a self-acting, railway incline. At its top there had been a wooden drum mounted on two stone pillars. Around the drum was wrapped a wire rope connected to descending and ascending trucks. I was readily able to understand this because I had often watched similar railway systems operating just a few yards away from my home, Dhu Stone Inn (now named Rowan Cottage).

The bottom of the incline opened out to a large, flat area created from spoil. This was where Alf spent much of his young life scything unwanted weeds.

On the southern side of the flat area were two charge kilns. The one on the left was filled with rubbish and scrub and a tree had fallen across it; the roots ripping the kiln top apart and causing much damage. Alf knew this kiln to be of considerable depth and when the industry closed down a horse had fallen into it and was killed. This resulted in the kiln being filled with disused bricks, rubble, and scrub planted to prevent further accidents. To the right he pointed out a significant dip around and in which had grown a number of hawthorn trees. Beneath the dip was the second similar kiln.

Taking us to lower ground he pointed out the entrance to the left hand discharge kiln. Due to the tree damage above a great deal had collapsed but the arched entrance was still in excellent condition.

Further along at that level Alf Reynolds showed us a most wonderful, secret site: a pair of superb ancient arches leading to two tunnels beneath the kiln below the 'dip' he had shown us on the flat open area above. This was as exciting as finding the proverbial secret garden.

Inside the arches were in superb condition. Small stalactites hung from perfectly preserved limestone and dhu stone roofs.

Even in 2013 the levelled track is obvious. Note the considerable piles of removed waste on either side.

Looking down the incline track :- from where the wooden drum was situated, mounted on two stone pillars. The light at the bottom of the incline is where it opened out to a flat area built from spoil.

Arched entrance to the left hand kiln. The author showing Clee Hill school children the three hundred year old arch still in good condition and the collapsed area above caused by tree damage.

Alf described the part these tunnels had played in the industrial process. Low down on the central arch wall there were two discharge holes opening from the kiln above into both tunnels. Horses backed their empty carts into the tunnels. Small lumps of lime were raked out from the bottom of the discharge kiln and loaded into the carts by hand. From here it was transported,   piled in fields and covered with soil to avoid it effervescing; before being spread when convenient as a crop fertiliser.

Other lime was used as mortar for building purposes; more mixed with water to form lime putty for plastering walls and diluted even more to be used as lime wash.   In my childhood all our outside toilets, washhouses and cowsheds were lime washed with this product. Poultry houses infested with red mite were sprinkled with lime powder. If not treated I have seen pullets pecked raw by other birds.

Many of our local squatter's cottage walls were smoothed and plastered with lime putty and it was porous so allowing thick walls to 'breathe'. In recent years modern waterproof finishes have been the norm for interior church and cathedral walls. However there is always a residue of moisture within thick walls and it must be remembered that many of them are two or more feet thick. Modern finishes, after a while bubble and flake off as a result of a change in temperature at different times of year; or heat inside a building drawing moisture to the surface. Architects realising that these thick walls must be allowed to 'breathe' are reverting to the use of traditional lime plaster and washes. History has its uses!

How was the lime stone rock treated and broken down? He described the following process. The kilns were deep enough to project down between the two arches. Into their base was thrown a quantity of dry kindling wood.   This was set alight through the draw holes and a quantity of coal placed on top. When burning steadily the kiln was filled up with blocks of limestone rock.

Alf Reynolds remembered to aid the firing more coal was placed on the limestone when the kiln was about half filled. More limestone was transported to the lime kiln until it was filled. Heat was maintained and as a result the limestone gradually disintegrated to lime as we would recognise it being spread on fields today.

Model section of a discharge kiln made by the author. It was made initially for illustration in a video entitled, "Up the Lane and Back Again" produced for the Author by his friend John Hughes .

Both kilns were kept in use, one cooling off as the other one was being filled. Alf was unable to tell me how long the process took other than , " a considerable time".

He continued that a railway track ran from the incline to each kiln allowing full trucks to be easily tipped. He mentioned there were other kilns within the Nuvvers but these two were where he had been involved.

In 1973 I had a series of black and white slides made from old black and white photographs given to me by miners and quarry men. This sparked me to do further recordings of the industrial heritage for our first intended book, "Titterstone Clee Hills.....". The cost of possible publication was frightening but Round Table friends Harry Conod and John Crofts encouraged me to begin illustrated talks and tours of the Clees to promote publicity and the area.; because no grants or financial help was available. After ten years collating information and 300+ subscribers I was able to publish "Titterstone Clee Hills, Every Day Life, Industrial History and Dialect" in 1983. Unexpectedly it became an instant success and I was contacted by Colin Richards, Environment Officer for South Shropshire. With the owner Ken Oram we visited the Nuvvers damaged kiln. Colin obtained some funding for contractors to cut up and remove the fallen tree which had caused extensive damage creating a collapse to the draw tunnels below and damage to the kiln mouth too.

Taken in 1970s for author's Book "Titterstone Clee Hills......":-Not only does it show the tunnels to the discharge kiln but also the height of the kiln too. Small stalactites hang from the lime block and dolerite supported roof.

2013 Photograph taken by Author :-of mouth of the same discharge kiln tunnels.

Damaged Kiln fenced off. Damage created beyond it by a fallen tree. Remains of the cut up tree in the background.

Colin informed us from what he had seen of the industrial complex that it had been a much bigger enterprise than he would have first assumed. He also stressed how local industries had been dependent on each other for success. Local bricks had been used to re-enforce tops of kilns and pit shafts and local coal for firing. He felt Nuvvers could even be three months kilns unlike most local ones which had been three day kilns.

Determined to prove or disprove Colin's theory, the owner of the Nuvvers Ken Oram, friend and video specialist John Hughes and I decided to try and clear the left hand kiln to discover its depth and shape.

Having no lifting gear we resorted to hand methods. An extension ladder was placed across the top of the kiln and covered with scaffolding planks. We hacked and cleared brambles and bushes and with ropes and buckets began the laborious task of hauling out a large quantity of bricks. John had the most back breaking task of hauling full buckets up for tipping. As we cleared, a second extension ladder was used for Ken and me to descend and continue digging and bucket filling. The tremendous amount of clever construction, became apparent. Beautiful blocks had been positioned in a circular, progressive wall, topped near ground level with local bricks.

As we got deeper the kiln narrowed until its shape resembled a huge ice cream cone with a gradual vertical curve. In places the wall blocks had fallen creating unstable walls.

Over a period of three months of working one whole day each week Ken and I found ourselves in a confined space not more than a yard across and at a depth of more than twenty feet. There were signs of instability above and slight movements. We believed we were not more than a yard from the draw holes; but; we had to reluctantly abandon our dig.

Although we had nearly given ourselves heart attacks we were convinced that we had proved Colin's theory that these two kilns at the Nuvvers were indeed three month kilns. You may notice that I have used the spelling of my childhood for the Novers as "Nuvvers".

Colin surveying our digging to date and the pile of bricks removed:- He pointed out the black specs in the bricks reminding us that coal had been used in their production as a releasing agent.

Digging out a kiln at Nuvvers:- John Hughes sitting on scaffold planks ready to haul up full buckets of rubbish.

Ken Oram owner of the Nuvvers and Alf Jenkins over 20 feet down. Note the walls from which lime blocks had fallen creating instability. Ken was a wonderful supporter and friend of TCHT.

We had to give up due to danger above. Bucket and tools in place at the bottom of the kiln.

Tours of Titterstone Clees

My lectures to promote the Titterstone Clees began in the 1970s and this enthused many groups to ask for a tour to actually look at important sites of industry and heritage. Demand from all sorts of societies escalated. Tours times varied from half, to a whole day or on occasions two days. Some historical societies from as far away as Birkenhead stayed in the area to see a slide show during an evening then take two whole days to be conducted around. Over the last forty years I have had the pleasure of conducting literally hundreds of people to experience the exceptional industrial heritage of our area. Organisations have included Ladies Groups and Luncheon Clubs, WIs ; YFCs; Round Table; Probus; Rotary; Masonic Lodges; History Societies; The Black Country Society; Birmingham University; Shropshire County Council Staff; London University and Birkenhead Industrial Society. By using a combination of mini bus and private cars it is possible to visit as many as fifteen sites; arrange a picnic or pub lunch at mid day and accommodate all ages. We can claim to have promoted Titterstone Clees popularity to a very large number of visitors resulting in five reprints of our first Book, "Titterstone Clee Hills......" With the help and expertise of friend John Hughes we have produced two DVDs namely "Up the Lane and Back Again" and "Discover South Shropshire's Titterstone Clee Hills" as well as a CD, "Wagons to Wheelbiers". In addition we have produced two books about life in North Herefordshire. I have been asked so many times "What will happen when you cease to be able to take groups?" The most important legacy for Ann and me is to make a written record of as much as we are able, to preserve our life's experiences of this wonderful area. Marjorie Hammond, ex head teacher of Clee Hill School has always been enthusiastic to pass on our heritage to pupils by encouraging them to experience ideas and hear stories of their ancestors.

Clee Hill Primary School Pupils: Traversing the man made railway track from the Lime quarry Tunnel

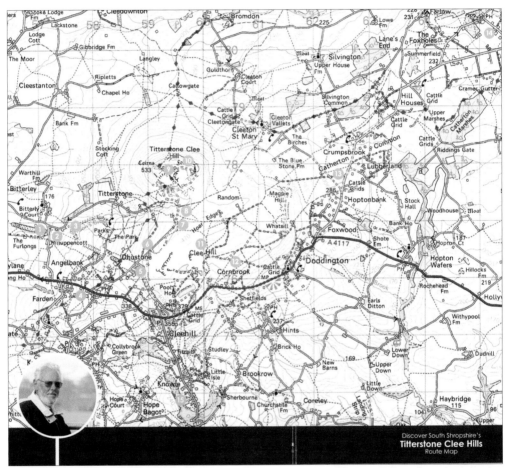

OS map which is included with our DVD, "Discover South Shropshire's Titterstone Clee Hills,":- It shows the major sites around the Hills and we endeavour to visit all of them. Two are on private land necessitating permission to visit.

Clee Hill children at the entrance to a tunnel leading to a Lime Quarry; Taken at the Nuvvers.

Brimfield Border Quilters' Society Members: They include friends Marion Basett (Left) and Ann Harris (Right).

Brimfield Border Quilters decided to use Clee Tour to produce collages with numerous materials.

Collage of Brimfield Border Quilters:- Depicting their tour of Clee Hills.

Border Quilters wonderful collage:- Includes Three Forked Pole ;Overhead Railway; and Brick Kiln.

Ann and I were absolutely delighted to be presented with the two illustrated collages by Brimfield Borders Quilters. The Collage of visited sites is indeed very special

2006:- Part of a Clee Hill group tour:-L to R Val Simpsom; Lorraine Wilkinson; Violet Proxton and Alf Jenkins

John Pitt's Group (2008)

Part of Ludlow Masonic Lodge No 611:- 2008. One of the last photographs I was able to take of Trevor Sutton (right).

Ludlow Museum Course. (2009):-Taken at Oreton Brick kiln. Note mobile cider press on left.

2009 Kinsham Historical Society Tour

2009:- Jan Vail's Clee Hill Group:-Neil Sutton, Son of Trevor back left. The cottage behind was constructed with bricks made in the Sutton Kiln situated in the yard opposite.

2009:- Shropshire County Council Tour:- Colin Richards (Environmental Officer) far left. Titterstone Quarry in the background.

2010 Wistanstow Ladies on tour. In the background Titterstone and the sign pointing to Bedlam.

2010. Alvis Cumming's Group:- Near to the viewing point at Dhu Stone Quarry.

2010. AONB Staff and associates tour.(Area of Outstanding Natural Beauty) On the floor of Titterstone Quarry.

*Presenting copies of Author's
book "Titterstone Clee Hill..."
to pupils of excellence at Clee
Hill Primary School awards
and sports day.*

Dialect

Since the heyday of Clee Hill's Coal Industry men have come to this area from all over England and Wales to seek work. This influx was expedited with the development of the railway system. Families brought with them industrial phrases which became imposed on our South Shropshire dialect to such an extent that Clee Hill folk were not readily understood in Ludlow, just five miles away.

I wrote about our dialect in some detail in "Titterstone Clee Hills......" and included a glossary of words commonly used during my childhood. The dialect and its origins is a comprehensive study in itself and I have broadcast programmes from Birmingham's BBC Studios about it and had Degree students interview me about 'Clee Hill Talk' in recent years.

Due to the fact that our local dialect was becoming almost obsolete, in 2006 I contacted Miss Marjorie Hammond , the Head teacher of Clee Hill Primary School and discussed with her the possibility of my writing the Nativity in Clee Hill Dialect. The idea had been given to me by a friend who had seen such a play performed in Black Country Dialect. Due to many working people moving back and forth between the two areas I discovered there were many words in common, although the pronunciation was different .

Being a lady of local origin Marjorie recognised a great number of the words in my script but doubted whether the children would be able to tackle them . However we decided to pilot some ideas by sending play parts home with them. To our great pleasure we discovered that older members of families especially grandparents were entirely at 'home' with the words; so with Marjorie's encouragement I ploughed ahead.

I produced the following and as a result of much hard work by Marjorie, her staff and the pupils a very successful Christmas production took place at Clee Hill School in 2006 to very large, appreciative audiences.

In the following script I have tried to help interpretation by inserting the following over the top of appropriate words. Short vowel sounds:- ˘ Long vowels:- ‒ Elongated vowels:- —. I have tried to spell words phonetically to assist pronunciation.

The Nativity

Narrator:- Thĕyēr wŭs a wench called Mary and 'er wŭs left tŭ clān the ĕs/ole. All of a sudden the mĭstle lifted and the parlour wŭs lit up. Er spun round and thĕyēr wŭs a yūkin stōndin by the winder ŏŏth a light round is yūd. Er wŭs frĭttĕnĕd tŭ dyŭth and ŏmŭst fell in the fĭnder.

Mary:- Ŏŏ bĭst thēē? Thēē dĭstnŭ ŏŏf give me the collies.

Angel Gabriel:- Dŭ be scāyered. I binnŭ gwăn tŭ ert thŭ. My name's Gabriel. I'm an angel thēē nŏst.

Mary:- Thēē bĭstnŭ bĭst?

Gabriel: I bē ; and I've come tŭ tell thēē sŭmmuŭt.

Mary:- Ō āst thēē?

Narrator:- 'Cause er thought this wŭs a queer ŏw dya do.

Gabriel:- Thēē bĭst gwăn tŭ ave a băbby.

Narrator:- Sŭrrĭ that shook er and er stāyered at im and said:-

Mary:- Dă talk daft. Thēē bĭst off thy yŭd. I bĭnnă mŏrrĭd yŭt.

Gabriel:- That dŭnnă mĕk no ŏdds. If God sĕz thēē bĭst gwăn to 'ave a băbby – thēē bĭst – its curtains. And thēē bĭst gwăn tŭ call 'im Jāsŭs.

Narrator:- Mary wŭs flummoxed so the angel saidn:-

Gabriel:- I'll tell thēē sŭmmŭt else an' all. Thēē bĭstnŭ the only one whose gwăn to. Thy cŭsant Elizabeth's 'avin' one an' all, and ers an auld 'ŏŏman.

Mary:- Well if thēē sĕz so – that's it. I cŏnnă do nothing about it; but my financy 'ŏŏl be all ĕspled.

Narrator:- When 'ēēd gwŭn Mary sat in the chāyĕr. 'Ĕr wŭs a bit out of sărts see. But! ătter a bit 'er got 'er yŭd round it and thought 'ĕrd gŏŏ tŭ see Elizabeth. So 'ĕr sŏŏbled 'ĕr fĕĕs, put on 'ĕr Sundays and went off tŭ Juda. When ĕ got thāyer Elizabeth wŭs lāning on the wicket and when'ĕr sĭd Mary 'ĕr shouted:-

Elizabeth:- Sŭrrĭ; ĭnt I glad tŭ see thēē; but thēē shouldnă 'ave trēĕpsed to see we in thy stăăt.

Mary:- An angel came and sĭd mŭ and saidn I be gwăn tŭ 'av a băbby in December.

Narrator:- Thăy went in and Elizabeth pŭt the kettle on and mĕĕd a cup a tāy. 'Ĕr saidn tŭ Mary that 'ĕr ōde chap Zecharias didnŭ believe 'ĕr when 'ĕr tode 'ĭm 'ĕr wŭs gwăn tŭ 'ăve a băbby.

Elizabeth:- 'Ē couldnŭ săăy nŭthin. 'Ē cŏnnă say nŭthĭn even 'ătter a wĭk.

Narrator:- Mary's fancy mŏn wŭs called Joseph. When Mary tōde 'ĭm about the băbby 'ē dĭdnŭknow what tŭ mĕk on it.

Joseph:- Thy mother 'ŏŏl give thēē some chŏllŏp. 'Ĕr'll say, "It's thy fault. I'll bŭzz thy ear 'ōle." And; the curtains 'ŏŏl be flappin frŭm 'ēre tŭ Bedlam. It ĭnnă no lŏffin matter Mrs.

Narrator:- Any road 'ē didnŭ get really ĕspled, but went up the 'ŏŏden ŭns tŭ 'ave a kip. An angel căăm tŭ 'im in a dream and saidn:-

Angel:- Dŭthēē get ĕspld 'ŏŏth Mary about this băbby. Just remember its God's son 'ĕrs 'avin. 'Is năăm 'ŏŏl be Jāsŭs. Somebody's got tŭ 'ave 'im or 'ēē wŭnna get bărn and God's pŭcked thy Mary. So get mŏrrid bŭttĭ. There ĭnna nŭthin tŭ get wĕrrited about.

Narrator:- Sŏŏn ătter thăăy wŭn spliced.   Thăăy lived in a plăăc called Nazareth.

Joseph popped in fer some snappin and saidn tŭ Mary:-

Joseph:- I've 'ad a sŭmmŭns frŭm the tax mŏn.; and that Caeser sez wēēn got tŭ gŏŏ tŭ wēĕr we wŭn reared tŭ be taxed. So wench, wēēn 'ad tŭ trēĕpse all the wăăy tŭ Bethlehem next wĭk.

JOURNEY

Narrator:- Mary cut a fēōw sandwiches and packed two skyŏmucks a căăk and some ŏpples; then măăd a bottle of cold tāy; (thăy didnŭ know about thermoses see) and cooked a fēōw rashers of fat bĕĕcon. Jospeh got the donkey sărted, pŭt Mary on 'is back and toddled off.

Joseph:- Cheer up Mrs. It inna far surri. Thee cŭst see the lamps of Bethlehem down theyre.   Wēē'n soon 'ave some kip. I wŭnna be sorri neither. I cŏnna stŏnd this sand in my sŏndals.

Narrator:- Joseph knocked on the door of an inn when they got into town. The inn keeper appeared.

Jospeh:' Ăst thee got a spēĕs whāyre we cŭn kip surri?

Inn Keeper:- No I annu. Sorri butti. I cŏnna 'elp thă. Wēēm 'aving 'ŏŏth all these newcomers come fer the tax mŏn. Thăăm kippin everywhāyre.

Narrator:- The next inn wŭs the săăm but Jospeh wŭs desprĭt and showed it.

Joseph:- Ăsnŭ thēē got any wāer we cŏn kĭp? My Mrs is out theyre on a donkey, AND 'ers gwăn tŭ 'ave a băbby afor lŭng. Thēēst 'ad tŭ do sŭmmŭt.

Narrator:- The inn keeper scratched his yŭd and saidn-

Innkeeper:- I've got an idea. Wēēn clāned the cow'ŭs and stĕĕble atter tāy, so it inna mucky. If I shifts the 'ŏsses and our camel thee cŭst gŏŏ in thāyre.

Narrator:- Joseph didnu bother tŭ ask Mary. 'Ē wŭs so plāzed.

MANGER

Narrator:- In the night sǔmmǔt 'appened. Mary shouted:-

Mary:- Joe

Joseph:- Is thāyre sǔmmǔt up or sǔmmǔt?

Mary:- The bǎbby's 'ere.

Narrator:- So as the Bible says, "they wrapped him in swaddling clothes and laid him in a manger." The inn keeper came in ǒǒth 'is Mrs and gǐd Mary some milk. 'Er wǔs real plāāzed. They thought Jāsus wǔs a bǒstin little bǎbby.

Inn Keeper:- Thēēst better come in and 'ave a noggin tǔ wet the bǎbby's yǔd.

Narrator:- So 'ē did. The Inn Keeper's Mrs tōde everybody; but wǎrned 'ǔm:-

Inn Keeper's Wife:- (To the crowd in the Inn) Āy you lot, thāyrs a 'ǒǒman in the cowus an' 'ers 'ad a bǎbby. 'Er needs tǔ get 'er yǔd down. So shut thy larrup or thēē bǐst out.

UP IN THE HILLS

Narrator:- It wǔs a starry night. Up in the hills thāyre wǔn some shepherds looking ǎtter their shǐp. It wǔs a bit chert so thǎy wǔn hǔtched up by a fire. Thāyre dogs wǔn wětchin whilest the shepherds 'ǎd some fǐttle and a fag. Suddenly the sky lit up like bonfire night and an angel popped up. Thǎy wǔn frǐttened tǔ dyǔth.

Angel:- Thēē bǐst a rum bunch. I bǐnna gwǎn tǔ 'ěrt thu. I got sǔmmǔt important tǔ tell thǔ. There's a bǎbby bǐn bǎrn in Bethlehem. 'Is name is Jāsus and 'ēs God's Son. Thēēst better gǒǒ and 'ǎve a gwaup at 'ǐm. 'Ēs in a stable lying in a bǒǒzi

BETHLEHEM

Narrator:- The shepherds went down the lěsǔs into Bethlehem and kept on about them angels.

Shepherd 1:- Fancy angels comin tǔ see the likes ǒ' we. We inna muchers in Bethlehem. We ǎnnǔ got much clout. We ǎnnǔ got a klět between us..

Shepherd 2:- It wǔn a good tune them ǎngels sung. I cǒnnǎ remember it all but thǎy saidn summut like, "Glory tǔ God in the Highest."

Shepherd 3:- When we gets wǔm wēn 'ǎd tǔ put it down on a slab o' stǒn.

Narrator:- They must 'ǎve done – otherwise we wouldnǔ 'ǎve known about it.

CAROL – WHILE Shepherds.

Narrator:- Any wǎy they kěm into town and thǎy wǔn a bit flǔmmoxed.

Shepherd 1:- It's all right 'ǐm sǎǎyin wēēn find a bǎbby in a bǒǒzi; but thāyres cowǔses and stǎǎbles all over the plǎǎce. We could be 'ǔntin fěr wǐks.

Shepherd 2:- Why dǔstnǔ thēē stop moanin. Two on us ǒǒl 'ǎve a gwǒǒp this side and you two 'ǎve a gander over that un.

Shepherd 3:- It ǐnnǔ much good lookin at cowǔses whāyre the doors bǐn shut.

Shepherd 1:- No; and if thāyres a bǎbby thāyre, thǎǎn sure tǔ 'ave a lantern.

Narrator:- They 'ěard thāyre buttǐ whistle, and they fǔn stěěble built in a cave. One whispered:-

Shepherd 2:- Dǔnnǎ měk a clatter. Wēēn be 'ēre.

STABLE

Mary:- Come in.

Narrator:- The shepherds take off thāyer 'ăts and go in on tip toe.

Shepherd 1:- Ŭw bĭst Mrs? An ăngel tōde us tŭ come and 'ăve a look at thy băbby.

Narrator:- Mary beckoned them in and smiled broadly.

Joseph:- 'Ēre 'ē is sŭrrĭ. Come and 'ăve a look. 'Ē's a real klinker. But! dŭnnă thēē brēathe on 'ĭs fēĕc.

Narrator:- The shepherds knelt down on thāyer knees and gyŏŏpped.

Shepherd 1:- Sŭrrĭ ĭnt 'ē tiny!

Shepherd 2:- Ănt 'ă got little dŏnnies.

Shepherd 3:-Course 'ē's tiny yŭ daft yăpputh. 'Ē's new ĭnt 'ē?

Shepherd 1:- I knows that.

Shepherd 4:- But thēē dŭstnŭ expect God tŭ be a little 'ŭn dŭst.

CAROL:- AWAY IN A MANGER

Narrator :- The shepherds turned to gŏŏ.

Shepherd 1:- I sĭd 'ĭm smile.

Shepherd 2:- No thēē dĭstnŭ. It wŭs wind.

Narrator:- But thăy wŭnnă sure. While all this wŭs gwăn on, three wise kings was in the country looking at the stars. One pŭt down 'ĭs telescope and hŏllered:-

King 1:- Āye you lot. Come 'ēre quick. I've sĭn a star as wŭnna thāyer afor and sŭrri ĭnt 'ē a big ŭn.

King 2:- Thēē bĭst right bŭttĭ.

King 3:- I bet it's the one ŭz 'ŏŏl tell us whāyer that new king's bĭn bărn.

Narrator:- Thăăy checked up and it wŭs. They journeyed to Jerusalem and came tŭ the palace – because of course that's whāyer thăăy expected tŭ find a king.

PALACE

Narrator:- King 1 knocks on the dōwĕr.

Sentry:- Ŏŏ bĭst theēē? O thēē bĭst kings. What dŭst thēē wănt?

King 2:- Is the king in bŭttĭ?

Sentry:- 'Ăf a mō I'll 'ăve a gănder

Narrator:- The King's name wŭs 'Ērod and 'ē wŭs in.

Sentry:- Thāyer's three kings 'ēre tŭ see thēē.

Ērod:- Oh! Whĕyĕr?

Narrator:- Ērod 'ăd the collies when the sentry saidn thăy wŭn outside. But 'ē saidn:-

Erod:- Thēē cŏstnŭ 'ave kings stŏndin on the door step. Get 'ŭm in.

Narrator:- Kings enter.

Ērod:- Well 'ŏw bist? Good tŭ see thŭ. What dŭst thēē wănt?

King 1:- We be lookin fĕr a new king as wēēn 'ĕrd 'ē's bin bărn and we wondered if 'ē wŭs 'ēre?

Ērod:- No 'ē ĭnnŭ 'ēre. But! if thēē claps thy eyes on 'ĭm, give me the wink and I'll gŏŏ and 'ave a gănder at 'ĭm mĭ sĕn.

Kings:- Right ō Ērod. So lŭng.

Narrator:- The kings went on thãyĕr way and Ĕrod saidn:-

Ĕrod:- That's a right 'ŏw dya do. Thãyĕr's only room fĕr one king 'ēre and that's me thēē nŏst.   When I knows whãyĕr this băbby is, I'll 'ăv 'ĭm killed.

Narrator:- The Kings went on thãyĕr wăăy and the big star stopped over the plăăs whãyĕr Jāsus wuŭs. And thay fun 'im; not in a palace but in a manger.

THE MANGER

Narrator:- The kings went in quietly and knelt down and in turn gave little Jāsus gold, frankincense and myrrh.

Narrator:- Mary looking so plăăzed:-

Mary:- Thank yō kings. Thăăm lovely presents. But! if thēē dŭstnŭ mind I'll kip 'ŭm in mĭ bottom drōwer until 'ē's a yŏŏkin.

Narrator:-The kings took off their crowns and went out backŭts. They didnŭ wănt tŭ see Ĕrod, cŏs thăy thought 'ē wŭs a terrible bloke. So thăy went wŭm another wăăy 'cause thăăy didnŭ wăănt 'ĭm tŭ kill little Jāsus

THE END

Snippets from Wellington Journal; Church Stretton Advertiser; Ludlow Advertiser;

With gratitude to Alan Brisbourne.

1 June 1867:- Clee Hills. Strike...amongst men employed at the stone breaking machine at the Dhu Stone works in consequence of a reduction of 2d per ton being made. Through the strike there are about 40 or 50 men thrown out of work. It is thought men will in a few days go in to work again at the former rate per ton.

15 June 1867:- Clee Hills Club anniversary of CH Benefit Society at the Club Room, Crown Inn, Knowbury.... led by Leintwardine brass band, marched to St Paul's Knowbury for sermon by Rev JB James...then visited houses.. and returned to Club Room for dinner of hosts Mr and Mrs Bowen...

22 June 1867:- Clee Hill boy drowned. On Saturday, little Charles Bowen 2, son of John Bowen, Crown Inn, Knowbury was missed from the house. A search was instantly made and the poor little fellow was discovered by his mother in an old cistern....HTW (Weyman, solicitor, Ludlow) inquest at the Crown.. jury verdict Accidentally drowned.

28 November 1868:- *Jasper Moore MP (late Jasper Moore's Grandfather) sitting MP for S Shrops...who loses his seat at election...no thanks to the intimidation of voters by the hired thugs of Clee Hill)*

(Church Stretton) Polling. Monday being the day fixed for polling the votes of district, the town at an early hour began to fill with electors and others intent on a general holiday. The shops were all closed and inhabitants warmly engaged in the exciting business of the day.   For some hours the street in front of the polling booths were filled with parties waiting for admission to record their votes. ... and by 12pm the majority of voters had polled. It was expected that Col. Corbett in this district would head the poll... Corbett C 340, Moore L 278....Herbert C 257. It was generally believed and hoped that the Liberal and useful member JM would be successful even by parties who voted with the assistance of the screw, for the Conservative Candidates....and when the state of the poll was known, the excitement was intense and there were but few who did not express surprise and dissatisfaction at the loss of the best rep which S Shropshire has had for some years. The Conservative trick succeeded well and great numbers of electors who split their votes not expecting such a result may now see the error of the system, and lay defeat at their own doors. To be openly defeated among so many friends and supporters is a lasting disgrace to S Shropshire.

The weather throughout the day was fine and but for the unfortunate disturbances created by a mob of lower class all would have passed off well. Soon after 3 pm however signs of riotous conduct were observed, the smashing of the Conservative committee room windows, and those of the CS Hotel, was wantonly indulged in, and huge stones, glass bottles etc were thrown with great force through the windows into the rooms thus rendering them unsafe for the occupants. Nor was this conduct confined to the destruction of property for numbers of gentlemen were grossly assailed and assaulted, their clothes torn and besmeared with mud, many having to make their escape good by stealing away through the back premises and others by taking refuge in the hotel, which was guarded by police. The greatest confusion and excitement prevailed throughout the day, and about dusk the police very prudently cleared the public houses and marched the mob (which by this time had greatly diminished)out of the town. . Order was then restored.   The hotel company's windows having been specially insured, the expensive plate glass of which they are all composed, will be made good. It is much to be regretted that the names of very respectable parties are associated as having tendered bribes and otherwise incited the commission of the wanton mischief. The declaration of the pole took place on Wed morning 12pm. Mr Moore (JM) the defeated candidate accompanied by many of his friends and supporters, arrived at the hustings at the time fixed where he waited more than half an hour for the arrival of the sheriff and successful candidates who at length came up, **followed by about 300 hired roughs from the neighbourhood of Clee Hills.** JM had previously requested his supporters not to indulge in 'Hurrahs' for him as it might create a disturbance from parties who were opposed to him....

3 February 1877. Clee Hill Accident. On Wed, when men working, a large stone fell suddenly from top of the quarry injuring Edward Hughes working nearby. He was taken home and contractor Mr Elijah Wright went to Ludlow for medical help and returned Dr Southern who dressed wounds. Progressing.

16 June 1877. Clee Hill...HTW Inquest... on body of Mary Edwards five months, inquest at Clee Stanton Gate, Mr Dodson foreman.

16 June 1877. Clee Hill fatal stabbing... labourer Charles Hodgkiss of Little Hereford, been drinking with Edmund Williams at Victoria Inn when quarrelled.. blows and left Inn...When near Shibbery Lane, quarrelled again during which Hodgkiss attacked Williams with clasp knife... Williams managed to reach home and his wounds were attended by Dr Sweet of Tenbury.. Hodgkiss went to a cottage and said what he had done. Conveyed to Burford Police Station. Williams died on Wed.

23 June 1877. Clee Hill stabbing (above) ...inquest HTW held at Golden Cross Inn on Edmund Williams... witnesses said been haggling over pint of ale...Hodgkiss had run off and caught by police... Prisoner said he 'would swing for it'... He was sorry for his wife and child. Jury returned verdict of wilful; murder... prisoner committed to Salop Assizes.. At PS at Tenbury.. an arrangement for the transaction of Shrops and Worcs business. Great excitement prevailed... and crowd gathered to see prisoner, appeared a quiet, inoffensive youth. Repeat of evidence....Prisoner saying it was in self defence to having his brains knocked out with a stone that he pulled his penknife out...(sounds as if Williams was a bully). Committed by Bench on Manslaughter charge to Salop Assizes.

25 August 1877. Clee Hill rejoicing at Granite Company Works....A very large gathering on Wed for company recently purchased business property of the Clee Hill Colliery Company and proprietors gave substantial tea to all work people of the two concerns in a tent on the common.   300 men and wives sat down to tea provided by Mr EW Askey, after sports of various kinds including donkey and pony races, pole climbing etc. The Clee Hill Band under Mr Martin played during the afternoon and at the public meeting held after tea, when Mr Thomas Roberts senior member of the firm presided. Partners listed... and resident manager Mr Yates, company present of 400. Stirring speeches rendered to trade of the Clee Hills and neighbourhood.

8 September 1877. Clee Hill ...fire in large hay rick of Mr Small at Hilluponcote Farm...lost rick but saved another large rick adjoining.

22 September 1877. Clee Hill Wesleyans....new minister Rev FH Pendrith preached ...etc...school under new master Mr JJ Phillips has much increased of late. Miss Small presided at harmonium, Mr Charles Hammond played the violin and Mr Samuel Small the bass viola. At each service a great number unable to gain admittance....Tea meeting on Tues held in school and public meeting after... Chair taken by Mr James Yates, deputy manager of the Clee Coal and Stone Company... The present chapel is in a most dilapidated state and friends are trying to get a new one.

20 October 1877. Clee Hill ..harvest at Bitterley Church....texts, wreaths, moss, fern and berries had pleasing appearance. The pulpit adorned with rich corn and in the chancel window stood a neat sheaf of wheat and also at each side of the front entrance of the church. Sermon by Rev J Walcot of Bitterley...efficient choir.. collection in aid of parish expenses.

25 May 1878. Clee Hill death of Emily Bissall, 12, found dead in bed...inquest at the Oak Inn, before dep coroner Mr T Griffiths, jury returned verdict 'died by the visitation of God'.

25 May 1878. Bitterley Clee Hill.. fatal accident... to Thomas Duce 44, a labouring man killed in stone quarry at Cleeton. He was getting stone with John Purslow when a fall of rubbish took place and both men covered in debris. Purslow extricated himself and with another pulled Duce out but dead. Inquest at school house, Cleeton, HTW,...Accidental death.

31 August 1878. Clee Hill... the new Wesleyan Schools, foundation stone laid last Sat for Sunday and day school...procession of children headed by Clee Hill Brass Band under Mr Martin...marched to large office of Granite Stone Company, and also Mr C Adkin residence, then to site of new schools. First stone laid by Mr Thomas Roberts manager for and senior partner in Granite Company who put £20 on it. Two ladies also put £15 on the same stone, 6 other stones were laid afterwards, on each at least £10 placed. Then came the pleasing sight of children laying bricks and placing sums of 2 to 5 shillings. The total sum amounted to £150. After, tea in tent in field next to Victoria Inn. Tea provided by Mrs Whittaker. Meeting held afterwards... addresses. Following day 3 sermons preached. In tent.. amount raised to £180.

23 August 1879. Clee Hill accident in sand hole... to Benjamin Turner, in employ of Mr Bate, Golden Cross Inn. Turner was working in a hole with Mr Bate jnr when gave way and buried Turner. Rescued after 10 minutes by Mr Bate. Injuries little although clothing damaged.

23 August 1879. Clee Hill excursion of employees of the Clee Hill Dhu Stone Company, had annual excursion, destination Liverpool. A special train had been chartered under the direction of Mr David Lewis, excursion of GWR. Start made from Ludlow at 6.40am and train arrived Shrewsbury after 8...onward via Wrexham, Gresford, Hooton, Bromsborough, Spital, Rock Ferry to Birkenhead for 11.30. Passing on to Woodside ferry, two of the company's boats were in waiting to convey the passengers over to Liverpool. Arriving there the duties of cicerone were entrusted to Mr C Bright... who took the party over the principal places of interest in the town. Afterwards by the kindness of the chief officer they visited and inspected the large ocean steamer Adriatic, lying in the river.

They then visited New Brighton by steamer and had a very pleasant trip returning to the landing stage for Birkenhead where they left at 7.25 arriving in Ludlow at 11.20...delighted with their day.

7 May 1881. Clee Hill Accident. On Monday last, the new incline from Bitterley to Titterstone was opened and just as a load of stone was about to be started from the quarry at the top, the hook at the end of the wire rope connected with the waggons snapped and the waggons descended with rapid velocity till they reached the 'turn out' when the whole of the waggons left the rails and were smashed to atoms, the contents being hurled in all directions. Two children were in a field adjoining the incline and when they saw the waggons descending with such frightful rapidity were so terror struck that they held fast by the fencing and were afraid to move. Some of the stones from the trucks hurled past them with terrible force. Fortunately there were no injuries sustained by anyone.

7 May 1881. Clee Hill Foundation of New Prim Meth Chapel... for long while, efforts have been made to find a site and finally last autumn negotiations concluded for a piece of land on the roadside from Angel Bank to Bitterley. To be built of brick, with blue brick string courses in front with ornamental cornice. The window arches are to be of blue brick, the window frames of iron... etc...to accommodate 100 and will cost £200. Plans of Mr B Weale, Ludlow. On Wed last the memorial stones were laid....hymns and prayers... stones being laid with donation by Mrs Key (Long House), Mrs Howell (Bitterley), Mr Weale, Rev J Pickwell. Tea meeting afterwards in barn at Long House. (Author says Chapel was closed and sold in 2013).)

18 June 1881. Clee Hill visit of Manchester scientific students Association... under Messrs RT Burnett, FGS and G Yates FSA. They were conducted from Ludlow by Mayor Mr Thomas Roberts, MD of Clee Hill Granite Company...to inspect company's quarries and famous basalt. The outcrop of the famous seam of great coal had been cut through to make an entrance to the great basalt... in this section there were

sections of fireclay, clunch, coal, shales and metamorphic rocks. Angle of dip 30 degrees... Party witnessed a 'blast'...short of time... and unable to visit company's limestone quarry and mass of fossils...area in which Sir Roderick Murchison found some chief items which allowed him to elaborate his 'Silurian Period'....etc.

6 August 1881. Clee Hill, shocking accident. A man named William Tonks was thrown out of a truck at Dhu Stone works on Sat and two trucks went over his legs, cutting them...He was taken home in a trap and lies in a precarious condition.

20 May 1882. Clee Hill Wesleyan Band of Hope. ...gave monthly entertainment at day schoolroom...chair taken by Mr D Roberts who said object was not merely to reclaim drunkards but to lead them to the path of everlasting life. He strongly condemned so called moderation, and entreated all who had not done so to take the pledge at once.

18 July 1882. Clee Hill drowning whilst bathing...HTW inquest at the Golden Cross on William Boyer 18, settmaker at Granite Quarry. Joshua Beddoes said he was a settmaker at works. On Sat last he, Boyer and George Jarvis went to pool at Magpie Cover to bathe....would not go in for many rocks at bottom. Boyer went in several times...got out of depth and called for help. Could not get boots off in time to help. (stopped to get trousers off). George Jarvis said he went to bathe on Sat last... deceased was the only one who got in pool. When deceased was plunging in water, he ran to Magpie Coalpit for help. Coroner asked why when a man was drowning, he ran away. Said Panic. Amos Chapman, settmaker said he heard that deceased was in pool and went and got him out. He was dead. Verdict 'drowned whilst bathing.'

19 May 1883. Clee Hill...Old English sports on Whit Monday; programme carried out by Mr G Lysall of the Victoria Inn and Committee listed... witnessed by 3-400. Results..includes female race for 1lb of tea... Stone contest (40 stones one yard apart)...1st Joseph Brown 3s...etc Match J Williams v Horse .. won by Williams.

2 June 1883. Clee Hill presentation at Granite works on Friday week. Before resuming work after breakfast, Mr Charles Jones, timekeeper was presented by manager Mr James Yates at mass meeting on behalf of men, neat and choice electro plated tea and coffee service with inscription given...from fellow workmen,... Mr Yates spoke in eugenic terms of his appreciation. He also said Mr Jones had taken a second wife and men thought it good opportunity to testify their feelings towards him.

4 August 1883 Clee Hill open air services ...of Wesleyans held in field at Clee Hill of Mr J Webster... good attendance. On Thursday the Wesleyan Sunday schools treat for 120 was held in the Day schoolroom... then adjourned to field where foot races and various games...prizes, nuts and sweetmeats were distributed.

11 August 1883. Clee Hill attempt to commit suicide at Nine Springs, Bitterley on Thurs by cutting throat. Mr Southern surgeon at Ludlow was called...rash act attributed to lowness of spirits.

10 May 1884. Clee Hill Fair. The annual Clee Hill Fair was held in a field at the back of the Golden Cross on Saturday and not withstanding the depression of trade in the district and the inclemency of the weather a large number of people gathered together. Hobby horses and swing boats were well patronised.

30 August 1884. WJ letter re recent Clee Hill letter....replies that late Miss Jackson in Shropshire Word Book standard of dialect made no connection of scores of words in use here...where recesses of the hills have nothing in common with other Shrops towns etc. I am pleased to contradict my death and to vindicate my word Book...area was well worked.

(Alf Jenkins read this book at the time he was writing "Titterstone Clee Hills...." and reported that he could not recognise any of the ' Shropshire dialect words' that Georgina referred to either. He stated that Diddlebury where the book was written would have been considered foreign land to Clee Hill).

13 September 1884. WJ letter continues 'Amongst Clee Hill' correspondence (Georgina Jackson) we learn... at Burwarton, one of the most beautiful and artistic village schools to be met with between Lands End and John O'Groats..

Crossing Horseditch from Titterstone towards the south you come to what is known as ' Clee Hill' in the proper sense of the term. It was in this latter that the famous seam of Great coal was discovered more than 100 years ago and supplied the surrounding districts....Out of this hill has come some of the richest iron ore ever dug from mother earth. Here the blast furnaces have belched ....here the puddling furnaces have extracted the carbon from the boiling cast metal... and here too the ponderous forge hammer has beaten the massive burning balls into their proper shape...which Mr Lewis marked 'Best,Best,Best'...It is on this latter hill chiefly that the famous Dhu Stone trade is carried on. It was developed some 18 years ago under the able management of Mr Thomas Roberts of Ludlow. Within the last two years, the enterprising duo of Field and Mackay have built the incline from Bitterley up to the south west side of Titterstone Hill where they opened a quarry in that basalt rocks for paving and macadam purposes...accommodation can be obtained at the Angel, the Oak, the Golden Cross and the Victoria...The PO is not kept by an old woman.. the post mistress both by her education and manner is fit to adorn a drawing room..and passes through her hands in the course of a year £3k.

The plant at the quarries and collieries are not very far behind the time. The quarry masters have steel rails and steel wheels on their tramways as well as good steam engines to work their crushers, and I am told they use nothing but solid steel tools in their quarries. The Titterstone Company have telephonic communications between Bitterley and Titterstone..There are Cleehillites in NZ, Australia, The Cape, Canada, the US...etc signed Clee Hill.

3 January 1885. Clee Hill. Trap accident. On Saturday evening, accident to Mr Kenhard's cartcarrier between Hopton Bank and Ludlow. Mr Kenhard with 8 passengers was returning when near Henley, horse stepped on a stone and fell throwing Mrs Kenhard and a passenger out with great violence. The wheel passed over both legs...but no bones were broken. The passenger thrown out escaped with a severe shaking.

23 May 1885. WJ Caradoc Field Club...visited Titterstone and Clee Hill.. proceeded from station in three large brakes to Bitterley Court and examined various historical documents etc and lunch by Rev J Walcot. Made way by side of Titterstone until reached boulders black with age on mossy top. Here chairman discoursed on great basalt caps which crown hills...and forces required to lift it to its present position. The described elements of its composition and the same made up hornblendic and trachytic kinds. The difference caused by speed of cooling. Party proceeded across dyke to Clee Hill through Granite Company's Quarries. Met at Victoria Hotel. Conveyance taken to Feathers Hotel..

11 June 1887. Clee Hill. Jubilee Committee at Mission Room..Vicar of Knowbury presided. 20 guineas collected.. tickets to be supplied to managers of schools for children's tea and also to children between 10 and 13 for those up to 14. Tenders offered for 80 teas for aged and widows at Mission Room.. Mr William Edwards of Pool House offered field for use of sports.

18 June 1887. WJ letter from Offley Wakeman listing the Jubilee bonfires of Shropshire..this included mention of electric light on the summit of Titterstone Clee. (AJ asks what powered this???)

25 June 1887. Clee Hill Jubilee on Tuesday Divine service in St Paul's Knowbury with vicar Rev FM Williams. Then public procession to Bennet's End;; here Mr B Martin's Excelsior Band accompanied by a large number of Foresters, Oddfellows and people from the Hill Side, together with 40 men, youths and maidens mounted on horses, decked in patriotic colours assembled to meet Capt Giles of Hope Court and the villagers from 'Hope Poetic Dell'. When they arrived the band struck up NA. The secretary Mr James Yates, then gave out a verse from a song composed for the occasion, and the company sang it. Capt Giles formed the procession headed with banner of the Oddfellows; the Foresters followed, then the band and 40 horsemen. The procession went 'up the Clee'. Resting at the Crown for refreshment, the procession increased by those 'round Knowbury dwell'. The secretary rode forward to the Firs where the vicar and schoolmaster Mr Wigmore were waiting to join with their 250 scholars who headed the procession and marched up Office Lane en route for Angel Bank. Arriving at the Oak Inn, met by the Wesleyan School from 'up the Clee'. Here children sang a composition of Mr Yates. Procession went on to greet those from Doddington and returning were given a ticket for refreshments. The young, robust and strong ascending to the grounds known as 'Top of the Rabbit Hole' for sports. The Aged, widows and children assembled for sandwich tea in the Mission Room supplied by Mr George Roberts. Ladies presided at tables listed....The vicar spoke kindly to the old people and Col Hill attended to comforts and wants. In the meanwhile on the bleak mountain top. Sports.... The committee dined at the Victoria Inn. Vicar in chair. Toasts...Adjourned to grounds for sports. Evening bonfire and fireworks. Sir Charles Rouse Boughton's electric light at Titterstone Clee Hill was very brilliant. (Author:- Where did the supply for this come from? Was it Bitterley hydro?).

28. April 1888. Clee Hill fatal accident...when on Monday, Mr Robert Kennish farmer returning from Ludlow market went over Clee Hills to Aston Botterill when near Doddington Church he turned on a bye road to old disused pit known as Church Pit. In passing another old pit, known as Bailey's Pit he was pitched out on very rough road and killed on the spot. He was discovered half an hour later by shepherd Turner in employ of Mr Beddoes of Ditton Farm. Horse was on top of him with heel s in the air. Body was removed to Victoria Inn, Clee Hill....leaves widow and 13 children, most grown. HTW inquest...details...includes mention of Noah Martin, shoemaker of Angel Bank, who told him he had come wrong way...advised to go by Gate Hangs Well and then round by the Bush.... Mrs Martha Trow at Cornbrook Bridge saw deceased earlier going very slowly ...Verdict Accidental death.

(Author says:- The Gate Hangs Well a public house at the east end of Catherton Common is now a private house; but there used to be a large oak tree outside the pub with an ornate sign with a gate and caption, 'The Gate hangs well and hinders none.'

12 May 1888. Clee Hill Pleasure Fair. On Sat, annual pleasure fair held in field in front of Golden Cross, Steam Circus, swing boats, military band organ, shooting gallery and coconut bowling provided for amusement of visitors. There were several stalls and two side shows all of which were well patronized.

14 July 1888. Clee Hill Granite Company's Picnic. On Monday, company gave all employees and wives, a handsome treat of a picnic coupled with a programme of athletic and other sports. The picnic took place on Hill Top overlooking the company's extensive quarries. Postponed from Saturday due to weather. Arrangements under the guidance of Company's resident manager Mr James Yates.

At 2 pm workmen assembled at Workmen's Dining Room on the works, were met by two of the three partners Messrs Thomas Roberts and W Pitman of Ludlow. About 40 of the men were mounted on horseback, mostly their own horses. A procession was formed of horsemen, the Mr Benjamin Martin's Excelsior Band, then settmakers , mechanics, quarrymen, loaders, machine men, followed by colliers who brought up the rear. The gay cortege proceeded via Craven Place, past Victoria, down to the Golden Cross, then back again and up the steep incline to Hill Top, where elaborate preparations had been made both for the sports and the requisite refreshments. The catering was placed in the hands of Mr George Roberts, who had provided apparently enough to feed an army. The sports were at once started with a catch trick, called on the programme, 'Reaching the Prize'. A platform was erected over which was put a cross beam; on the top of which were placed three elaborate looking objects, purporting to be prizes, from the gilded tinsel of which was suspended a cord just sufficiently high above the platform for any boy to jump at and reach. 100 yards from the platform was placed five roughish looking lads stripped for the race, waiting for the signal to run and 'reach the prize'. The race was exciting, the scramble on the platform equally so. The cords were reached and down came three hidden tin cans, spilling over the competitors their liquid contents of raddle, whiting and blue. The red, white and blue together with the loud peals of laughter from the hundreds of spectators did not appear very much appreciated by those who had so eagerly reached the prize. The programme was well sustained throughout and not withstanding the saddened state of the ground there was some good racing, and very credible feats of jumping and other athletic performances. The tug of war was a tug indeed. Ten, tall, fine, able bodied men contended and tugged with ten more well chosen and equally well weighted and muscled. The strength and weight were so equally matched, that the excitement of the spectators became intense as with a kind of desperation the warriors strove to win. If the sustaining powers had been equally matched with the strength and weight, the tug would have been an almost endless one. Here Captain Jones prevailed. His team was not stronger than Capt Williams, but perhaps a very little better able to sustain their strength under vigorous exertions. Hence their victory. At 4.30 there was a break in the sports for tea. Rustic tables were extemporised and loaded with an ample meal. The kind ladies of the neighbourhood had been invited to preside at these festive boards and had come up in the cold, damp mountain mists, and did excellent service. They were Mrs Watson, Mrs Green, Mrs Taylor, Mrs Askey, Mrs Yates, Mrs J Genner, Mrs B Genner, Mrs Edwards, Mrs Corfield, Mrs Lynal, Mrs Bate, Miss Bate, Mrs Webster, Mrs J Martin, Mrs B Martin, Mrs Whittaker, Mrs Leaworthy, Mrs T Key and Mrs John Martin. When the feast was over the sports were resorted to, and Mr Martin's band played a choice selection of music. The whole of the proceedings were marked by a total absence of wrangling or any angry word having been spoken. The Granite Co have intimated that it is their intention to have the festival an annual one, and their employees, about 400 in number appear to be heartily appreciating the kind intention of their employers.

.A goodly number of visitors from Ludlow and other places did honour to the occasion. It is estimated that about a 1000 persons were on the grounds during the day.

21 July 1888. Clee Hill. Wesleyan Day School examined by Mr JC Colville HMI and his assistant MR CH Cowley on Monday in the presence of Mr W Putman when 122 boys and girls were presented by Mr Leeworthy for inspection.

25 August 1888. Clee Hill Accident. A man named John Benbow 51, of Oreton...drawing coal with mare and cart from Watsill Colliery...going down steep bank, breech band broke, causing mare to become restive...ran away and knocked wall down of Mr Morris...later Benbow fell and wheel went over him...cart continued and lost wheel when hit a large stone. Mare eventually stopped by James Edwards and little injured. Benbow conveyed home in a spring cart and Dr Thomson of Cleobury Mortimer attended...however died on Thurs. Inquest held at Plough. Accidentally killed returned.

8 September 1888.

Clee Hill Foresters' church parade on Sunday afternoon of court 'Victoria Pride' 5651 of Shrewsbury district at St Pauls Knowbury...procession formed at Victoria Inn by 80 members headed by Mr W Martin's Brass Band. To church for service...offertory of £1 9s 9d for SI.

27 July 1889.

Clee Hill. Serious accident. To William Dovey of Dhu Stone Company...engaged on face loading stone when one fell against his leg and broke it. Conveyed home at Crump's Brook where surgical aid was obtained.

Fatality to William Whatmore of 44 Winthill's Cottage Knowbury...died Tues morning from blow of stone to back of head from Dhu Stone rock falling that morning. HTW inquest that evening....he said he had been informed that the quarry was not safe for men and thought they (jury) should visit it and form their own opinion. They inspected it with Mr Hammonds, foreman present. Place where accident had happened had been covered with 100 tons of stone....the mode of getting the stone was explained viz when the men were at work in gangs there were two men told to watch the rock above, in order to warn the men below of any expected fall of rock. After inspecting the quarry, the jury returned to the Oak Inn and evidence taken. Benjamin Allerton son in law of deceased said he lived at the Buildings, near the Dhu Stone works... as a labourer at the quarry...Coroner said the quarry appeared to be a dangerous place and adjourned the inquest...It was only right and fair to the workmen and the owners of the quarry that an inspector should inspect the quarry. He would ask the police to obtain evidence of the other accident that day; also the man hurt on Sat (above) in the same quarry. They had all seen the amount of stone fallen and had the men been working, the result would have been more serious....Adjourned to next Friday. HTW asked Mr Hammond if the men would be able to get off at five pm and was told they were only paid for the time they were there. He was not authorised to say they would be paid after they leave...Jury bound over to attend.

3 August 1889 (continuation of above)...Inquest continued; on July 23rd of William Whatmore.Present included Mr Townsend one of the proprietors of the quarry, Mr Hammond, foreman. Thomas Beddoes who lived at Silvington Tump, was on the same cutting as the deceased. He showed jury the place. He was one of the watchers...saw the stone fall on Sat 20th and one piece struck William Dovey and broke his leg. He shouted and all the men ran except Dovey...He was present on the 23rd when accident happened to Whatmore..he was watching some stone fall. Here lumps dropped from face of rock. He saw the stone strike the deceased on the head. There had not been any grumbling by the men that there were no watchers. Samuel Martin of Crump's Brook gave evidence of accident to Beddoes.

Mr Montford on behalf of proprietors called following to give evidence of safety of working in quarry. Joseph Parker, John Garbet (ganger in quarry) John Morris and Benjamin Hammonds (foreman) all of whom said quarry was worked same as it was at the starting.

John Breeze surveyor of Wellington said he had seen quarry two years ago and did not consider it any more dangerous than any other....all were more or less dangerous. HTW said he had adjourned inquest in hope to get an inspector to examine quarry. He wrote to Home Secretary on matter and read reply...which said quarries are not subject to Mines and Regulation Acts and not a duty of an inspector to attend an inquest held in respect of a fatal accident in a quarry...

Coroner summed up evidence and after consultation, jury returned verdict that Whatmore's was an accident and that present system of working the quarry was rather dangerous, and hoped company would continue to take every precaution for the safety of the men and remember the widow of the deceased. Mr Montford said the company would arrange that.

5 September 1890. Broome; death of William Davies 27 waggoner. HTW inquest at Railway Tavern in employ of Mr Woolley at Rowton when he fell off shafts and was run over by wheels. Accidental death..... In separate item; the unfortunate fatal mishap opens up the question as to the best manner to be adopted to prevent such disasters. Davies case was the same as many others. He had been to Clee Hill Colleries for a load of coal and on the way home got on shafts for a rest. He went to sleep and fell off – wheels of heavily loaded wagon passed over him. Accidents like this are not uncommon and so long as drivers of such vehicles are subject to the physical exhaustion on long journeys...It is a matter in which it is next to impossible to impose conditions calculated to effect...

26 July 1890. MW Ward meeting...Surveyor instructed to purchase about 1000 tons of Clee Hill Dhu stone for main roads.

28 May 1892. Clee Hill serious accident when William Brown of Tenbury Bank at Granite Company's Works was at work in the quarry and was struck on head by a piece of falling stone. Badly cut and conveyed home and Dr Watson sent for...progressing.

28 May 1892. Bitterley accident on the Clee Hill railway. On Sat, one load of four waggons was coming down, pulling empty trucks up and one of the links broke and waggons came down at terrific speed and ran into dead block at bottom and waggons and contents thrown over embankment into road... waggons smashed, no one injured. A breakdown gang was sent from Shrewsbury to repair the damage.

26 January 1899. Wanted 100 stonebreakers for regular work, good wages – apply to Mr W Edwards Clee Hill Granite Company, Craven Place, Clee Hill.

22 March 1900. Tunnels being driven under Clee Hill (*Birmingham Welsh Water).*

14 June 1900. Article about S African War. Feed 200,000 men. 50,000 followers, 40,000 horses, 30,000 mules every day. Pretoria was as large as CS. JM speaking at Farlow said his son was in Imperial Yeomanry – trouble brewing in China. Told him to form a rifle club on Clee Hill.

23 January 1911. Ludlow County Police case of drunk in charge of a steam engine (Author says these travelled at about 4 mph). Edward Radnor, Titrail Cottages, Clee Hill...engine on Bromfield Road going to CA when complaints received by group of men. PC Phillips said at 3.40pm on March 6th he telephoned to PS Pearce at CA and proceeded on his bicycle. He met PS Pearce at Onibury where engine was at standstill at 4.20pm. The driver Radnor was very drunk and unfit to be in charge. They refused to allow him to proceed and got a man named Jones to take the engine into the yard of Mr Jones at Onibury. Another man was got later and the engine continued on its journey to Broome. The defendant went by train. Fined £1 and costs of 5s. He asked for time to pay and Bench said no...the alternative was 28 days in custody.

3 August 1911.A Bitterley tragedy. Labourer's fatal fall. Thomas Rigby going to Clee Hill tarmacadam works at 4am saw a man lying in road and recognised him as Donovan...doctor sent for and conveyed to Ludlow Cottage Hospital where he died. Assumed fell over a wall...seen at 10.30pm and assumed to be drunk... inquest accidental death.

9 May 1912. Ludlow Co. Marston complains at SCC use of Denbighshire stone over Clee Hill.

19 December 1912. Clee Hill Stonebreakers' Case. Compensation injury etc. Mr John Ward MP interested himself in case, so case brought before Judge. Piece rate, paid 2s3d for every ton of stone broken. As the stone was broken it was weighed periodically and applicant paid. Accident on 19th July when a small piece of stone flew up and into left eye being serious. Incapacitated. Kept in EET a week and attending there ever since. Lost sight in the one eye. Protracted legal argument but agreement reached. Applicant awarded 2s11d a week to make up lower rate of pay. Now earning of 10s7d a week at company's quarry.

14 June 1913. Clee Hill RH asked President of Board of Education whether he knew of Wesleyan Schools which had been burnt down last November...and though school had been rebuilt in April, it had not yet opened and 100 children were without any school to attend. He was told: that the premises would be opened next Monday.

2 August 1913. Clee Hill ...lad Henry Didlick who worked in engine room at Titterstone Quarry caught clothes in machinery and was whirled round fifty times before falling out. All clothes torn off him including his boots...ankle and right arm broken and his hands and toes smashed. He was conveyed to Ludlow Cottage Hospital where critical.

2 August 1913. Clee Hill Horticultural show. ...detail...Punch and Judy, Turnouts etc.

2 August 1913. Clee Hill Wedding. At Doddington Church on Wed afternoon. Mr John Roberts, son of Mr Thomas Lee Roberts (chairman of the directors of Clee Hill Granite Company Ltd) and Miss Edwards (daughter of late Mr and Mrs W Edwards of Poole House, Clee Hill). Large gathering...Rev Arthur Roberts of London brother of groom officiated. Bridegroom is a director of Clee Hill Granite and esteemed in district. Over fifty guests...couple drove to and from church in motor cars lent by friends...After, retired to Poole House for reception...refreshments in marquee on lawn. Later couple left in motorcar to Worcester where train for south of England...then to Continent. Will be away six weeks before taking up residence at Hope Bagot Rectory. Many presents including clock and bronzes from workpeople of Clee Hill company etc.

16 August 1913. LA: Clee Hill. Man killed by fall of stone...at No 3 quarry Dhu Stone works on Monday when George Mapp 34, who was working on the face of rock beneath was buried in the debris...Extricated and found to be dead. HTW inquest at Golden Cross Inn...adjourned for HM Inspector of Mines inquiry. Deceased had worked in 3 quarries all his life and had been working on Dhu stone for a number of years... Mr King on behalf of company expressed condolences.

26 March 1914. Mass meeting of workers in Mission Room Clee Hill on Tuesday...orderly crowd listened to Mr S Hotchkiss read report to Secretary of National Union of Quarry Workers...on terms offered and accepted by workers and owners: for

1. 9d per ton on all 3 inch setts; 6d a ton on all others. 4x12 kerb to be 2d per foot.

2. 2d per ton on all sizes of hand broken.

3. 3d per day advance for day men at all quarries, the age to be 17 to become a full labourer. No one to work under 3s 6d per day on attaining 17 years of age. The minimum to be raised from 3s 4d to 3s 6d.

4. Engine drivers to be paid the advance equal to 3d per day and two shunters to receive 3s 6d or 3d per day advance.

5. Hours of work. On Saturday to cease at 1.00pm. No one to start work after 7.30am on Sats.

6. Drilling to be raised from 2s to 2s 6d. Sixpence a foot advance. Drillers to be supplied with tool carrier and to carry tools for settmakers if required.

7. Tippers at Bitterley Yard to be advanced to 1d per ton on all tipping, including stock.

8. Loaders at Titterstone Quarries to be raised to 3 and a half pence per ton all round (half d per ton advance).

9. No advance on loading muck at either quarry.

10. Contractors at Titterstone Quarries to receive their own money at office on pay days, and to be provided with slips.

11. Overtime rate: to time and a quarter for overtime; time and a half for Sundays and double time for holidays.

4 January 1917. Military appeal Trib Ludlow RDC. A Clee Hill Haulier and owner of traction engines (a lady) appealed for her son 27 single, passed Class B2, described as a manager, and for a man 35 married and 5 children. She said she had 2 engines running all the summer and 4 rollers; there were 5 engines and 5 rollers altogether. The number of men left is 14 including the son appealed for. The tribunal considered the son would be a useful man on the roads in France and refused the application in his case. The other man's case was adjourned for him to attend a Medical.

31 May 1917 Boy killed by motor car on Clee Hill. Clifford John Gittens 4 who ran out into the road. Inquest HT Weyman with jury of 7 – first time under new regs. (usually 12). Driver from Liverpool was exonerated.

28 June 1917. L RDC. The military appealed against the condition attached to the exemption (provision of an efficient substitute) granted the son(25, single Class A) of a Clee Hill baker and grocer – Respondent said three of his sons were serving. The son in question baked 1000 4lb loaves a week – The Military Representative thought the bakers of Clee Hill could make some arrangement to combine. Respondent said he baked more bread than anybody else on Clee Hill; to take the place of three men he had lost he now had two girls. Some of the bakers on Clee Hill only baked 300 loaves. At his other shop, 5 – 6 miles away, he could only bake half the quantity he could sell owing to the shortage of labour. The son in question also never missed a day baking at either place except Sundays. The Tribunal dismissed the military appeal and confirmed the previous decision.

(Author says there were a great number of appeals, mostly unsuccessful at the time).

4 October 1917.   Clee Hill suicide of Emily Hayden widow 61; from a nail on back of door. Inquest held at Dhu Stone Stores. (Hedgehog preservation centre now).

3 January 1918. Clee Hill. Our readers will be pleased to know that Signaller Jonathan Evans son of Mr Samuel Evans, 10 Rouse Boughton Terrace, Clee Hill, has been awarded the MM for conspicuous bravery in the field in Salonika; his brother, Charles Evans gained the DCM early in the war at the battle of Loos. We join in congratulating these two brave Clee Hill boys.

3 January 1918. Clee Hill. A children's operetta entitled 'The Babes in the Wood' was performed at   the Council School on Thursday last week under the supervision of Mrs J Hammond. The principal   parts were: The Babes Miss Elsie Hickman and Nancy Breakwell (Cissie Davidson as their nurse); The   Robbers, Miss Mag Webster and EG Whitaker; The Robber's wife and Servant Emily Cadwallader and Freda Patterson; Witch Miss Hilda Andrews; Fairy Queen, Muriel Edwards; The four Robins and Fairies must not be forgotten; All the artistes who were trained by Mrs J Hammond did their parts extremely well. Miss Mag Webster and EG Whitaker caused roars of laughter as comics;

Muriel Edwards made a charming Fairy Queen, especially when she defeated the witch, whose determination overcame her discretion. Freda Patterson made a pert servant, while Emily Cadwallader a first class robber's wife. Mr J.E.Roberts, JP as usual made a very efficient chairman. The accompaniments were capably performed by Miss Doris Hammond. The hand painted scenery presented by Mrs Steel was very effective. The schoolroom was packed by 6.30 and several had to go away disappointed, which shows how popular Mrs Hammond's plays are. The proceeds were in aid of Soldiers' Comfort Fund of the Clee Hill and Knowbury Working Party, of which Mrs FA Steel is president. About £12 was realized including donations.

13 June 1918. Clee Hill Fallen Shropshire Officers. Rev Charles Whitefoord of Whitton Paddocks, Clee Hill, was for a year one of the clergy at the Roman Catholic Cathedral, Shrewsbury and went out to the front as Chaplain to the Forces in the autumn of 1916. He was educated at Rugby and Merton College, Oxford and received into the Catholic Church at Chartres Cathedral. He was wounded on May 29th and died in hospital the following day.

28 November 1918. The local football supporters were treated to a good match between the Ludlow discharged soldiers and the discharged men of Clee Hill on the Mill Lane ground on Saturday. Both sides were well represented. The game opened evenly, but....the visitors soon took the lead but was won by the home side. The game was strenuously contested and was in aid of PoW Fund and the Discharged Soldiers' Federation.

28 November 1918. Clee Hill. Mr JC Mackay JP has deposited with the Board of Agriculture the plans for the Ludlow, Knowbury and Doddington Light Railway. The station will be at the back of the Electric Light Works and the railway will run alongside the Bromfield road for a short distance turning to the right under the main line to Shrewsbury and join the Clee Hill road at Rocks Green. The stations will be at Ludlow, Bromfield Road, Fishmore, Rocks Green, Bridgnorth Road, Henley, Snitton, Bitterley wharf, Angel Bank, Knowbury, Caynham Road, Clee Hill, Cornbrook, Doddington, Earlsditton and Hopton Wafers. (Author:- this did not sadly happen mainly due to the development of motor transport).

24 July 1919. Clee Hill. Arrangements are being made to establish motor bus service between Ludlow and Clee Hill. It is to run a down and up service morning and evening on Mondays, Weds, Sats and as required.

11 September 1919. Ludlow. A case of anthrax discovered at Mr Charles Hotchkiss, Stone House, Clee Hill. The carcase, a milking cow was cremated on the farm by PS Williams and PC Lloyd.

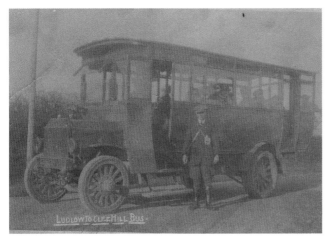

Believed to be a photograph of the first motor bus on Clee Hill:- Observant people will notice it had solid tyres and was chain driven. The conductor is dressed in the usual uniform of the day. By his right arm is his cash bag for taking fares and his roll of tickets.   On his left side hangs his ticket punch. A hole in a ticket showed it had been paid for.

11 September 1919. Ludlow. A motor bus service between Ludlow and Angel Bank, Clee Hill and Doddington was inaugurated on Monday morning. Dozen passengers leaving Galdeford for the initial journey. At present the bus will run on Mondays, Wednesdays and Saturdays making two journeys each way on those days. (Was this the first use of a bus here?).

1920. Extracts from Clee Hill Housing-Commissioner's Inquiry:- Mr Courtney Clifton (M.Inst.C.E._ held a conference of Local Authorities interested in housing needs in the Clee Hill area. Those present included Dr Wheatley (Med. Offr .for County), Dr White (Med. Offr .for health for Ludlow R.C.)Mr Whittaker (Chairman), Mr Millichamp (Sec. Of Clee Hill Quarrymens' Union), Mr G Randles (Trade and Workmen's Union). Mr J Mackay and Mr WR Field (Rep. Titterstone Quarries); plus many others there too. Mr Millichamp hoped the quarry owners would follow the Rural Council's requirements.   He said on C.H. the conditions were very bad. There was overcrowding in several houses. More houses were required – between 20 and 30. Present houses were very small. Some had only one room up and one down. Some had two small bedrooms. Five people were living in many. Mr Randles worked on the mineral train to C.H. and heard what the men said. At Bedlam there had been some houses built by Field and Mackay; good houses; but all tenants had to take in lodgers. Married men complained because they were separated from their wives, had to lodge because there was nowhere else to go. Some live five or six miles away from work. They lost time through bad weather and quarry output suffered. Being wet brought on illness. He would like to ask for houses to be built from concrete instead of bricks (plenty of material available in the quarries). He considered all houses should be built round the quarries. Commissioner asked what rent could be expected. Due to quarrymen receiving quite good wages, it was thought 9 shillings a week. It was reported that some men walked six miles from Ludlow and one man from Highley. Houses would cost £450 to £500. (dispute about this because thought they should cost less).

Dr Wheatley made a report about conditions. He said they were the most disgraceful he had come across and for years nothing had been done. Mr Millichamp said housing conditions affected capacity of work. Large numbers were living in damp houses with dilapidated roofs, rooms unventilated, overcrowding and insufficient accommodation. There were examples of two families in one house, of husbands and wives being separated and in one instance children being sent to the workhouse. Most of the houses could not be renovated because they were in such a poor state.

19 February 1920. Clee Hill Motor Bus. An improved postal service between Ludlow and Clee Hill is announced to commence on Monday next by the introduction of a motor combination mail in place of *a horse and trap* . Correspondence from the Clee Hill, Knowbury and Bitterley districts will be delivered about an hour earlier than hitherto. The night mail dispatch will also be made much later. The latest time for posting being Clee Hill 6pm, Knowbury 6.15pm and Bitterley 6.30pm. A clearance at Bedlam letterbox will in future be made at 1.30pm daily except Sundays. (*Have services improved a century later?*).

9 September 1920. Onibury. Fire. Monday 12.11pm the Ludlow Fire Brigade received a call for a fire at Mr Frank Bach's Farm Onibury. Call gave the details asked some time ago by Capt Packer in the case of country fires, viz that it was a rick fire and the nearest water supply was 400 yards away. When the brigade arrived at Onibury Station, Mr Bach was waiting and directed the brigade to the nearest way by the river. The fire engine was towed by the Clee Hill motor bus from the Ludlow Motor Garage and the engine was on the scene within 13 minutes of the call of the outbreak.

23 September 1920. At Ludlow County Court application for a cinematograph licence by Mr Stubbins for Mission Room , Clee Hill. Mr Stubbins proprietor of picture house at Tenbury; had always shown high class films as the police would agree.   Building is of brick and tile, used as a church on Sundays by vicar and wardens. Magistrate wanted to speak to the trustees. The Mission Room was built for certain purposes which the application conflicts with.   Told to be present as it was used for concerts, dances and entertainments. Proposed to use the hall two nights a week for a start at weekly rental of so much a night. After trial of three months could have a lease for five years. Bench still wanted to see trustees or their approval and adjourned the matter. Before the court rose, applicant drove over to Knowbury Vicarage and obtained letter from Rev J Hughes Parry but alas not what was wanted by the Bench. Solicitor asked that they granted provisional licence not to exceed three nights a week on condition that a tenancy agreement was drawn up by the trustees. Supt Williams said he had inspected the building and there were three doors which opened inwards and if application was approved, he should like a condition made that they open outwards and the licence be granted subject to the engineer's certificate as to the safety of the apparatus. Solicitor said fine. Bench had further discussions and reverted to original position of adjournment causing frustration and ill-feeling.

7 October 1920. Ludlow County Court. Cinema on Clee Hill. Solicitor showed tenancy agreement. In reply to court, said that only the chancel was consecrated. He was asked whether the machine was going to be inside or outside the building. Inside. The police said the doors in question were to be chained open as done on a previous occasion.

19 October 1922. Clee Hill last Friday quite a stir amongst the local corps of the Salvation Army, when the members united with Ludlow Corps in giving a welcome to Brigadier A Hadden, divisional Commander from Stoke on Trent. At 7pm there was a rally at the Cross, brigadier in charge. Good number present. Inside the Citadel an interesting meeting took place, the officers present being Captain Duncan and Lt Hewitt of Ludlow. Capt Curl and Lt Brown of Clee Hill...song, stirring words.....etc. *(During the author's childhood the very active Salvation Army was based in a building down Tenbury road about 100 yards from the cross road on the left hand side. The Salvation Army band played every Sunday outside Clee Hill pubs including the Dhu Stone Inn, E Flat Bass player Mr Jones walking from the Knowle bottom to do so).*

19 October 1922. Clee Hill fatal fire. Itinerant violinist and artist burnt to death. Harry Jarman's sad end. About 2.45 on Sunday morning the Ludlow Fire Brigade received a call to an outbreak of fire in some outbuildings adjoining the Angel Inn Clee Hill.   The alarm was given by a servant girl who set out on a bicycle. She was overtaken on the road by a motorcar, the driver of which gave her a lift into Ludlow, she leaving her bicycle in the roadside, and in this car Engineer Teale and two firemen returned to the scene of the conflagration, a shed containing a large quantity of straw, situated between a cow shed and a garage.... discovered by Mrs Clent at 2am...one cow was burnt to death. Within five or six minutes every member of Ludlow Fire Brigade had answered the call and the engine was on the street ready to start but again there was a delay in getting the Clee Hill motor bus ready to tow the engine to the scene...church clock was striking four when the engine moved off with its full complement of men. PS Powell accompanied them and

During 1922 and 1923 Speed trials were held on Angel Bank , Clee Hills:- Above 23-9-1922, shows GS Boston on the starting line at the bottom of Angel Bank.

23-9-1922. V Hawkins on the Start Line near the bottom of Angel Bank:- He was driving Bayliss-Thomas. Long House Cottage on the left. Large crowd watching OK 3960.

23-9-1922:- GS Boston on the right and Hassell on Left. Boston's Vauxhall 30?98 (left) and on the right TB 3 wheeler.

23-4-1923. GS Boston in speed trials on Angel Bank:- Half litre Austro-Daimler on the way up Angel Bank Clee Hill.

on arrival there were stories that an itinerant violinist who had made his headquarters at the CLH in Ludlow Henry Jarman, had perished in the burning shed and a search among the debris soon led to the discovery of things which left no doubt....last seen leaving the Angel Inn by the front door before nine on Saturday... Inquest states parts...PS said discovered remains....found two violin pegs and an umbrella frame...knew the fiddler personally...and he had an appointment in a chapel in Ludlow for Sunday morning and did not keep it. He has not been found. He was a heavy pipe and cigarette smoker and also addicted to drink...Jury were satisfied that it was the old fiddler. Brother identified his paint box.

14 December 1922 Clee Hill WI Xmas party 60-70 present. President Mrs Clegg. Committee gave each member a present. Guest of the evening was late President Mrs Flora Steele of Cheltenham who gave an address to the women of their duty as women of the British Empire...a nice programme of music and recitations followed by games. *(Mrs Flora Steele was a very prominent and influential lady of the suffragette movement).*

19 July 1923. Clee Hill Wooden legged Man's fatal Fall. Jas Davies 62 quarryman fell from cart. Had a wooden leg for three years. Sale of timber at Angel Inn. Neighbour helped move some planks he had bought. Fell backwards out of the cart. Sent for wife. He had broken his wooden leg in fall. Said on Tuesday he had slipped on the boards. Suffering from fractured dislocation of spine.

20 September 1923. Clee Hill WI garden fete and sale held at Knowbury House by invitation of Dr and Mrs Watson. Hon Mrs Wheeler, Bitterley Court opened proceedings with Mr Clegg who spoke of the valuable work done by the WI...During the afternoon, the late President Mrs Flora Ann Steele and daughter motored over from Cheltenham and received a hearty welcome....The Hopton Brass Band played selections of music...proceeds for Institute's Building fund.

4 September 1924. Clee Hill Show report. A record show in spite of adverse conditions. Field sodden with rain and more fell...record entries..first rate animals in livestock section...veg, flowers, needlework, baking, butter making and children's work.

11 September 1924. Ludlow accident. Mr JD Griffiths 70 of Clee Hill, V Chair of Ludlow RDC, while returning from Council and Guardians...made journey on bicycle collided with Ford motorcar driven by Mr Green of Hopton Hall...thrown through windscreen; taken to Ludlow Cottage Hospital and in precarious condition.

18 December 1924. Clee Hill. Branch of Ludlow Divisional Labour Party is being formed at Clee Hill.

1 January 1925. Clee Hill Red Letter Day. Dhustone Company and their employees. Mr P Lane secretary of the company. Tuesday when by generosity of the company, employees wives and families were entertained at a Xmas party on a most sumptuous scale. One of the most happy and brilliant the village has ever seen and good feeling exists between the two...in Mission Room, Clee Hill magnificently decorated...afternoon party for the children. 170 guests...each employee receiving a present when entering of tobacco and cigarettes, given by the company....

28 May 1925. Clee Hill Village Carnival. Shropshire Education Secretary at crowning of May Queen...carnival procession disrupted by a thunderstorm the same as last year...picturesque scene with small boy on a small horse and decorated bicycles...when they got to Clee Hill rains poured again. Crowning in Mission Room. Miss Doris Williams was crowned by Mrs Penddlebury, wife of County Secretary of Education.

25 June 1925. Clee Hill Wesleyan meeting quarterly held for the first time in 12 years at Clee Hill when Rev FF Benson chair of District visited. Local preachers meeting in the morning, followed by lunch at WI. Afternoon Rev Benson preached to a crowded congregation. In the evening Rev Benson lectured on 'Wilberforce' drew a packed audience...and the famous preacher made a deep impression. Captain R Lee Roberts chaired.

22 October 1925. Clee Hill trade union official sent to prison. Pleads guilty to embezzlement and falsification charges. Ben Millichamp 43, quarryman...stole £31 5s 6d and other sums as Union employee and made false entry in cash book...

14 January 1926. Clee Hill. Brightening the Workers' lives...We the undersigned quarry workers, colliers and others living on the Clee Hills in Shropshire, six miles from any place of amusement, protest at the unfair attack on the BBC transmission. Our crystal sets, mostly home-manufactured give our children a

delightful hour, and our evenings, after our hazardous occupations, have become a time of pleasure instead of weariness. It matters not whether the transmission is high brow, low brow, educational or frivolous, it makes life brighter for us. (then followed 62 signatures). Radio Times.

29 April 1926. Article on St John Ambulance Association, Clee Hill Branch...at Mission Room where awards were distributed....Inspector Hodnett gave resume of history of class..demonstration given by Clee Hill Granite Company Team of a broken thigh (lady's) with stretcher work. The Clee Hill Dhu Stone Company's Team gave a demonstration of a broken leg; carried patient over obstacles. Shunter Bond demonstrated individual work...PC Hall gave demonstration of artificial respiration and Inspector Hodnett demonstrated the triangular bandage and its adaptability...names on certificates... Doc Watson was presented with a case of pipes for members.

12 August 1926. Clee Hill Danger. Brum Boy's tragic death. Party of 6 Brum boys under 10 walking on Titterstone Hill, attempted to climb rocks. Joseph Burford 8 fell. Went for help at Bedlam but boy found to be dead. Boys been sent to Bedlam from Brum through Children's Welfare Society. Inquest in reading Room, Bedlam. Father attended and quite satisfied to allow son to attend holiday at Clee Hill....looked after by their foster mother Mrs Ainge who could not keep an eye on them all of the time. Coroner said it was a most dangerous thing to allow boys to run over the Hill. She had had 4 groups for their holiday that year...she fed and housed boys for a fortnight...At Bedlam there were about 16 boys on holiday...no one to supervise over herself except when the Secretary visited....She had told the boys the Hill was dangerous and they must not go up too far.... Fractured skull... Coroner said seemed no observation exercised over the children...accidental death. Children's Welfare Society represented by Secretary Miss Abrahams.

19 August 1926. CSA letter re Clee Hill stone, from T Harwick asking where the men unemployed at the quarry and on dole could find work, for 'as long as Conservative Councils buy foreign road material for their roads and their candidates motor in foreign cars to preach Tariff Reform, there is, not much hope for quarrymen.'

21 October 1926. Labour prospective candidate at Clee Hill, Mr A W Johnson JP..held in Bedlam Reading Room.

6 January 1927. Clee Hill. Col Windsor Clive and the Quarry workers. Meeting at Clee Hill in canteen. Conservative Member addressed luncheon hour(*salubrious name for their usual 'snappin' time)*...arranged by Field and Mackay.

6 January 1927. Article Clee Hill Dhu Stone Christmas treat for workmen, wives and families held in Mission Room on Friday...about 140 sat down to tea in gaily decorated room...kiddies were enchanted with the crackers and balloons provided for each child..miniature gun practice... Father Christmas, each child given a gift.

5 January 1928. Clee Dhu Stone Company's Beneficience...employers and friends entertained... fourth time reporter invited in Mission Room on Sat evening. Each kiddie receiving a present from fully decorated Xmas tree... following distribution, short concert two songs, 'Pack up your Troubles' and 'Cock Robin' by 8 little children...recitations. Male employees received tobacco and cigarettes.

12 January 1928. Clee Hill Xmas party. CH children's welfare held in WI on Wed pm when 38 mothers and babies present. Address by Mrs H Higgins, Ludlow on care and upbringing of children; then tea and each baby presented with a porringer.

26 April 1928. CA Golden Wedding of Mr and Mrs Hough... married 1878...Mr Hough well known had **unique experience of working the only passenger train ever to run on the Clee Hill branch line.** For 30 years he worked between Crewe and Swansea, 25 years in charge of passenger trains. At retirement he was one of oldest engine drivers on LNR. He had 53 and half years experience. His service was remarkably free from accidents. His two hobbies were gardening and bookkeeping on Stokes PC...(*it is well documented that the Clee Hill Branch line had been expected to be a passenger line as well as mineral line. Tickets had been produced for the purpose but were not used. AJ*).

29 January 1929. Clee Hill young hooligans annoying decent inhabitants by booing, calling names, throwing cinders, removing gates and during frost, making the road to Golden Cross dangerous by toboggan slides.

This culminated on Monday by the removal of cushions from closed Waggonette, belonging to President of WI during a meeting. What are the police about?

25 April 1929. Clee Hill dance in aid of Mission Church Funds, 100 present with Havana dance band from Cleobury ...£8 raised.

25 April 1929. Clee Hill enjoyable concert at Schools by Wesleyan Roosters Concert Party. Large attendance... party of 13 attired as negroes and loudly applauded...circuit funds.

11 July 1929. Football. Large photograph of the successful Knowle Rangers FC all named of men engaged in quarrying on Clee Hill and who had picked up many cups.

8 August 1929. Ludlow RDC. Clerk resigns. Mr Weyman had been clerk for 35 years. Ill health. MO reported on cases of over crowding at Clee Hill, of 4 adults and ten children in two rooms. Notice to be served on owner.

19 June 1930. Clee Hill 7th Carnival, on Whit Monday. 700 present raising £50 for Clee Hill Nursing Assn. Led by the Clee Hill Salvation Army Brass Band,the carnival processed through the village, children portrayed periods in the history of Clee Hill, followed by competitors in fancy dress and decorated vehicles. Included in the entertainment were Maypole and Country dances...well known entertainer Professor Dan Leano greatly amused by clever conjuring, ventriloquist and Punch and Judy shows...dog show.

21 August 1930. First annual outing since amalgamation of Clee Hill Granite and Clee Hill Dhu Stone and Titterstone quarries took place on Saturday when 250 men and wives journeyed to Southport for the day. Left early in the morning; 10 charabancs conveyed to Ludlow station. Embarked at 7am. A beautiful day attended outing. Party arrived home in early hours after a thoroughly enjoyable trip.

1 January 1931. Clee Hill. Mystery death of George Hopewell 80, retired sett maker, of Cornbrook, Clee Hill. Inquest at Salvation Army HQ, Clee Hill...had burn on knee which could not be explained.

5 February 1931. Ludlow By Pass; to be opened by Sir Henry Maybury native of Ludlow and director of Clee Hill Quarries. Number of men at Clee Hill has been considerably reduced owing to introduction of machinery...Sir Henry is greatly interested in Shropshire Soc in London which included some of the most famous and distinguished men in Shropshire. A description of the work done was given by Borough Surveyor Captain Lane..representations made in 1923 and later in 1928 to SCC...Road was 404 yards in length and 30 wide and 40 feet on bridge. Road surface was Clee Hill stone pitching, coated with Clee Hill tarmac... bridge constructed of reinforced concrete...50 feet wide allowing one and a half times more water flow on bridge. ...cost of work £10,961. Sir Henry spoke of the splendid work SCC had done in improving the roads in Shropshire and made special reference to the English and Atcham bridges.... following ceremony, luncheon at Angel Hotel...speeches. Sir Henry Maybury said motor traffic would increase and this was a good thing for trade but not for the railways...increased output by 26,000 tons, but not got all the men they wanted. Setts were coming from Norway and Sweden and their manager at Clee Hill, Mr Donald Mackay, was anxious to get men as sett makers at Clee Hill Quarries where they would be well paid.

12 March 1931.Motoring death on Clee Hill; one killed and many injured. Morris Lorry, skidded on Angel Bank when brakes failed..knocked over petrol pump and overturned..all occupants injured..Ludlow police and motor ambulance there quickly..(must have been men in the back).

Early 1930s. Eric Gitten's grandmother, Mrs Gittens lived at Coronation Terrace Clee Hill died in the dentist's chair whilst having treatment. The Dentist was Mr Clee who had a practice in Ludlow but held a surgery on Clee Hill two afternoons each week. This was a great shock and Mr Gittens was left with four young family; Winnie, Norman, Stella and Doris. Winnie being the eldest was about 16 years old and from then on acted as house keeper and mother. She wonderfully responded to all family emergencies. Winnie married Norman Fletcher who had joined the RAF from Ludlow Grammar School. He was athletic and an excellent footballer. When home on leave he played for Clee Hill United. Stella married Wallace Morgan who joined the army but was killed on active service. He trod on a mine and was blown up. Stella married again later. Mr Gittens was an ardent church man and his wont was to call at the Golden Cross for a pint every Sunday evening. One such evening he was enjoying his usual pint when he collapsed and died; a second tragedy for the Gittens family. (Notes kindly given by Mr Alan Johnson).

23 April 1931. Ludlow RDC Clee Hill the great British Quarrying Combine of Clee Hill of which Sir Henry Maybury is MD requires a large number of settmakers, and, for each employed would be able to employ a couple of unskilled men. The company could find sett makers but could not house them on Clee Hill...could find families for 30 houses if Ludlow RDC could house them. Demand for setts came from Lancashire and London. Chairman of RDC stated Dr White condemned housing on Clee Hill 12 years ago and the condition was worse today. Question asked why company did not do something and take advantage of Government grant.

288 August 1931. Clee Hill prosperity, all quarries working full time; at a recent meeting of Surveyors in London it was said that Clee Hill stone for macadam and chippings was not to be surpassed in GB. Almost no unemployment on Clee Hill. Latest machinery, electronically driven has been installed.

1 October 1931. British Legion. Successful meeting at Clee Hill.. at WI on Tuesday evening of ex-Service men. Captain Donald Mackay in chair....advantage of ex-Service men in district to become members. Chair read a list of activities the Legion was doing in all parts of the country.

26 November 1931 Clee Hill WI held concert at WI for Electric Light Fund. Songs,glees by the Welsh singers.. recitations..monologues.

21 January 1932. Clee Hill British Legion AGM held in WI on Friday..Capt JD Mackay in chair... need for own hall...a timber and corrugated iron building could be erected for £200. ..could borrow the money, citing Titterstone Canteen Fund (much laughter), then could hold whist drives, concerts or have boxing matches and gymnasium work, or use room for meetings.. had 92 members.

25 February 1932. Interesting article...Clee Hill..big contract completed.. Makes Brum roads. Exhibition of surfaces at Brum to which all the road stone used in demonstration as well as granite setts are supplied from Clee Hill Quarry belonging to the British Quarry Co Ltd which is the biggest quarry company in the country if not Europe... In the last few years since the three well known quarries on Clee Hill which had been working for 70 years or more, had been owned by the British Quarrying Co Ltd...being re-organised and re-equipped and electrified throughout .

7 April 1932 Clee Hill...foul weather on Monday, main road frozen...deep drifts of snow...on Tuesday when sun shone and scene was dazzlingly brilliant resembling Switzerland. Many from Ludlow on Hills...thaw causing flooding...in Ludlow Corve Street flooded.7 April 1932. Clee Hill Cookery Lectures being held at WI on Clee Hill. First by Miss Morgan on Tues. Demonstrated cooking of savoury dishes and sweets.

26 January 1933. Clee Hill Scouts First Troop red letter day. When an investiture took place at HQ Tenbury Road...1st investiture on Clee of 7 boys will form foundation...Scout Master Mr Lowe, Ludlow performed... Emphasised ideals etc...afterwards, knot tying was given by Troop Leader Lawton blindfolded followed by an attractive display of tumbling by a band of Ludlow Scouts. Scoutmaster Mr W Edwards, Chapel Farm, assistant Mr W Cadwallader and Cub Master Mr F Edwards of Chapel Farm. To an unprejudiced observer no praise can be too high for the splendid unselfish work carried on by Scoutmasters and their helpers in their efforts to give the rising generation something worthwhile physically and morally. They surely deserve the unstinted support of all those concerned for the welfare of the very young citizen.

16 March 1933. Clee Hill Fatality. Walter Roberts 60, retired publican of PO, Clee Hill found at level crossing leading from Granite Works on Saturday. .. for some years proprietor of Dhu Stone Inn. Inquest held in WI room.. by HT Weyman who inspected scene adjacent to a number of coal trucks of British Quarrying Company.

20 April 1933. Clee Hill Scouts and Cubs made first public appearance as a troop on parade. Headed by local Salvation Army Band, marched.. route given.. at morning service, troop flags were dedicated. Vicar spoke words of welcome in his address...return march via Caynham road with 21 members and 3 officers; promise for the future.

1 June 1933. Clee Hill Scouts' combined camp Service. Clee Hill and Tenbury Troops walked to the summit of Titterstone and picnic tea and camp service under Scout Master Mr W Edwards.. Mr JH Owen gave an inspiring address.. concluding with hymn and blessing from Scouts Service Book. Later Troops indulged in community singing and ramble.

1 June 1933. Clee Hill meeting of Amalgamated National Union of Quarryworkers and Sett Makers at WI to consider a merger.. of great interest to all those engaged in the quarrying industry..

8 June 1933. Clee Hill Fair. Mr W Ryan visited CH on Frid – Tues with his Fair...roundabouts, swing boats, and many sideshows. On the last night Mr Ryan held a competition for those who would eat a treacle bun the first to get into his jacket, which was turned inside out, and whistle...very amusing tussle for the competitors because they could not touch the bun with their hands, for they were tied behind them. J Mansly was the winner received half a crown and A Greatwich was second.

15 June 1933. CSA letter. In welcome Ludlow. Sir, in passing over Clee Hill on Whit Sunday and Monday, I noticed scores of motors drawn in on the grass, and the happy owners spending a lazy holiday – some reading, some with gramophones and others with a portable wireless. Now, coming into Whitcliffe Common, I noticed that some misguided persons had had the audacity to dig a trench to stop motorists drawing on to the grass.. This as an attempt to fence in the common land. I think Ludlow would do well to welcome all visitors, no matter where they parked their cars on Whitcliffe and if litter was left it would pay the borough to send a man to clear it up.

23 June 1933. Clee Hill held a mannequin parade...dresses made at recent dressmaking classes of Miss Askwith.

25 August 1933. Clee Hill Choir trip of 22 from Mission Room, visited Rhyl on Wed...reached 3,15pm..on sands and promenade...returned 8.25pm,home by midnight.

1 Septermber 1933. Clee Quarrying...item 'To quarry away the crests of Titterstone and Brown Clee would be nothing short of a National Crime, if permitted. Those responsible for those cutting into the crest of the Brown Clee must have no souls. A more pitiful quarry I have never seen. Untold millions of tons of dhu stone can be got from the Clees without committing such a desecration as removing crests. How the 'proud' Salopians can watch the crime committed, unmoved I cannot understand. Beyond doubt the Clees, or the main line of the crests, should be taken over by the nation as a national park. In proper hands they would mean as much to Shropshire as do the Malverns to Worcestershire.

9 February. 1934. Clee Hill death of Mrs Clara Davies 74 of WH following accident at home when she was airing a mattress before the fire and knocked down a saucepan of boiling water onto her foot. HTW inquest at Ivy House with injury...Nurse had dressed scald and Mrs Davies was eventually moved on doctor's advice to the Hospital.. Had had a wound on her leg before. Nurse Bayfield, District Nurse of Criterion Cottage, Clee Hill... Accidental death.

9 February 1934. Damson dispute. Ludlow County Court on Wed...George Genner, unemployed Clee Hill claimed £71 from Probert Ltd, the Factory, Bromfield Road, Ludlow, balance for damsons supplied by Genner.. Counter claim of £26...was laid by Proberts for failure to deliver. Contract made by Proberts July 1933 to purchase 10 tons of damsons at £14 ton. Genner, grocer's assistant said manager of Proberts came to him at Clee Hill and asked him to supply with damsons which they would collect from the growers...he made arrangements and whole of 10 tons were coming from outside Tenbury...Defendants fetched 2 loads and then no more saying they would not take them unless he got them to Clee Hill...he told them he had 28 bushels of damsons but when came to collect he did not release as they had no means of packing...the growers were waiting for empties in which to pack the damsons. Defendant said he had got into trouble for not fulfilling contract...for he was selling at £10 a ton. He was buying at £11 and selling at £10 to Messrs Smedley of Evesham. He made contract to buy at £14 a ton. Makes no sense. Fined for plaintiff and granted costs.

2 March 1934. Clee Hill Exchange...name change to Clee Hill due to confusion with exchange near Cheltenham named Cleeve Hill.

29 June 1934. Clee Hill.. Ludlow County Court when Richard Ripard of Knowbury, given 1 month HL charged with stealing a pair of brown shoes valued at 5 shillings from gipsy pedlar John Lock...shoes were on back of a cart...stopped to talk...and then disappeared. Ripard said he found them in road...Locke was traced to Newnham Bridge and identified them as the shoes.

27 July 1934. Clee Hill inquest of George W Harris 58, quarryman held at Titterstone Reading Room known as Bedlam.. found by daughter in shed with throat cut...been hay making recently.. but quiet...pocket knife produced...suicide while temporarily insane...

17 August 1934. Presentation to Mr James Williams of Doddington, Cleobury of Gold medal for 61 years long service . Presentation made by Sir Henry Maybury supported by Capt Donald Mackay and Mr JE Roberts....Sir Henry's speech...to have worked in such an arduous industry for such a long time is no mean record....Men trained in such an industry were invaluable to the country in the trying years of 1914 to 1918...should remember how much they owe to the skilled quarrymen...capable of performing the most exacting service. To live and work on Clee Hill for 77 years is a record.. It was no doubt men of the sterling qualities of Mr Williams whom AE Housman had in mind when describing, 'The Shropshire Lad'.

19 October 1934. Clee Hill motor cycle fatality...Widow knocked down..died 5 weeks later.

Miss Sarah Thomas ...Inquest. Harold Thomas of 10 Rouse Boughton Terrace, Clee Hill a stone crushing plant feeder...said mother had been knocked down by a motorcycle...taken to Kidderminster General.. unconscious.

16 November 1934. Clee Hill accident with a humane killer when Harry Bate was having his dog destroyed by local butcher Mr Alfred Martin. Bullet which killed the dog entered Mr Bates' leg and Dr Hunter called. Progressing.

25 January 1935. Ludlow Schoolboy in trouble. 10 years old boy from Clee Hill, in children's court for stealing football value 3/6d from SCC from Clee Hill School and with stealing flash light. Step father agreed to case being heard in Court...An elementary teacher said boy was pupil. During stock take, ball was missed...denied it but older boy sent to his house and recovered it.

8 February 1935. Ludlow County Police court when interesting and unusual case of one farmer suing another for food and water consumed by 3 ponies impounded by former for straying on his land at Clee Hill. Wellings Davies of Hope Court Farm, Hope Bagot claimed £6 from William Bodfield of Hill Top Caynham... found 3 ponies on his land and following day they enticed his horses out on to the road.. He recovered his stock but ponies returned and he put them in a building. Bodfield denied they were his.. Ponies were advertised as strays...Police said they were Bodfield's and he has not been seen since. Witness said he has been wandering about the Hill and is not responsible for his actions. Judgement was made for payment in 14 days.

13 February 1935. Clee Hill Scouts and Cubs entertained at supper at Hope Court, residence of Mr and Mrs CP Leese...afterwards Mr Leese gave a cinema show and games were played.

13 February 1935. Clee Hill death of Mr Samuel Hall 68 resided all his life in district and was formerly employed by Granite Quarrying Company as a carpenter...Funeral at Bitterley.

19 April 1935. Clee Hill. Abandoned car found on Clee Hill having been reported missing in Brum previous night. PC Michael while on patrol noticed the car without headlights and investigated...had run out of petrol.

3 May 1935. Clee Hill Playing Fields opened on Wed at School by Mr JV Wheeler.. Mrs AR Clegg presided... Mr Hinton HMI and Mr JH Owen HMS.

10 May 1935. Clee Hill death of Mr Tom Price 70, Cleobury Mortimer discovered by employ of Granite Quarrying Company foreman Mr George Jordan at bottom of cliff. Had it not been for dog Nell, none of the quarrymen would have been able to identify him...must have fallen down quarries in the middle of the night. HTW inquest with jury in canteen...fond of a drop of beer...George Poyner licensee of the Victoria Hotel, said he saw Price at 10pm.. second visit of the night. Price's watch stopped at 11.15.. verdict accidental death...lost his way in the dark.

20 September 1935. Midland Red Extension...new service Ludlow to Clee Hill. Service currently operated by Messrs Edwards Bros of Hopton Wafers. Ludlow, Clee Hill, Hopton Bank will be taken over by Midland Red on 30th Sept.

6 November 1935. A solution to unemployment . A correspondent advocates work on Clee Hill by creating a second Switzerland. Writer says that to do work to benefit generations to come...Why not open Bedlam to Clee Hill by a good road across the Parks, put a bridge over Dog Ditch (*Benson's Brook*)...charabanc parties etc...In severe weather, skiing on Titterstone...etc.

20 March 1936. Clee Hill woman charged with stealing £330 savings... by man's sister-in-law...Rose Fish Housekeeper...property of Thomas Hughes of The Parks, Bitterley. Bailed.

9 October 1936. Clee Hill heroine...still very ill. Dorothy Jones 11 who though terribly burned ran three quarters of a mile to place her baby sister in safe keeping was still very ill...in Bridgnorth Infirmary...but improving.

27 November 1936. Clee Hill disastrous fire early on Sunday damage estimated at four figures when one of the largest buildings in the village consisting of working men's library, three shops and living apartments gutted...Alarm raised..Ludlow Brigade called...total loss of one of Clee Hill's chief business premises. Mr and Mrs Tommey were away from the village and arrived to find nothing left of home and business. Cause unknown.(Author always wondered why Tommey's Bakers shop was so modern looking compared with other village shops. Problem solved)

18 December 1936. CSA letter re coal on Clee...from experience as a coal and mining expert, I know that there is any amount of virgin coal, ...not only in Knowbury.. but under Angel Bank and Bitterley Moor up to the Old Dhu Stone Pit...I know from my divining experience that there is coal enough to find work for a large number of men for upwards of 50 years...if a small company was formed the writer would take up a share...Mineral expert.

26 February. Clee Victory Motor Cycle Trials on Sat attracted 89 entries...53 mile course...won by Bert Perrigo, Brum, competition rider on 350cc BSA. One irate farmer who claimed one of the sections near Coreley was his private road, stopped in the path of competitors and refused to allow anyone to pass.. Officials pointed out OS map road but he refused to recognise it...decided to by pass the section.. Various cups listed..

25 March 1937. Clee Hill death of Mrs Martha Crowther 88...Leaves behind a very large family.

1 October1937. Clee Hill...harvest festivals across the district...At Clee Hill a piece of granite was among the offerings.

8 October 1937. Clee Hill Nurse's Home formally opened by Mrs CP Leese...original appeal had been for £500... Whist Drive and Dance to be held at Xmas...House Debt will be cleared.

14 January 1938. Clee Hill accident...while unloading corn from a wagon at Titterstone Quarries Benjamin Millichamp slipped and fell.. His right leg, amputated some time ago was broken above the knee. Removed to RSI. (*Ben was the 'osler' who looked after Tittersone Quarry horses and ran a small shop for quarrymen*). 21 January 1938.Ludlow County Court. Thomas Martin of Pool Farm, Clee Hill guilty of taking hold of a moving vehicle for purpose of being towed...PC Jones said on duty in patrol car on Angel Bank on Dec 29th when saw defendant being towed by British Quarrying Company lorry and driver said he had not given permission to catch hold... Defendant said he was in a hurry. Fined 5 shillings.

8 July 1938. Clee Hill suffered severe hail storms; drifting 6 inches in places....white carpet still next morning. Crops damaged especially potatoes.

15 July 1938. Clee Hill Sett Makers...and apprentices.. Disagreement at Belfry Quarry. Sett making is only trade connected to quarrying and boys have to serve apprenticeship of 3 years under qualified sett maker.. Originally cost borne by Unemployment authorities but this was stopped. Arrangements were made to receive 5s per week, parents to pay a small sum to the sett maker who was teaching... A dispute arose between parents and sett makers who are not demanding a fixed rate.. Until there is agreement there are no apprentices at Belfry Quarry.

22 July 1938. Clee Hill mutual service sale of work in aid of the Hut...Opened by Mrs Watson of Knowbury House..said Mutual Service Hall had fulfilled a great need in life of village... previously no place for working

people to gather......room could be used for handicrafts etc...Day concluded with a successful dance.. raised £9...intended to purchase land upon which building stands.

23 September 1938. Clee Hill Salvation Army journey to hop fields at Rochford, Eardington, Lindridge etc on Sunday...where more than 20 bus loads of visitors...open air services held in fields.

28 October 1938. Clee Hill ARP on Thurs, Mr R Harrison a Grade 1 instructor of Ludlow addressed meeting of wardens etc in Council School on aerial warfare and civil population. Capt Scott in Chair area organiser of ARP who illustrated his lecture with diagrams and blackboard sketches. He outlined the necessity for ARP, methods and aims of bombing aircraft and described the features of air attack in their order of importance, viz HE, incendiary bombs and gas. Each feature was fully described, emphasising the panic and loss of morale were gravest dangers in the bombing of open towns and the civilian population.

Caynham Parish Council

Extracts from Caynham Parish Council Records. 1895 – 1980.

I wish to thank Councillor Adrian Coles for encouraging me to include the following notes and arranging for me to loan the Minute books. Please note the earlier way of spelling Caynham as Cainham.

Clerk's salary 1895- £5.00. 1925- £10.00 (Author's salary as Orleton's Clerk in 1965 was £5.00).

30 January 1895. Councillors were E.W. Askey, T. Edwards, F. King, H. Leeworthy, G Roberts, Dr H Watson and Headmaster of Clee Hill School.

  The Knowbury National School was the meeting place and a fee of 1/- (one Shilling) was to be paid for each meeting.

The Clerk was asked to write to the Highways Board about the state of the road leading from the Golden Cross to the Railway Goods Shed. Also Dr Watson proposed that the Clerk write to the Clee Hill Railway Company and lay a complaint against one of their servants forbidding people passing over the line. The Clerk to write to the County Council on the state of the main road leading from Clee Hill to Cainham after severe snow storm. The snow had been allowed to remain there for an unreasonable amount of time.

It was proposed that all ratepayers be admitted to all meetings.

6. March 1895.Mr Smith proposed that there should be 2 constables appointed; one for each ward. – Carried.

29th March. 1895. The Annual Meeting of the Electors was held at the Wesleyan School, Clee Hill.

17th April 1895. Proposed by Mr Ed Small that Mr William Edwards of Pool House be appointed overseer for the Ward of Knowbury – passed.

9th October 1895. Two wells were much complained of, the water not being fit for use. Pollution by cattle etc a concern. More wells should be sunk.

11 June 1896. Mr Edwards proposed a letter to the District Council recommending a footpath be made by the side of the main road leading from the Victoria Inn to the Royal Oak Inn. Very dangerous in the dark. – passed.

21 April 1897. Dr Watson proposed that the Clerk write to the Postmaster at Ludlow and ask that the Mail Cart be allowed to come to the Royal Oak Inn and Office Lane to collect letters. – carried. Dr Watson – Clerk to write to Chief Constable of Shropshire to ask for further police supervision of this neighbourhood and point out the recent outrages committed to property.

15 December 1897. Clerk to ask District Council to protest against the Railway Company's action in trying to close the footpath crossing the Clee Hill Railway near the Dhu Stone Drum House. It was proposed that

a petition be got up and signed by the inhabitants of the neighbourhood, protesting against the Railway Company's action.

20th July 1898. Clerk should write to Postmaster General asking him to reconsider the postal arrangements on Clee Hill and Knowbury Post Offices and hope he will allow the post boxes to be open from the outside and all letters taken to Ludlow and stamped.

19 April. 1899. Proposed the Clerk should write to the Chief Constable to ask for better police supervision on the Clee Hill and point out the great advantage it would be to have a station and lock up on the Hill for the neighbourhood; especially now as the B'ham Water Works was so near – it causes a great deal of drunkenness.

22nd July 1897. Very important. Proposed by Mr Leeworthy that the well in Mr Griffith's land be cleaned out, bricked up and protected. Expense not to exceed £10.00. Mr Small proposed disused well in Mr Sam Bates meadow be cleaned out and sunk a further 6 feet to prove water could be found. The cost not to exceed 10/- (50p).

19 October 1899. Mr Roberts proposed that the Clerk should get the pump at Knowbury in proper working order.

14th May 1901. Cainham P Council; had thoroughly gone into the water question with rate payers and come to the unanimous decision that the present water supply from Public Springs is totally insufficient for the inhabitants. We therefore desire the Ludlow DC to take steps to send a qualified engineer to take levels and consider....water at the Green to be rammed up...Nine Springs; Corn Brook;Three Forked Pole and any others.

22 April 1902. Meeting to consider what steps should be taken to celebrate the Coronation of King Edward VII. Proposed that the Council - the rejoicings to be taken by voluntary contributions.

16th July 1903. The Clerk should write to the Inspector of Nuisances to say the water coming from the Golden Cross to the side of the road leading to the Goods Station *(the top of Goods Shed Lane by the side of the railway),* was very offensive.

20 April 1905. It was unanimously agreed that the Chairman and V Chairman should represent the parish at a meeting to be held in Ludlow on 5th May to consider the necessity of providing Secondary Education under the Education Act of 1902.

18 October 1906. Mr Griffiths proposed to accept the offer of lectures on Higher Education. They would approve those on Gardening and Cattle...to be held at the Wesleyan School.

31 October 1907. P Council had received a petition signed by many inhabitants of Clee Hill asking that the Rt. Hon. The Earl of Plymouth would allow them to take a small strip of land from a grass plot to make the Bridle Road into a Cart Road. They think if the present Bridle Road leading from Tenbury Main Road to the Titrail common was made wide enough to allow vehicles to pass over it – it would be a great boon to the neighbourhood.

15 October 1908. P.C. to consider numbering of cottages. Proposed the Clerk make a list of cottages with owners throughout the Parish in the various roads.

30 September 1909. Resolution that a Parish Room be built at Knowbury for the convenience of holding P. Council and parish meetings upon a piece of land belonging to the Parish; lease to be borrowed from Local Government Board.

29 January 1913. P.C. to consider the proposal of the County Council to build schools at Clee Hill for the accommodation for 200 children. Three quarters of the expense will fall on the whole of Caynham Parish *(note change of spelling).* There was opposition to this because of repairs and extensions to the Wesleyan School being in hand to accommodate 130 children.

26 March 1913. Resolution passed, Clerk to write to London and Salop Education Authorities drawing attention to the fact that for over five months 100 children have been unable to attend any school, owing to the Wesleyan School having been burnt down *(see our other publications of photograph of burnt*

down school being examined); and the meeting urgently request immediate steps to provide emergency accommodation. "We also point out that the Vicar of Knowbury has offered the Mission Room *(Clee Hill Church)* for infants or part scholars. Children's education is suffering due to enforced idleness.

28 April 1913. Much dissatisfaction expressed to the Education Authority's continued objections to not open the Wesleyans School. The children are running wild.

16 April 1914. The Council beg to call to the notice of the Assessment Committee of the Ludlow Union the extremely low rental value at which Clee Hill Dhu Stone Company is at present assessed namely £750.00.

27 April 1915. Rhum Spring in Cainham Road has had an accident; has become tainted with surface water and is unfit for human consumption. This well is much used by a large population in the district.

24 April 1925. The Clerk to draw the attention to the deplorable state of Dhu Stone Lane; this road leading to the most thickly populated place in Cainham Parish.

26 June 1928. It was reported that the tap to Clee Hill well had been wilfully damaged; instruction given for it to be repaired as soon as possible and the police to be asked to investigate the damage and a reward of £1 offered for information leading to offenders.

13 February 1929. That a letter be forwarded to Ludlow RDC concerning a petition signed by 29 householders concerning the deplorable, dangerous state of Dhu Stone Lane. Minor accidents had occurred.

26 February 1929. That the petition respecting the Dhu Stone Lane be sent to the Ministry of Transport pointing out that despite repeated protests to LDC nothing had been done to repair the road; although the state of the road was largely due to the hauling of stone for the RDC.

1 April 1930. The attention of the RDC be again called to the dangerous turn at the top of Caynham Road. It is suggested the present hedge be replaced with farm railings.

13 June 1930. Caynham P Council would welcome any scheme for the improvement of the water supply of Clee Hill and District.

Housing:- owing to the cases of overcrowding in the Clee Hill District. The Parish Council urge the consideration of a housing scheme for the locality. It is understood in Caynham Parish alone there are 12 houses containing 20 bedrooms and housing 81 occupants.

6 October 1931. Wells in a bad state of repair and polluted.

3 January 1933. Caynham P Council pleased to note there is an early possibility that a housing scheme will be put in hand for Clee Hill District -- this would be a great boon to the present workers of Clee Hill where unemployment is very pronounced.

17 April 1934. As the housing shortage is very acute the Caynham Parish Council hope the RDC will give the resolution favourable consideration.

15 March 1935. King's Jubilee:- Proposed and carried that a rate of 3d be levied on the Parish for the purposes of the Jubilee Celebrations. The amount collected is estimated to be £50 Upper Ward and £25 Lower Ward.

4 October 1938. Proposed that a payment of 2/6d per meeting for the school room be authorised.

22 April 1939. Clerk's salary £2.10 shillings per annum.

8 March 1939. Petition on Unemployment. Arising from correspondence from Col Windsor Clive MP re this petition on unemployment. The following resolution was passed with reference to the petition re unemployment in the Clee Hill District. It was decided to send a letter of appreciation to Col Windsor Clive MP for his efforts with the Ministry of Labour in the direction of lessening unemployment; and if further influence could be brought to bear for extra orders of stone from Clee Hill it would be of decided benefit locally; also asking for permission to publish his letter.

Letter sent to RDC re proposed water supply for Knowbury. Was there any hope of the water scheme being extended to Knowbury in the near future because complaints have been received that water at Butley Moor Well is again unfit to drink.

No meeting in 1941 due to War.

11 April 1942. The Chairman referred to the vacancies on the council caused through members joining HMF. It was decided to leave them vacant.

27 March 1943. A tablet had been placed in the church Knowbury in memory of Dr Watson; also 2 oak candle sticks with a brass plate on each for use at the Font; also an oak cover for the Font. The cost of the above raised by contribution was £32.18 shillings.

The Clerk asked to be released from his office. It was difficult for him to call and attend meetings owing to war work which takes him away from home at 6.45 am until 8.30pm. Members requested he remain in office.

15 April 1946. Chairman gave a welcome back to F G Edwards and E Davies who had returned from serving in His Majesty's Forces. A contract was accepted to pipe the water from Clee Hill main to the village of Knowbury.

20 December 1947. Food gifts from the Dominions via the Red Cross distributed to needy and poor; 42 families Clee Hill and Dhu Stone and 28 at Knowbury; 6 in Caynham and 6 in Hope Bagot (82 families). Gifts to be distributed by WH Jordan, FG Edwards, W Greenhouse, T Morgan, H Stanton and Hope Bagot Mrs Leese.

17 April 1948. HH Everall stated in cases of emergency, no hired cars were obtainable in Clee Hill, Coreley or Bitterley. It was proposed to support the application for Mr HV Roberts of Clee Hill for extra petrol, who has agreed to do this hire work.

25 September 1948. Support given by WH Jordan and HH Everall supporting an application of Mr Sid Smith, The Cafe, Clee Hill (Tenbury Road) for a licence to run a hired car for the Clee Hill District.

30 October 1948. A letter from the Lord Lieutenant of the County asking for the co-operation of the Council in obtaining the names of those who gave their lives in 1939 – 45 World War:- Names William Ernest Edwards – Private – RASC; Thomas William Jones – Gunner – RA; Wallace Morgan – Private – Light Infantry; Frederick James Penny – Private – KSLI; Donald Harwood Stanton – Officer's Steward – RN; Charles Speake – Air Craftsman – RAF; Civil Defence:- Stanley Benjamin Unitt – Warden AA Gunner – 185 (HG) AA2 Battery;

26 February 1946. Council members:- FG Edwards (Chairman); John Edwards; HH Everall; FGH Edwards; A Wiltshire.

2 March 1949. A licence to run a hired car application by Sid Smith, Clee Hill was turned down. It was turned down a second time but was granted to Mr GG Martin Cornbrook Bridge, Clee Hill. The Parish Council did not feel satisfied with the Regional Petroleum Officer's decision and ask the Clerk of Ludlow RD Council to make a further application for Mr Sid Smith, " who was by all reason the most suitable and convenient person to run a hired car for the District."

21 May 1949. A request made for a telephone kiosk to be installed at Lion Lane, Knowle. This had been placed on the list.

17 December 1949 Food parcels were delivered via Parish Council to 52 Clee Hill homes; 22 at Knowbury; 7 at Caynham.

11 February 1950. Alfred Richard Jenkins is applying on Monday 6 March 1950 for a Justice's Licence authorising him to apply for and hold an Excise Licence to all by retail the following intoxicating liquor viz:- " wines for retail by consumption either on or off the premises known as the Dhu Stone Inn, Clee Hill" (*Until this time Dhu Stone Inn had been a beer and cider public house only. It is now a private house known as Rowan Cottage).*

9 May 1950. Animals:- A petition from the residents of Clee Hill Village requesting Parish Council should do all in their power to stop the nuisance and damage of straying animals off the Common were doing.

2 December 1950. In connection with the Festival of Britain for the tidying up of Clee Hill Village that P Council order 9 new street bins.

17 March 1950. The Chairman stated it was very probable he would be able to obtain a grant of £50 towards the proposed bus shelter at Clee Hill to celebrate the Festival of Britain.

26 May 1951. The Rural District Council wished to receive a name of the New Housing site road. It was proposed by Mr W Jordan and seconded by F G Edwards to be called Festival Avenue. Proposed by FG and seconded by A Wiltshire the road from the Victoria Inn Clee Hill to Mr Hodgson, Critereon Stores be called the High Street.

12 January 1952. Council submitted two names for the 16 New Cornish Houses in Clee Hill Village; Railway Crescent and The Crescent.

16 February 1952. The P Council stood in silence for the death of King George VI th.

30 January 1953. The agreement was received from the MEB for the Street Lighting of Clee Hill Village.

21 May 1955. P Council to write to RDC to enquire if it would be possible to have a public convenience at Clee Hill.

11 June 1955. The RDC wish to know where was space to build a public convenience.. Proposed FG Edwards and Seconded by T Morgan that the land by the Cornish Houses let to Mr E Selly would be suitable.

14 January 1956. Repairs required to Dhu Stone Railway Bridge. It was passed. RDC should write to British Railways.

1 March 1958. P Council concerned at the report in the local press that when the present District Nurse retires the CC are not considering appointing another in her place.

18 April 1959. Public Meeting in the school room Knowbury. As no members of the public were present the meeting closed. (This happened frequently).

26 September 1959. £10 given by Mr Moore for a payment by Clee Hill May Fair. It was proposed to give £2 each to Clee Hill Boy Scouts; Knowbury Memorial Hall; Clee Hill WI; Clee Hill British Legion and Clee Hill Social Services Room.

3 January 1960. A complaint had been received with regards to the bad state of the footpath and fence along the side of the Railway Line from Clee Hill to Dhu Stone.

28 September 1963. Proposed to write to Ludlow RDC to see if it would be possible to put a sewerage works at Dhu Stone Clee Hill.

2 May 1964. Proposed development for Tenbury Road. No Objection but would suggest bungalows so as not to take the view from the houses on the top side of the road.

22 October 1966. The Council was asked to give a name for the Clee Hill Old people's dwellings.

15 March 1969. Proposed that we advertise for a Clerk. Salary £10 per year.

7 September 1969. A letter had been received from the Brewery relating to the closing of the Crown Inn Knowbury.

(*Author noted that there was a great deal of improvement in detail of minutes of the Parish Council from this date*).

11.July 1973. The RDC should be asked to remove the rubbish from the rear of the New Clee Hill Primary School; the grass and weeds in front of the school rails and indeed the whole place needed to be tidied up.

The Tenbury Doctors should be asked if a surgery could be provided at Clee Hill and Knowbury.

5 September 1973. Midland Red stated there was request stop at Three Crosses Clee Hill and if any driver refused to stop he should be reported. Ratepayers of Dhu Stone were still pressing for a sewerage scheme.

4 October 1973. P Council proposed that it join the National Association of Local Councils and the idea of a Clee Hill Village Community Centre. Dr Atlee asked if something could be done to the sound proofing of his surgery so that discussions with patients could not be heard in the waiting room.

7 February 1974. The question of whether numerous old pit shafts were sufficiently protected. A map was to be produced to locate them and address the matter.

9 July 1974. It was brought to the notice of the P Council that S C C did not encourage the appointment of teachers as managers because the Teacher's Union was against this practice. Also other teachers might object. Under the circumstances the proposal that ....be offered the managership of Clee Hill School was withdrawn.

14 July 1974. A school manager for Clee Hill School had to be elected in place of HH Everall who had been manager for 30 years but under new regulations because he was 70 was obliged to retire. (HH did not think much of that).

15 May 1975. Field at Knowle (2.75 acres). It was proposed and carried the P Council purchase this field for £1,050. Also that this plot be then sold to Clee Hill United and Knowle Football Club for £1,050, the purchasers to pay all costs and fees.

1 April 1976. County Surveyor advising strengthening of side roads which have to take increased amounts of heavy traffic during the period of the construction of Ludlow bypass.

1 July 1976. Councillor King suggested that small bungalows for elderly people and young married couples without children, should be built at Clee Hill. Elderly people living alone in 3 bed roomed houses could move into the new bungalows and their houses rented to big families. 3 February 1977. Notice boards to be erected on the Wall of Miss Hammond's Shop at Dhu Stone and be made by Mr T Lloyd of Bridge Farm.

7 July 1977. There was concern about the closure of Ludlow Cottage Hospital and transferring patients to East Hamlet.

4 August 1977. Clee Hill Village Hall Committee were interested in the old Clee Hill School (Ludlow Road) which was for sale but required further details of price and the possibility of obtaining vehicular access.

2 February 1978. The Council said, "We meet with sadness this evening after the death of our Chairman Mr Harley Everall. He has been a member of this Council for over 30 years and Chairman for 20 years. There are many things for which we remember him; his fairness as a Chairman; his great courage and humility. The community and Council will miss his wise counsel. It was proposed that a donation be made with a view to providing some permanent memorial to Mr Everall.

3 March 1978. Rev I Williams of the vicarage Clee Hill informed the P Council of confirmation at Knowbury Church on Sunday 30th April for 15 candidates. (*How things and attitude have changed*).

20 April 1978. Reports there would be a new Sports Centre in Ludlow but not before 1980/81.

2 November 1978. Note:- Cleaning of Knowbury and Clee Hill Bus Shelters; £6 for 6 months each respectively.

2 November 1978. There was a threat of post boxes in the area being closed. Currently it costs 61p per box per collection.

15 April 1979. It was reported that the County Council Works had involved spending of £150,000. Snow clearance and other winter costs had been £750,000 and snow and frost damage repairs would cost in excess of £2,000,000.

24 April 1979. Councillor Coles reported there were 600 people on the Housing waiting list of South Shropshire County Council.   The proposed new Village Hall for Clee Hill had been shelved due to lack of interest by the village.

6 September 1979/4 October 1979. Telegram sent by the Parish Council:- "On behalf of your people of the parish of Caynham I tender their loyal greetings and inform you of their horror at the circumstances and sincere sorrow at the untimely death of Lord Louis Mountbatton of Burma (Chairman). Mrs Marina Clent was welcomed as a member of the Parish Council. Chairman organised a civic service of St Pauls, Knowbury to commemorate the new pole and flag.

6 March 1980. School Transport charges cost almost £2 million per year. Proposed parent cost £300,000. Mr Keyse, Headmaster of Clee Hill C P School asked if it would be possible for a small group of older pupils to attend part of a Parish Council Meeting.

Full Circle

From Clee to Eternity began with incidents of the childhood of my sister Marina and me and memories of our immediate industrial environment at Dhu Stone Inn, Titterstone Clee Hills. We return to my life seventy years later.

It is with enormous gratitude I have the good fortune of the gift of a truly wonderful wife, my soul mate and friend Ann; three special , hardworking children all thankfully married to considerate partners and six delightful grandchildren.

In addition to still being fully occupied in community life, having more than enough to look forward to each day plus a strong faith – what more could one wish for?

Ann and I do however regret not having recorded the thousands of funnies blurted out to us during our long teaching careers but we did not; thinking we could remember all in detail. We have however jotted some gems from our own grandchildren during the last twenty years. Enjoy them with us.

Grandad talking to Grandson aged 7. "How is your friend Horace? Are you still good mates with him?" GS:- "Well Horace is a bit like Grandad's dog Tarzan, sometimes he likes you and sometimes he doesn't."

Grandson aged 4, carrying a bunch of squashed, half dead snowdrops said, "Nanny, I have brought you some raindrops to make you feel better."

Our son rang to say that Grandson (4) had left his toy lion by a 'service' tree at our house and could we have a look for it because it was a bedtime comforter. Ann remarked we hadn't got such a thing as a service tree and in any case it had been pouring with rain and GS had not been outside. He had been playing all day in the Conservatory. At this point our son burst out laughing. We all now refer to the Conservatory as 'The Service Tree'.

 Great Grandson chatting to Great Grandma:- "Nan you are very old aren't you? You'll die soon won't you? Great Grandma:- "Well I expect I shall." " And will you go to Heaven?" G Grandma replied, "Well I do hope so." GGS, " Well what will happen when it's full?" *(we have all been wondering the same thing).*

Granddaughter (7) :- " Nanny Ann we were doing tie and dye at Kids' Club today, but only had time to tie this week, so I am going to dye next week." Nanny Ann ," Oh! I hope not." GD, "Oh don't be silly Nanny, I mean the material."

Granddaughter (5);- "I love you in the world Nanny Ann."

Nanny Ann knew the Doctor very well and had taken Granddaughter aged 5 for an appointment. Granddaughter, "Nanny would you like to be a child again?" Before she could reply the Doctor with a wicked smile said," Well you are approaching your second childhood."

Grandson (4). "Nanny you are very old and I am very new."

Granddaughter (5). On asking her Mummy about a neighbour who had died recently said with tears in her eyes, "Mummy you aren't going to die are you; because I can't take the top off the marmite jar yet."

Grandson aged 6 who had an excellent vocabulary had been watching a James Bond video with Grandad said, "Do you like watching James Bond videos Grandad?" Answer " Not particularly." GS, "Well I wouldn't have expected an elderly, intelligent man like you to be really interested in him."

Granddaughter (6) turned to Grandad while having lunch said, "This smells lovely." Nanny Ann interjected saying, "Grandad can't smell anything, not even honeysuckle or bacon frying or anything like that." GD looking earnestly at Grandad, "Can you still breathe?"

Grandson (8) playing with model dinosaurs, " "Grandad do you know what happened to dinosaurs when they died out?" Grandad, "Well I expect the same as happens to everything that dies." GS, "No Grandad they went to the Natural History Museum."

On a visit to Clee Hill with Grandsons aged 5 and 8. Nanny Ann said, "That's called the Glass House and that one is called The White House." GS, "Oh is that where the President of the United States lives?"

Raising money for cancer Nanny Ann was making out a list of names for 'Name the Teddy'. Granddaughter was looking intently at the list, began to giggle and said, "Nanny, you have written Fanny here; that's what the boys at school call private parts – Oh! this is even worse. Look you've got Willie."

The Team vicar was called Gareth and one of the Churchwardens was a wonderful person who loved children and always greeted our grandchildren with real warmth. Grandson (5) said, "Is Gareth the vicar?" "Yes he is." GS, "And is Winnie an Angel?"

Our local Grapevine Magazine had a page for a children's colouring competition. Grandson (6) was busy colouring in his entry when he looked at his Great Grandma and said, " Have you coloured in your picture?"

Grandson (6) was curious about a story he had heard at Playgroup. Grandson, "I think that story is rude. Why would a princess have a pea in her bed?"

Grandson (8). When his cousin was born 9 weeks prematurely said, "Crikey Nanny; will she have arms and legs?"

Grandson (8). My best mate is Elliot, but he is grumpy at times and we had a bit of a fight; but we shaked hands and maked it up."

Grandson (7). Looking at the new calendar for next year being put up said," Nanny aren't those snowdrops beautiful. The old calendar is still as good as new. You can keep it until 2005 comes round again."

Grandad hardly ever finds it necessary to wear shorts and no top. On one such very hot day Granddaughter (8) whispered to her Nanny, " Oh! I can see Grandad's tits."

Granddaughter (2) often praised and complimented by her mother was at the stage where she also wished to be complimentary. When Grandma came out of the toilet Granddaughter said, "Good boy Grandma. Well done."

We have a stuffed barn owl in our Hall known as 'The Inchmoor Barn owl' because it flew into wires at Inchmoor Farm. Granddaughter (2) looked at the owl and said, "Wow Nanny! Look at that big robin." – much to the amusement of an older cousin.

A favourite drink for the grandchildren is blackcurrant. A Grandson(4) when asked what he would like to drink said, "Black – la- crunt please."

Grandad Alf wears a tie most of the time which is not seen as being in the fashion nowadays. Grandson (10) asked, "Grandad why do you always wear a tie? My Dad doesn't wear a tie."Answer, "Oh he does when he goes to something special or a funeral." Grandson, "Yes but you wear one all the time. Why?" Grandad, "Well I don't like the draught going down my neck."

Two of our Grandchildren have a Dad who is a Lifeboat Helmsman and they often see a helicopter assisting with a rescue. Granddaughter (2) came running into the kitchen and said, "Nanny, Grandad, come and look

– a copter." We responded, quickly going into the conservatory and looked up to the sky but couldn't see one. Then we saw her little hand pointing to the conservatory fan blades.

In our multi-cultural society it is deemed necessary to introduce even primary school children to different religions. The following comment came from our 9 year old Granddaughter after a primary school lesson. "Mum I want to be a Muslim." "Why?" "Because I like pitta bread."

As was her usual practice, great Grandma put her false teeth in a glass of water over night. On seeing them next morning Great Grandson carried them to her asking, "What are these G/Grandma?" Answer, "Those are my teeth." To which he asked, "Are they alive?"

Granddaughter; picking blackberries with her Mother. " They are a bit sharpy Mum."

On going to the toilet small Granddaughter shouted, "Oh look Nanny, a big webcob."

Nanny Ann has a birthmark on her leg. Small Granddaughter on seeing it asked, "Did you hurt yourself Nanny?" Answer, "Yes I did." GD, "Did Grandad pick you up?"

Granddaughter aged 3 had enjoyed singing carols at Nursery School especially 'Away in a Manger'. Later that day when shopping with her Mother at Tesco's and traversing the aisles they were singing together. An elderly lady tenderly said, "May I join in with you my dears. It is so delightful that some little ones still learn about Christmas."

Granddaughter aged 3. Now well toilet trained but still often taken to the toilet. But! being independent is left by Mummy with these words, "Call me if you need any help ." While staying with Nanny Ann she said, "I will not be long. I am going to the toilet. Very soon a little hand appeared round the door and a voice said, "Are you alright Nanny? If you want anything just call me."

Speaking to a Granddaughter aged 4 on the phone who had a brother aged just 1. Nanny Ann, "What is Charlie doing Jessica?" Answer," Oh, he's just texting". Nanny, "Who is he texting?" GD, "Just one of his friends from Nursery School; but he can't get through so he's thrown the phone on the carpet."

Recently our younger Daughter and family visited Guernsey and hired a car. Grand Daughter to Nanny Ann, "Did you and Bampi LOWER a car when you went to Cornwall?"

Very young Granddaughter chatting to a friend at Sports Day. "Miss is going to have a baby soon." Other child, "Yes and she is going on eternity leave."

At Playgroup, Grandson had been playing with Anghared (Welsh name). When queried who he had been playing with GS answered, Oh! King Herod."

Grandson aged 9 being queried by his Mum. "What part are you playing in year 6 Production?" GS," I don't know they haven't finished partitioning yet." His Mum, "You mean auditioning." GS , "Yes that's the one."

It was Ash Wednesday and Grandad had been to the 'Ashing' service.   When he arrived home he showed Granddaughter (5) the cross of ash on his forehead.   After a simple explanation to her she said, "It's a bit dull Bampi. Don't they put a red or white mark on." Bampi (Grandad) was a little mystified but then realised that while watching rugby on TV the coloured cross was often seen on fans.

Nanny Ann hearing children read at the local school. Nanny Ann, "Where do you live?" Answer from a small boy, "I don't know, but it's along 2 straights and round 3 corners."

A Grandson (4) had been listening to the Christmas Story at school and said, "Nanny and Grandad, did you know that Horrible Hedwood wanted to kill all the little boys?"

Grandson (3) at Christmas Time. "You be Daddy Bear and I will be the Inn Keeper."

Son-in-law chatting to his son(3). S-in-L, "Today is Mother's Day." GS, "What's that?". S- in- L, It's a day when we say thank you to your Mummy for all she does for us." GS, "Are we going to have a children's day?"

An uncle took a Grandson fishing. GS was really excited while unpacking the rods etc. Uncle ultimately demonstrated how to cast the line. They sat there quietly for what seemed a long time. GS after a huge sigh said, "Do you know anything about fishing uncle?"

Ann still goes into our local school to hear little ones read. While reading 'The Hungry Caterpillar' one child excitedly said, "The caterpillar changed into a racoon."

Grandson (4) had been learning about Van Gogh at Nursery School. He was asked to stand up and say what he had learnt. Later he rang his Grandma and said, "Nanny Ann, my name has been put on the Board because I knew about Llandoch (the name of the local hospital in Penarth).

Mr Summers always takes the trouble to chat to our two youngest grandchildren from Penarth when they visit our village shop. When they were 7 and 4 Andrew the proprietor said to the Granddaughter, "Thank you for coming to look after Grandad. Is he a lot of trouble?" Grandson, "No not really." Granddaughter, " He takes an hour sometimes to get home because he stops and talks to everyone and Nanny Ann worries where he is. But I've heard most of the stories before."

On another occasion the Grandchildren had scooters. Grandad, "Don't go so fast you two and stop at the edge of the pavement by Damsons Close. " Grandson, "Grandad, you are a bit slow. You need some more exercise."

We often have chicken roast on Sunday, followed by cold chicken on Monday and chicken soup on Tuesday. Our Grandchildren do not appreciate this 'saving' routine. On arrival of chicken soup our one very young Grandson looked a little downcast and was asked, "What soup would you like then?" Answer, "Mr Stroney.".

We were driving from Penarth to Orleton with two Grandchildren at the time Olympics were very much in the news. A hooded cyclist went past us when we were waiting at the traffic lights. He continued and ignored the next traffic lights while they were on red. Grandson (5) said, "He's got no common sense. I've got plenty of common sense." Encountering numerous sets of traffic lights in Cardiff the same cyclist over took us and Grandson commented, "I 'spect he is training for the Olympics."

Youngest Grandson was being dressed for his cousin's 18th birthday with the help of safety pins. He piped up, "Oh look Nanny Ann, I've found a tasty pin."

Visiting Penarth to stay in the regular chalet, our two youngest grandchildren Charlie 6 and Jessica 9 asked if they could come for a sleep over. Great Grandma, Nanny Inchmoor has accompanied us for a number of years. Looking at the dining table Charlie said, "Nanny Inchmoor should be sitting there."

Having visited Great Nanny Inchmoor at the nursing home, on leaving Charlie was very quiet. Then he suddenly said, "Grandad, if I had special powers I would make all the old people there well again." How touching that was.

MBE

An accolade, not sought but humbly accepted on behalf of Titterstone Clee Hill People for their courage, determination and physical 'slog' over many generations resulting in its landscape we have today.

I was invited to Pebble Mill Birmingham the then BBC studios in the early 1970s to give a programme about Clee Hill Dialect. Very unexpectedly for me the broadcast was heard by my ex history master, Fred Reeves, who by then was an elderly man. He wrote me an extensive letter asking me to terminate my research and impressing on me to record my memories and knowledge of this amazing area; and to let him have a copy of my work before he 'passed on'.

Many readers will know that our first book "Titterstone Clee Hills, Everyday Life, Industrial History and Dialect" was published in 1983 after 10 years research. It was followed by our publications about country life in North Herefordshire; then with the help of friend John Hughes two DVDs and a CD about this little bit of Heaven, Titterstone Clee Hills.

Unbeknown to me Major Adrian Coles a local Councillor at the time and a number of like minded people applied for an award on my behalf saying, that in their opinion I had done more than anyone else to promote Clee Hills far and wide and "put them on the map". Incredibly my name came out of the hat.

I was asked by St. James' Palace if I wished to accept an honour of an M.B.E. I had no hesitation in accepting. I have always been an admirer of Her Majesty Queen Elizabeth II and what an overwhelming and truly humbling occasion that Award day turned out to be.

On Friday 10th October 2008 I was presented at an Investiture at Buckingham Palace with my MBE by the Queen herself; an occasion I will never forget. No matter what individuals think of royalty such an experience is truly awesome.

A wonderful bonus was, to be able to take my wife Ann and our three children Graham, Helen and Karen into the Palace for the presentation. They were more than a little worried as to how I would cope with such a complicated process,being deaf. I was apprehensive too but need not have worried. The preparation was thorough. On entering the Palace we were met by Members of the Irish Guards, looking absolutely resplendent. My wife and children were separated from me, conducted by one of four ushers to the magnificent Ballroom and seated about four rows back from the front. Ann was in an excellent position to see all. Music was being played by a band of the Irish Guards and on command guests were instructed to stand.

The Queen entered the Ballroom attended by two Gurkha Orderly Officers. The Queen was accompanied by the Lord Chamberlain.   The National Anthem was played and all the guests seated.   The Queen took my award from a velvet cushion held by a senior member of the Household. Usually the Master and the Secretary of the Central Chancery of the Orders is responsible for making sure the correct decoration is distributed and an Equerry in Waiting reminds the Queen who each recipient is.

Going my separate way, on each magnificent staircase, gallery and room, adorned by most scintillating paintings I was greeted by gentlemen with "Good morning sir. This way". I kept looking round thinking someone else was being addressed.

We were given a briefing as to how to greet Her Majesty and what the procedure would involve. We were divided into groups of ten and as part of the process passed through numerous rooms, in each being asked our names and validity details.

To be in such deserving and eminent company was so surreal. The gentleman next to me at the presentation was Billie Beaumont, ex England Rugby Captain. What a charming fellow! He offered to sign my award list, had a very informal chat and later we saw his three sons.

Also near me was a tall gentleman in pristine, forces uniform . He asked me why I was there and what public work I had been involved in. Having told him about my experiences, I noticed he had a pronounced scar on his cheek and so I asked him what was his award for. He said, "I don't deserve to be here. My episode did not last years as yours did; it was a mere fraction of a second.

He continued that he was leading his platoon of men on active service when he spotted an object protruding above the sand. He instinctively dropped his radio etc on top of it. He recalls that he woke up in hospital to be told that he had saved the lives of his men. We saw him later on TV being interviewed about his award. What a privilege to meet such special and modest people.

My group of ten arrived at the penultimate room and I could see into the magnificent Palace Ballroom. The person ahead of me was signalled to go forward. I saw him turn left and approach Her Majesty.

My tummy began to churn. I did not hear my command to proceed; but I received a gentle push from behind and there I was in front of the Queen. This absolutely charming person with such an engaging smile bent forward from her dais and pinned my award on my left lapel. I had not realised that she was very little taller than my 5 feet 7 inches even when on the dais. As though I was the only person in that special room she asked me about my work; gave me an opportunity to describe it to her and to my great surprise said, "Oh Prince Charles has mentioned this work and how he is trying to reintroduce such historical practices in Romania to assist the development of their infrastructure." Quite unbelievable! I was well aware that

OCTOBER 2008:- *An occasion I will treasure for the rest of my life. Receiving my M.B.E at an Investiture in Buckingham Palace for publishing work about the **Industrial, Social History and Dialect of Titterstone Clee Hills in South Shropshire, England.***

there was a person standing behind the Queen giving her information but there were 94 people at the Palace on that occasion and I know they were all given quality time.

The Queen gave everyone of them time to converse.

I was able to join my wife and children before they left the Great Ballroom and filed out with them down yet another resplendent staircase into the inner courtyard's gleaming sunlight.

Official photographs followed before we made our way to the outer courtyard to be met by crowds collected outside the railings. Our family of fourteen was determined to share the occasion and as we emerged they began to shout and cheer with others.

At the time granddaughter Jessica was just four and on seeing us jumped up and down uncontrollably and shouting, "Nan and Grandad." The two policemen on duty were obviously touched by this small child's exuberance and unexpectedly let her through those gates to run into our arms. What a superb human touch by those officials!

Sister Marina Clent was also awarded an M.B.E. two years earlier. She has lived at Clee Hill for the majority of her life, contributed to the community in many ways and received her award for having played the organ at three parish churches for sixty years. What a record! It is impossible to contemplate this could possibly have happened to a brother and sister, born in a little country pub on Titterstone Clee Hill. What would our Mum and Dad have said?

TCHT

Titterstone Clee Heritage Trust

Towards the end of the 1990s and the beginning of the New Millennium I was finding a little more time to look around Titterstone Clee Hills and I became increasingly concerned about industrial artefacts of my childhood that were disintegrating and many having been 'carted' away and disappeared.

In desperation I wrote to numerous Government Departments seeking grants and advice but in spite of polite replies I had very little material success.

At Titterstone's old quarry some re-enforced iron rods inserted into remaining concrete, stone crusher bases were corroding badly, bins were open and dangerous to people and animals, small, remaining buildings were unsafe and stone setts had been stolen from railway incline stanchions . At Bitterley the dam wall built to retain the reservoir dammed up from Benson's Brook, now silted and dried up, was beginning to show signs of deterioration and Bitterley Yard was suffering too. Each of my visits showed new signs of setts having been removed from the railway wharf wall and parts of the yard were no longer recognisable. Titterstone railway incline route was still clearly discernible but sections had been privately acquired.

At Dhu Stone the railway route was overgrown, some bridges had been removed, parts of the route had been sold off, Dhu Stone bridge had been rebuilt and a large water pipe inserted beneath it. Some squatters' cottages I had entered when I was a child were no more than piles of rubble. The signal box, drum house, tarmacadam plant, engine house, workmen's stores no longer existed and most disappointingly to me Dhu Stone Inn, my old home had closed and was renamed 'Rowan Cottage'. I have never been in favour of renaming properties which have had an important historical connection. The Dhu Stone Inn was such a place. Will Rowan Cottage create the same impact?

Ken Oram owner of the Nuvver's ancient lime industrial remains and thirty acres of woodland encouraged me to continue conducting interested parties around that area and I decided that before more damage was done to produce a pictorial representation in DVD form of what I remembered the area to be like.

I invited Colin Richards, Environmental Officer for South Shropshire to visit the Nuvvers and other areas to supplement my knowledge. Colin is such an unassuming gentleman with incredible knowledge of industrial and social history. I respect him so greatly. As described earlier, friend John Hughes, Ken Oram and I dug out, very laboriously one Nuvvers kiln and to Colin's surprise it was so deep he decided it was a three month kiln and therefore had been a part of a much larger industry than had been previously thought. Thus the majority of my time during the first couple of years of the new millennium was occupied, with John's filming expertise producing, "Up the Lane and Back Again." This valuable record of social and industrial heritage becomes more precious everyday and is enhanced by a dialect contribution of Dennis Crowther , the bard of Clee Hill now sadly passed on.

Soon after this time Ken's wife Eve was taken seriously ill and much against his will Ken decided he would have to move nearer her home and put his beloved Nuvvers on the market.

What could be done? I knew if this invaluable microcosm was sold to the wrong hands the woodland would be flattened, kilns destroyed by a bulldozer and valuable evidence of railway lines and inclines be annihilated. This was very serious.

In 2006 in desperation I contacted Major Adrian Coles MBE TD and told him of my plight. His advice was, "No matter what publicity you have striven to give Clee Hills you will not get any constructive help or grants unless you form a Community Group. There is an important meeting to be held at Cleobury Mortimer this week with a representative from AONB, Colin Richards, Tom Britnall, archaeologists and others. Go and tell them what you are concerned about."

I attended, explained my deep concerns, especially the urgency of the Nuvver's Sale. I had productive chats with Clare Fildes (AONB) and met archaeologist Glynn Barratt; who I discovered had lived on Clee Hill awhile at the bottom of Hopton Bank. Glynn readily cottoned on to my enthusiasm for our area. At the end of the meeting he asked if we could have a chat. We travelled to Craven Place, Clee Hill and sat in a car park near the ex quarry offices (Craven Place Cafe and Tea Rooms until 2013) and looked into the valley below. The view before was one we both greatly treasured.

This chat resulted in the formation of Titterstone Clee Heritage Trust in October 2006, "to preserve, enhance and promote the Industrial and Social Heritage of Titterstone Clee Hills."

The Establishment of Titterstone Clee Heritage Trust:- Alf Jenkins left (Founder Chair) and Glynn Barratt (well known archaeologist).

Legal advice was given and a constitution formulated by Nancy Webb a specialist in that field at Gabbs Solicitors, Leominster. Four Trustees were recommended and appointed. I was nominated founder Chair assisted by Glynn Barratt, John Hughes and Marjorie Hammond. A Committee was formed; the Trust began work and most of those stalwart Committee members are still with the Trust.

In 2007 the Trust asked John Hughes and myself to capture memories by interviewing elderly folk who lived in the area. Both of us had been born on The Hill; knew many folk in the district and John was an expert camera man with much experience. It was decided that I would do the interviewing. We met various people who had carried out similar projects and as a result drew up a list of specialist equipment we would require. We estimated mileage involved; prepared a time schedule and a standardised questionnaire.

I applied for a £10,000 grant from 'Awards for All' and Major Adrian Coles MBE TD agreed to act as appointed 'referee' for the project. After searching questions, interviews and much form filling we secured the grant. "Awards for All" however insisted we finished the project within a certain time span; one year. Marina Clent MBE, Ann Sutton and others who knew communities well recommended people who may be interested in the project and willing to be interviewed. All interested participants were asked to sign an agreement to be interviewed. This they did. Time wise every day that passed was vital. We needed to start the project immediately. Every participant needed to be given an appointment to suit themselves and have time too to think about what we were likely to ask. The whole process of filming, editing and producing a DVD, with Cam 3 of White Grit producing the final satisfactory format, took just the year permitted, of concentrated work and interviewing. So into being came "Heard Around the Hill." John designed a special sleeve cover to include railway lines and a sett maker. The inner leaflet and back cover included all the parish Churches. A photograph of all participants and an Ordnance Survey Map of the area involved was also added. TCHT has in its possession an invaluable archive of the lives of fifty three special Clee Hill people. The DVD is still available via the Trust but sadly already eleven of those recorded have passed on.

Knowing that the Trust was being formed, Mr Ken Oram wanted to make sure that it had the first realistic option of purchasing the Nuvvers. He therefore took the property and woodland off the market to give time for grants to be applied for. The whole Committee agreed enthusiastically that the Trust should do all it could to secure the Nuvvers. As a result of heroic efforts by Glynn Barratt, and generous gifts from the general public the asking price of £60,000 was achieved. A dream was as far as I am concerned fulfilled. The Nuvvers and its microcosm of precious lime industry and the only woodland on Clee Hill was secured hopefully forever and a day .

The Trust has experienced one continual stumbling block and that has been to secure enough cash flow, not part of the grants for Nuvver's work, to send out regular communications by post to all those who have supported and are interested in the work of the Trust. But; it is determined to overcome this hiccup.

The Trust has organised many and varied craft courses in the Nuvvers, Ludlow and other places; numerous lectures, informative tours of the Clee Hills and a number of Country Fairs both on Clee Hill and at Mahorall Farm, Nash. Those events have been very popular and more are asked for. However, they are very expensive to organise and the Trust no more than breaks even.

Regular working parties are held at week- ends in the Nuvvers, improving footpaths, clearing scrub, planting trees and aiming to produce a Forest garden. The woodland is gradually being managed and hopefully facilities will soon be available to assist the organisation more educational courses. The Trust is always looking for more week- end help at the Nuvvers.

One major aim of the Trust was from its inception and still is to facilitate a resource/educational/information, distribution centre in the area to help the Trust promote Titterstone Clees. Unfortunately every vacant, possibly suitable venue has proved too expensive to purchase and renovate but in 2012 we had what seemed the perfect solution. Hopton School closed and its Trustees approached TCHT saying that the deeds of the school stated that if the school closed its future use should include an educational element. The school Trustees felt that going on its past record TCHT could provide this.

The buildings were in perfect condition, positioned at the 'east end gateway' to Titterstone Clees and only running expenses and up keep would be required from the TCHT. The Trust devoted a great deal of time investigating the viability of this possible future project and held two public meetings, one at Clee Hill and another at Hopton Wafers. Both meetings were very well attended and the general consensus was for the Trust to go ahead do more detail costing and relevant research. The Hospice Group from Cleobury was looking for more accommodation and was enthusiastic about teaming up with TCHT.

Unfortunately at a further meeting of joint Parish Councils held at Doddington to which the Trust was invited, there was vociferous opposition from a Hopton Wafers contingent. Sadly the Hospice and TCHT decided not to expend further valuable time on what could have been a golden opportunity to assist the whole of Clee Hill's community. The Trust continues to be determined to pursue future possibilities.

At this juncture, 2014, TCHT is working in conjunction with AONB (Area of outstanding Natural Beauty) based at Craven Arms and Clee Hill Partnership to acquire a £1.6 million grant to preserve and enhance a considerable portion of Titterstone Clee's Industrial artefacts. I sincerely hope this bid is successful and TCHT will continue to go from strength to strength.

Who knows? Ann and I may be lucky enough to live to see this come to fruition.

Many species of flora and birds are more readily seen. That does not however mean there are larger numbers. That is certainly not the case with skylarks and curlews.

With a decreasing workforce in the quarries from hundreds to less than a score, local public houses are less frequently visited. Mobility gives greater choice. People travel further afield and the 'local' is no longer the essential hub. A few years ago The Angel Hotel, Royal Oak, Golden Cross, Victoria Hotel, Golden Lion, The Craven Arms Inn (The Kremlin), The Dhu Stone Inn and The Lady's Finger were all well patronised and important farm sales were held regularly at The Angel. Sadly only two public houses remain on the Hill top.

Titterstone Clee Hill has a special place in my heart and Cleeton St Mary a special one for Ann. The views are some of the best in the world. These Hills have been a hard, isolating but unique area for many, many generations where they have toiled and carved the landscape to make it as it is. It has created an indelible imprint on our lives. Will Eternity prove to be as challenging and fulfilling? It is only time that will tell.

Ann and Alf with their lovely family in 2014.

Words and phrases

Carve – a wooden box on skids pulled by mining boys in Clee Hill coal pits.

A todd bellied mon; and e could nu see over the pulpit.- He was a man with a fat belly and he could not see over the pulpit.

Well e could nu be lying ere if they annu found im. - He could not be lying here if they haven't found him.

Chips. - Baskets made from flat, very thin strips of wood used as containers for plums and other fruit in which to be taken to market.

Wum . – Home.

Annu. – Have not.

Wunna. – Will not.

Didnu. – Did not. Dunna.- does not. Ooth. – with. I inna gwan. – I am not going.

Snappin. – food or quick snack.

Tips. – Mounds of spoil from the stone quarries forming considerable hills.

We adnu got much time fer snappin and we wun dry. So the fust un didnu touch the sides. – We hadn't got much time to eat our food and we were very thirsty. So the first pint of cider/beer did not touch the sides of our gullet.

Screen. – High backed wooden seat to keep off draughts. Summut tu ate. – Something to eat.

We adnu got a klet. If we wun lucky ween goo down to Fairy Glen and put our fit in the bruck. – We had not got any money. If we were lucky we would go down to Fairy Glen and put our feet in the brook.

Frum taters. – Small pig potatoes. Swill tub. – Swill for the bacon pig in a tub.

Wallers. – Alder trees.

Boster. – 28 pound hammer used in the stone quarries to break stone.

Ween ad tu goo down tu Ludlu tu see the daay light. – Because of the low lying mist making the day so dark we will have to go down to Ludlow to see the day light.

Glat. – A Herefordshire word for a hole in a hedge.

Tallut. – Loft store for hay or grain.

Trous. – Herefordshire word for hedge brushing.

The sweep. – A word used in the public house for a draw of chance for the winner of a race, or the highest football score of the day.

By gom er wus a good lookin ooman. – My goodness she was a good looking lady.

Surri boy this is klinkin. – Good gracious boy, this is very good; excellent.